MORTAL GODS

MORTAL GODS

Science, Politics, and the Humanist Ambitions of Thomas Hobbes

TED H. MILLER

The Pennsylvania State University Press
University Park, Pennsylvania

Chapter 3 is a revised version of "Thomas Hobbes and the Constraints that Enable the Imitation of God," *Inquiry* 42, no. 2 (1999): 149–76.

Library of Congress Cataloging-in-Publication Data

Miller, Ted H., 1965–
Mortal gods : science, politics, and the humanist ambitions of Thomas Hobbes / Ted H. Miller.
p. cm.
Includes bibliographical references and index.
Summary: "Argues against the accepted idea that Thomas Hobbes turned away from humanism to pursue the scientific study of politics. Reconceptualizes Hobbes's thought within early modern humanist pedagogy and the court culture of the Stuart regimes"—Provided by publisher.
ISBN 978-0-271-04892-5 (pbk. : alk. paper)
1. Hobbes, Thomas, 1588–1679.
I. Title.
II. Series.

B1247.M49 2011
192—dc22

Copyright © 2011 The Pennsylvania State University
All rights reserved
Printed in the United States of America
Published by The Pennsylvania State University Press,
University Park, PA 16802–1003

It is the policy of The Pennsylvania State University Press to use acid-free paper. Publications on uncoated stock satisfy the minimum requirements of American National Standard for Information Sciences—Permanence of Paper for Printed Library Material, ANSI Z39.48–1992.

CONTENTS

Acknowledgments vi

1
Introduction 1

2
The Humanist Face of Hobbes's Mathematics, Part 1 9

3
Constraints That Enable the Imitation of God 35

4
King of the Children of Pride:
The Imitation of God in Context 55

5
Architectonic Ambitions:
Mathematics and the Demotion of Physics 81

6
Eloquence and the Audience Thesis 115

7
All Other Doctrines Exploded:
Hobbes, History, and the Struggle over Teaching 137

8
The Humanist Face of Hobbes's Mathematics, Part 2:
Leviathan and the Making of a Masque-Text 161

9
Conclusion 201

Appendix: Who Is a Geometer? 221
Notes 239
Bibliography 303
Index 333

ACKNOWLEDGMENTS

I have accumulated many debts in writing this book. I can't begin to repay them. I nevertheless wish to thank those who were there from the very beginning, and those who have come along later as the work continued. I am particularly grateful for the assistance I have received from Tracy Strong, who saw this work from its earliest and now distant inception. I also have Gerald Doppelt, Alan Houston, Arthur Lupia, Steven Shapin, and Don Wayne to thank for their early comments and assistance. I've been sustained by good intellectual company as the ideas in this book made it to the page. For this I also owe thanks to Chris Dugan, Elizabeth Ellis, Verna Gehring, Bernard Gert, Christina Haddad, John Hughes, Nancy Luxon, Utz McKnight, James Murphy, James Philipp, Hans von Rautenfeld, John Richardson, Arlene Saxenhouse, Verity Smith, Pat Snyder, Marek Steadman, and Elizabeth Wingrove. Chris Laursen's encouragement and comments from afar have always been more than helpful. I offer especially heartfelt thanks to Samantha Frost. She and Dean Mathiowetz were steadfast in their assistance. They allowed this work to reach a safe harbor.

I owe particular thanks to Terry Royed for her companionship and encouragement. She has kept me going. J. David and Susan Miller were always there, interested and patient. Karen, Alan, Elana, and Michael Rubinstein were rooting for me.

I also wish to single out Sandy Thatcher for his interest, and his integrity as an editor. Dan O'Neill gets the credit for sending me to Sandy. I have also had the good fortune to work with Kendra Boileau and Stephanie Lang. I'm grateful for their invaluable assistance.

I thank those institutions whose support was crucial to the completion of this project. This study would not have been possible were it not for the generous grant and institutional assistance I received from the Huntington Library, the British Academy, the Earhardt and Mellon Foundations, Dartmouth College, and the University of Alabama. I also wish to thank the Chatsworth Devonshire Collection, in particular Andrew Peppitt and Peter Day, the librarians at Chatsworth, and Diane Naylor for her assistance in procuring the images from the collection used in this book.

1

INTRODUCTION

Alexis de Tocqueville is not, perhaps, the first name readers of an interpretation of Thomas Hobbes would expect to see. For some, it will correctly stand as a marker of the eclecticism of North American political theory. Nevertheless, every interpretation must have an origin, and this one is no exception. It emerges from within the broad, relatively fragmented and freewheeling constellation of curiosities of political theory as it is primarily practiced in departments of political science in the United States and Canada. These departments are staffed by a community of practitioners long interested in Hobbes, but often resistant to those readings which celebrate him as a pioneer of social science, or hold up his work as an early model of analytic philosophy.[1] This reading is, in part, an extension of that tradition of resistance.

De Tocqueville declared history's trajectory to be the inevitable growth and progress of equality. Equality was an "irresistible revolution advancing century by century."[2] There is a straightforward way to connect Hobbes to this master narrative. By making men equals in the state of nature, Hobbes rejected the premises that sustained the hierarchical ways of understanding the natural, social, and political orders rooted within the doctrines of the schools, churches, and courts. As such, he is a part of the history of equality's progress.[3]

As de Tocqueville insisted, though, that progress was (and still is) haphazard. One can imagine, says de Tocqueville, an "extreme point" where liberty and equality would "meet and blend."[4] All having an equal right to participate in government, and all being equal, no one would be able to exercise tyrannical power. Along the way, however, the two principles are realized neither at the extreme nor simultaneously, but distinctly and unevenly. Here again, a connection to Hobbes can be made. Hobbes moved from the equality of his state of nature to the gaping inequality embodied in the absolute sovereign's relation to his or her subjects. In accord with the ideology of absolutism, Hobbes declares that the sovereign must outshine all the other subjects like the sun outshines the stars.[5] The thirst for equality, de Tocqueville thought, could bring about tyranny. It could be of the absolutist variety, or the tyranny of the majority, which he feared most. Both the absolute sovereign and the sovereign majority might be compared to gods; they are likened to entities that dwarf all others with their power (and make them more equal to each other in their common subjection).[6] When Hobbes speaks of his sovereign as a "Mortal God,"[7] it is useful to think of what he hoped to assemble, but also, with de Tocqueville, what he was taking apart. His work was also an assault on the intermediary institutions between the sovereign and the people such as the established church,[8] the nobility, and the courts. In so far as his philosophy insisted upon a unified form of sovereignty that need not take the form of an assembly, it was also an assault on Parliament.

For my immediate purposes, however, these initial points of connection to de Tocqueville can give way to another, perhaps less straightforward link. It concerns not merely de Tocqueville, but also the sometimes tangled relationship between some committed Tocqueville scholars and the audiences that make use of de Tocqueville for their own purposes. Alan S. Kahan, author of *Aristocratic Liberalism: The Social and Political Thought of Jacob Burckhardt, John Stuart Mill, and Alexis de Tocqueville*, wrote of de Tocqueville (and his two other subjects) that "the interpreters of aristocratic liberals are all too often ready to ignore the issues and circumstances . . . [these thinkers] thought crucial. Instead of asking the three what their questions were, we ask them our own questions, and as a result get an answer that is distorted and misunderstood."[9] Hobbes scholars have undertaken their own reclamation efforts. Hobbes, they have declared, must be spared our purposes and given back to his own. Among Hobbes scholars, these sentiments will bring to mind the "contextualist" approach of the Cambridge School historians. I will discuss the relationship between contextualist readings and the status of "his own" below.

In light of the goals of this interpretation, de Tocqueville's would-be rescuers offer a more poignant dynamic. They, of course, resist certain presentist readings by insisting that we understand de Tocqueville as a man of the nineteenth century (if not a man whose life was primarily determined years before by the French Revolution). They also, and more interestingly, caution against reading de Tocqueville as if his intended audience was in fact (or at least necessarily) the society of relative equals within the United States. They urge us to consider that his foremost audience may have been the frightened aristocrats of his native France. In short, they raise the possibility that *Democracy in America* was not aimed toward the sensibilities of our time and the political events that consume us. *Democracy in America* is not "ours," they suggest, because it was not written to appeal to today's egalitarians, much less those whom it describes. The book critically defends democratic ways to an inegalitarian aristocratic culture still trying to find its footing in early nineteenth-century France.[10]

For whom did Thomas Hobbes write? My purpose is not to duplicate the reservations urged upon readers by the de Tocqueville scholars. Hobbes is not warning one class that another is coming to replace it. The differences between our society and Hobbes's are in many ways unlike the differences between our society and de Tocqueville's. In both cases, however, our democratic sensibility is offended by the suggestion that the texts of these two men are not immediately *ours*.[11] Nevertheless, the example of de Tocqueville should prompt useful questions about how to approach Hobbes. Why should we be more attentive to where Hobbes's audiences stood within the hierarchical cosmos of seventeenth-century Britain? In short, because doing so gives us a better appreciation of Hobbes's politics. We should therefore ask: what did it mean to address oneself, or to offer a philosophical doctrine, to a sovereign one would make absolute? We can gain new and important insights into Hobbes's politics if we try to discern how he negotiated (in the full sense) these distinctly seventeenth-century contexts and their attending practices. More specifically, I will read Hobbes in light of the practices of humanist education, patronage, and what I call the high culture of practical mathematics that were a part of seventeenth-century Britain's most imaginative plastic arts.

Against the trajectory of this—or any contextual—approach one might raise a hermeneutic objection. Any reader—in fact, all readers, whether they acknowledge it or not—will reveal that the text they interpret is always *for* them because it cannot be otherwise.[12] My interpretation always makes a book *mine*, and your interpretation makes it yours. In a broader historical frame, we, today, make the books we interpret *ours*. This argument seems to me undeniable, but if we must always make an author *ours*, the example of de Tocqueville suggests that one of the more fruitful ways to make an author *ours* is to make him untimely: "acting counter to our time and thereby acting on our time."[13] That is, the interpreted author who will necessarily be made *ours* can be *ours* in the way we make them *not theirs*. In this case "*not theirs*" does not mean denying authors their contexts, or more aptly, what we think of as their contexts. It means working from those contexts to pull him or her away from some of our contemporaries. In fact, this reading works toward a doubly untimely Hobbes. I make arguments for taking Hobbes away from his scientific admirers,[14] and for bringing him, I hope, too close for comfort to those who typically think of themselves as having achieved maximal distance from him.

We should therefore consider that Hobbes's works were written for a different society, and likewise for someone other than ourselves. We may hold to this effort even while acknowledging that this "other" and the historically distinct society are never independent of ourselves because we (and not the dead) are the ones who declare and articulate these differences. Hobbes can and should be useful to us, but it does not mean that we need assume that his purposes are our purposes. This interpretation has been developed with this thought in mind, and with particular focus on Hobbes's claim to offer his readers a science.

Returning to de Tocqueville, I would like to suggest an inversion of the audience question as it applies to Hobbes. Both raise the question of unequal audiences. De Tocqueville was trying to convince one audience of how the world need not be so horrid once it is forced to give up some of its powers. Hobbes was trying, in part, to convince another audience of how, with his help, it might claim a tighter grip upon power. Hobbes was not defending democracy to aristocrats; rather, he was defending a democratic moment of authorization of (and to) an absolutist sovereign. In other words, Hobbes had set himself the task of convincing a would-be absolute sovereign, a ruler who might have imagined his or her rule legitimated by other means, such as divine right, to accept power from the bottom up.[15] In this respect Hobbes can be seen as the beginning of a de Tocquevillian nightmare: a man who joins the mandate of a dedifferentiated society in the state of nature to a central sovereign power who will rule without challenge.

As such, the greatest and first burden—and the central orientation—of Hobbes's work is the sovereign his doctrine would create. *Leviathan*, in particular, is a mirror for a prince, if an unconventional one. It is a grand, scientifically constructed mirror. It offers a gift to the sovereign-in-potential, who—if he likes his gift—will find his likeness in it. That gift is to become the soul of a mortal god. This sovereign does not exercise its power merely over its subjects, but over all matter within its reach. Hobbes was a court philosopher who offered a would-be sovereign (and patron) a form of control that we in the twentieth and twenty-first centuries have not yet fully imagined. And it is this sovereign that is the as yet unimagined "other" that we need to consider not only in *Leviathan* but also in all of Hobbes's major works.

In this book I try to reason through what I believe to be the most surprising implications of this concept of sovereignty and to show how it extends to domains of Hobbes's thought not yet considered in the Hobbes literature.[16] The most contentious claims will violate some contemporary scientific pieties, but I also hope to disturb some of the pieties among modernity's critics that have been a long-standing part of political theory. Sovereignty, in Hobbes's thought, was more than merely political in the conventional sense. Others have noted how "the political" in Hobbes's thought expands to exert its control over other domains of civil society, such as science, commerce, law, and religion, such that these domains lose whatever autonomous internal logic we might imagine they had. Such encroachments do indeed occur, and have been described by Carl Schmitt.[17] Nevertheless, Schmitt and others (including Leo Strauss)—while mindful of Hobbes's "mortal god" claim—did not fully appreciate just how thoroughly Hobbes proposed to make man the imitator of God through his science.[18] God's sovereignty over nature, as creator, was an implicit model for the activity of Hobbes's science. His concept of philosophical inquiry, I will argue, was not so much a science of discovery as we often imagine it today, but a science of creation.

Although my purpose is not to make extensive comparisons of Hobbes and Francis Bacon, the broad outlines of this interpretation can be sketched in light of some fundamental differences and similarities. Hobbes embraced Copernicus and mathematics. Francis Bacon embraced neither. Because of this Hobbes is thought to have not been strongly influenced by him, in spite of his early employment as Bacon's amanuensis. The differences between Hobbes and Bacon are substantial, but where they were alike is in their understanding of the purpose of knowledge. Each thought the end of knowledge was power, and more specifically state-power.[19] Both men also advocated a new and total beginning to philosophy itself.[20] Both men embraced conceptions of the practice of science to which the power and resources of the state were integral. Bacon imagined an army of investigators, each meticulously doing a small part in a collective effort to make nature yield up its secrets to the political elite. Hobbes, by choosing mathematics—and geometry in particular—imagined the state as a grand manipulator of all matter. Science was what taught this manipulator of matter to build the effects it desired and to maintain its own body politic in a state of peace and prosperity. God was a grand geometer. So might be the mortal god. Those who reverence both Hobbes and a notion of science as a systematic means of discovering, verifying, or even merely investigating and disconfirming inaccurate accounts of a reality independent of ourselves will be disinclined to agree with this reading of Hobbes.

I hope that this reading will also trouble and provoke in a friendly way those who have faulted Hobbes for having trod the path of modernity condemned by Heidegger and many others. That is, those who condemn him for having taken this independent reality for granted, for having duplicated the presuppositions that give us the Cartesian subject.[21] If my Hobbes troubles them, it might be a kind of guilt by association. For against those who hope to master the world through grasping its inherent and inalterable principles, many critics have argued that the world is contingent, conditioned, and always already constituted by our gaze and our discourse. Nowadays these arguments seem a bit moldy, and those of us who are in sympathy with their self-appointed task of thwarting hidden sources of domination in modernity must, nevertheless, ask whether or not something has been overlooked in this struggle, since so many robust sources of domination exist and continue to reproduce themselves.

In the conclusion I will approach this question more systematically. In spite of many efforts to convince others that the wish for sovereignty is an impossible and dangerous dream, we have not fully understood what it has meant to aspire to sovereignty. A different understanding of Hobbes can help us address this problem. In his time and in his own way Hobbes was more aware of the fluxious character of the world than most of his contemporaries. We are too facile if we declare ourselves his mental, political, or ethical superiors because we know that no amount of scientific inquiry will ever exhaustively describe the world that we ourselves are always constituting. Showing the scientific world its reflection in Procrustes is often apt, but the shock value would have been lost on Hobbes. Those who chop into pieces in this philosophy are not looked upon so harshly, provided they know how to construct what they will out of the basic elements.[22] In spite of his materialism, his seemingly reductionist assumptions about human nature, Hobbes cannot be chastened by the figure of Procrustes. This is not merely because his conceptions of human activities often reveal themselves as more sophisticated than the stereotypical visions of *homo economicus*, his predecessors, or his new replacements. It is because Hobbes's will to dominate nature pursues a more direct path toward its end than anticipated in our cautionary tales about the unintended, or even devious, consequences of reductionism.

After positing, rather than defending, his assertions about the material universe, Hobbes never, conceptually, denied the world its contingency, its sheer protean possibility. On the contrary (as I shall argue) there were times when he insisted upon it in the face of rival conceptions of philosophy—especially natural philosophy—that claimed knowledge of creation, of its secret powers or its mechanisms. Hobbes's goal was not to offer a superior account of nature (that which God is said to have created) but to teach the foremost member of his audience, the sovereign, to be like a creator god in mustering the causes necessary to produce desired effects—peace instead of the reigning chaos, as well as the things that make for "commodious living." De Tocqueville offered his (aristocratic) foremost audience laments and reassurances in the world of increasing equality. Hobbes in his grand translation of all into matter in motion promised the foremost member of his audience the chance to be a god. The mediating institutions de Tocqueville (later) hoped to preserve (and some he did not) were the very ones that Hobbes threatened. These institutions, the universities, churches, and other elements of existing political and social authority, fought back.

Hobbes's language of "mortal gods" has been available to us for some time.[23] Discerning the grand scope of his ambition, however, requires more than an apprehension of the social and historical dynamics that de Tocqueville brings to our attention. We must also dispense with a modern presupposition that has informed most Hobbes scholarship. Hobbes was said to have "discovered" geometry in a library in France in midlife.[24] We have assumed that when Hobbes moved toward geometry, he was moving away from his earlier humanist training. Hobbes is thus said to have had two phases, an early, prescientific humanist phase, and a second, (New) scientific phase that began when he discovered geometry. Others maintain that Hobbes, upon further reflection, decided that philosophy alone was unable to accomplish its task in the real world, and so, especially with *Leviathan*, he reconciled with humanism, and with its most important political tool, rhetoric.[25] That would constitute a third phase.

My contention against such readings is that Hobbes had a single phase, that is to say, no such distinct scientific and humanist phases, in his thinking. Like most humanists, he had disagreements with other humanists—especially those who used their eloquence for *popular* oratory—but what we have assumed regarding the relationship between mathematics on the one hand and humanism on the other is anachronism. The Renaissance humanists, who were especially good at pointing to the likeness between human excellence and divinity, were always a part of Hobbes's intellectual repertoire.[26] It is correct to say that unlike prior humanists, who located man on a great chain of being—somewhere above the beasts but beneath God—Hobbes's thoroughgoing materialist metaphysic radically leveled this hierarchy. This is because he no longer counted upon "Nature" or God to enforce its hierarchy and orders upon the world, including the political realm. Hobbes can be folded into the narrative of the modern world's disenchantment and secularization. On the other hand, Hobbes came from a world in which order and the promise of peace took the form of a divinely ordered hierarchy. If Hobbes lost faith in an animate nature that would restore itself and its order, he nevertheless proposed to those who might find themselves at the top that he had the means of creating a substitute, a grand artifice,[27] which might even be superior to what nature was once said to have created. In a world of divinely sanctioned hierarchies, Hobbes's philosophy was one of "do it yourself." (Strauss is therefore correct in linking him with Machiavelli, but incorrect when he asserts that Hobbes's science somehow masks the decision to "do it himself.") When nature (and God's) false promise of order failed, Hobbes proposed a philosophy that would establish human sovereignty over chaos.

To argue, as some have, that the world is never without remainder, always more contingent and chaotic than modern science's categories have allowed, is not incorrect, but here it misses the mark. Hobbes's example illustrates that it is possible both to acknowledge, even trumpet, the world's chaotic and contingent nature, and to wish to impose order upon it, regardless of the futility of searching out a natural order. We have grown accustomed to modern forms of domination that extend their reign over us through a claim of knowledge over what is declared the natural order. Having become accustomed to this, we tend to forget (especially when discussing science) that the will to dominate also operates independently of the will to know. Hobbes can help remind us of this sorry fact where we are most inclined to forget it.

The argument proceeds as follows. Chapter 2 begins to chip away at the dichotomy between humanism and mathematics. Chapter 3 describes how the imitation of God is integral to Hobbes's conception of philosophy. Chapter 4 discusses the will to imitate God in the broader context of Renaissance humanism and speaks to the question of Hobbes's conception of human being. Chapter 5 enters into a discussion of what it meant for Hobbes to reinvent science, and how Hobbes's approach should be understood as his attempt to win an intellectual war on behalf of mathematics (and his own vision of geometry) *against* natural philosophy. For Hobbes it was a contest for dominance, not a plea to allow mathematics to join in the task natural philosophy had already set for itself. Chapters 6 and 7 address the questions of rhetoric and Hobbes's notion of how his state would actually come into being. Chapter 8 returns to the topic of humanism and mathematics and courtly persuasion. There I argue that *Leviathan* may be read as equivalent of a grand court-masque, a stage genre cultivated in the Stuart era. The conclusion, Chapter 9, discusses implications for our understanding of sovereignty and the relationship between politics and reason.

2

THE HUMANIST FACE OF HOBBES'S MATHEMATICS, PART I

In this chapter I intend to start picking up the stakes that mark a false boundary within our understanding of Hobbes. This boundary is between Hobbes's alleged humanist "phase" and subsequent "phases" in which Hobbes is said to have (at least for a time) abandoned humanism for mathematical reasoning for more modern scientific endeavors. As regards mathematics and humanism, Hobbes had a single phase. He never ceased to be a humanist. Having not ceased to be a humanist, Hobbes did not make a return journey. I do not deny that his thought changed over time, or that he became increasingly interested in harnessing the power of mathematical reasoning and defending his reputation for possessing this power. I do deny, however, that we can adequately understand Hobbes's affinities for mathematics without understanding the affinity for mathematics of the humanists who had preceded him and which continued to inform his conception of what mathematical, and scientific, thought was meant to achieve. These humanist affinities for mathematics, cultivated among the gentlemanly patrons and pedants, have been known to others, but they have been erased in the grand narratives that inform Hobbes scholarship. They need to be recovered and juxtaposed with Hobbes's thought. In this chapter I undertake to recover some aspects of the humanist face of Hobbes's mathematics. After further consideration of Hobbes's philosophy, Chapter 8 and the appendix on the Hobbes-Wallis dispute bookend the process by adding to the portrait.

Hobbes, Humanism, and Modernity's Abrupt Beginnings

There is a strong temptation to describe the history of Hobbes and geometry as a conversion story.[1] Aubrey's account of Hobbes's discovery of geometry seems to offer a glimpse of a key moment in the history of the scientific revolution. Aubrey writes that he was "40 yeares old before he looked on geometry; which happened accidentally. Being in a gentleman's library in . . . , [Aubrey's ellipsis] Euclid's Elements lay open, and 'twas the 47 El. Libri I. He read the proposition. 'By G—,' sayd he, 'this is impossible!' So he reads the demonstration of it, which referred him back to such a proposition; which proposition he read. That referred him back to another, which he also read. *Et sic deinceps*, that at last he was demonstratively convinced of that trueth. This made him in love with geometry."[2]

There are good reasons to doubt this story of a sudden conversion to the church of mathematical worship. Book 1, proposition 47, of Euclid is the Pythagorean Theorem. Upon its discovery, Pythagoras is said to have sacrificed one hundred oxen to the gods. Aubrey's account, with its reference to divinity and Hobbes's joy upon seeing the truth of something he first thought impossible, may be a creative seventeenth-century inversion allowing us to imagine Hobbes experiencing the same revelation centuries later. This story, which has Hobbes encountering a book of geometry in the same way enthusiasts encounter an open Bible, bespeaks as much humanist continuity as it does sudden transformation.[3] Our first doubts, however, should be cast upon our own view of what it must have meant to be mathematical. It is incorrect, in spite of Aubrey's account, to assume that Hobbes's love of mathematical ways and practices truly began with a love affair with Euclid's geometry. This judgment is affirmed by looking into the mathematical affinities of his contemporaries, and indeed Hobbes's own account of his early interests. Hobbes reports his youthful devotion to the things produced by practical mathematicians: maps, celestial charts, and geography were strong preoccupations during his time at Oxford.[4] In the very year of the supposed conversion, 1629, Hobbes had already made himself an accomplished practitioner of a mode of mathematically informed humanism.

In that year he published his translation of Thucydides. This work is rightly viewed as a sign of Hobbes's strong commitment to humanist learning in his early years. Aside from turning Thucydides's ancient Greek into English, Hobbes was particularly proud of having created an accompanying map of ancient Greece. Unlike other maps available, he claimed, his would help readers of the history by adequately locating the regions that corresponded to the place-names in Thucydides.[5] While the map was not the work of his own surveys, except through Thucydides and other historical accounts of the geography,[6] it was something we can now recognize as part of a larger element of contemporary humanist culture.

By adding, and boasting of, the map, Hobbes was walking on a path already trod by fellow humanists, one guided by an affinity for the products of mathematical practitioners. It was by this time an intellectual common ground where mathematical practitioners and humanists walked together. They met most often at the points where court patronage might provide sustenance.[7] (These locations will be further explored in Chapter 8.) It has been argued that the very subjectivity of some key humanists of the preceding era was constituted by and through a cartographic imagination.[8] Henry Peacham's *The Complete Gentleman* embodied and promoted humanist ideals of gentlemanly identity. Peacham endorsed an education in mathematics and geometry, and like Hobbes he spent his school days "hanging over maps."[9]

Hobbes's early participation in this aspect of a mathematical connoisseurship, however, is not enough to fully refute the view that his career had two phases. This is because it is not merely a matter of chronology, of determining when Hobbes's mathematical and scientific curiosities were first piqued, but a deeper question. We need to consider how to conceive Hobbes's ongoing affinities for mathematics and how these manifest themselves in the works recognized now as his most scientific. The first step is to review the investment we have in an understanding of Hobbes that insists his work had at least two phases, if not more.[10]

Those who hold the view that Hobbes's career had multiple phases make Hobbes's own transformation from a classically trained, yet imprecise, intellect to one of mathematical rigor a synecdoche for the transition from one age to the next. A line would seem to have been crossed on the way to the modern world in this library in France. Ferdinand Tönnies and Richard Peters, for example, purposely set out to link Hobbes to narratives of modernity's abrupt awakening.[11] According to this transformation narrative, Hobbes abandons his humanist approach to politics in favor of the search for law-like certainties in political life.

Perhaps the best evidence for the depth of our commitment to this view of Hobbes's career has not been those authors who celebrate him as a member of the scientific revolution. It has, rather, been the way some of Hobbes's interpreters have tried to blur this line between phases. Some attempt this by showing that Hobbes continued to use his humanist skills—particularly his rhetorical skills—after the so-called scientific phase began. Important examples are Leo Strauss and Quentin Skinner, neither of whom easily discounts the influence of humanism.[12] Both, however, maintain that Hobbes "discovered" geometry, and that this discovery meant his humanist period was on the wane.[13] Strauss nonetheless held that Hobbes's most important moment—his decision to abandon the morality of the ancients—occurred *prior* to his discovery of mathematics. On this reading Hobbes's mathematical phase obscures the genesis of his philosophy. This yields a thesis that implicitly accepts and maintains a "two-phase" view; Strauss's critique is of the conventional assessment of our *view* of the transition, not on the transition itself.[14]

For Strauss's subversion to take place, the transition must occur and our eyes drawn to the wrong side of the divide. This leaves us with a different way to see the origins of modernity (and opens up upon a much larger and more complex part of Strauss's view of the question), but it reinforces the notion that Hobbes's discovery of Euclid moved him outside the humanist orbit. In his recent work, Quentin Skinner makes much of what he sees as key transitions in Hobbes's intellectual career. He argues that Hobbes was forced later in his life to realize the mistake of rejecting humanism's signature political tool, rhetoric, and elected to return to some of resources he once thought he could forgo.[15] Even more radical approaches to the question of the relation between Hobbes's rhetoric and his science, such as Victoria Kahn's, do not efface the distinction between mathematics and humanism. She reveals the rhetorical character of what are considered some of Hobbes's most purely scientific works of political philosophy. The force of Kahn's reading is in compelling Hobbes's contemporary philosophical admirers to acknowledge the rhetorical character of Hobbes's claims to a scientific method.[16] There is a revelatory character to such arguments. Hobbes must be revealed to be dependent on a humanist skill that he (and contemporary positivist admirers) claims to have left behind. Instead of arguing that Hobbes changed his mind, she argues that we ought to change ours. One can agree with the force of this reading and still maintain, as I do, that the links between Hobbes's mathematical ways and his humanism need further investigation. There is, in fact, something other than a *covert* humanism at work in Hobbes's mathematics. The question we need to ask is why that something, which should be visible to us, has become invisible.

Hobbes is not strictly identical to his mathematically inclined humanist precursors (and they do not, in any case, speak with one voice), nor is his debt to his humanist predecessors total. I am not denying Hobbes's originality or his radicalism in pushing for a mathematicized philosophy. I argue that Hobbes took a set of preexisting humanist arguments in favor of mathematical learning and pushed them yet further. Just how far he pushed them will be most apparent against the background of the sixteenth-century educator Richard Mulcaster's boosterism for education in mathematics. We can, therefore, have it another way. Instead of showing the humanism masked by Hobbes's mathematical face, we can show that his mathematics has a humanist face. The place to begin, however, is with the early work by Hobbes that most clearly establishes his beginnings in Renaissance humanism.

Although Hobbes's first widely recognized publication, *De Mirabilibus Pecci* (*The Wonders of the Peak*) in 1627,[17] is relevant to our concerns, the work that put Hobbes on the map as an accomplished man of letters was his translation of Thucydides in 1629. This work, again in print, is recognized as a particularly fine translation,[18] and it alone has often been enough to establish Hobbes's *bona fides* as a humanist. He was, notably, proud to claim another distinction for his work. Other English translations of Thucydides at the time were translations of translations, from either Latin or French sources. Hobbes's was a translation directly into English from the Greek. This is one of the hallmarks of humanist accomplishment as it has been traditionally understood. Hobbes was a part of the ongoing project to unearth the ancient texts either lost, or in this case inadequately preserved, by earlier scholars because they lacked the requisite competency in the text's original language.

Indeed, Hobbes himself and Aubrey testify to what a fine humanist he was going to become from the earliest known point of his education under the young Oxford scholar Richard Latimer. In his autobiography, Hobbes boasts that prior to entering Oxford's Magdalen Hall at age fourteen[19] (in 1603) he had had six years of Latin and Greek, and could speak four languages. Aubrey records that Mr. Latimer "delighted in his scholar, T. H.'s company, and used to instruct him, and two or three ingenious youths more, in the evening till 9 a clock." He further boasts that Hobbes had "turned Euripedes' *Medea* out of Greek into Latin iambics, which he presented to his master."[20]

But skills with ancient languages were not all that might make a humanist, and here too we can see in the materials that accompany Hobbes's translation a solid marker of his participation in the practices associated with humanists. Hobbes writes in the prefatory writings and dedicatory that it is not merely that he loved Thucydides and wished to make the text available to others (in the way he himself experienced it in the Greek).[21] It is also that Thucydides's *History of the Peloponnesian War* was a text that could do something for, and indeed *to*, the reader who approached it in the right way. In the dedicatory he recommends it to his new young charge, William Cavendish, in this way:

> I could recommend the author unto you, not impertinently, for that he had in his veins the blood of kings; but I choose rather to recommend him for his writings, as having in them profitable instruction for noblemen, and such as may come to have the managing of great and weighty actions. For I may confidently say, that notwithstanding the excellent both examples and precepts of heroic virtue you have at home, this book will confer not a little to your institution; especially when you come to

the years to frame your life by your own observation. For in history, actions of *honour* and *dishonour* do appear plainly and distinctly, which are which; but in the present age they are so disguised, that few there be, and those very careful, that be not grossly mistaken in them.[22]

It seems likely that Hobbes intended his translation of Thucydides (whom he celebrates as an antidemocratic hero in his accompanying essay, "Of the Life and History of Thucydides")[23] as a commentary on Charles I's conflicts with Parliament amidst efforts to assert personal rule.[24] Hobbes's elitist (and promonarchical) politics carry over into his prefatory "To the Readers," where he tells "the multitude" that his translation has already passed muster with those whose judgments, unlike theirs, he truly respects. It is only out of prudence, he tells them, that he begs the "terrible" multitude to read his work with an open mind.[25] This element of Hobbes's self-presentation as a humanist who teaches virtue to the select few capable of acquiring it relates to what I stated in the introduction concerning Hobbes and questions of audience, but for the moment I wish to dwell on Hobbes's pedagogical claims in this translation.

His translation, Hobbes asserts, could do something for the young nobleman Cavendish's "institution." Reading this book for what it was, rather than its (evidently, still "not impertinent")[26] source, might make him a better, more worthy, nobleman. If the world of Great Britain in the 1620s was perhaps a time in which honor and dishonor had become confused, a good history such as this could remove their disguise, unmask false honor and separate the authentic from the counterfeit. Reading Thucydides might therefore make a nobleman live up to his responsibility, especially if he is the kind to take on "great and weighty actions."

I wish to focus on how Hobbes frames the value and character of useful learning. It is already well known that humanists valued learning that aided persons in the domain of the *vita activa;* it is clear that Hobbes wishes to provide learning that makes a nobleman capable of participating in political life, although not the political life designed to sustain a self-governing republic. It is not merely the domain that must interest us, but what Hobbes, as a humanist, suggests about the characteristics of useful learning itself. For Hobbes and humanists before him, such learning is a particular kind of *possession.* Moreover, it was meant to be a possession that conferred, or more aptly, generated specific powers and advantages.

It is not just that Cavendish will now have a copy of the history by Thucydides on his shelves. If he actually reads the work when he's ready,

Hobbes suggests, it will do something to him, to *his* "institution." He will possess it in a different sense than mere claim right on the physical entity as property. It can, with his effort, have an impact upon *who* he is, or who he might become. This particular sense of learning as a possession that also helps craft an identity is also to be found in the passages where Hobbes praises (possibly falsely)[27] Cavendish's recently deceased father. The dead earl employed Hobbes, thereby having created the debt of gratitude he references in the dedicatory. Nevertheless, he tells his student there could be no better person to dedicate the book to than his father even if that debt did not exist. This is because "there was not any, who more really, and less for glory's sake favoured those that studied the liberal arts liberally." This general virtue, which redounded to Hobbes's benefit particularly, is in part a reference to the library Hobbes was able to use and build while in the previous earl's employ. Hobbes tells the son that it created a house in which no man "should less need the university" than his own. Here again, however, Hobbes is careful not to attribute mere superficial possession to the previous earl's learning. He writes: "For his own study, it was bestowed, for the most part, in that kind of learning which best deserveth the pains and hours of great persons, history and civil knowledge: and directed not to the ostentation of his reading, but to the government of his life and the public good. For he read, so that the learning he took in by study, by judgment he digested, and converted into wisdom and ability to benefit his country: to which also he applied himself with zeal, but such as took no fire either from faction or ambition."[28] Possessed learning becomes a part of an identity constituted by virtues when it is digested, internalized, and converted into "wisdom and ability" for the country's sake. And he continues with further testimony to the virtues the elder Cavendish possessed as a result of his studies. He could give sound advice, express himself clearly, and handle difficult matters both public and private. He was "one whom no man was able either to draw or justle out of the straight path of justice" (*EW*, 8:iv).

Nor is this notion of learning as an internalized possession restricted to the praise of Cavendishes. In his opening remarks in "To the Readers," the same concepts are at work. Thucydides himself is to be ranked among the most highly regarded ancients, for he is "a workman no less perfect in his work" in history than "Homer in poesy, Aristotle in philosophy, Demosthenes in eloquence" (ibid., vii). History's "principal and proper work" is "to instruct and enable men, by the knowledge of actions past, to bear themselves prudently in the present and providently toward the future" (ibid.). No one, says Hobbes, does this more naturally and fully than Thucydides. Just as readers of histories may come to possess various virtues, so historians may also be compared.

Do they possess the virtues necessary to the production of worthy histories? Other histories may delight with fantastic stories, or reflect the historian's talents in speculating on motives, but Thucydides's history is most instructive because "he filleth his narrations with that choice of matter, and ordereth them with that judgment, and with such perspicuity and efficacy expresseth himself, that, as Plutarch saith, he maketh his auditor a spectator" (ibid.). Here we can recognize some of the forms of eloquence Hobbes is said to have reconciled himself to after having returned to rhetoric and humanism after supposedly having largely spurned them for geometry and a scientific approach to politics.[29] Thucydides is one who makes "word-pictures," a technique Hobbes is said to have used himself in *Leviathan* and *Behemoth*.

Without wishing to disagree with the claim that Hobbes admired and used "word-pictures," my argument is that this hook is too weak to hold the claim that Hobbes abandoned the humanism that informed works like his translation of Thucydides when he took up mathematics. There are, to be sure, elements of this translation's accompanying material Hobbes no longer embraced after he offered the world a science of politics. This would include, obviously, the praise of Aristotle and the assertion that honor and dishonor might be discerned merely on the basis of a superior character, rather than by the fiat of a sovereign. This, however, does not amount to an abandonment of humanism, or humanism's understanding of learning. Still, if the basis for sustaining the view that Hobbes moved from a humanist phase to a mathematical phase is weak—and I will argue that it is weaker still—there is a need for a more positive case.

Why should we believe that Hobbes remained a humanist in his approach to mathematics? The straightforward answer is as follows: First, and contrary to another implicit and flawed presupposition of the "phased" view of Hobbes, being a humanist in the seventeenth century and before did not mean being amathematical. It is (according to the phased view) as if picking up mathematics meant that Hobbes had to put down his humanist understanding of what it meant to possess useful learning. In fact, as I will argue momentarily, mathematical skills were also skills that many humanists understood one could "possess" in the way I have described, just as one might possess other moral or intellectual talents. Second, Hobbes continued to participate in this way of praising and practicing mathematical knowledge skills himself. Third, the possession of these skills was sufficient for Hobbes to claim a science of politics. Importantly, he was willing to make this claim on a basis quite foreign to the announced (if not implicit) contemporary standards of the scientific (and in some cases philosophical) knowledge of politics. Finally, and as mentioned earlier, the humanist affinities for mathematics translated into a high culture of mathematical products, not least as a refined Stuart and Elizabethan appreciation for the plastic arts, theater, and architecture.[30] As I will argue in Chapter 8, Hobbes's *Leviathan* is a work that participates in this appeal to this high culture's consumption, especially as that culture fed the ideology of absolutism in the Stuart Court. For present purposes, however, I now wish to turn to the sources and writings of humanist educators and their discussion of what one might come to possess through mathematical learning.

Humanist Education and Mathematics

Conventional narratives of the scientific revolution and Hobbes's place among the scientific revolutionaries have made it unnecessary for Hobbes scholars to consider the full range of possible connections between the philosopher and his humanist predecessors. In this part of the chapter I will focus on one, particularly glaring, omission: those humanist teachers who made mathematical learning a part of their students' curriculum. I will begin with a key source for mathematical humanist pedagogues, Quintilian.

QUINTILIAN

In Quentin Skinner's very extensive treatment of Hobbes, rhetoric, and humanism, there is probably no more important classical source than Quintilian.[31] He is an authoritative source on figures, tropes, and ornament, and a critically important figure for attempting to untangle the relationship between the good speaker and the good man. For all the detailed attention he receives in Skinner's treatment, one part of the *Institutio oratoria* goes unnoticed: Quintilian's ringing endorsement of mathematics.

After a complete copy was discovered in 1416, Quintilian's *Institutio oratoria* became key to humanist conceptions of education.[32] Given that the *Institutio oratoria* is dedicated to equipping the young and promising orator with superlative skills, Quintilian's inclusion of mathematics is both surprising and noteworthy. In fact, Quintilian may have anticipated his reader's shock and seems to have thought of this as all the more reason to press forward:

> What, say some, has the knowledge of the way to describe an equilateral triangle or a straight line got to do with the pleading in the law-courts or speaking in the senate? Will an acquaintance with the names and

intervals of the notes of the lyre help an orator to defend a criminal or direct the policy of his country? They will perhaps produce a long list of orators who are most effective in the courts but have never sat under a geometrician and whose understanding of music is confined to the pleasure which their ears, like those of other men, derive from it. To such critics I reply, and Cicero frequently makes the same remark in his Orator, that I am not describing any orator who actually exists or has existed, but I have in my mind's eye an ideal Orator perfect down to the smallest detail.[33]

Quintilian did not assert that training in mathematics *is* training in oratory, but that training in mathematics is part of a general education (παιδεια) (*Institutio oratoria* 1.10.15, 22–26). It makes for a complete orator, and he insists that this is an element of what is necessary to achieve his goal: to craft an orator who would not falter under any circumstances (1.10.1, 5–6). Quintilian's student, like the students tutored in Plato's works, would be an "ideal sage who is to be consummate in all knowledge and a very god incarnate" (1.10.5). The advantages conferred by the mathematical part of this education are not in most instances immediate. Rather, they bolster the orator's capacity and supply him with subtle strengths. An orator whose education is supplemented with mathematics acquires skills that "do not reveal or intrude themselves in actual speaking, [but] supply hidden forces and make their silent presence felt" (1.10.7).

Musical harmony and rhythm were a traditional part of mathematical learning. The orator needed to learn music, and Quintilian would convince his reader of the nobility of the subject. Orpheus and Linus studied music; it was considered both divine and one of the oldest arts. Awareness of the mathematical principles behind harmonies yielded philosophical knowledge:[34] "Pythagoras for instance and his followers popularized the belief, which they no doubt received from earlier teachers, that the universe is constructed on the same principles which were afterwards imitated in the construction of the lyre. . . . As for Plato, there are certain passages in the *Timaeus* which are quite unintelligible to those who have not studied the theory of music" (1.10.12–13).

More pertinent to the practice of declaiming, knowledge of both harmony and meter was particularly effective in controlling the mood of one's audience. Music "soothed the savage breast" (1.10.9). The armies of Sparta were "fired to martial ardor by the strains of music"; the greatest generals "played on the lyre and the pipe." The abilities one gained though an education in music were truly profound: "Give me knowledge of the principles of music, which have the power to excite or assuage the emotions of mankind. We are told that Pythagoras on one occasion, when some young men were led astray by their passions, to commit an outrage on a respectable family, calmed them by ordering the piper to change her strain to a spondaic measure" (1.10.32). He recollects a fictitious story, a myth he approves as indicative of the learnedness of its author. A piper is accused of manslaughter because he played a tune in the Phrygian mode as an accompaniment to a sacrifice: the person officiating went mad and flung himself over a precipice (1.10.33).

Are there points of connection with Hobbes's affinity with mathematics? Thus far, I have emphasized particular elements of Quintilian's argument for mathematical education that would have likely met with Hobbes's disapproval. Hobbes directed his suspicions and invective toward those who sought to manipulate crowds by playing on their passions. Testifying to the power of an education in music by illustrating how it might be used to drive men mad might have impressed Hobbes, but would not have pleased him. Hobbes devotes only the smallest space to consideration of why harmonies are a pleasing sensation. He does so in the *Elements of Law*, where he also takes note of Galileo's findings on harmony.[35] Hobbes's contemporaries, however, took the search for harmonies that reflected the divine ordering of the universe very seriously. Marin Mersenne envisioned ambitious plans for the study and use of harmonies as a means of moving closer to understanding and expressing the workmanship of divine creation.[36]

Quintilian's praise of another branch of mathematical learning, geometry, is more pertinent to what Hobbes himself appreciated. Echoing his contemporaries, Quintilian asserts that the value of geometry does not so much lie in the knowledge that it yields, but in the way the practice of geometrical reasoning actually "sharpens [the] wits and generates quickness of perception." He goes so far as to assert that geometrical skills are useful to the orator in their concrete application: the ability to manipulate lines and figures, for example, will make an orator more capable of handling cases where the opposing sides dispute the boundaries of their property. Most of his arguments, however, are variations on the connection between mathematics and sharp wits.[37]

Quintilian associated mathematical reasoning with syllogistic reason.[38] Typically, we think of rhetoric in terms of its deviation from syllogistic practice. Rhetoricians use enthymemes (arguments with an implicit premise) rather than syllogisms. For the sake of including mathematics within the fold of his education, Quintilian argues the opposite. Because the enthymeme is almost like a syllogism, those who learn to reason syllogistically with mathematics also train themselves in a skill that neighbors the rhetorical:

> But geometry and oratory are related in a yet more important way than this. In the first place logical development is one of the necessities of geometry. And is it not equally a necessity for oratory? Geometry arrives at its conclusion from definite premises, and by arguing from what is certain proves what was previously uncertain. Is not this just what we do in speaking? Again are not the problems of geometry almost entirely solved by the syllogistic method, a fact which makes the majority assert that geometry bears a closer resemblance to logic than to rhetoric? But even the orator will sometimes, though rarely, prove his point by formal logic. For, if necessary, he will use the syllogism, and he will certainly make use of the enthymeme which is a rhetorical form of syllogism. Further the most absolute proof is that which is generally known as linear demonstration. And what is the aim of oratory if not proof? Again oratory sometimes detects falsehoods closely resembling the truth by the use of geometrical methods.[39]

Whether *we* find Quintilian persuasive is not particularly important. He could be said to have stretched his rhetorical abilities to the limit to include geometry within the orator's training—indeed this might have been his purpose. What is important is that Quintilian's writings on mathematics shaped the arguments of the many Renaissance humanists who took an interest in and promoted mathematical learning.[40] Mathematics, still a long way off from creating the calculating and calculable world which seems so far removed from humanistic pursuits as they are often conceived today, would be situated, at times tenuously, within the *vita activa*.

Later Renaissance Pedagogues: Mathematics, Character Construction, and the Conflict Between Scholastic and Humanist Educational Ideals

Although recent scholarship has illustrated the need for caution when drawing rigid distinctions between humanists and scholastics, it remains the case that one of the defining features of Renaissance humanism was the antagonism many humanists harbored toward the proponents and defenders of traditional scholastic methods of education.[41] The humanist affinity for mathematics can be understood as a part of this larger conflict. One way of engaging in the struggle against the schools was to celebrate the parts of the curriculum that they neglected, and mathematics and mathematicians were marginal figures in most medieval institutions. Humanists took up the cause of mathematics, and there found a number of virtues that allowed them to reiterate a key claim in this conflict: that the humanists were the champions of useful learning while the scholastics had lost themselves in meaningless abstractions and debates. Although not all of the prominent humanist educators were in favor of mathematical learning, they all understood mathematical education as a matter of character. Would it, or would it not, help produce students who could usefully and skillfully interact with the world? Would it grant them the kind of learning they could possess? Would it supply them with a reserve of intellectual powers which might serve to make them better gentlemen? Would the mathematically trained person prove worthy of patronage, be a useful and skilled person? And, finally, in that being mathematical had become synonymous with worldly merit, what might threaten the credibility of those who truly possessed mathematical virtues? Were the critics merely jealous, and were there some who sought the recognition for being mathematical without actually possessing the "real" virtues that mathematical skills imparted? I will begin this brief survey with the Spanish humanist Juan Luis Vives, known as "the second Quintilian."[42]

Vives: Mathematics with Reservations

Vives played a significant role in the development of English humanism prior to the Henrican (English Protestant) Reformation. Following his dedication of *Commentaries on the Civitas Dei* (1523) to Henry VIII, Vives found himself the successful client of the Crown. He was invited to teach at Oxford, at Corpus Christi College (in 1523).[43] Vives devoted an entire chapter of *De tradendis disciplinis* (1531) to mathematics. Some of Quintilian's claims were left behind, many were echoed, and some new claims were added.

Like Quintilian, Vives presents mathematics as part of a well-rounded education.[44] Unlike Quintilian, he does not argue that skill in mathematics makes one a better orator. He recommends mathematics as a way of cultivating diligent mental habits. Mathematics, he asserts, can lend greater gravity to distracted minds, and quiet babbling tongues: "Young men should be led to the study of the mathematical arts, in order that muteness may succeed talk, and silence may be imposed on a tongue previously busy."[45] He wrote:

> The mathematical sciences are particularly disciplinary to flighty and restless intellects which are inclined to slackness, and shrink from or will

not support the toil of a continued effort. For they engage these minds and compel them to action, and do not suffer them to wander. Forgetful minds are not suitable for these studies. . . . In this subject, there is a necessity in what is taught of the idea of series and a perpetual string of proofs. We can thus easily let them slip, unless they are frequently made use of and thoroughly impressed upon the mind.[46]

Geometry in particular is associated with systematic thinking, and in ways that will resonate with Hobbes's views: "In Geometry there will be set forth the explanations of all the terms used in the subject. Then those principles which seem to be most in agreement with the constitution of our minds, and which we possess as though they were impressed upon our mind as anticipations (i.e. axioms). Then come theorems and their proofs which (in accordance with what is granted) not merely satisfy us, but also compel us, and take by force our assent."[47]

The admiration for the capacity to produce proofs that do more than merely satisfy, but which force assent, is noteworthy in another respect. A key part of the humanists' polemic against their scholastic opponents was to accuse them of endless disputation. Their interminable disputes, the humanist critics charged, served merely the needs of arrogant men who liked to make fine distinctions and argue, but no one else. Agricola, an early champion in the North of humanism over scholasticism, suggested that mathematics had not been cultivated in the schools precisely because it did not admit of the quibbling and noisy disputation favored there.[48] Geometric demonstration, they liked to point out, could be carried out in complete silence—a point that resonates with Vives's claims concerning the quiet tongues created through a mathematical education.[49]

The humanists who endorsed mathematical training were not unequivocal in their praise of it. Vives's treatment exemplifies some of these reservations: "If anyone allows himself to follow up deeply these reflections and observations, he will be led by them into the infinite: and anxious inquiry into such mathematical problems leads away from the things of life, and estranges men from a perception of what conduces to the common weal."[50] The well-rounded public servant couldn't become too absorbed in such studies.

This theme was reiterated by another humanist reformer, Roger Ascham. He warned schoolmasters to "marke all Mathematicall heades, which be onley and wholy being to those sciences, how solitarie they be themselves, how unfit to live with others, and how unapte to serve in the world." Such as have "over moch quickness of witte, either given by nature, or sharpened by studie, doth not commonlie bring forth, eyther greatest learning, best maners, or happiest life in the end."[51] A man in training to become a master of civic affairs should have the benefit of training in mathematics, but he should guard against acquiring a scholar's preoccupation lest he become withdrawn. Mathematicians, as Steven Shapin has documented, were not immune to the suspicions cast upon scholars in general: their training might turn them into rude and abrasive pedants, unfit for civil conversation—a vice particularly damning in one hoping for a life as a courtier. They might be too determined to stand on a point rather than give way, as a gentleman might in order to preserve the civility of conversation.[52] Although I will not try to cover the issue here, this became one of the most common criticisms of Hobbes.[53]

Vives's criticisms against the bookish indulgences of the mathematician are, however, mediated by a third theme. If mathematics should not lead away from practical affairs, its proper practice is nevertheless credited for yielding particularly useful forms of knowledge. We ought to learn numbers: besides sharpening the wit, they make us proficient in things that are essential to daily life: "No part of life can be devoid of the use of numbers."[54] Geometry is recommended because from it are developed optics, perspective drawing, architecture, "and the art of measurement, all of which have great usefulness in ordinary life for protecting our bodies; for movement and position of heavy weights.... Then follows the study how to measure fields, mountains, towers and buildings. How great comfort does architecture bring to us in our dwellings!"[55]

Like Quintilian, Vives praises the use of knowledge of harmony as a way of calming weary minds, as well as the student's savage nature. He cautions against allowing the students to train in the wrong kind of music.[56] Astronomy should not be put to use to divine the future, but it can be used to help us better describe and determine the seasons, thereby aiding farmers. It is essential to navigation: "Without this knowledge the sailor would wander in uncertainty amidst the greatest and most grievous dangers."[57] He goes on to recommend several mathematicians suitable for teaching, singling out Euclid: "I wish him to be very carefully explained."[58]

Richard Mulcaster
English humanist enthusiasm for mathematics runs high in Richard Mulcaster. As a part of his plan for university reform, Mulcaster recommended a radical reorganization of school colleges on the principle that individual colleges ought to be devoted to the distinct subjects taught at specific phases of a student's education. This curriculum would include a college devoted to training

in mathematics. Here again mathematics is lauded for its capacity to sharpen the intellect. Those who acquire the science are exemplars of mental acuity and the intellectual cautiousness of the truly diligent thinker. I have mentioned Ascham's warnings against "Mathematicall heades." Mulcaster put himself forward as Ascham's competitor, and in the case of mathematics, he illustrates his anxiousness to outshine his opponent. He goes to some lengths to defend the practice against Ascham's cautions.

Criticism of mathematics, Mulcaster asserts, comes from persons who do not "know the force of these faculties bycause they neuer thought them worthey their studie as being without preferment, and within contempt, do vse to abuse them, and to mocke at *mathematicall* heades."[59] In short, those who berate mathematics do not know mathematics, and their ignorance is indicative of deficiencies in their character. They are too preoccupied with a shallow conception of the skills necessary to preferment to notice its true worth. In the *Scholemaster* Ascham had expressed admiration for Sir John Cheke (provost of King's College, Cambridge, from 1548 to 1553 and tutor to King Edward VI). Mulcaster recounts Cheke's devotion to mathematics: "In the middest of all his great learning, his greate eloquence his sownd judgement, his graue modestie, feared the blame of a *mathematicall* head so litle in himselfe, and thought the profession to be so farre from any such taint, . . . as he bewraid his great affection towards them most euidently."[60] Moreover, Mulcaster notes, Cheke made efforts to ensure that the students of King's College were educated in mathematics: "for the better encouraging of them to that studie gaue them a number of *Euclides* of his own coste."[61]

Furthermore, the "*mathematicall* head" possessed a number of virtues sometimes mistaken for flaws, or merely parodied by those who posed as mathematicians. The practice was being dragged through the mud by those who could only pretend to understand it. Those who know mathematics know the virtues that it requires, and therefore have the capacity to develop and appreciate those virtues. Hobbes had suggested to Cavendish that history might allow him to cultivate a capacity for moral judgment. Here Mulcaster deploys an extension of the logic of cultivated capacities to turn the tables on the critics of mathematical learning: "The studie [of mathematics] . . . requireth attentiuenes, and such a minde, as will not be soone caried to any publike shew, before his full ripnes, but will rest in solitarie contemplation till he finde himself fledge [i.e., fit to fly]. Now this their meditation if they be studentes in deede: or the shadow of meditation, if they be but counterfettes, do these men plaie with all, & mock such mathematicall heades, to solace themselues with."[62] It's sour grapes for the critics of mathematics: their scorn is a masked confession of their own incapacity. On the other hand, those who do master the practice will indeed possess—unlike the counterfeiters and their "shadow" meditations, presumably—talents and capacities that will run deep: "In the manner of their teaching they do plant in the minde of the learner, an habite inexpugnible by bare probabilities, and not to be brought to beleeue vpon light coniectures, in any other knowledge, being still drawne on by vnfallible demonstrations: In their similitudenaire applications, they let one see by them in sense the like affection in contemplative, and intelligible things, and be the surest groundes to retourne vnto in replies and instances, either vpon defect in memorie, or in checke of auersarie, contraire to the common similitudes."[63]

Mulcaster goes on to suggest that there is a basic and immediate character to mathematical learning that other disciplines lack. He makes the point with reference to Plato's[64] comparison between philosophers and pilots aboard ship who go unheeded, achieving an expression of *ressentiment* to rival Plato's along the way:

> For when ye compare the common weale to a ship, and the people to the passangers, the application being vnder saile, maye be out of sight, when ye seeke for your proofe. But in these sciences the similitudinarie teaching is so certain in applying, and so confirmed by effectes: as there is nothing so farre from sense, and so secret in vnderstanding, but it will make it palpable. They be taken from the sense, and trauell the thought, but resolue the minde. And though such as vnderstand them not, do mislike them, which yet is not reason in them, nor any disgrace to the thing misliked by them, seeing ignorance misliketh: yet those that vnderstand them, maye boldly mislike the mislikers, and oppose the whole aunceint Philosphie, and all well appointed common weales against such mockmathematicalles, without whose helpe they could not liue, nor haue houses to hide their heades, though they thanke not their founders.[65]

Those who mock mathematics—the "mockmathematicalles"—are no disgrace to mathematics, merely themselves.

Mulcaster recollects the memory of one of his own teachers, "one master *Bukley*, somtime fellow of the saide colledge, and very well studyed in the *mathematicalls*."[66] William Buckley had been brought to King's by (the aforementioned) John Cheke, the Regius Professor of Greek, and another early humanist admirer of mathematical education. Buckley's *Arithmetica memorativa*[67] is indicative of how mathematics and the didactic practices of humanism could permeate each other. In this work Buckley had put the rules of mathematical practice into Latin verse (to make them easier and more pleasant to learn) and distributed copies to students. Mulcaster's memories of learning Greek at Cheke's King's College are intermingled with his learning of Euclid: "My selfe am to honour the memorie of that learned knight, being partaker my selfe of his liberall distribution of those *Euclides*, with whom he ioyned *Xenophon*, which booke he wished, and caused to be red in the same house, and gave them to studentes, to encourage them as well to the greeke toungue, as he did to the *Mathematickes*."[68]

Mathematics was thus a part of Mulcaster's gentlemanly education at Cambridge, and he thought it appropriate to continue and augment the practice. At the time of his authorship tradesmen were already pursuing mathematical skills. Indeed, part of the trouble experienced by advocates for genteel mathematical education was the risk of pollution—gentlemen who involved themselves with the practices beneath their station risked their status as gentlemen.[69] Mulcaster stood firm. At the time he published *Positions*, Mulcaster had been master of the Merchant and Taylor's School, and took great care, nevertheless, to laud mathematics for its use in the trades: "These sciences bewray them selues in many professions & trades which beare not the titles of learning, whereby it is well seene, that they are not prating, but profitable, grounds: not gay to the shew, but good to be shewed, & such meanes of vse, as the vse of our life were quite maimed without them."[70] This learning would be suitable for "marchaunets" (merchants), carpenters, masons, shipmasters, "maryners," "deuisours," and architects, and if they need to learn Latin to acquire these skills, then let them do so. Mulcaster announces that he is undeterred by those who would note that these professions have already served the nation without such erudition. His rebuttal: imagine how much better they will be once they augment their abilities with such training.[71] With this defense, Mulcaster openly defies the pollution concerns of gentlemen in the name of utility: let the tradesman become erudite, for the good of us all. The question of what is "gay to the shew" (flashy and insubstantial) should be ignored in favor of what is "good to be shewed" (useful). In fact, mathematically educated persons were making a living in the manufacture of (and instruction in) flashy—although not necessarily utilized—mathematical instruments for gentlemen. They sold their works to those who wished to associate themselves with the fruits of practical mathematical learning and the accomplishments associated with it (surveying their lands, gunnery and warfare, navigation—and therewith, imperial adventures).[72] There may be no better testimony to the connection between the *vita activa* and mathematics than the fear Mulcaster expresses concerning the fashionable, showy but shallow taste for things mathematical among gentlemen. I will return to this topic in Chapter 8, but I will now turn to the things that connect Hobbes to the authors I've just reviewed.

Hobbes and the Humanist Affinity for Geometry

Quintilian had argued that the study of mathematics made one a better orator. The (Late and Northern) Renaissance humanists adopted only a part of this argument.[73] They echoed Quintilian's claim that mathematics was a useful part of a general, well-rounded education and repeated his arguments celebrating the virtues of training in mathematics, just not his assertion that skill in mathematics contributed to skill in oratory per se. Vives and Mulcaster reiterated some of these arguments, and then developed and added to the list of laudable characteristics. Mathematics was the cure for the flighty mind. Persons whose thoughts buzzed about unsystematically might have this unruly characteristic tamed by the rigorous and methodical practice of mathematics. The mathematical thinker, particularly the geometer, began with carefully elaborated first principles and worked, one step at a time (*Et sic deinceps*), until he reached the conclusion. Although Hobbes does not simply mirror this line of reasoning, this notion of the systematic mathematical head is a critical part of his basis for recommending mathematics and, most of all, his own mathematically inspired philosophy.

THOUGHTS REGULATED AND UNREGULATED

The parallels emerge in some of Hobbes's most basic discussions of ways of thinking. Indeed, Hobbes's discussions of thinking equal what one might (anachronistically) call the humanist's phenomenological sensitivity to the mind at work. Hobbes speaks of two kinds of thought, "unregulated" and "regulated." Unregulated thought resembles the travels of the flighty minds referred to by Vives and the other humanists. According to Hobbes, it is "*without* design, and inconstant."[74] There is no desire to guide the thought, and nothing seems to govern the relation between the conceptions that pop into the unregulated thinker's head. There is something dream-like about this kind of thought. Who experiences Hobbes's unregulated thought? Vives's student's "flighty head" is the demeaned counterpart to the mathematically trained head. By comparison, Hobbes is in some respects less censorious.

He acknowledges that none of us are immune to unregulated thoughts; persons left alone have them. Moreover, he suggests that even in one's "wild rangings," a person might "perceive the way of it" and possibly discern some connection between the thoughts that follow one another. Hobbes gives an instance of his own:

> For in a discourse of our present civil war, what would seem more impertinent than to ask (as one did) what was the value of a Roman penny? Yet the coherence to me was manifest enough. For the thought of war introduced the thought of the delivering up the king to his enemies; the thought of that brought in the thought of the delivering up of Christ; and that again the thought of the 30 pence which was the price of that treason; and thence easily followed that malicious question; and all this in a moment of time, for thought is quick.[75]

(It must be noted that Hobbes was writing in 1651, shortly after the publication of *Eikon Basilike* in 1649, which was said to be the most popular book of the century. In this work issued after his execution, Charles I likens himself to the martyred Christ.[76] The "coherence" would have been, therefore, "manifest enough" to more than just Hobbes. This should be read as an opportunistic assault on Charles I's executioners.)

Nevertheless, the general portrait of the unregulated thinker is not particularly flattering. A person whose experiences do not go beyond unregulated thought would appear an idler, possibly addle-brained. We learn that unregulated thought is typical of those "without a care of anything," whose thoughts are busy, but without harmony. Hobbes compares their thoughts to "the sound which a lute out of tune would yield to any man, or in tune, to one that could not play."[77]

Regulated thought is a clear improvement, but in Hobbes's rubric it is not strictly identical with geometric or mathematical thought. According to Hobbes, a passion toward some concrete end may be enough to pull our thoughts into rough order.[78] However, the most strictly regulated thoughts are those of persons reasoning according to the dictates of science, and this form of reasoning *is* modeled after the ways of the geometers. The content that carries over from the humanist affinity for mathematics is the sense of orderliness, and the importance of building on clearly stated principles. For Hobbes, thought may be conducted without words, but we vastly improve our thinking with the aid of words. Words augment memory and help us form general concepts to cover the attributes of a vast number of particulars;

words of course facilitate our capacity to communicate, and they can record and codify our reason. In his discussions of how persons think, words remain Hobbes's basic currency.

The implicit framework of possessed capacities is at work here too. When we interrogate the character of others' thought, Hobbes instructs us to ask: Do they keep track of their definitions? Do they combine their words into propositions that fit their definitions? Do the propositions come together to form syllogisms, and do these form a longer chain that instructs us in a useful knowledge of cause and effect? Orderly thought, in Hobbes's framework, is expressed and developed in terms of the orderly use of words.

Within this framework, mathematics and geometry in particular are Hobbes's chief exemplars of the most orderly thought we can achieve. He writes in *Leviathan:*

> Seeing then that *truth* consisteth in the right ordering of names in our affirmations, a man that seeketh precise *truth* had need to remember what every name he uses stands for, and to place it accordingly, or else he will find himself entangled in words; as a bird in lime twigs, the more he struggles the more belimed. And therefore in geometry (which is the only science that it hath pleased God hitherto to bestow on mankind) men begin at settling the significations of their words; which settling of significations they call *definitions*, and place them in the beginning of their reckoning.[79]

Flightiness of mind is something that Hobbes is willing to excuse, so long as we can cultivate the discipline necessary to generate more ordered thoughts when we need them. Flight, nevertheless, has made its return in Hobbes's philosophy, and in a tropic form just as demeaning as Vives's "flighty head," when Hobbes considers whose diligence with definitions falls short of his standards:

> For the errors of definitions multiply themselves according as the reckoning proceeds, and lead men into absurdities, which at last they see, but cannot avoid without reckoning anew from the beginning, in which lies the foundation of their errors. From whence it happens that they which trust to books do as they that cast up many little sums into a greater, without considering whether those little sums were rightly cast up or not; and at last finding the error visible, and not mistrusting their first grounds, know not which way to clear themselves, but spend time in fluttering over their books, as birds that enter by the chimney,

and finding themselves enclosed in a chamber, flutter at the false light of a glass window, for want of wit to consider which way they came in.[80]

Hobbes and his humanist predecessors have filled the intellectual aviary with a wide variety of species. If Mulcaster's true students of mathematics only take off when fit to fly—when "fledge"—the bird-wits within these passages from Hobbes bespeak spastic, undignified flight. The mind unlike that of the geometer's flutters and makes itself a victim of its own sloppy practices with language. The kind of carelessness against which Hobbes preaches includes the thoughtless acceptance of another person's words, especially those of a scholastic authority. For Hobbes, practice in geometry is a possession that helps thinkers avoid awkward flight.

Bickering Scholastics, Silent Geometers

I noted that humanists such as Vives and Agricola celebrated mathematics for the indisputability of its conclusions. Humanists used this characteristic of mathematical thought's reputation to make unflattering contrasts with the bickering of their scholastic opponents. Although often cited as an example of what separated Hobbes from his premodern opponents, the likeness between Hobbes and his humanist predecessors could not be greater when it came to making this kind of argument. Like Mulcaster, Hobbes is happy to trumpet the "inexpugnable" mathematical knowledge and to make it a goad to his school-trained opponents. In this context new light is shed on the claims of the "Epistle Dedicatory" of the *Elements of Law*, often cited as evidence of his rejection of scholastic learning, but which we should now see as also joining him to a tradition of humanist condemnation of scholasticism:

> From the two principal parts of our nature, Reason and Passion, have proceeded two kinds of learning, mathematical and dogmatical. The former is free from controversies and dispute, because it consisteth in comparing figures and motion only; in which things truth and the interest of men oppose not each other. But in the later there is nothing not disputable, because it compareth men, and meddleth with their right and profit; in which, as oft as reason is against a man, so oft will a man be against reason. And from hence it cometh, that they that have written of justice and policy in general, do all invade each other, and themselves, with contradiction. To reduce this doctrine to the rules and infallibility of reason, there is no way, but first to put such principles

down for a foundation, as passion not mistrusting, may not seek to displace; and afterward to build thereon the truth of cases in the law of nature (which hitherto have been built in the air) by degrees, till the whole be inexpugnable.

There are innumerable examples in which Hobbes rails against the disputatious nature of the schools, and then draws a contrast between their practices and the intellectual virtues he celebrates in geometers. In chapter 46 of *Leviathan*, for example, Hobbes makes such a comparison:

> But what has been the utility of those schools? What science is there at this day acquired by their readings and disputings? That we have of geometry, which is the mother of all natural science, we are not indebted for it to the schools. Plato, that was the best philosopher of the Greeks, forbad entrance into his school to all that were not already in some measure geometricians. There were many that studied that science to the great advantage of mankind. But there is no mention of their schools; nor was there any sect of geometricians.[81]

The contrast continues: the philosophy of the schools was more "dream than science." It was "set forth in senseless and insignificant language." Only those who learn geometry can cure themselves of these ills. The moral philosophy of the schools "is but a description of their own passions." Hence, "they make the rules of good and bad, by their own liking and disliking: by which means, in so great diversity of taste, there is nothing generally agreed on; but every one doth (as far as he dares) whatsoever seemeth good in his own eyes, to the subversion of commonwealth."[82]

These commonalities with the humanist proponents of mathematics are important. Why have they gone unnoticed? Hobbes has been understood as a part of the wave of thinkers who ushered in the "New Science." And, indeed, Hobbes was a full participant in this moment, and an admirer of Galileo. By drawing Hobbes a bit closer to Renaissance humanists, are we pulling him away from his affiliation with the New Science? Only if we assume that the New Science itself was not also a participant in the practices of Renaissance humanism. Work in the history of science shows us that we should not make this assumption.[83] Showing the continuity between Hobbes and his humanist predecessors in matters mathematical is thus not to shove Hobbes back down the ladder of a predetermined history of ideas. It is, however, to question some of the assumptions of that history. We have tended to laud the "New

Scientists" for using mathematics (or hoping to use mathematics) to *discover* things about the universe. It is what they did to modify our view of this grand *object* that has captured our attention. The humanist side of the turn toward a more mathematical approach to thinking, however, held out the possibility that achievements in philosophy and science were not necessarily a matter of what one might know about a given object, even the grandest objects of all. The criteria for accomplishment retained the humanist ideals that a form of learning had to do something for the person who possessed it. Great learning made great persons, persons whose learned possessions made them capable of great things. Such learning was meant to produce distinction, and Hobbes should be seen as a participant in this, perhaps vain, humanistic culture of intellectual accomplishment. His embrace of mathematics, and geometry in particular, was a part of this culture, not a departure from it.

Where Hobbes does distinguish himself from the humanists we have reviewed is in his single-mindedness in turning mathematical ways of thought into a source of power. Mulcaster's trenchant defense of mathematical training will help illustrate this point by comparison. Both Mulcaster and Hobbes would likely agree that rather than being isolated from the world by his discipline, the mathematically trained person serves his fellows as well or better than any other. Hobbes, however, goes further. The spirit of Ascham's and Vives's criticism reflects, at least in part, a fear that mathematics will become an obsession. While Mulcaster does not express this fear with regard to mathematics, his educational philosophy includes many of the traditional subjects that were designed to prepare a well-rounded individual. His basic educational philosophy was a part of a larger movement of humanist educational reformers such as Vives, Erasmus, and even Ascham. His goal was to use education to bring what he thought of as man's God-given abilities to their perfection: the justification for doing so was that it pleased God, and it served the commonwealth. Hobbes's intentions for mathematical thought, however, are more intellectually imperial. His sustained attention to matters of method, and his willingness to make the geometer's methods the standard across a wide variety of disciplines, *is* a basis for distinction.

Even for Mulcaster, there is such a thing as trying to go too far with one's mathematical knowledge. A brief, but for our purposes not insignificant, example can be found in Mulcaster's *The First Part of the Elementary*.[84] He asserts that the end of education is "to help natur vnto hir perfection, which is, when all hir abilities be perfited in their habit."[85] In his view God grants us a set of natural abilities that permit us to continue our existence and to flourish,[86] but it is incumbent upon us to develop and cultivate them. God put into our hands the capacity to catch and throw, but it is an ability that we must develop by our own efforts. Education is a process whereby these natural abilities are both cultivated, and then also by further efforts brought to even greater perfection—as when we go beyond mere catching and throwing to refinements that make us the most effective in these practices. Mulcaster takes a similar view of the education of mental capacities.[87] It is in the context of outlining these educational ideals that Mulcaster inserts a brief note of caution. He suggests that his education follows the lead of nature, fulfills our end on earth according to God's intentions for us, but this program, in spite of its "resemblance of natur," must not be taken to mean a counterfeiting of nature: "This is that resemblance of natur, which I do mean, not to counterfeat hir in soe other work, as fondlie comparing, or frowardlie bragging with the effects of natur, like som *Apelles* in [painting], or som *Archimedes* in motion, but when consideration & judgement wiselie marking, whereunto natur is either euidentlie giuen, or secretlie affectionate, doth frame an education consonant therevnto, to bring all those things to perfection by art, which natur wisheth perfit, by franknesse of hir offer."[88] Hobbes celebrates accomplishments that go beyond these limits. He not only promises to teach philosophers to imitate the effects of nature (if not the causes of these effects), but goes even further in what he calls the *a priori* sciences where he teaches men to imitate God.

What Hobbes has to say in praise of mathematical training is not radically different from what his humanist counterparts said. What they say differs in the degree to which they make their educational cures depend upon these mathematical virtues. Hobbes is much more dependent; much hinges on the particular virtues he assigns to the geometrically reformed mind. As we shall see, the geometrically trained mind will make the difference between those Hobbes describes as "having no science" and those who do. Such a mind is also a check upon the possibility of possessing something worse, having internalized false rules of reasoning.[89] Here we also begin to see the glimmers of a distinctly modern enthusiasm for a technological fix-all intermingling with a more traditional humanist optimism/propaganda for the efficacy of educational improvements. The characteristics that the humanists appreciated remain in Hobbes's work, but they are put to use in Hobbes's works in new, more focused and aggressive ways. It is the singular dedication to making the world right by mathematics that makes Hobbes stand out against this background.[90]

3

CONSTRAINTS THAT ENABLE THE IMITATION OF GOD

Hobbes greets readers of *De Corpore* with a bold claim. His philosophy can teach one how to imitate God:

> Philosophy, therefore, the child of the world and your own mind, is within yourself; perhaps not fashioned yet, but like the world its father, as it was in the beginning, a thing confused. Do, therefore, as the statuaries do, who, by hewing off that which is superfluous, do not make but find the image. Or imitate the creation: if you will be a philosopher in good earnest, let your reason move upon the deep of your own cogitations and experience; those things that lie in confusion must be set asunder, distinguished, and every one stamped with its own name set in order; that is to say, your method must resemble that of the creation.[1]

Discovering philosophy within oneself may mean following the example of "statuaries" (sculptors), who claim to "find" their object in the raw material by removing the superfluous, but to be what Hobbes would consider a "philosopher in good earnest" one must learn to do as God did. One must imitate creation. One must make order out of confusion, and it is the capacity to do this that Hobbes seems to promise his readers.

Such promises do not sit comfortably with conventional views that assign Hobbes a role typically more modest than imitator of the omnipotent.[2] We have learned to think of Hobbes as a student of the natural order, and of human nature in particular, not as a creator. He is said to have grounded his systematic political philosophy in assumptions that posit permanent human characteristics. To better their condition, he did not seek to craft or create humans, but strove to compensate for, and accommodate, them.[3]

The conventional understanding of this process of accommodation and compensation is roughly captured by the notion of "constraints that enable." The constraints are most often associated with Hobbes's laws of nature.

They enable us to overcome and even take advantage of even the undesirable characteristics of human nature. We follow our self-interest and seek our own survival, and we are willing (and in the state of nature, even entitled) to do this at great cost to others. When unconstrained, the way we pursue these goals gets in the way of our capacity to cooperate with one another. Such a life has, famously, "no account of time; no arts; no letters; no society; and which is worst of all, continual fear, and danger of violent death," and the life of man is "solitary, poor, nasty, brutish, and short."[4] These would seem to be the conclusions of a detached observer of humanity, of a thinker content to work with our inconvenient characteristics. The constraints we impose are designed with these root-level motivations in mind. We try to channel them toward more productive ends (sometimes promising to turn disadvantages into advantages). They count on our reasoning, perhaps our self-interest, or our selfishness, but most important, they modify the rewards and punishments that attend loyalty or the temptation to betray. The constraints, therefore, do not modify basic human nature (however conceived). Instead, they create the circumstances under which beings assumed to have these characteristics can be predicted to cooperate with one another.

Against this perspective, I want to focus on a different set of constraints and a different set of promises to enable. The laws of nature are undoubtedly important, but there are more constraints in Hobbes's philosophy. Instead of working around an inviolable subject (who must bounce and rebound off the institutional structures of the state according to scientific prediction, but who remains whole and essentially unchanged), the constraints that Hobbes proposes are like those imposed by the hands of a craftsman. They are designed to refashion the subject. Those who submit themselves to Hobbesian constraints are to be crafted into forms suitable to a well-ordered commonwealth. They can be compared, as Hobbes indeed does, to the stones made to fit together by a mason into a well-constructed building—if our sharp edges and odd shapes prove too hard to trim, the stonemason may throw us away as useless.[5] Indeed, Hobbes not only does not think the subject inviolable, but alterable, and radically so: "The common people's minds, unless they be tainted with dependence on the potent, or scribbled over with the opinions of their doctors, are like clean paper, fit to receive whatsoever by public authority shall be imprinted in them."[6]

Hobbes did not, however, wish to be rid of the "doctors" (i.e., scholars), and so one must ask who he thinks will scribble on the minds of the scribblers. Hobbes's lessons in philosophy are meant to mold the minds of the doctors.

He wishes to craft new doctors, and their new education in philosophy, the science they will learn to possess, will be the foremost concern of this chapter.

Constraints on Truth and Language

Hobbes places limits on truth. Specifically, he places limits on what can *count* as truth. Truth only emerges under specific circumstances: it is restricted to the realm of words. This limitation suggests nominalism, but truth's limitation to the realm of words represents a more comprehensive confinement, of which nominalism is a key part.[7] Taken as a whole, these limits can be seen most clearly when made to stand in the foreground against the truth claims of worldly, especially factual, experience.[8] There are several components to the barrier Hobbes erects between the experience of things outside ourselves and the realm of truth.

He tells us, for example, that prudence (the wisdom acquired through experience)[9] cannot produce truth. Although Hobbes's devaluation of prudence is sometimes overemphasized,[10] there is no question that he draws a sharp distinction between prudence and the knowledge made available through (his) philosophy.[11] The distinction is perhaps most marked when Hobbes allows that even beasts can be prudent.[12] The prudent person may "recon" (recollect) the images in his head, compare them with present circumstances, and use signs to form indispensable judgments. When one considers that Hobbes states that our minds are prone to a chaotic "wild ranging,"[13] this certainly counts as an accomplishment. The prudent individual's desires and curiosity may allow him or her to tame the chaos, to regulate the train of thought and sweep through his or her memories like a spaniel searching out a scent.[14] Whatever the prudent person's efforts, the results do not represent the best that humans can do. For that we need "the help of speech and method." With this help "the same faculties may be improved to such a height as to distinguish men from all other living creatures."[15]

Only when we have moved to this higher level, where the order of our thoughts is tamed by the order we impose (or could impose) on our words and discourse, will Hobbes allow us to speak of truth and falsity. Mere mental discourse, either the chaotic flurry of our fancy or thoughts strung together in order, may be useful. Nevertheless, these fancies, unassisted by the aid of words, are not the materials out of which truth can be constructed.[16]

In *Leviathan* Hobbes considers speech as technology. It is one of our most ancient inventions, standing in his estimation above all later innovations in communication. Hobbes grants printing recognition, but he recommends greater reverence for the unknown individual who invented letters—invented, he asserts, to help us memorize the different words that we can create with our tongues and other "organs of speech." We ought to be that much more impressed with speech:[17] "the most noble and profitable invention of all . . . consisting of *names* or *appellations*, and their connexion, whereby men register their thoughts, recall them when they are past, and also declare them one to another for mutual utility and conversation, without which there had been amongst men, neither commonwealth, nor society, nor contract, nor peace, no more than amongst lions, bears, and wolves."[18] Speech secures two fundamental advantages. It helps us remember our conceptions, and to communicate those conceptions to others. With speech we "transfer our mental discourse" into "verbal" discourse. We transfer, that is, "the train of thoughts into a train of words." Words keep our conceptions from slipping out of our memory, but speech does more than help with immediate sense impressions. Whenever we calculate, words help us retain conclusions we would otherwise ultimately lose. Words are thus a technology that facilitates reasoning itself. They allow us to speak of classes and categories of things. A person without words cannot generalize the conclusions of his thoughts to cover common circumstances. Language can be used to codify and preserve our conclusions: with it we can teach them to others.[19]

Other things can be done with words.[20] With speech we may acquire help from one another by letting persons know "our wills and purposes."[21] We can also use speech "to please and delight ourselves and others, by playing with our words, for pleasure or ornament, innocently."[22]

Not long after listing the possibilities made available by speech, Hobbes dwells on the disadvantages that also result. Speech is a double-edged sword. Truth has no "place but amongst such living creatures as use speech."[23] This assertion suggests more than a claim about the relative intelligence and dignity of creatures capable of using speech. Speech-using creatures *can* stand above the rest in that they possess the necessary equipment for making truths, but the same equipment that allows them to make truths also gives them the privilege of speaking falsely, and not just falsities but absurdities. For example, the absurdity "incorporeal body"—the way some refer to the bread of the Eucharist—is created when we allow ourselves to combine words that belong to categories properly kept apart. Worse yet, such mistakes are covered over by words (often invented by the schools) as abbreviations for these "unfit connexions." The abuses of speech are such a dangerous source of confusion that we may self-destructively pull ourselves down to depths that less capable creatures need never fear.[24] In *De Homine* Hobbes writes:

> It is easily understood how much we owe to language, by which we, having been drawn together and agreeing to covenants, live securely, happily, and elegantly, we can so live, I insist, if we so will. But language also hath its disadvantages; namely because man, alone among the animals, on account of the universal signification of names, can create general rules for himself in the art of living just as in other arts; and so he alone can devise errors and pass them on for the use of others. Therefore man errs more widely and dangerously than can other animals . . . . Therefore by speech man is not made better, but only given greater possibilities.[25]

We may find ourselves trapped in a tangle of absurdities, but a key part of philosophy's task is to find a way out: "For speech has something in it like a spider's web . . . for by contexture of words tender and delicate wits are ensnared and stopped; but strong wits break easily through them."[26]

Hobbes thought himself a strong wit and took on the task of breaking through the absurdities that had accumulated through centuries of abuses committed by the schools and their deficient philosophies. If philosophy is to live up to its promise, if it is to grant us a possession worth having, it has to teach us to regulate—to place constraints—on our speech so that we might reap the benefits.

Hobbes imagines multiple ways we might become ensnared in speech. Some abuses of speech are deliberate. Persons lie: they use words to "declare that to be their will, which is not." They speak metaphorically by using words "in other sense than that they are ordained for."[27] They abuse the technology by putting it to use in grieving one another. These, however, are more subtle areas of potential abuse: he holds that there are circumstances in which the practices used in grieving another constitute an appropriate use of speech. These involve governing and instruction: "For seeing nature hath armed living creatures, some with teeth, some with horns, and some with hands, to grieve an enemy, it is but an abuse of speech, to grieve him with the tongue, unless it be one whom we are obliged to govern and then it is not to grieve, but to correct and amend."[28] Correcting and amending are Hobbes's near constant preoccupations; they are a necessary loophole. His dispraise for those who fail to define their words or remain unaware of how others define theirs is a good example.

Some abuses of speech are not deliberate. Human beings have given names to their conceptions, but they are not always as diligent in keeping track of these conceptions as they should be. Moreover, the definitions we supply ought to create a picture in the mind of the listener of the conception we name. The definitions of things that have conceivable causes, moreover, ought to resolve the causes (i.e., supply us with the necessary "accidents" of the matter under consideration that, when brought together, generate the entity).[29]

Unlike the conscious abuses of speech, these are not understood to be unequivocally deliberate. If working with only well-defined words is a strict mental discipline that must be achieved through diligence, then most abuses of speech are partially attributable to lapses in discipline. As was seen in passages quoted in the previous chapter, Hobbes is fond of drawing comparisons between the thinker who is not sure of the conceptions that attach (or should attach) to words and the troubles created by delinquent bookkeeping. Trusting an author's words is akin to the actions of

> a master of a family, [who] in taking an account, casteth up the sums of all the bills of expense into one sum, and not regarding how each bill is summed up by those that give them in account, nor what it is he pays for, he advantages himself no more than if he allowed the account in gross, trusting to every of the accountants' skill and honesty, so also in reasoning of all other things, he that takes up conclusions on the trust of authors, and doth not fetch them from the first items in every reckoning (which are the significations of names settled by definitions) loses his labour, and does not know anything, but only believeth.[30]

Because we hate to acknowledge our mistakes, however, the risk of duplicitous accountants remains a key part of the problem. The schools have built their philosophies out of nonsense, and therefore have an interest in maintaining their deceptions, whether they began as victims of these deceptions or designed them deliberately to hide their own ignorance and incompetence.

But Hobbes's mathematical simile for the compounded confusion that occurs through the careless use of speech is indicative of something more. Hobbes's model of the proper use of speech was rooted in his admiration for the mental habits of competent mathematicians. He wanted these habits of mind, their prized possession, to spread across the learned disciplines. All reasoning, according to Hobbes, ought to be understood as reckoning: the adding and subtracting of mental parcels.[31] It is possible to conduct these operations without the aid of speech (for Hobbes can imagine that conceptions or phantasms generated from sense impressions might be compounded one with the other), but the operations are, again, greatly facilitated and improved with the aid of language.[32] Our conceptions may be culled and organized under the general terms, and these terms may be compounded into propositions (or affirmations) that suggest the causes of our conceptions;[33] propositions may be compounded into syllogisms, and syllogisms may be strung together to reach conclusions that supply us with knowledge of the complex causes of things that we wish to produce.[34]

What is the model for the right use of speech? Whose example ought the philosophers to follow? Of all mathematicians, we know that Hobbes had the greatest admiration for the geometers. In particular, he wanted the careful habits cultivated in geometry to become the model for philosophers.[35] As I noted earlier, geometers begin with definitions. Their self-discipline in using definitions is the guide the strong-witted adopt to break through the confusion created by the risks of using language: "Seeing then that *truth* consisteth in the right ordering of names in our affirmations, a man that seeketh precise *truth* had need to remember what every name he uses stands for, and to place it accordingly, or else he will find himself entangled in words; as a bird in lime twigs, the more he struggles the more belimed. And therefore in geometry (which is the only science that it hath pleased God hitherto to bestow on mankind) men begin at settling the significations of their words; which settling of significations, they call *definitions*, and place them in the beginning of their reckoning."[36]

Against the background of trapped birds or insects (in the aforementioned spider's webs) the claim that geometry is God-given is particularly interesting.[37] It is worth noting that this claim forms the second half of a minor theodicy drama that Hobbes crafts in chapter 4 of *Leviathan*. If God has given us geometry as a way to escape from the turmoil brought about by the inconstancy of our words, it may be a form of compensation for the confusion he caused when he punished humanity at the tower of Babel. God was the first author of speech, but Adam and the generations that followed augmented our supply of words.[38] At this time human beings spoke a single language. Hobbes mentions that this language lacked the terms necessary to philosophers or orators. As punishment for our sins, however, God deprived us of a common tongue: "But all this language gotten, and augmented by *Adam* and his posterity, was again lost at the tower of *Babel*, when by the hand of God every man was stricken, for his rebellion, with an oblivion of his former language. And being hereby forced to disperse themselves into several parts of the world, it must needs be that the diversity of tongues that now is proceeded by degrees from them, in such manner as need (the mother of all invention) taught them; and in tract of time grew everywhere more copious."[39]

Thereafter, the opportunities for absurdity grew. To overcome this hardship (as we shall see), man had to make himself godlike.

Nominalism

As a part of the discipline Hobbes imposes on the use of language, true and false are only to be spoken of in the narrow context of statements that take the form of a proposition.[40] Thus "true" and a true proposition are one and the same thing, as are "false" and a false proposition. More precisely, things that admit of evaluation as either true or false can and should be reduced to words joined by a copula, in English the word "is." For Hobbes the proposition "X is Y" is true if when we say "X," it can be said to "name the same thing" as when we say "Y." This, Hobbes states, occurs when "X" is comprehended in "Y."[41] By this rule, "man is a living creature" is true because "man" *is* comprehended under the more abstract name "living creature." Likewise, "whatsoever is called, *man*, the same is also called *living creature*."[42] "Man is a stone" is false because what we name "man" is not comprehended under the notion of "stone."

This leads to the question, what is the determining ground on which we declare one name comprehended in another? Many persons, both Hobbes's contemporaries and we ourselves, are likely to consult sense.[43] They would make our sense experience of the world the arbiter. Hobbes is determined to cut off this avenue. Instead, he refers us to the power that man has to impose names, to attach names to the particular conceptions that have their beginnings in sensation, but which possess their names because of man's fiat. Names are not assigned according to some independently established truth that existed prior to the imposition of names themselves. He writes, "From hence it may be deduced, that the first truths were arbitrarily made by those that first of all imposed names upon things, or received them from the imposition of others. For it is true (for example) that *man is a living creature*, but for this reason, that it pleased men to impose both those names on the same thing."[44]

He reiterates and clarifies his identification of "true" and "a true proposition" in *De Corpore*:

> Now these words *true, truth,* and *true proposition*, are equivalent to one another; for truth consists in speech, and not in the things spoken of; and though *true* be sometimes opposed to apparent or *feigned*, yet it is always to be referred to the truth of proposition; for the image of a man in a glass, or a ghost, is therefore denied to be a very man, because this proposition, *a ghost is a man*, is not true; for it cannot be denied but that a ghost is a very ghost. And therefore truth or verity is not any affection of the thing, but of the proposition concerning it.[45]

Hobbes is reinforcing the barrier between the experience of the outside world and the realm of words and propositions. Even when the temptation to assess truth claims in terms of the real or the apparent—to test, for example, descriptive truth claims against the existence or nonexistence of something—is strongest, Hobbes erects this barrier. He redirects philosophers back into the closed circle of propositions and to truths that are strictly formal. Under Hobbes's regime a witness who sees a ghost and claims to have seen a man may be said to have spoken a falsehood. This claim of falsehood, however, cannot be grounded in empirical fact. Truth or falsity cannot be determined because someone can show that the witness saw a "true" man (e.g., someone who affirms that the witness saw John) or a "false" man (e.g., a claim that the witness saw a reflection or a ghost). Determining falsehood on this basis would do exactly what Hobbes wishes to disallow; it would assign, he insists, truth or falsity to the entities themselves rather than propositions. Only the witness's *statement* can be submitted to the test of truth or falsehood: if his statement amounts to the proposition that a ghost is a man, then the proposition is false. This must be strictly related to the conclusion that "ghost" is not comprehended under the name "man." Claims about the world, the impression of sense, even refined ones that might keep us safe from what we would call misperceptions, are disallowed as arbiters of truth and falsity.

I am not particularly concerned with the viability of Hobbes's nominalism, or whether the broader set of restrictions that he imposes on philosophical thought could be successfully adopted. I would note, however, that a number of scholars have resisted these characteristics of Hobbes's work. They seem to fear that Hobbes disconnects himself from knowledge of the real world, and this concern is reflected in questions often directed toward Hobbes's account of our exit from the state of nature. Scholars want to know, "*Is* this in fact the way rationally self-interested individuals act?" and "Can we assume that persons will act in rationally self-interested ways, even if Hobbes actually understood what rationally self-interested persons would do?"[46] Hobbes's limitations on truth and his nominalism are obstacles for those who seek this kind of reassurance. Their fears are justified. The verification these scholars seek is ruled out by Hobbes's decision to limit the realm of truth to the realm of words.

Satisfied with Less?

Rather than try to salvage Hobbes's philosophy, we ought to try to consider how Hobbes could have remained satisfied with something that has dissatisfied so many contemporary readers. I justify this claim as an interpretative strategy, not as an attempt to assist Hobbes as a philosopher.[47] The best way to do this is to focus on Hobbes's definition of philosophy: specifically his strict insistence that philosophy teach us about cause and effect, and his equally firm demand that philosophy be rooted in the practices of manipulating and understanding the actions and interactions of bodies in motion.

Hobbes identifies philosophic knowledge ("true ratiocination") with knowledge of cause and effect. In *De Corpore* he defines philosophical method as "the shortest way of finding out the effects by their known causes, or of causes by their known effects."[48] To consider an additional barrier between Hobbes's philosophy and knowledge of the world, it must be noted that causal knowledge does not in this case imply knowledge of reality. His demand for causality is also accompanied by his insistence on the conditional character of such knowledge: " . . . for the knowledge of consequence, which I have said before is called science, it is not absolute, but conditional. No man can know by discourse that this or that is, has been, or will be, which is to know absolutely, but only that if this be, that is, if this has been, that has been, if this shall be, that shall be, which is to know conditionally; and that not the consequence of one thing to another, but of one name of a thing to another name of the same thing."[49] Hobbes defines reason as a process of either determining the conditional causes of effects, or the conditional effects of given causes.[50] For enthusiastic readers at the turn of the century such as Ferdinand Tönnies, these mechanistic aspects of Hobbes's writing were evidence of a path-breaking philosophy: it was the first step in revealing the working structures of the social world.[51] One can acknowledge that Hobbes's philosophical account of the world was machine-like; Hobbes strives for well-ordered cause and effect relations that describe with precision the conduct of matter in motion. However, because it provides strictly conditional knowledge of cause and effect, and because of Hobbes's nominalism, Tönnies's leap cannot be accepted.[52]

Hobbes's arguments concerning the deceptiveness of sensation further erode the possibility of a connection between Hobbes's philosophy and the practice of making descriptive truth claims.[53] He traces the beginnings of all conceptions to sensation. Everything imagined or remembered,[54] every element of a person's train of thought, is built from the conceptions that have their beginnings in sense. Strictly counting on sensation, we may go as far as prudence, but such knowledge cannot make universal conclusions, and at its root, it is merely uncritical "knowledge of fact."[55] Reason, however, does not apply itself to sensation per se. It is applied, rather, to the words we put to sensations (in particular, those names that stand for sensations that we class together).⁵⁶ We are thereby channeled back into the nominalist stream.

The wedge between the realm of sense and the realm of science is further reinforced in chapter 9 of *Leviathan*, "Of the *Several* Subjects of Knowledge." He notes:

> There are of Knowledge two kinds, whereof one is *knowledge of fact*, the other *knowledge of the consequences of one affirmation to another*. The former is nothing else but sense and memory, and is *absolute* knowledge, as when we see a fact doing, or remember it done; and this is the knowledge required in a witness. The latter is called *science*, and is *conditional*, as when we know that *if the figure shown be a circle, then any straight line through the center shall divide it into two equal parts*. And this is the knowledge required in a philosopher, that is to say, of him that pretends to reasoning.⁵⁷

From a contemporary perspective it may be tempting to assume that Hobbes must allow all knowledge, perhaps especially the "absolute knowledge" of fact, to count as philosophical or scientific reason. The foregoing passage argues against jumping to this conclusion. The boundaries are important for Hobbes; not all knowledge qualifies. Those who "pretend to reasoning," by which Hobbes does not mean making a false claim, but making an identity claim for oneself ("I am a philosopher"), must find the proof of their reasoning skills elsewhere. *Having* reason, or being a philosopher, Hobbes here asserts, means mastery over this domain of words and the conditional conclusions they make possible. The knowledge of witnesses, the knowledge recorded in histories (and we may infer the knowledge achieved through prudence), is not scientific/philosophical knowledge. The conclusions drawn from considerations of experience (be it witnessed personally or recorded in a history) simply do not count as philosophical reasoning. Paradoxically (at least from the perspective of contemporary scientific inquiry), the "absolute" character of factual knowledge further divides it from the philosophical knowledge: knowledge of consequences, that is to say, scientific knowledge, is (as we noted before) conditional. Allowing the "absolute" knowledge of fact to become a part of Hobbes's inherently conditional philosophical knowledge would imply a contradiction. Finally, it is with the consequences of "affirmations" (words and propositions), and not the consequences of facts, that Hobbes's philosopher must concern himself.

There is another factor at work in Hobbes's limitation on reason. This concerns man's ability to know the works of God. The world is God's creation, and like many who held to the voluntarist theological view, Hobbes claimed: "There is no effect which the powers of God cannot produce in many several ways."[58] This means that whatever we witness in nature might have been produced in any way that God pleased. To suggest otherwise would be to place a limit on God's capacity as the omnipotent creator, a matter which he forbids in others.[59] We cannot know with certainty how the world was created because the creator himself is so far above us that we dare not presume to learn how he has produced it.[60] For us mortals, it should be enough for us to know that he is omnipotent, the creator of the world, and that his dictates always agree with the dictates of right reason. Hobbes used this voluntarist veto against his philosophical opponents, particularly those who made claims that went beyond the limits Hobbes imposed on his own philosophy—notably, claims about the world.[61] In light of these limitations, Hobbes instructs philosophers to rest satisfied with the contingent conclusions that reasoning makes possible in natural philosophy: these will always (only) be about the possible means by which things that we see in nature might be generated.[62]

Thus far, Hobbes's philosophy emerges as a complex trade-off. It teaches the proper means of producing truth with language, the means of avoiding falsity (and absurdity). Nevertheless, it leaves these truths permanently bound within the realm of words. One could say that reason's conclusions are established by "true fictions."[63] Is this satisfactory? Here it is worth taking note of Michael Oakeshott's view. For Oakeshott, this was indeed enough.[64] Oakeshott was deeply impressed with Hobbes's philosophic rationalism, but was also concerned that this kind of thinking be kept within its proper limits— that it not migrate to places such as politics, where (in his view) it did not belong. On this reading, Hobbes teaches us to be guided by the thread of reason to the exclusion of all other influences. He is said to pursue these fictions not merely because they achieve generalizable knowledge, but (as fictions and no more) because "reasoning can go no further."[65]

I am arguing, however, that this standard would have been insufficient for Hobbes. Oakeshott's reading underestimates the practical intents of Hobbes's philosophy. We reason by true fictions, but the purpose of doing so is for the sake of making these fictions "come true." Of course, Hobbes had a strictly linguistic conception of truth; thus in saying that his true fictions are made to "come true," I am departing from his conception, but it is to make a larger point concerning the concrete expectations that Hobbes attached to his science. Truth for Hobbes *was* nothing other than a true proposition, but the true propositions that reason establishes are not self-justifying. Hobbes pursued knowledge of cause and effect so that we might produce concrete effects for ourselves. Hobbes's philosophy was indeed to be a useful possession, even if its path to usefulness was not that mapped out for it by retrospective positivists. In *De Corpore* he wrote: "The end or scope of philosophy is, that we may make use to our benefit of effects formerly seen; or that, by application of bodies to one another, we may produce the like effects of those we conceive in our mind, as far forth as matter, strength, and industry, will permit, for the commodity of human life."[66]

This may present something of a quandary. Can one affirm that Hobbes's philosophy does not strive to inform us of how the world really is, and also maintain that Hobbes's philosophy was meant to produce effects in the world? Here is another instance where grasping Hobbes's work requires that we move beyond the limits imposed by readings that seek to assimilate Hobbes to the tradition of predictive or explanatory sciences. At best, these give Hobbes permission to merely model, rather than actually capture an accurate picture of, the world. A model need not get the world right in every detail. A model works when it proposes a scheme that offers a simplified notion of the world, and our observations allow us to say that the world functions "as if" it were in fact constructed this way. It is difficult to see how Hobbes could have belonged to even this more permissive form of inquiry. The practitioners of social scientific modeling are (in theory) ready to test their models against empirical reality. A good model may not capture all of reality, but it ought to predict it. Hobbes's nominalism, and the myriad other barriers between his truths and the world, disallows the grounds on which to describe a hypothetical account of true or false in terms of its relation to the real world. In fact, Hobbes makes it clear that demonstration is not possible when we try to give accounts of the causes of the things we observe. Both the modelers and some of the earlier readings that claim to find something like a modern social science in Hobbes assume that he, or anyone else who seeks to produce effects, first needed to come to some understanding that at least reflected the world as it really is (or was).

This point of view fails to consider a more radical, if much less practical, possibility. Hobbes need not maintain that his philosophy's fictions are empirically true (i.e., a matter of fact, or an approximation to reality, or even a model of reality) to "make use to our benefit of effects formerly seen . . . for the commodity of human life." If our goal is to produce effects, then a form of reasoning that teaches us how things *could* be generated has already done enough. Hobbes suggests this in several places. He tells the king in the "Epistle Dedicatory" in *Seven Philosophical Problems:*

> The doctrine of natural causes hath not infallible and evident principles. For there is no effect which the power of God cannot produce by many several ways.
>
> But seeing all effects are produced by motion, he that supposing someone or more motions, can derive from them the necessity of that effect whose cause is required, has done all that is to be expected from natural reason. And though he prove not that the thing was thus produced, yet he proves that thus it may be produced when the materials and the power of moving are in our hands: which is as useful as if the causes themselves were known.[67]

He repeats this claim in *Decameron Physiologicum*.[68] In short, there is something more than philosophical knowledge (truth) to be had from Hobbes's philosophy. In arguing his view of Hobbes, Oakeshott wrote that philosophy's utmost end is to reflect the real world in the rational mirror. It yields a picture that is merely analogous to the world, but philosophy sacrifices accuracy for the advantages of knowledge that strictly adheres to the demands of uncompromised reason.

Hobbes goes much further. He does more than sacrifice accuracy. In pointing to the sufficiency of knowledge that allows us to produce effects for ourselves, Hobbes in effect gives philosophers permission to give up mirroring completely. Put in a more philosophical vein, Hobbes need not hold his philosophy to a correspondence theory of truth. We may be indifferent about whether reason shows us how things were actually produced. This indifference is not the product of the satisfactions of achieving a philosophical conception. Hobbes encourages our indifference with a much grander claim that he will teach us how to produce the effects observed in nature for ourselves by our own means. Here is an example of the expansiveness of Hobbes's claim to supply his students with a grand possession, but as we shall see in the next section these do not exhaust the philosopher's capacity to assert his resourcefulness.

Not unlike other visionaries of the seventeenth century, Hobbes embraced designs that were oriented toward practical ends, but, nonetheless, still idealistic in their means. This particular, yet determined, practicality emerges again in the specifics of Hobbes's discussion of the admirable traits of geometers. Hobbes drew on geometry because it exemplified systematic thought, but also because it yielded mankind "commodities": it gave us the capacity to measure matter and motion, to move large bodies, gave us architecture, navigation, and instruments to study the motion of the stars, "parts of time," aided geography, and so on.[69] These more pragmatic—in particular, more architectural—uses for geometry illustrate instances of an intellectual practice that yields both truths and commodities, without having to tell us something about a reality that exists independent of ourselves. Things accomplished with geometric knowledge are not true before we make them "come true." These elements resonate with Hobbes's reflections on the purpose of philosophy:

> For the inward glory and triumph of mind that a man may have for the mastering of some difficult and doubtful matter, or for the discovery of some hidden truth, is not worth so much pains as the study of Philosophy requires; nor need any man care much to teach another what he knows himself, if he think that will be the only benefit of his labour. The end of knowledge is power; and the use of theorems (which, among geometricians, serve for the finding out of properties) is for the construction of problems; and, lastly, the scope of all speculation is the performing of some action, or thing to be done.[70]

Imitating the Creator

Hobbes placed great importance in our ability to produce effects for ourselves. Our capacity to do so carried weighty implications for human autonomy: both with regard to what we could know, and with regard to what we could do on our own (without calling upon the further assistance of God).[71] The closer we look at Hobbes's remarkable claims, the more we appreciate the importance of these boasts to his enterprise. The best evidence is found in the categories that inform his classifications of the sciences.[72] Hobbes was concerned to divide the sciences according to relative degrees of what, for want of a better term, might be called creative autonomy. In *De Homine*, he notes that geometry exemplifies the highest degree of such autonomy: "Since the causes of the properties that individual figures have belong to them because we ourselves draw the lines: and since the generation of the figures depends on our will; nothing more is required to know the phenomenon peculiar to any figure whatsoever, than that we consider everything that follows from the construction that we ourselves make in the figure to be described. Therefore, because of this fact, (that is, we ourselves create the figures), it happens that geometry hath been and is demonstrable."[73]

In the physical sciences, unlike geometry, it is not we but the creator who initially brings about the effects: "On the other hand, since the causes of natural things are not in our power, but in the divine will, and since the greatest part of them, namely the ether, is invisible; we, that do not see them, cannot deduce their qualities from their causes. Of course, we can, by deducting as far as possible the consequences that we do see, demonstrate that such and such *could* have been their causes."[74] A science such as geometry therefore stands higher than physics. Being able to make things ourselves yields a superior form of demonstrability. We can always know what we make much better than we can know what God has made. Beyond the relative certainty of demonstrability, however, there is also a radical claim for human abilities contained in this distinction, and this brings us back to the context of God and man.

As noted, in the address to readers at the beginning of *De Corpore*, as well as in the introduction to *Leviathan*,[75] Hobbes invites his readers to imitate God. The distinction I am pointing to suggests that there are more and less dignified ways to imitate the creator. One may either attempt to create what God creates by our own means (and remain uncertain of how God himself created these things), or we may play the part of creator in a more daring and independent way. Instead of merely fashioning our own versions of what the creator has already made, we pursue the less slavish form of imitation. That is, we imitate God *as a creator*. We use philosophy to turn ourselves into creators. Instead of remaking what God has made, we make what we wish. We become more dignified by creating something original, not something that merely emulates a thing created by someone else (even if that someone is God himself).[76] Furthermore, we can know what we create ourselves with the utmost certainty.

In spite of this ambitiousness, Hobbes did not claim to share knowledge with God. He was not claiming to give us the knowledge of *the* creator (or the creator's own knowledge), but promising to help man turn himself into *a* creator. Hobbes willingly admits that we cannot know how God created the world. In this respect, his thought conforms to the voluntarist theological tradition.[77] He is anxious to put us in a position where we might become indifferent to this ignorance. This indifference does not proceed from a mood of philosophical detachment, but from the knowledge that we might (by our own means) produce like effects to God's own by causes that we ourselves control. Hobbes promises to turn us into forceful, original creators (and not just re-creators), and this promise "to enable" fosters that much more indifference toward our inability to know the world as it actually is.

Mathematical Method and the Science of Creating

Earlier I noted that reason's accomplishment consists in escaping the confines of sense experience. This captures the trajectory of Hobbes's efforts, but Hobbes's distinctions between the sciences allow us to add to it. According to Hobbes, some of the sciences guided by reason are more detached from sense experience than others.[78] This comes out in the distinction he makes between sciences that depend on either mixed or pure forms of mathematics. According to Hobbes, "Those sciences are usually called mathematical that are learned not from use and experience, but from teachers and rules."[79] Examples of pure mathematics include geometry and arithmetic, and these "revolve around quantities in the abstract so that work in the subject requires not knowledge of fact."[80] By contrast, the mixed (or impure) mathematical ventures force us to become involved with matters of fact: "Those mathematics are mixed, in truth, which in their reasoning also consider any quality of the subject, as is the case with astronomy, music, physics, and the part of physics that can vary on account of the variety of species and the parts of the universe."[81]

This distinction can be restated in terms of Hobbes's two methods of causal reasoning, resolution and composition. In resolution one begins with a whole and works one's way down a causal chain (i.e., from a specific effect to its composite causes, all the way down to the most elemental parts of the whole).[82] In composition, one begins with the elemental parts and works one's way up to the whole (i.e., compounding causes until one has constructed the desired effect).[83] Although all of Hobbes's sciences entail both resolution and composition, those that Hobbes classifies as pure in their mathematics may (always) begin by means of composition. In the case of the pure sciences we learn (at first from instructors) and practice the means by which the most elemental matter may be combined to produce certain effects. By contrast, sciences such as physics begin with an observed (i.e., factual) whole, which then must be resolved into elemental parts before we can apply the constructive techniques of composition.[84] In *De Homine*, Hobbes calls the pure science's form of demonstration *a priori;* that of impure science, *a posteriori*. (Although in *De Corpore*, Hobbes states that demonstration only occurs in those sciences that are pure in the sense just described.[85] In all cases the pure sciences are always held in higher regard than the mixed.) Hobbes was certainly not the first to use the distinction between a priori and a posteriori demonstration, and to argue in terms of synthetic and analytic methods. It was in fact a part of the traditional case made on behalf of the certainty of geometrical demonstrations.[86] What is notable about Hobbes's use of this distinction is the way he puts it to use in asserting the worthiness of his science of politics and how the distinction is linked to the way we are said to imitate God.

The relative degrees of dependency upon sense map onto the distinction between what I have identified as less or more dignified ways of imitating God. The natural sciences teach us how to produce, by our own means, the effects that we observe in nature; the a priori sciences teach us how to generate what we wish. In the latter, we direct our efforts toward goals (things to create) that we choose ourselves: we are not imitators of the outcome of another's creation. Instead, we choose our own ends, constructing whatever we are capable of by our own means. In this sense, the a priori sciences make us the brasher, more independent imitators of God. The independence from sense, from matters of fact, or as Hobbes puts it in *De Homine*, "the irrevocable past,"[87] is also a step in the direction of becoming more independent creators.

These distinctions do not simply illuminate the differences between geometry and the physical sciences. They are also tremendously important for understanding the ambitious nature of Hobbes's science of politics. Hobbes included his science of politics among the a priori sciences.[88] The science of politics does not teach us to direct our efforts toward reproducing things observed in nature, matters of fact, or from the "irrevocable past." Indeed, the very idea of a polity as the subject of an empirical study is very much at odds with his vision. Like the concatenated planes, lines, and figures of geometry, or the guidance we provide ourselves in the science of navigation, the laws and covenants that form the materials of the science of politics are our own creation.[89] Continuing his analysis in *De Homine*, Hobbes writes: "Finally, politics and ethics (that is the sciences of *just* and *unjust*, of *equity* and *inequity*) can be demonstrated *a priori;* because we ourselves make the principles—that is, the causes of justice (namely laws and covenants)—whereby it is known what *justice* and equity, and their opposites *injustice* and *inequity*, are. For before covenants and laws were drawn up, neither justice nor injustice, neither public good nor public evil, was natural among men any more than it was among beasts."[90]

In the introduction to *Leviathan*, Hobbes plays with the distinction between ways of imitating the creator, ultimately affirming politics as a higher form of imitation. He begins by noting that nature, "the art whereby God hath made and governs the world," is, by "the *art* of man," imitated. We are capable of creating an "artificial animal." Hobbes is referring us to the lesser form of imitation, and suggests a series of equivalencies between natural animal life and the life that might be created through artificial means already within our power to create: "For seeing life is but a motion of limbs, the beginning whereof is in some principal part within, why may we not say that all *automata* (engines that move themselves by springs and wheels as doth a watch) have an artificial life? For what is the *heart*, but a *spring*, and the *nerves*, but so many *strings*, and the *joints*, but so many *wheels*, giving motion to the whole body, such as was intended by the artificer?"[91]

In each case, something divinely produced (hearts, nerves, and joints) is linked to an equivalent in the realm of things we can produce for ourselves. The heart, nerves, and joints, the creator's own handiwork, are pulled back down into the orbit of potential human creation. As natural bodies receive their motion from the heart, nerves, and joints, so may man-made bodies receive artificial life by the means at our own disposal. The effects observed in nature are reproduced by our own means: by springs, strings, wheels, and joints. The foregoing passage has been read by some as a reductionist reconceptualization in mechanical terms of humans and the rest of the world.[92] Although many readers have assented to this reading (some enthusiastically), the enterprise Hobbes is here evoking is *not*, fundamentally, a matter of conceiving of the world in simplified mechanical terms. The capacity to create for ourselves obviates the need to describe and conceive of the world precisely as God made it. When Hobbes suggests that the heart is but a spring, his efforts are not so much a matter of reductionism as they are a proclamation of equivalency between divine and human creation. God may make a heart, but we may make a spring—and that is all we need do. In the face of this remarkable prospect, the goal of knowing the world as it really is becomes less important. Our springs may do for us what God's handiwork has done in creating a heart (i.e., we may re-create the effect); and having produced the same effect, we need not know how an actual heart functions.

The imitation of the creator's effects is certainly grandiose, but this form of imitation is not the highest in Hobbes's hierarchy of sciences. After the passage just quoted, Hobbes writes:

> *Art* goes yet further, imitating that rational and most excellent work of nature, *man*. For by art is created that great LEVIATHAN called a COMMONWEALTH, or STATE (in Latin CIVITAS), which is but an artificial man, though of greater stature and strength than the natural, for whose protection and defense it was intended; and in which the *sovereignty* is an artificial soul, as giving life and motion to the whole body; the *magistrates* and other *officers* of judicature and execution, artificial *joints; reward* and *punishment* (by which fastened to the seat of the sovereignty every

joint and member is moved to perform his duty) are the *nerves*, that do the same in the body natural; the *wealth* and *riches* of all the particular members are the *strength* . . . Lastly, the *pacts* and *covenants* by which the parts of this body politic were at first made, set together, and united, resemble that *fiat*, or the *let us make man*, pronounced by God in the creation.[93]

The first sentence is particularly interesting. Our art will go further when it imitates the rational and excellent work of nature, man. Hobbes is not speaking here of making (or even remaking) a human being. "Imitation" in this context is suggestive of something *on the order of* making a human being. As original creators in our own right, we create (like God creates) after our own image, but our artificial man is not a re-creation of what God made. "Art" goes further because unlike the springs, strings, and wheels that merely form a substitute effect for God's natural effects, we are in this instance told we might imitate God's fiat. Unlike what I have referred to as the less dignified form of imitation, we are not using our skills to remake what God has made. We are using them instead to create something that God has not made himself. Better still, our artificial man is "of greater stature and strength than the natural." The Leviathan is not a mere man, but a man-made man; not a singular man, but a composite of men. Hobbes is so bold as to suggest that as creators in our own right, we can surpass God's creation (i.e., ourselves).[94]

To conclude, we would seem to have a particularly potent example of a claim to enable. Hobbes measures God's accomplishments and claims that humans who use his philosophy may imitate (perhaps even outperform) God. Specifically, he claims to teach the art of political creation. We sometimes speak of the tendency among moderns to imagine themselves as starting afresh.[95] Hobbes's claim concerning what his philosophy can accomplish certainly illustrates this tendency.

4

KING OF THE CHILDREN OF PRIDE:
THE IMITATION OF GOD IN CONTEXT

> Law is for subjects and if it is my will, I can abolish old law and impose new; the universe is divided: Heaven belongs to Jove, but the scepter of worldly power is mine.
>
> —NERO, IN MONTEVERDI'S *Coronation of Poppea* (1642), ACT I, SCENE 9

I have argued that Hobbes cultivated useful learning as a kind of possession. It was a possession that could help establish and constitute the possessor's identity. A person could be known by the practices and talents made possible by it. Attentiveness to these connections and a claim to be able to cultivate these talents in others were a part of what it meant to be a humanist. This aspect of humanism carried over into Hobbes's approach to philosophy, and to mathematics in particular. In Chapter 3 I described the prized possession Hobbes promised to the students of his philosophy: they would learn to imitate and even rival God.

What are we to make of a philosopher who makes such claims? They would be ridiculous were they made today. Chapter 3 has already located these claims within a relatively narrow philosophical framework in which they can make sense, but there is more work to be done if Hobbes's claim of divine imitation is to be taken seriously. Today it would be difficult to resist the conclusion that any philosopher making a claim to imitate God has lost his way. The matter becomes all the more pressing when we consider that Hobbes expected his philosophy to yield practical results. One might be driven to mockery. Did Hobbes, great imitator of God, expect to exercise supernatural powers? We know from the prior chapter that his philosophy set itself to the task of manipulating material causes, but under what circumstances would such a claim to manipulate causes be credibly compared to exercising godlike powers? The chief purpose of this chapter is to contextualize claims to imitate God, to locate Hobbes's place within these contexts, and to speak to the practicalities involved in implementing Hobbes's political program.

A second question is bound inextricably to claims to imitate God. Not only must we learn how to take Hobbes seriously when he makes such promises, but we must also turn to the conception of human being (we typically speak of Hobbes's conception of "man") that accompanies such claims. This is an immense topic that cannot be exhausted here. I will therefore limit my discussion to those elements that relate to my own claims about his science. The conventionally understood Hobbes is quite well known for his pessimistic views of human nature. In Chapter 3 I have shown that Hobbes's approach to science prohibits claims to factual knowledge. These basic claims about human nature therefore exist in some tension with Hobbes's own philosophical methods.

Nevertheless, these basic claims have filled an important gap between Hobbes's philosophy and how many readers imagine his political program coming to fruition. They have allowed Hobbes's twentieth- and twenty-first-century scientific admirers to see him as working within a familiar framework. Hobbes's "man" is calculating, self-interested, self-preserving, fearful, and at least potentially rational. In light of these characteristics, we ask, what kind of behavior, what choices, can we reasonably expect from such a creature? Critically engaging Hobbes has therefore often been an exercise in either adjusting his views on human nature, or arguing that his conclusions about what we would or should do (to exit the state of nature) do not necessarily follow from his premises.

When Hobbes discusses human nature and formulates philosophically or scientifically guided political advice, is he working from the same conception of "man" that our contemporaries have in mind? Following Foucault on a general level, we ought to consider the possibility that "man" is not a universal, but a historically situated entity, and that the calculable "man" of today's social sciences and philosophy may not have been what Hobbes had in mind when he wrote of human beings.[1] Indeed, an understanding of the framework in which it makes sense to compare human talents with God's bespeaks a different conception, one that operates by its own logic and concerns itself with a rather different set of questions.

Such a conception begets questions such as "Where do we stand within a grand hierarchy?" Are we located above animals? Thinkers such as Machiavelli and Erasmus asked these questions in their own works of princely advice and rendered divergent forms of guidance.[2] This framework considers whether we could, or should, sometimes behave more like beasts than human beings.

Moral choice and the question of "our nature" are woven together here in ways that still link entities to their positions on a chain of being. Debate within this framework typically asks: How do we stand when we are at our best, and what is this "best?" Do we come close to the level of God? How do we resemble him? Might the most godlike have achieved their status through the most beastly forms of conduct? This is a framework which is therefore asking what human beings can do, and about their potential for good or evil deeds. In the case of more radical thinkers such as Machiavelli and Hobbes, it asks more daring questions: What is our capacity to define or redefine what good and evil might be? Even as Hobbes and Machiavelli ask questions that erode the confidence that might have been invested in settled conceptions of the natural order, they do so within a framework that is centered on the consideration of human capacities and talents.

If this is Hobbes's subject, then we will require a different understanding of what he had in mind for the implementation of his political program. Instead of counting on a creature who always manifests the particular characteristics of his reliably calculable "nature," we can find a more malleable subject within Hobbes's thought. When asking about the practicality of Hobbes's political designs, we need to attend to the hopes he pinned on education and the teaching of his doctrine. Likewise, if Hobbes's "man" is not the human individual of contemporary predictive social science and philosophy, than we will also need an explanation for why Hobbes makes generalizations about human nature, especially in light of the tensions I have referred to.

All of these themes come together in the dedicatory and the preface (added in 1647) to *De Cive*. In the dedicatory to the Earl of Devonshire, Hobbes turns to the question of human nature in the context of his dispute with partisans of republican government. They accuse kings of being predatory beasts. After asserting that history shows the bestial nature of the Roman citizenry, Hobbes affirms a more general perspective. He declares true the maxims that "Man is a God to man, and Man is a Wolf to man" (*De Cive*, dedicatory, 1). He is a god, says Hobbes, in the relations of the citizens to each other, and a wolf in the relations between commonwealths. Justice and charity are exercised among human beings in a commonwealth, and in these "virtues of peace" we resemble God. The "virtues of war"—force and fraud—are necessary to the self-preservation of commonwealths (*De Cive*, dedicatory, 1–2). Men in the state of nature are also entitled to act in the pursuit of their own preservation (*De Cive*, 1.7–12), and so also act in the wolfish ways Hobbes attributes to commonwealths. It is only when civil science is actually achieved and followed that true godlike virtues are actually realized.

The aforementioned logic of *possessed* sciences is also at work in Hobbes's claim in the preface to provide readers with a fully accomplished civil science. As he did in his introductory writings in Thucydides, Hobbes begins by testifying to the utility and dignity of what he has to teach. He evokes an image of a possession once so prized that it was at first hidden, sought after for many years, and finally revealed in full in his own work. The wise men of "remotest antiquity," Hobbes asserts, valued this possession to such a degree that they only passed such knowledge on to posterity in secret form. They kept it shrouded in "pretty poetry or in the shadowy outlines of Allegory." Their hope was "to prevent what one might call the high and holy mystery of government from being contaminated by the debates of private men" (*De Cive*, preface, 2). In a lost and unrecoverable "golden age" human beings simply obeyed sovereign powers and revered them as "a kind of living divinity" (6). Later, when civil science became the subject of wider attention, no less than Socrates was the first to fall in love with civil science, even though in these early times it was only partially visible "through the clouds."[3] It is testimony to the dignity of the science that Socrates begat so many imitators: Plato, Aristotle, Cicero, "all the other Greek and Roman philosophers" sought this prize. It is also sought by "gentlemen . . . in their leisure hours," who stand accused here of radically underestimating how easy it is to obtain it. Reiterating the connection between learned practice and identity, Hobbes adds: "What most contributes to its dignity is that those who think they possess it or are in a position where they ought to possess it, are so very pleased with themselves for the semblance of it which they do possess, they will gladly allow specialists in the other sciences to be considered intelligent, learned and erudite, and to be called so, but they never want them to be called Statesman. Because of the preeminence of this political expertise they believe the term should be reserved to themselves" (3).

In the preface to *De Cive* Hobbes not only appeals to the logic of possessed knowledge and the dignity of his learned accomplishments, he also states that he will be appealing to "a Principle well known to all men by experience and which everyone admits, that man's natural Disposition is such that if they are not restrained by fear of a common power, they will distrust and fear each other, and each man rightly may, and necessarily will, look out for himself from his own resources" (10). A conception of "man" that appears very familiar and modern comes together here with a set of residual humanist conceptions that link human virtues with a nearness to divinity and human vice with animality. How and why do these come together in Hobbes? The place to begin is with others who had encouraged human beings to imitate God.

The Imitation of God in Context

The preeminent Elizabethan theologian Richard Hooker (1554–1600) supplies an important example in the English context of just how mundane such claims could be. In "The law whereby man is in his actions directed to the imitation of God," book 1, chapter 5, of *Of the Laws of Ecclesiastical Polity*, Hooker argues that all things that exist participate to some degree in God's goodness, for God is the supreme cause of all things. Moreover, "every effect doth after a sort contain, at leastwise resemble the cause from which it proceedeth," and "all things in the world are said in some sort to seek the highest, and to covet more or less the participation of God himself."[4] Mere existence is a prerequisite for the imitation of, or at least the resemblance to, God. It hardly seems to be a basis for distinction. Hooker's assumption, however, that all things "seek the highest" and that things "covet" the highest allows a basis for distinction to reassert itself.

Of all things created by God the one that strives the hardest to imitate its creator is man: "This does nowhere so much appear as it doth in man: because there are so many kinds of perfections which man seeketh." Perfections which adhere in God have corresponding human perfections. These include "'the desiring the continuance of their being." God is everlasting. Man is not, but he can propagate himself through procreation. God is immutable. We are not, but we can seek after this kind of perfection through our own efforts at "constancy." There are others, but the greatest degree of goodness is found in our capacity to reason:

> By proceeding in the knowledge of truth and by growing in the exercise of virtue, man amongst the creatures of this inferior world, aspireth to the greatest conformity with God, this is not only known unto us, whom he himself hath so instructed, but even they do acknowledge, who amongst men are not judged the nearest unto him [i.e., pagans]. With *Plato* what one thing more usual, than to excite men unto the love of wisdom, by showing how much wise men are thereby exalted above men; how knowledge doth raise them up unto heaven; how it maketh them, though not Gods, yet as gods, high, admirable and divine? And Mercurius Trismegistus speaking of the virtues of a righteous soule, Such spirits (sayeth he) are never cloyed with praysing and speaking well of all men, with doing good unto every one by word and deed, because they studie to frame themselves according to THE PATERNE of the father of spirits.[5]

Mixing scriptural guidance with Platonist influences, writers could argue that we were most like the Deity in our most perfect faculties, and our most perfect faculty was reason. Hooker's example makes clear that the range of possible ways men, and other things, might be said to resemble God was terrifically diverse.

It is this very diversity, and its metaphysical sources, which might prompt a quite reasonable objection to Hooker's juxtaposition with Hobbes. Hooker is still thinking within the parameters of a view of the cosmos that Hobbes very explicitly rejects. When Hooker notes that man seeks his perfection, he draws on the authority of Aristotle.[6] Hooker's man pursues the very *summum bonum* that Hobbes declared nonexistent (see *Lev.*, 11.1). He is guided by a telos; Hooker's man pursues, by nature, a final cause. Hobbes's man merely pursues one thing and then another as his particular desires and aversions dictate. This Hobbesian man, and all other entities in Hobbes's cosmos, is mere matter, and the only cause relevant to their motions and actions is efficient causality. Hooker is a sincere theologian, *the* theologian of the Anglican Church. Hobbes was in all likelihood an atheist, and was certainly accused of atheism by those trained in the tradition Hooker helped create. When Hobbes therefore says he is teaching his students how to imitate God, perhaps the only appropriate response is to smile since we know that Hobbes did not actually believe in the being he boasted of imitating. Doesn't Hobbes's philosophy, so to speak, remove the chain of being from its holy hook in the heavens and let it tumble down and make it impossible to distinguish between one link and another, between the rarest of spirits and mere dirt?

Is the gap between Hooker and Hobbes really the difference between night and day? Hobbes does what he can to amplify the differences between himself and his theological opponents. He associates their thought with "The Kingdom of Darkness" (*Lev.*, pt. 4), a particularly brash maneuver if we credit the view that he was a nonbeliever. We can grant that for Hobbes the transition from one system of thought to his own made all the difference he himself could imagine. However, we should try to avoid confusing his image of a great difference with the differences or similarities that we can see from our yet greater distance from them both. Whether or not Hobbes was a believer is an interesting question, but at least as interesting (if not more so) is the question of what it could mean to lose, reject, or supplant faith in these contexts. Answers suggest themselves from within the world in which humans claim to imitate God. It echoes the same immodesty that I described in Chapter 2 when I compared Hobbes's views to Mulcaster's concerning the natural and theological limits that man ought to observe in the pursuit of his own excellence through mathematics.

Renaissance historians have, in varying degrees, already charted a path from divine imitation to impious human assertion. The historians have recognized a latent (and in some cases more than a latent) possibility among Renaissance humanists.[7] Humanists could pave the way from the pursuit of godlike perfections that God himself intended, to the point where human intentions might supplant God's. A creature with godlike perfections would one day decide to totally replace God, especially as God himself and the order he was said to warrant throughout the universe seemed to be crumbling. This, I am suggesting, is the trajectory Hobbes was on. We need not require Hobbes to have ever been a particularly pious person, or a believer in God, to find this son of a drunken clergyman on this path. Situated in a framework in which human improvement takes the form of godlike accomplishments, Hobbes need only have worked on the far edge of a customary system of thought. Having let the chain of being tumble into an undifferentiated mass of mere "matter," we find Hobbes, the absolutist philosopher, erecting a scaffold from which a new hook and a new order might be hung.

The Imitation of God and the Humanist Tradition

Although Hooker supplies us with a more immediate context for understanding Hobbes's boasts, Hooker's tone, at once a celebration of human perfections and a goad to achieve them, reflects contributions from earlier humanists.[8] These humanists struggled to reconcile recovered or newly revered classical texts with traditional medieval Christian pessimism. Out of this tension, new arguments for the dignity of humanity emerged. An important element of these arguments celebrated man as a maker (*homo faber*), and here the notion of a human divinity was a commonplace, and one that resonates with Hobbes's own view of human accomplishment.

Giannozzo Manetti (1396–1459), a Florentine orator, ambassador, territorial governor, translator of the New Testament and of the Psalter, the *Nicomachean Ethics*, and the *Eudemian Ethics*, and author of *De dignitate et excellentia hominis*, synthesized classical appreciation of man's creative skills with Christian virtue by describing man as a second creator:

> After that first, new and rude creation of the world, everything seems to have been discovered, constructed and completed by us out of some singular and outstanding acuteness of the human mind. For those things are ours, that is, they are human, which are seen to be produced by

men: all homes, all towns, all cities, finally all buildings in the world which certainly are so many and of such a nature that they ought rather to be regarded as the works of angels than of men. . . . Ours are the paintings, ours the sculptures, ours the arts, ours the sciences, ours . . . the wisdom, ours, finally, lest we dwell too long on single things since they are almost finite, are all discoveries, ours are all the different kinds of languages and literatures.[9]

Our mechanical inventions also entitle us to this praise. Like the artificial man referred to in the introduction to *Leviathan*, Manetti describes them as examples of how human beings improve upon what God has provided in nature: "Indeed these [inventions] and others of the same sort are everywhere seen to be so many and of such a quality that the world and all its beauties seem to have been first invented and established by Almighty God for the use of man, and afterwards gratefully received by man and rendered much more beautiful, much more ornate and far more refined."[10] No wonder then "that the first inventors of the different arts were worshipped as gods by the early peoples."[11]

Marsilio Ficino (1433–1499), who supplied the standard Renaissance Latin translation of Plato, made similar, "second creator" arguments in *Theologica Platonica*:[12]

> The force of man is almost similar to the divine nature since man by himself, that is through his intelligence and skill, governs himself without being in the least limited by his physical nature and imitates the individual works of the higher nature . . . .
>
> In these industrial arts it may be observed how man everywhere utilizes all the materials of the universe as though all were subject to man. He makes use, I say, of the elements, the stones, metals, plants, and animals, and he transforms them into many shapes and figures, which animals never do. Nor is he content with one element or a few, as animals, but he uses all as though he were master of all. He tramps the earth, he sails the water, he ascends in the air by the highest towers . . . . How stupendous the structures of buildings and cities. How ingenious his works of irrigation. He acts as the vicar of God, since he inhabits all the elements and cultivates all, and present on earth, he is not absent from the ether . . . . Universal providence is proper to God who is the universal cause. Therefore man who universally provides for all things living and not living is a certain god. He is the god without doubt of the animals since he uses all of them, rules them, and teaches some of

them. He is established also as god of the elements since he inhabits and cultivates them all. He is finally, the god of all materials since he handles all, and turns and changes them.[13]

If Ficino's celebrations of the human capacity still seem somewhat exaggerated, and too distant from Hobbes's time, we can jump to those authors who began to encroach upon godly powers by turning instead toward the very things that seemed to testify in favor of supernatural powers, miracles. Would-be natural magicians (including Francis Bacon)[14] aspired to find the latent, undiscovered, natural causes of the extraordinary. Many who pursued such study took the precaution of noting that some miracles, particularly those recorded in the Bible, were, in fact, true miracles. They could not be accounted for except by the unknown (and unknowable) forces of God. Using naturalistic explanations to account for the so-called miracles of pagan literature was one thing, taking this approach to miracles of the Bible quite another. Not all were so cautious.[15]

The Paduan scholar Pietro Pomponazzi (1462–1525) insisted on finding causal explanation for all miraculous events, even those in the Bible.[16] Later followers of Pomponazzi were burned as heretics (with, it should be noted, the approval of Mersenne).[17] Such examples suggest a very different context for understanding Renaissance claims to imitate deities. The notion carries with it the suggestion of accomplishment, of the cultivation of man's reasoning and even mechanical capacities. It does not necessarily suggest an attempt to exercise supernatural powers so much as the possibility of their human replacement.

A stunning example exists in Thomas Hill's *Naturall and Artificiall Conclusions*, a work published in 1581, and republished often, purporting to be an English translation of "sundrie scholars of the University of Padua."[18] Hill includes directions on how to turn water into wine and how to walk on water. The secrets behind these effects are quite mundane (if not greatly improbable on a practical level): "For to doe this, take two little Timbrels, and binde them under the soles of thy feete, and at a staves end fasten another, and with these you may walke on the water, unto the wonder of all such as shall see the same: if so be you often exercise the same with a certaine boldnesse and lightnesse of the body."[19] In some editions, an illustration of a man in puritan dress walking on water with the assistance of this device accompanies this very irreverent how-to guide (see fig. 1). In others (the editions of 1581, 1584, and 1586),[20] a man dressed only in loincloth and hat treads the waters. Hill advertised his work as an appropriate source for wits to entertain themselves (however dangerously!) in their spare time.

Fig. 1 "How to Walk on the Water," in Thomas Hill, *Naturall and Artificiall Conclusions* (1650). British Library, E.1380 [1], Oxford University, Bodleian Library. Shelfmark: Wood. 727 [2]. Wing (2nd ed.), H2018. © The British Library Board.

In other contexts the imitation of the divine carried different implications. We can also find late sixteenth-century claims to divine imitation in works written in defense of poetry. Courtiers cultivated poetic talents to express their opinions on court life, the king's rule, and—because court life often required them to supply proofs of their worthiness in the competition for patronage— as a demonstration of their intellectual virtues. As such, poetry itself came under criticism, and was in turn defended.[21] In England George Puttenham begins *The Art of English Poesy* by declaring that poets resemble God: "A Poet is as much to say as a maker. . . . Such as (by way of resemblance and reverently) we may say of God: who without any travell [travail] to his divine imagination, made all the world of nought, nor also by any paterne or mould. . . . Eve[n] so the very Poet makes and contrives out of his owne braine, both the verse and matter of his poeme, and not by any foreign copie or example."[22] Puttenham later complicates the picture by claiming that poets also imitate what they encounter in the world in ways that are "true" and "lively." These claims suggest a likeness between Puttenham's boasts concerning the poet and Hobbes's, perhaps in parallel with the ways of imitating the creator that I have described. It suffices to note, however, that in each case, godlike abilities are claimed for the purpose of lending dignity and legitimacy to a particular practice.

Philip Sidney's *The Defense of Poesy* makes similar arguments, although his reference to God is more oblique.[23] He describes rival learned practices, including those of astronomers, geometers, arithmeticians, musicians, natural philosophers, and lawyers. Each is compared unfavorably with the poet for merely "looking upon" nature. All are "compassed within the circle of a question according to the proposed matter." Poets, Sidney suggests, break outside such restrictions: "Only the poet, disdaining to be tied to any such subjection, lifted up with the vigour of his own invention, doth grow in effect another nature, in making things either better than nature bringeth forth, or, quite anew, forms such as never were in nature."[24] What Sidney praises in poetry Hobbes would seem to appropriate for philosophy.[25] The truly skillful can not merely re-create nature, but exceed it.

The question we have to ask in light of these examples is, why rival God?

We can look to the work of René Girard, who finds mimetic rivalry (and concomitant violence) an undeniable part of human nature.[26] There are several points of connection between what Girard has suggested, especially between the man who seeks kudos, and the Hobbesian sovereign. He ends all violence by being the most violent.[27] The connection is possible, but it begs a historical question. Why did God's rivals, Hobbes included, become so aggressive when they did? Thomas Hill, for example, turns godlike achievements into impious jokes for crafty pranksters. Why, we might ask, did Hill and others like Pomponazzi wish to convert the miracles of the past into the human creations of their own day? Behind the cleverness and the search for new human powers, there may be something of a grudge against the maker of the universe.

Commenting on Pomponazzi and earlier contemporaries, the Renaissance historian Eugenio Garin observed that we can become facile in our readings of the humanistic praise of man if we do not understand the price that had to be paid for it. Garin refers to their having to abandon a worldview still sustained by the schools and which held together the social fabric of the Middle Ages: "One had to pay for the freedom to fight in a world that was stubbornly opposed to any effort and in which progress was difficult by relinquishing the reassuring idea that a given order existed. One also had to abandon the belief in a justice which would always in the end, albeit sometimes by very obscure means, triumph."[28] On Garin's view, what came to replace this world was one in which faith was beginning to fade. In politics this meant a world that tried to operate without illusions, "in which people were buffeted by forces without pity and in which the vanquished were eliminated without compassion."[29] The coldly realistic politics pioneered by Machiavelli is recollected here, and it is fair to say that Hobbes's politics emerges from the same frame of mind.

Regarding God himself, Garin observes: "People began to sense that everything in the world was frail and that God, if a God remained, was terribly far away and ineffable and likely to issue unintelligible decrees to punish the just and save the sinner—a God to Whom it was vain to address prayers."[30] In addition to Machiavelli, Garin lists Pomponazzi, Michelangelo, Copernicus, Bruno, Galileo, Luther, and Calvin, who each live with the faraway God. Hobbes is not on Garin's list, but he belongs.

Hobbes's Political Imitation of God

Like those thinkers on Garin's list, Hobbes lived in a world that was tearing itself apart. In an attempt to better understand Descartes's context, Stephen Toulmin has noted the connection between the political chaos of the Thirty Years' War and the search for new foundations to replace the old.[31] Hobbes and the earlier humanists of the Italian Renaissance also illustrate that crises may lead to the search for new foundations. Beyond, and in some respects against, the received view of this stage in the "quest for certainty," the search for new foundations may also lead to the search for new practical powers to supply the defects of a collapsing old order.[32] The certitude Hobbes claimed for himself and his new science was not a certitude about the world to replace the old and tired certitudes, but a program to replace the old source of order itself.

In accord with this new standard, Hobbes's claims therefore go beyond that of the poets. Part of Hobbes's task (particularly in *Leviathan*) was evoking a lively image of what could actually be created. He claims that the laws and covenant laid down in his doctrine will, if followed, produce a stable, well-ordered commonwealth—something more concrete than supplying a conception. At the close of the first half of *Leviathan* Hobbes considers some of the impediments to the realization of his artificial man. He was interested in offering more than a conception of a well-ordered commonwealth:

> Considering how different this doctrine is from the practice of the greatest part of the world . . . . I am at the point of believing this my labour as useless as the commonwealth of *Plato* . . . .
>
> But when I consider again, . . . that neither Plato, nor any other philosopher hitherto, hath put into order, and sufficiently or probably, proved all the theorems of moral doctrine, that men may learn thereby both how to govern and how to obey; I recover some hope that, one time or another, this writing of mine may fall into the hands of a sovereign who will consider it himself . . . and by the exercise of entire sovereignty in protecting the public teaching of it, convert this truth of speculation into the utility of practice.[33]

Hobbes expected to orchestrate the creation of concrete, utilizable, results. Here, and against the conventional view of Hobbes's science, we might ask why he connects the conversion of his "truth of speculation" into "the utility of practice" with the (protected) public teaching of his doctrine?

Typically, when we ask how Hobbes intended to see his commonwealth built, we turn him back into the kind of social scientist that I have said he is not. We note that Hobbes had a particular conception of human nature. It was a pessimistic one, but one rooted in generalizations that allowed him to predict what people would do if the proper institutions were, or were not, crafted to get them out of the state of nature and into a commonwealth. It is with regard to Hobbes's generalizations about "mankind" that he seems to stray furthest from the model of science I have attributed to him. He might be thought to deviate from his own philosophical standard of truth, for example, when he asks readers to consult themselves if they think his view of human beings too uncharitable.

For example, after having famously turned the state of nature into a state of war in chapter 13 of *Leviathan*, he admits that "to some man that has not well weighed these things," further arguments must be made. If the argument that draws upon "inferences made from the passions" to derive a state of war is not enough, "Let him therefore consider with himself—when taking a journey he arms himself, and seeks to go well accompanied; when going to sleep, he locks his doors."[34] He makes similar claims in *De Cive*,[35] appealing to men's opinions and actions to acknowledge a truth about themselves that is not, strictly speaking, a mere propositional truth.[36]

Even in his more rigorous demonstrations of the inevitability of a war of all against all, in our natural condition, Hobbes's "inferences from the passions" do more than assert conditional knowledge. They seem to be asserting matters of fact, and specifically fundamental, metaphysical facts about man as a species. It is mankind's "general inclination" to seek "power after power"; we are competitors, we are diffident, we are glory-seeking creatures. We are curious, we are fearful, we are moving machines that have not only the right but the natural urge to preserve ourselves.[37] It is because of these generalized facts about man that we, in our natural condition, live in a war of all against all. If Hobbes's science is not a science of facts, but a science of conditional constructions, what are we to make of these well-known, grand, and (seemingly) factual assertions?

As noted, Hobbes sometimes identifies these assertions, particularly those that lead to conflict in the state of nature, as "inferences from the passions." It is as though they were merely inferences about what we *would have to be* within the terms of his philosophy. They stand as the conclusions of deductive causal reasoning and not observation, things that *must be so* if we are also creatures who seek our own felicity in moving from one object of desire to the next. In some of his more aggressive assaults upon natural philosophy Hobbes draws the conclusion that follows from the prohibitions on factual truth assertions we reviewed in the previous chapter. He pointedly states, for example, that "it is supposed that in the natural kingdom of God" there is no way to know anything other than by "natural reason," "that is, from the principles of natural science, which are so far from teaching us anything of God's nature as they cannot teach us our own nature, nor the nature of the smallest creature living."[38]

In spite of these moments, we ought to see these fundamental factual assumptions about the world and ourselves for what they are. Hobbes's list of conditional assertions comes to an end in a basic assertion concerning the state of the world and life within it. If felicity "of this life"[39] is continual success in moving from one object to the next, it is because "life itself is but motion, and can never be without desire, nor without fear, no more without sense."[40] His view of human being thus seems to be at least partially rooted in factual assertion, even if his science rules out factual assertion. (Hobbes's philosophy even gives us reason to contest the philosophical truth of these assertions, on his own terms. If all things that exist are matter in motion, than all things, including those things conventionally called dead or lifeless, are, on Hobbes's terms, living. The matter from which they are composed does not cease to move.)

But if it must be acknowledged that Hobbes hits bottom with some basic assertions about the world and "life itself," it does not follow from this that his science must go on to make further factual assertions or predictions. This runs contrary to his own philosophical rules and trajectory. It also does not follow that his philosophy must take the form of a science that proves its worth by verifying the truth of hypotheses about the world. The tensions in Hobbes's thought are more interesting if we don't paper over them by converting him into a familiar scientific inquirer.

Why, then, assert fundamental matters of fact? Hobbes, I would suggest, thought that he first had a responsibility to shatter what he saw as the dangerous, and even negligent, illusions of the crumbling orthodoxy. He opposed an old metaphysics with a new one. His thoroughgoing materialism is an undefended condition of his philosophy. It is not proven by his methods, but it is the prerequisite for his philosophical practice. Although he can reconstruct the effects he posits about human conduct through a posteriori reasoning, his basic factual assertions about human beings function in much the same way. The old orthodoxy had a place and a purpose for man within the grand scheme. Hobbes rejected this. He asserted an alternative metaphysical starting point. His philosophy dictated a much-diminished set of expectations for human beings who expect to count upon a natural order. Were they not to rely upon their own talents? They had to use these talents to make an order for themselves. No order could be expected to spontaneously, or "naturally," emerge of its own accord.

His assertions each contribute toward the rejection of the old telos. That old order may have located human beings in a position greatly inferior to that of God, but it also reassured them of a place within an established divine order. Hobbes's dictates for a constructed order create a substitute for what was rejected. Hobbes's human beings are thus no longer the kind of creature that can expect a divinely sanctioned hierarchy to determine their place for them. In Hobbes's commonwealth, position will be determined by the sovereign's will.[41] Nature or God will not place talented men in a position to lead, or punish those who might challenge God's anointed order. It will be up to the subjects to report those who would disturb the peace to their sovereign, and those who are punished by the sovereign are reminded that it is a punishment they themselves authorized when they consented to join society.[42] In the state of nature, there is no binding law, no just or unjust. In Hobbes's commonwealth, the sovereign is the source and the condition for the laws, but not bound by those laws. The sovereign is identified with God, as an omnipotent lawgiver of the state, and thereby also becomes the political substitute for God.

As I noted in the introduction, prior writers have considered the link between Hobbes's sovereign and God, but there has been a tendency to underestimate just how "godlike" Hobbes sought to make his political and intellectual accomplishments. This is because the tendency is to credit the magnetic pull of a particularly Cartesian vision of science on Hobbes's thought. I've argued the characteristic mistake of this approach is to assume that the pull toward the mathematical approach to politics requires a corresponding withdrawal from what preceded it, including the influence of humanism. Carl Schmitt was among those who considered Cartesian reasoning to be key to understanding Hobbes's thought. Like many others, he underestimated how godlike Hobbes's ambitions were.

Carl Schmitt's Cartesian Hobbes

Carl Schmitt considered the juridical place of Hobbes's sovereign—as the state's omnipotent lawgiver—particularly important, and his view has been amplified recently by Giorgio Agamben.[43] Schmitt used Hobbes's thought as he saw fit within his circumstances in Weimar and Nazi Germany.[44] Schmitt requires attention here because today he is considered the writer most identified with the tendency to stress the mortal god concept in Hobbes's writings,[45] and because his reading, though brief, contextualizes what he sees as Hobbes's secularization of Cartesian theological concepts of God. In light of what I have argued, there is reason to contest this contextualization.

There are, however, problems with engaging Schmitt. Because of his abhorrent politics, correcting Schmitt's reading of Hobbes is not unlike debating the characteristics of munitions with an enemy soldier—an analogy he would have appreciated. There are more urgent critiques that must take precedent, and so this treatment can by no means substitute for a full discussion of his thought. Nevertheless, because this reading and Schmitt's stress the mortal god, I would like to point to some important differences in how each deals with the topic. More immediately, this discussion will bring us back to Hobbes's conception of "man" and the imitation of God by mathematical means.

For Schmitt, Hobbes's "mortal god," his state, was an initially attractive framework for making the case against nineteenth- and twentieth-century liberalism. In particular, Schmitt was critical of liberalism's commitment to a constitutionally limited government. In periods of political turmoil, Schmitt advocated a stronger state power, one unlimited by the ordinary laws that apply during times of tranquility. He particularly admired Hobbes's conception of sovereignty. In spite of this admiration, Schmitt did not think Hobbes's model of state authority invulnerable. Schmitt's various approaches to Hobbes blended praise with (at times despicable) laments. The latter were directed against what he believed were the precursors within Hobbes's thought that overlapped with historical forces and trends he opposed: liberal, modern, and Enlightenment-inspired political and social perspectives. Schmitt thought these ultimately destroyed Hobbes's state from within.[46] From this point of view, Hobbes's state, in spite of his godlike sovereign, was insufficiently unified. Historical forces would reveal its weaknesses. The most prominent aspect of this criticism of the weaknesses of Hobbes's "state theory" was written in the late 1930s and blended Schmitt's own anti-Semitism with an analysis of what he saw as Hobbes's failure to fully control his sovereign's subjects by means of a state religion.[47] Hobbes's sovereign is head of both church and state, but Schmitt is mindful that Hobbes permits a distinction between what subjects must publicly profess, and what they may privately believe within their own hearts or consciences.[48] For Schmitt, a conservative inspired by nineteenth-century Catholic reactionaries, this was a fissure that would be exploited quickly by Jewish philosophers beginning with Spinoza. Those who did not truly believe might publicly profess insincere beliefs and gain acceptance within a community that they would eventually destroy. The freedom of private thought and belief was, Schmitt declared, the "seed of death that destroyed the mighty Leviathan."[49]

This aspect of Schmitt's critique, however, was accompanied by another histrionic, although somewhat more historical, account of potential weaknesses within Hobbes's account of state authority. Here our discussion of Hobbes's "man" and the connection between his science and the imitation of God is apropos. Hobbes's sovereign, his mortal god, contains another fatal flaw, and that is its fostering of an image of the state as a great machine, a view Schmitt asserts Hobbes absorbed from Descartes. In his earlier, more positive, views of Hobbes Schmitt describes a parallel between Descartes's God, and Hobbes's sovereign. Descartes's God was the singular rational architect of the universe and its laws.[50] Schmitt suggests that Hobbes's adoption of this model for his sovereign was a near inevitable expression of a common milieu, a part of a "continuous thread" that ran "through metaphysical, political and sociological conceptions that postulate the sovereign as a personal unit and primeval creator."[51] This "new rationalist spirit," embodied in Hobbes's sovereign, is identified with this rational creator God, a necessarily singular architect of the grand order.

Among contemporary Enlightenment thinkers, notably Heidegger, Descartes's impact was frowned upon.[52] In *Political Theology*, however, Schmitt finds something to approve, especially as it affected Hobbes's thought. It was this element of commonality with Descartes, Schmitt suggests, which contributed to the "decisionalist cast" of Hobbes's thinking. Without citing a reference, Schmitt notes that Descartes had once written to Mersenne: "It is God who establishes these laws in nature just as a king establishes laws in his kingdom."[53] In Schmitt's view, Descartes was establishing the sovereign as a secularized omnipotent God, who as the creator of the state's laws is also the one who can decide to operate outside them. The sovereign Schmitt admires is ever mindful of why he might have to do so; he is attuned to the possibility of threats to the existence of the state. In response to such threats (in what modern governments call states of emergency or crises) he has the power to "decide the exception."[54] This means he can declare a state of emergency: those he deems a threat, an "enemy," will be exposed to forms of violence ruled out by ordinary lawful, or constitutional, restrictions. That is, the enemy could be exposed to the unlimited violence deemed necessary for survival in Hobbes's state of nature, although in this case it will be violence exercised by the state rather than by fellow individuals.[55] Extending the secularization to the exception, Schmitt notes that "the exception in jurisprudence is analogous to the miracle in theology."[56]

Hobbes's sovereign is thus linked to a transcendent source, and so it is a mortal god who can perform the violent miracle of the exception, on Schmitt's reading. The transcendent source of law is not bound by law. Schmitt observed that this put the sovereign in an odd position. He stands outside the law, but nevertheless belongs to it.[57] Schmitt would note (in his later treatment of Hobbes) that Hobbes's sovereign is not himself created by the individuals who contract with one another, but remains both connected to the state he protects and in the state of nature. He retains his natural right of self-preservation, while the individuals contract with one another to make the sovereign their protector. They agree with one another to transfer to the sovereign rights they would have had were they not within a civil state.[58]

This transfer of rights had the ironic result of making the Hobbesian sovereign the most bestial precisely when he is exercising his most godlike powers. His capacity to perform miracles—that is to say, to declare exceptions to the regular law and order of the state—is also his prerogative to exercise the most unfettered forms of violence. Hobbes's sovereign is both god and wolf in one, and he may roam about threateningly among his people with impunity. This character of sovereignty is what drew Schmitt to La Fontaine's revival, during Louis XIV's absolutist reign, of Aesopian fables such as "The Wolf and the Lamb."[59] Recent work that draws on Schmitt has argued that the "empty space"[60] between unbounded adversaries in the state of nature was also made a part of the civil state. The tendency to declare states of emergency and exception with growing regularity in modern states has become an issue of particular interest to political theorists.[61]

Schmitt's reactionary sensibilities, however, are reflected in a sensitivity to the ways subsequent liberal-Enlightenment political conceptions, such as the rule of law, could undermine Hobbes's decisionalist sovereign. Even in his most admiring (early) descriptions of Hobbes, Schmitt considered that the philosopher's mathematical and scientific aspirations were ultimately at odds with his godlike view of sovereignty.[62] A transcendent God and a transcendent sovereign could perform miracles, and could exercise the exceptions to the laws they warranted. The tendency during the Enlightenment and within political thought in the nineteenth century was, Schmitt noted, against transcendence. The conceptions of the universe that arose in the eighteenth and nineteenth centuries focused on immanent, not transcendent, causes. The rational machine created by Descartes's God was now seen as independent of its creator. It functioned automatically. Likewise, the laws of the liberalizing states after the French Revolution were seen to have autonomous lives of their own:

> The exclusively scientific thinking has also permeated political ideas, repressing the essentially juristic-ethical thinking that had predominated in the age of the Enlightenment. The general validity of a legal prescription has become identified with the lawfulness of nature, which applies without exception. The sovereign, who in the deistic view of the world, even if conceived as residing outside the world, has remained the engineer of the great machine, has been radically pushed aside. The machine now runs itself . . . . God enunciates only general and not particular declarations of will . . . . The decisionalistic and personalistic element in the concept of sovereignty was thus lost.[63]

It is therefore a flaw, in Schmitt's view, that Hobbes's dictatorial solution to the disunity of the state was blended with "mathematical relativism,"[64] for it was this component of his thought that developed into a force to erase the memory of and reverence for the transcendent sources that Schmitt argued sovereigns needed for the construction of successful political theologies.

In his more sustained critical considerations of Hobbes, Schmitt turns again to what he claims are the connections between Hobbes and Descartes. In these later writings,[65] Schmitt highlights Descartes's understanding of man. Here, unlike his earlier discussion of Descartes's transcendent God, his narrative incorporates some of what have become more conventional (likely inspired by Heidegger) criticisms of both Descartes's and Hobbes's ontologies. Schmitt notes it was Descartes who made the "first metaphysical leap" and who stands responsible for the critical moment when "the human body was conceived to be a machine and the human being, consisting of body and soul, was postulated to be in its entirety an intellect intent on a machine."[66] Hobbes's mortal god, his Leviathan, may assimilate man to animal and man to god, but it is the vision of man as machine that Schmitt thinks more potent historically, and it is this element which he comes to stress as most central in Hobbes's political philosophy: "Hobbes transfers—and that seems to me to be the gist of his philosophy of state—the Cartesian conception of man as mechanism with a soul onto the 'huge man,' the state, made by him into a machine animated by the sovereign-representative person."[67] Moreover, in what appears to be a modern revision of Plato's inquiry into the huge man in *The Republic*, Hobbes is said to have "consummated" the modern understanding of man as a calculable machine: "After the body and soul of the huge man became a machine, the transfer back became possible, and even the little man could become an *homme-machine*."[68] When Schmitt writes that even the soul of the huge man has become a machine, he refers again to the loss of a transcendent sovereign and its replacement by an *unexceptional* regularly ordered state. Instead of being committed to the defense of substantive transcendent values, the nineteenth-century "bourgeois law-and-constitutional state" conceives of its fundamental laws as neutral, technical instruments. Schmitt thus declares Hobbes to be the "spiritual forefather" of this state.[69]

Hobbes is apparently, if we follow Schmitt, the originator of the mechanical state filled with mechanical men. Even Hobbes's laws for these people were moving in the direction of creating "mechanism[s] driven by compulsory psychological motivations." "Law" thus became a means of manipulating such compulsory motivations and a technical exercise in finding "calculable functioning that can serve different aims and contents" without a particular concern for substantive standards. For Schmitt, these elements in Hobbes, aided and abetted by his mathematical-mechanical proclivities, help destroy the transcendent within the state. States would no longer have a (non-mechanical) soul devoted toward a particular set of beliefs, as they did in an era when sovereigns claimed to rule by divine right.

While it is not my wish to show that Hobbes's state had the kind of transcendent soul that Schmitt wished to retain and defend (by force), I have shown why Schmitt's understanding of Hobbes's mathematics is flawed. I will not discuss the sweeping questions raised by Schmitt's assertions concerning

Hobbes's spiritual fatherhood of later liberal thinkers. I do wish to note that in Hobbes's contexts being mathematical did not, contra Schmitt, mean abandoning the goal of substituting man, and the sovereign, for God. Hobbes's view of the world does not so easily yield an image of the universe as a grand machine that would someday "run itself," especially politically. A proponent of efficient over ultimate causes, Hobbes did not lose the habit of imitating transcendent causes as readily as Schmitt suggests. Instead, Hobbes's wish to imitate God meant that the sovereign's rule remained central. The view of man as a machine may have become characteristically modern, but Hobbes's understanding of the godlike character of machine-builders was something Schmitt's account elides. Descartes sought to grasp the order of the rational God's universe with his own reason. This was not Hobbes's goal. Wishing to build like God does not necessarily imply, in this case, a search for the order God himself had established. Schmitt was mindful of how Hobbes's thought was intended to sweep away a medieval conception of order, but he did not fully consider what it meant to substitute one created order for another. Hobbes would be particularly resistant to visions of a regular and independent order in which a sovereign builder would be pushed aside. More like a building than a modern machine that runs on some fuel regularly supplied by nature, the foremost purpose of Hobbes's artifice was to remain standing and doing so required ongoing obedience to its sovereign.

Returning to our narrative concerning the imitation of God, we saw how the age Hobbes belonged to had not yet eradicated miracles. Some took it upon themselves (as with Pomponazzi, and the irreverent Hill) to domesticate the miraculous. Special persons, in possession of the right kinds of knowledge and practices, may not claim to perform miracles though God's own means, but they might find their own. In Schmitt's history there is too little middle ground between the transcendent (however secularized) and the mere mechanical and soon to be automatic, but this is where we will find Hobbes.

Hobbes's Responsible Politics

Before turning to Schmitt's Hobbes, I noted that Hobbes's will to displace the old telos could be seen as an effort toward an arrogant, but responsible, attempt to substitute the products of human virtues for the crumbling and disappointing order attributed to God. This assumption of responsibility does not occur by reviving nature (or creation's) power to order the universe. It is not a wish, in Hobbes's case, to at last discover and exploit nature's powers or patterns, or to reaffirm nature's perfection by claiming to finally find its true order. Nature (and nature's architect) had fallen short. With the right science, human beings could become the ordering power over nature. In Hobbes's philosophy the being that had been taught to perfect himself had not given up the habit of seeking godlike perfections; he had simply lost his humility.

Hobbes's human being, his "man," may have impulses and passions like the fear of death to help move him in the right direction when it comes time to build a commonwealth, but his attributes are not akin to the self-interested (or self-preserving) engines, or machines that continuously power and direct the actions of the more modern subject. The desire for self-preservation is fundamental for Hobbes. We must fear death rather than welcome it. We must, indeed, seek peace. Nevertheless, these are not forces of nature which he expects to continually harness; they are not the compulsory impulses to channel through institutional, or constitutional, designs. Human beings are, instead, malleable entities given over to a variety of impulses (some helpful, many harmful as regards their ability to live together in peace) who must be "made fit" for society because nature, contrary to Aristotle and the school's deficient doctrines, did not create them fit from the start.[70] Indeed, it is because some men welcome death for heroic or religious reasons that they must be reshaped.[71]

For Hobbes, materialism is therefore not an invitation to discover the order of nature hidden by the absurdities and nonsense of the scholastics. It is an invitation to sweep the imagined universe clean of false, mysterious, and seemingly autonomous powers. It must be done to clear the field for man to manipulate matter as he sees fit. The exercise of sovereign power over nature is understood here as commanding the skills and techniques for manipulating matter, making it move according to a well-ordered plan rather than channeling its inherent or calculable motions. Therefore, when Hobbes makes metaphysical assertions of fact about human nature, he is only glancing around a corner that may lead toward the modern conception of the subject. The plumbed, prodded, harnessed, and predicted subject is not yet on the scene. Hobbes will go so far as to posit disaster if human beings do not employ their talents and craft a suitable civil science, but on the road toward a peaceful state Hobbes would have us rely much more on his own philosophical talents than on our "nature."

He will not therefore wish to build on his claims concerning human nature in the way that the Newtonian physicist will build upon assertions about the laws of gravity. He does not make it his concern, therefore, to predict what *the* rationally self-interested person will *always*, or even usually, do. If we find

Hobbes lacking for not having done this, we are in fact trying to place him in a framework that his science and his own sovereign ambitions resist. This is to make Hobbes captive to a telos that can only congratulate him when he most resembles contemporary social science. We must, instead, pay attention to Hobbes when he says that his truth of speculation can be made real only through the teaching of his doctrine.

Hobbes, like the humanists and educators before him, still pursues his goals by teaching. It is a perfection he himself declares, rather than God, and rather than God's self-appointed agents, the clergy. Their telos is rejected, but neither the habits of the pedagogues who accepted that telos, nor the need for a grand architect's direction, has yet been abandoned in Hobbes's thought. This is why Hobbes's discussion "Of Man" in *Leviathan* (and the discussions in other works, such as *De Homine*) is in most parts *not* an account of the rational egoist (or some other modern "Man"), but is instead a return to the training (pedagogy) of how to understand and improve ourselves.

There he teaches his readers how to use what they have, not merely (or primarily) what it is they are. We learn how to conceive of sense, what to do to properly reason over sense impressions and memories. We learn how to use this reason to overcome our own destructiveness. Hobbes is still in the habit of teaching his fellow human beings how to become what they could be, even as he has rejected the old scheme, which dictated both the limits and the trajectory of human existence. Like his humanist predecessors, Hobbes plays a builder of human material. He, however, is akin to a builder who supplants the architect, appoints himself the new architect with his own designs, and goes searching for a new patron.

This is the context in which we should understand Hobbes's reference to the sovereign's decision to "protect the public teaching" of his doctrine. In other words, the concrete means of creating his commonwealth—the process that allows us to become creators, like God in politics—*is* education. A geometer may construct figures by moving matter on the page, an architect by directing the assembly of timbers and stones. Likewise, the commonwealth comes into being through the actions of the indoctrinated citizens and those who lead them at the sovereign's pleasure. To actually create the commonwealth, to truly imitate the creator, the doctrine devised by Hobbes must be taught and obeyed. Contra Schmitt, Hobbes's mathematical learning did not compete with his political theology; it was integral to his political theology.

Hobbes's doctrine is also not merely a defense of absolutism. Absolutism, and the kind of rigorous control of learning expected in such a system, is also the condition for its fruition. Hobbes required that the sovereign power make his doctrine the state's official doctrine. It had to be taught in the universities, and it had to inform the officers of the state, including magistrates and clergy. These persons, in turn, would be required to disseminate and enforce the doctrine among the people. His philosophy, his *doctrine*, is made real by institutional authority.[72]

In effect, Hobbes's politically educated citizens, their divines, their teachers, their magistrates, are all instructed to work in concert. All such persons subordinate to the sovereign are the matter Hobbes would have controlled according to the precise directions of his philosophically guided doctrine. Their motions, like the matter manipulated on the geometer's page, are precisely dictated. When combined, Hobbes promises, they will create the well-ordered commonwealth. One could call it a marching-band state. Subordinates and subjects generate, in precise formation, the peaceful commonwealth. Hobbes's philosophy generates an elaborate "how to" manual. Individual persons are to become his building blocks, but to play this role his doctrine must be written on them by their teachers. In conducting themselves in accordance with it, they make themselves pieces of a well-constructed, peaceful, artificial man.

Hobbes writes that nothing made by mortals can be immortal, but that commonwealths can at least live as long as "mankind, or the laws of nature, or as justice itself, which give them life."[73] Furthermore, if they do dissolve by "intestine disorder,"

> the fault is not in men as they are the *matter*, but as they are the *makers* and orderers of them. For men, as they become at last weary of irregular jostling and hewing one another, and desire with all their hearts to conform themselves into one firm and lasting edifice, so for want, both of the art of making fit laws to square their actions by, and also of humility and patience to suffer the rude and cumbersome points of their present greatness to be taken off, they cannot, without the help of a very able architect, be compiled into any other than a crazy building, such as, hardly lasting out their own time, must assuredly fall upon the heads of their posterity.[74]

Human beings, in other words, are an adequate starting material from which to build a commonwealth. A strong and enduring structure could be built out of them, but the task cannot be done without the help of a "very able architect."

During the period when Hobbes emphasized the potential to imitate God through his philosophy, he enjoyed (on and off) his most intimate access to the Crown and influential courtiers.[75] It is worth noting, therefore, that a key claim of Stuart absolutism was that kings are to their subjects as God is to man.[76] Although James I was long dead when Hobbes began to describe his mortal god, James's political works remained a resonant defense of absolutism during Hobbes's lifetime.[77] James I had told his heir, "as a King; seeing in him [God], as in a mirrour, the course of all earthly things, whereof hee is the spring and only moouer."[78] James continued to defend this aspect of his doctrine in his later works.[79] Although this last remark is suggestive of a creator role for the king (the Elizabethan courtier poet Puttenham did, in fact, suggest an identity between poet, monarch, and divine creators),[80] the divine aspects of kingship that James stresses most are not connected to God's role as creator. It was God's *authority* over men and the lessons regarding the king's authority that were more important to James's absolutism. It was unlawful to resist either.

Hobbes may have been motivated at least in part by the prospect of bettering himself and his proposal in the eyes of the sovereign by suggesting a compatibility between his doctrine and the Stuart fashioning of monarchical identity. In suggesting that his philosophy teaches the godlike art of creation, Hobbes may have been arguing that both he and Charles II might use their respective powers (intellectual and authoritative) to fulfill one another's aspirations. It is noteworthy that one of Hobbes's pleas for the public teaching of his doctrine occurs directly after one of his most noteworthy evocations of a sovereign who could imitate the divine. In chapter 30 of *Leviathan*, "The Office of the Sovereign Representative," Hobbes offers up his secular equivalent of the Ten Commandments. Upon completion of his description, Hobbes notes that the universities are the "means and conduits" by which the people will receive this instruction. Hobbes is much less permissive—and a great deal less liberal—in allowing the dictates of private conscience to weigh upon the subjects' minds than any Cartesian reading of his work could anticipate. Because psychological compulsion was not the method he had in mind, he intended to reform the institutions where seditious beliefs had at first become "so deeply rooted" in subjects. As a font of authority with the wider public, the universities that had planted false doctrine would now be compelled to "plant the true."[81]

Hobbes's philosopher is not a passive observer. Philosophers must imitate the creator. When philosophers find chaos, in language, in heads, or in politics, their task is to set it right by stamping an order upon it. They do not need a well-known and orderly universe to accomplish this. They need, instead, the skills of a builder; they need the skills of an "able architect." This does not mean that Hobbes found dealing with his fellow human beings easy. The opposite was the case: it is precisely because they were so prone to cause chaos that the imitation of God—the greatest orderer of chaos—became necessary. Hobbes's philosophy is a political philosophy of countermeasures. Quite literally, he was going to teach jostling humanity a lesson (a practice very much in keeping with the Stuart tradition of pedant kingship). The conventional view that I have questioned has frequently asserted that Hobbes's philosophy seeks to take steps to calm chaos and to create order. What this perspective has failed to grasp is how ontologically aggressive Hobbes was in his efforts to arrest our jostling selves. Developing a descriptive or predictive social science was not a part of Hobbes's attempt to solve the problem. He insists that nothing short of turning ourselves into creators will do. Hobbes's philosophy teaches us to respond to the threat of chaos by modifying and crafting the world and ourselves into a well-ordered artifice.

5

ARCHITECTONIC AMBITIONS: MATHEMATICS AND THE DEMOTION OF PHYSICS

> They that study natural philosophy, study in vain, except they begin at geometry; and such writers or disputers thereof, as are ignorant of geometry, do but make their readers lose their time.
>
> —Hobbes, *De Corpore*

In Chapters 3 and 4 I stressed several points. First, Hobbes did not pursue either descriptive or predictive accounts of natural phenomena. His use for physics was merely to re-create the effects observed in nature. Second, Hobbes assigned a lower rank to physics because it re-creates rather than creates originally. He assigned a higher rank to sciences such as geometry and the science of politics. Hobbes claimed that we know the products of these superior sciences with a greater degree of certainty because we create (or could create) their objects ourselves.

The purpose of this chapter is to show that behind these distinctions there was an ambition that can best be described as architectonic.[1] Not unlike his former employer Francis Bacon,[2] Hobbes wished to fundamentally reorganize the scientific curriculum. Had he been granted the power to reform the schools on the sovereign's behalf, Hobbes would have tried to impose this new ordering, and new hierarchy, upon the universities. Hobbes did not get his way. Our assessment of his conflicts in these matters, however, should take these ambitious goals into account. It was for Hobbes not merely a matter of whose scientific conclusions were true or false. As the epigraph from *De Corpore* suggests, it was also a question of how philosophy (science) was to be taught. Which subjects were to come first, and which were to be ranked higher or lower in the academic hierarchy? My interest here is not to defend

Hobbes's system of sciences, but to show how this architectonic ambition expresses itself with regard to physics and mathematics. The purpose of this inquiry is not to bolster Hobbes's reputation as a scientist, or to show the compatibility between Hobbes's pursuit of truth and present-day practice. It is to illustrate the rather aggressive, political, character of his participation in the domain of early modern scientific dispute.

Demoting Physics

Stephen Gaukroger has observed in his interpretation of Descartes that those who pushed for a mathematicized physics were not merely substituting new tools for physical inquiry, but challenging the very idea of what should count as an explanation in physics.[3] The same holds true for Hobbes's intervention into natural philosophy. Hobbes pursued some radical maneuvers to bring physics into the orbit of (his) mathematics. We can bring Hobbes into better focus by contrasting his claims for a mathematical philosophy with those of the same sixteenth-century Jesuit proponents of mathematics who may have also influenced Descartes.[4] The comparison allows us to draw contrasts between Hobbes and earlier mathematically inclined philosophers who wished to insinuate these methods into the study of physical phenomena. Before doing so, however, I will review some of the contemporaneous disputes over mathematics and physics within Hobbes's career and writings.

Because Hobbes has been so often associated with an effort to create a "social physics,"[5] these contemporaneous disputes bolster the evidence against this perspective. From Hobbes's point of view, he was doing more than reforming physics by making it mathematical. He was demoting—not extending—it. He was subordinating it to his own vision of mathematical and philosophical practice, and so we see the sparks fly not merely in his conflicts with "the schools" but in his conflicts with those closely linked with the development of more modern forms of mathematicized physics, such as John Wallis. In works such as part 4 of *De Corpore, Decameron Physiologicum*, the *Anti-White*, and to a lesser extent *Seven Philosophical Problems*, Hobbes takes on a particularly large burden. These are not merely attempts to refute the conclusions of rival philosophers; they are attempts to redefine what it should mean to do physics (i.e., what the schools would have considered natural philosophy). Thus, these texts do not begin with specific debates among natural philosophers, but with instructions in how to engage in natural philosophy, and how to avoid the errors, absurdities, and corruption of the natural philosophy he has rejected.

In the *Anti-White* Hobbes suggests that "mathematics" is derived from "*manthanein*, that is, to learn" because all the other sciences taught things open to question. From this he infers that "all the sciences would have been mathematical had not their authors asserted more than they were able to prove."[6] Throughout this work Hobbes periodically takes it upon himself, beginning in chapter 2, to reeducate his opponent in the proper means of performing natural philosophy in a geometrically inspired fashion.[7] In effect, Hobbes puts himself in the challenging, in fact radically aggressive, position of first demanding our assent to his reinvention of philosophy. Only then, after attempting to dictate the terms on which natural philosophy can be done, does he confront the conclusions of rival scientists and philosophers.

Hobbes's *Decameron Physiologicum*[8] begins with an extremely disparaging history of natural philosophy. In a work designed to convince a sovereign king to have his doctrines taught in the schools, Hobbes was not unhappy to employ a courtly tactic: attack one's enemies by attacking their lineage. Dig deeply into the genealogy of today's natural philosophers, Hobbes suggested, and you will discover ignoble roots. In this text he winds his way to a time prior to Aristotle (whom he mentions favorably, although he deems reading him unnecessary),[9] and turns a jaundiced eye toward the natural philosophers of North Africa. These first natural philosophers are described as having largely deprived the discipline of whatever dignity it might have achieved. Reflecting a more general human weakness, they abused their reputations for wisdom. If a person "obtain[s] the credit of an extraordinary knowing man," his desire to dominate and exploit others leads straightway to practices of deceit and self-aggrandizement. Instead of asking the question that natural philosophers ought to ask (How might these effects be produced?), they have sought and claimed to know the causes in nature. Failing in this, as they must, they have resorted to spouting nonsense.[10]

As a part of this narrative he turns to the ancient historian Diodorus Siculus to relate the origins of Greek natural philosophy out of Egypt. These natural philosophers, in turn, had received their natural philosophy from a group of astrologers from Ethiopia, who had convinced the people of that nation that they had, by predicting eclipses, "discourse with the gods." They were charlatans, Hobbes notes, and were eventually "put to the sword" by King Ergamenes. Prior to this action, these philosophers had such sway with the people that they were a threat to the monarchy. By that point, their philosophy had already spread to Egypt and Assyria. Egypt then taught it to the world. The history of natural philosophy then proves to be little more than the history of "needy, ignorant, impudent, cheating fellows." He compares the Assyrian community of natural philosophers—they "had their towns and lands assigned them"—known as Chaldees (Chaldeans) to Europe's other marginal community associated with North Africa, the "gipsies." The difference, however, was that the Chaldeans were "admired and feared for their knavery, and the gipsies counted rogues."[11] Having established his critical theme, Hobbes ultimately includes the pope himself among those who would control philosophical knowledge for the sake of preserving their own power. The natural philosophy of the schools has been nothing but a means of perpetuating his authority.[12]

Hobbes wrote this work as a dialogue between "A" and "B." The discussion quickly shifts to questions of causal knowledge. A observes that he does not find that "from the causes they [school philosophers] assign, the effect is naturally or necessarily produced."[13] B responds:

> You must not wonder at that. For you enquire not so much, when you see a change of anything, what may be said to be the cause of it, as how the same is generated; which generation is the entire progress of nature from the efficient cause to the effect produced. Which is always a hard question, and for the most part impossible for a man to answer to. For the alterations of the things we perceive by our given senses are made by the motions of bodies, for the most part, either for distance, smallness, or transparence, invisible.[14]

The issue of the smallness or invisibility of the motions[15] is one of a number of arguments Hobbes uses to make us question our capacity to ever reach definitive knowledge of the workings of the natural world. Most important, the interlocutors agree that the things we wish to explain outside ourselves are in fact "fancies," namely, the phantasms created in our minds through our interaction with the jostling bodies in the world.[16] Chapter 2 of the *Decameron Physiologicum* is then devoted to starting natural philosophy afresh. He begins by calling on natural philosophers to imitate the geometer's methods and supplies a series of definitions and axioms concerning the motion of bodies, and clarifications concerning causality and space. When A asks whether so much "niceness" is necessary, he is answered, "Yes. The want of it is the greatest, if not the only, cause of all the discord amongst philosophers, as may be easily be perceived by their abusing and confounding the names of things that differ in their nature."[17] Although they will never achieve better than a posteriori reasoning (i.e., from wholes to parts and back by man-made reconstruction), they will at least achieve a partial imitation of the mathematicians. It is a worthy goal since the mathematicians have a means of reasoning that need not cause confusion. Unlike the natural philosophers of old, the mathematicians busy themselves with the more important and dignified task of *making truths* by construction. Remaking nature by certain mathematical reconstructions is better than making impossible claims to know nature's actual workings.

Part 4 of *De Corpore* follows the same logic. After reintroducing readers to his definition of philosophy (seeking cause and effect) Hobbes states his modest definition of natural philosophy—the re-creation of observed effects, but not necessarily by the means by which nature (or God) made them. Working from his critique of White, Hobbes systematically rules out natural philosophy's capacity to offer answers to the ultimate questions concerning the age of the universe, its magnitude, and so on.[18] These things are the handiwork of God; the answers sought are impossible because it is impossible for the finite to measure the infinite. Already cognizant of opposition from rivals (John Wallis and Seth Ward), Hobbes chastises those who would allow mathematics to become a part of the absurd debates over such questions:

> And the men, that reason thus absurdly, are not idiots, but which makes the absurdity unpardonable, geometricians, and such as take upon them to be judges, impenitent, but severe judges of other men's demonstrations [i.e., Hobbes's own attempts to square the circle]. The reason is this, that as soon as they are entangled in the words infinite and eternal, of which we have in our minds no idea, but that of our own insufficiency to comprehend them, they are forced either to speak something absurd, or which they love worse, to hold their peace. For geometry hath in it something like wine, which, when new, is windy; but afterwards though less pleasant, yet more wholesome.[19]

This is not so much an admission of the fallibility of mathematics as it is anger with what Hobbes saw as the flaws of recent mathematicians who were setting about a rival program for mathematical contributions to philosophy.[20]

The possibilities for the science of politics are greater. Because the science of politics is classed, with geometry, among the a priori forms of knowledge, these may bask closer to the light of the architectonic science.[21] We find such themes, moreover, not just in the works where Hobbes considers the relation between the disciplines at length, but also in Hobbes's key political works. Thus, some of Hobbes's most renowned boasts on behalf of mathematics need to be considered not merely in terms of his opposition to the schools, but in particular, in terms of his opposition—as a mathematician—to traditional natural philosophy practiced in the schools. In *De Cive*, he writes:

> Now look how many sorts of things there are, which properly fall within the cognizance of human reason; into so many branches does the tree of philosophy divide itself. And from the diversity of the matter about which they are conversant, there hath been given to those branches a diversity of names too. For treating of figures, it is called *geometry;* of motion, *physic;* of natural right, *morals;* put altogether, and they make up *philosophy*. Just as the British, the Atlantic, and the Indian seas . . . make up *the ocean*. And truly the geometricians have very admirably performed their part. For whatsoever assistance doth accrue to the life of man, whether from the observation of the heavens or from the description of the earth, from the notation of our times, or from the remotest experiments of navigation; finally, whatsoever things they are in which this present age doth differ from the rude simpleness of antiquity, we must acknowledge to be a debt which we owe merely to geometry.[22]

In the review of the history of philosophy in *Leviathan* Hobbes writes,

> But what has been the utility of those [Grecian] schools? What science is there at this day acquired by their readings and disputings? That we have of geometry, which is the mother of all natural science, we are not indebted for it to the schools. *Plato*, that was the best philosopher of the Greeks, forbad entrance into his school to all that were not already in some measure geometricians. There were many that studied that science to the great advantage of mankind. But there is no mention of their schools; nor was there any sect of geometricians; nor did they pass under the name of philosophers.
>
> The natural philosophy of those schools was rather a dream than science, and set forth in senseless and insignificant language, which cannot be avoided by those that will teach philosophy without having first attained greater knowledge in geometry. For nature worketh by motion, the ways and degrees whereof cannot be known without the knowledge of the proportions and properties of lines and figures.[23]

Against my reading of the disparagement of natural philosophy, it might be objected that in the *Seven Philosophical Problems* Hobbes speaks of natural philosophy in his dedication to Charles II as "the most noble employment of the mind that can be." This superlative is better understood in its full context. First, Hobbes is speaking of his own conception of natural philosophy. Second, the full statement is, "Notwithstanding the absence of rigorous demonstration, this contemplation of nature (if not rendered obscure by empty terms) is the most noble employment of the mind that can be, to such as are at leisure from their necessary business." Hobbes is subtly reminding Charles II that there is in fact a more noble employment for those who need to attend to their "necessary business." A reasonable candidate for this more noble employment would be Hobbes's own civil science.

To more fully understand Hobbes's wish to so thoroughly overturn the standing of natural philosophy, we will have to discuss the standing of mathematics and physics in the schools in the sixteenth century, and the connections between Hobbes's arguments and the terms of this debate. Before doing so, however, I wish to turn to a recent treatment of Hobbes's conflict with the seventeenth-century mathematician John Wallis. The political stakes attached to this debate can be better discerned against the background of Hobbes's architectonic ambitions. Moreover, the debate helps illustrate that Hobbes was not necessarily trying to clear a path for the mathematicized physics we know today, but something very different.

Pure and Mixed Studies

We know Hobbes as an antischolastic thinker, but his most vitriolic and longest-lasting dispute was with a fellow mathematician, John Wallis. Aside from his contributions toward the development of calculus and his influence on Newton, Wallis is also known for his aggressive assault upon Hobbes's attempt to square the circle. (Hobbes was not the only one. Wallis himself made an attempt.) In fact, Wallis did more than this; he argued Hobbes's deficiencies as a mathematician in a variety of contexts. Following a painstaking and path-breaking study of Hobbes's mathematics and his protracted quarrel with Wallis, Douglas Jesseph confronts a key question. Hobbes came off the worse for this debate. Why, asks Jesseph, did Hobbes persist in an erroneous mathematics? His answer leads him to Hobbes's broader claims concerning his approach to philosophy. Hobbes had closely connected his mathematics to his particular way of doing philosophy; he therefore could not afford to allow the challenge to his competency to go uncontested, even to his dying days. As Jesseph notes, for Hobbes, "geometry is an integral part of philosophy and that continued failure in geometric matters must be symptomatic of philosophical ineptitude . . . . Wallis was right to characterize Hobbes as having 'set such store by geometry as to hold that without it there is hardly any thing sound that could be expected in philosophy.' . . . Hobbes ultimately saw his entire philosophical program threatened by the prospect of his inability to deliver the great mathematical results he had promised."[24]

I wish to make two points with regard to this conclusion. First, Jesseph is correct to conclude that Hobbes's mathematical squabbles point to something larger: namely, his reputation as a philosopher, or more specifically the standing of his vision of a philosophy rooted in the superior, mathematical approaches to reasoning Hobbes claimed to possess. Second, in light of this conclusion it is therefore strange that Jesseph (next) uses his conclusions to launch an attack on sociological approaches to the study of scientific knowledge. Jesseph declares himself opposed to approaches that reduce scientific controversies into accounts that see these disputes as "driven purely by social factors."[25] Here Jesseph offers us a false choice in pitting his conclusions against those which he thinks are concerned to reduce disputes to "purely" social factors. Moreover, his own best insights undermine the dichotomy he privileges. Surely, there can be no "purely social" domain against which we then say that we need not investigate the truth claims of the disputants. Rather, matters of truth and matters of social standing, competition, and conflict remain inextricably entangled.

With this in mind, I want to turn to Jesseph's treatment of the relationship between physics and mathematics in Hobbes's thought. Jesseph's approach to the question of Hobbes's mathematics begins by gauging Hobbes's conception of mathematics against that of his predecessors. One of the central features of Hobbes's mathematics—his insistence upon the materiality of geometrical entities—reveals itself nicely in Jesseph's account of a division, Aristotelian in origin, maintained by his predecessors. This is the division between pure and mixed mathematics.

According to this understanding of mathematics, pure mathematics studies quantities abstracted away from their physical or material circumstances. Mixed mathematics, by contrast, concerns itself with actual physical entities that are, in most cases, understood to merely approximate the more perfect mathematical abstractions studied by pure mathematicians. Mixed mathematics was the domain of astronomy, harmonics, and optics. By focusing on quantities wholly abstracted from their material aspects, pure mathematics was understood to be the superior part of the discipline by virtue of the perfection of these abstractions. Thus, for Hobbes's predecessor Christopher Clavius, mathematics should be seen as occupying a middle ground between physics on the one hand and metaphysics on the other. Physics was wed to the study of material bodies, and metaphysics to the wholly immaterial, such objects as God, the soul, or being in general. By insisting on the materiality of everything, Jesseph notes, Hobbes undermined this pure/mixed dichotomy.

As Jesseph goes on to argue, there is hardly an aspect of Hobbes's disputes with his fellow mathematicians that is not related to Hobbes's thoroughgoing materialism.[26] We find Hobbes not only arguing with Wallis over how to define the basic components of geometry (points, lines, and planes) but also offering correction to traditional Euclidean definitions that violate his rules of good mathematical practice. Hobbes insisted that geometrical entities be understood strictly in terms of matter, and specific geometric forms as particular motions imparted to matter. Hobbes's materialistic mathematics is rooted in a prior ontological decision. Here Hobbes makes it clear that all that *is* is matter, and reveals his commitment to resisting the common temptation to conceive of material things in immaterial terms. Like the famous "separate essences" that Hobbes combats in *Leviathan* and *De Corpore*, he sees the divorce between being and body as the route toward philosophical confusion at best, and chicanery at worst.

One of the areas where Hobbes's materialism therefore creates a source of conflict concerns the relationship between physics and mathematics. As Jesseph notes, Wallis frames his criticism of Hobbes in terms of a contamination of mathematical foundations by introducing physical principles. Is not our conception of a line, for example, merely clouded when we include the line's thickness, or introduce (as does Hobbes) a conception of a material point moving over a distinct period of time? According to Wallis, the material nature upon which Hobbes insisted merely served to emphasize the accidental, rather than essential, aspects of geometrical entities. This also undermined the pure/mixed (or as Jesseph here refers to it, the pure/applied) dichotomy upon which Wallis insisted as a means of ensuring the certainty and precision of mathematical foundations.[27]

In his reply, Hobbes turns back to his own foundational principles: all demonstrations must demonstrate by means of construction, and in geometry this means drawing lines, accounting for the real motions of matter as matter. From Jesseph's point of view, however, "This part of the controversy . . . reduces to a conflict over the proper demarcation between mathematics and natural philosophy. As such, it is not readily amenable to resolution, because such fundamental disagreements can rarely be overcome or even profitably debated. Hobbes continued to insist that the only proper foundation for mathematics must be sought in the nature of body, while Wallis viewed this program as an abandonment of the essential features of mathematics."[28]

Here I think there is an opportunity to discern something that Jesseph passes over. His analyses show that Hobbes's materialism is a critical factor in the debate with Wallis, and that the issue of the relationship between mathematics and physics is strongly connected to this point. Therefore, a further look into the relationship between mathematics and physics would seem in order, rather than allowing the issue to come to a rest with a gesture toward the futility of *our* debating the relationship between these disciplines. Even if one wished to accept the conclusion that the debate can be said to lead *us* toward an unprofitable set of disagreements, it surely appeared to carry stakes that Hobbes and Wallis were willing to pursue at some length.

Why would Hobbes and Wallis find themselves at odds over such a fundamental question? If, ultimately, this dispute between Hobbes and Wallis was more than merely a reflection of rival conceptions of mathematics (narrowly construed), then what were these things? Here is where we need to consider the scope of Hobbes's ambitions. Hobbes was not merely claiming to possess mathematical acumen, but to possess a method and program for the reform of philosophy. Moreover, the stakes attached to this debate concerned not merely reputation, but the larger goal. He sought to put his reputation to work: to push a program to bring the universities into conformity with his doctrines.

Holding Fast to Yesterday's Conflicts

One of the best ways to discern these stakes is by returning to a document that appeared at the beginning of the protracted conflict between Hobbes and Wallis. This is Seth Ward's *Vindiciae Academiarum* (1654), a work written primarily in response to the sweeping university reform plans of the radical cleric John Webster. Included with the work are appendices that attack Hobbes and another reformer, William Dell (who had been appointed by the Long Parliament master of Gonville and Caius College Cambridge). It also includes a preface critical of all three by another Oxonian, John Wilkins, the warden of Wadham College.[29] As Jesseph notes, this work represented a reply from Oxford to both the publications of critics of the universities, and it may be seen as a defensive measure in light of a potential threat from the Barebones Parliament, which had considered in 1654 a proposal to abolish the universities outright.[30] Ward's specific response to Hobbes is directed to the *Leviathan*, published three years prior. As noted, *Leviathan* strongly emphasizes the need for the universities to reform, and to do so by teaching Hobbes's doctrine. Ward's response is in larger measure designed to counter Hobbes on these points, and I shall go into these matters in greater detail in Chapter 7, including Ward's accusations and Hobbes's replies.

Of immediate interest is the fact that Ward questions Hobbes's competency as a mathematician and attempts to bait the philosopher into publishing his solution to the problem of squaring the circle. This, Jesseph argues, was likely the mathematical ambush that caught Hobbes in the decades-long fight. When Hobbes inserted his attempt at squaring the circle in *De Corpore* (1655), Wallis, it appears, had been waiting in the wings to pounce upon it.[31] Another interesting part of Ward's counterattack speaks to Hobbes's understanding of the state of mathematical education in the universities. Ward notes Hobbes's claim that geometry "till of very late times, it had no place at all. And if any man by the ingenuity of his nature had atteined to any degree of perfection in it, he was commonly thought a Magician, and his Art Diabolicall."[32] As Jesseph also notes, Ward informs Hobbes that there are already students at the university who may know enough mathematics to strip him of the reputation he claims to deserve. Then Ward adds the following: "The truth is Sir, about that time when Mr. *Hobbs* was conversant in Magdalen-Hall [his student days], the constitution and way of the University might (likely) be enclining to his Character of it; but now his Discourse seems like that of the seven sleepers, who after many yeares awaking, in vaine addressed themselves to act according to the state of things when they lay down."[33] Some Hobbes interpreters have taken such assertions at face value. As Jesseph's and other accounts of Hobbes's disputes show, there is reason to doubt that Hobbes was unaware of mathematical developments in the universities—nor were some of Hobbes's mathematical claims so wide of the mark of debates still contemporary among English mathematicians. Noel Malcolm's researches into Hobbes's London contacts during this period move in a similar direction.[34] Mordechai Feingold's research would suggest that the underestimation of mathematical education was a self-serving comment not only on Hobbes's part, but a strategy employed by Ward and Wallis as well.[35]

Nevertheless, there is at least a grain of truth in Ward's accusation. This is not because Hobbes was eons behind his fellow mathematicians, as Ward in other parts of his criticism gleefully suggests, but because Hobbes was in fact pitching his arguments to a debate that, while still current among mathematicians in the seventeenth century, stretched back to the sixteenth. For what this criticism suggests is that Hobbes's attachment to mathematics has the character of an intervention designed to thwart opponents whose target was not so much a particular approach to mathematics, but to mathematics itself as a discipline and its claim to respect. Some mathematicians in the sixteenth century wished to reach a position of equality with their counterparts in traditional natural philosophy (i.e., the dialectical physics of the schools).

The historian of mathematics Paulo Mancosu has recently argued the ongoing importance of a debate conducted between mathematicians and natural philosophers known as the *Quaestio de certitudine mathematicarum*—a debate that starts by asking how well mathematics matches Aristotelian standards of certainty in its demonstrations. For Mancosu, Hobbes's (and Wallis's) participation in debates that perpetuated some of the language of this dispute illustrates the surprising continuity of Aristotelian concerns well into seventeenth-century mathematics. (It is also worth noting that Hobbes may have had reason to believe that Aristotle was making an intellectual comeback. Thomas White had made it his project to restore Aristotelianism by illustrating its compatibility with the new science, and to make it the ground for a newly philosophically strengthened theology. Unlike his predecessors, White found a dignified place for mathematics in his thought. He fashioned himself a mathematical thinker, and published his own works—including his own attempt at squaring the circle—and was similarly accused of possessing an incompetent understanding of mathematics, one that betrayed a more systemic problem.)[36]

I will now review significant features of this debate. In the sixteenth century there was a mathematical vanguard in Jesuit institutions working to bolster the position of mathematicians in the universities of Europe. They were in the midst of a debate with natural philosophers, who resented what they saw as an encroachment upon their own, more exclusive, loftier domains.[37] As we investigate this debate, we will find that Hobbes and his mathematically inclined predecessors speak a common language regarding the advantages of mathematical certainty over traditional dialectical methods of reasoning. It is also against the background of their relatively ambitious claims for mathematics that Hobbes's radicalism as a proponent for mathematical methods truly emerges.

Mathematics in the Sixteenth-Century Universities

Why, one must ask first, did mathematicians feel they needed a defense in scholastic contexts? In the sixteenth-century Western European universities mathematics was a demeaned discipline. In the traditional scholastic curriculum students were first instructed in the *trivium:* logic, rhetoric, and grammar. Beyond this the schools recognized in principle, if infrequently in practice, a set of mathematical subjects, the *quadrivium*—arithmetic, geometry, music, and astronomy.[38]

On the whole, Europe's universities engaged in a wide range of mathematical studies—not just geometry and astronomy, but also optics, mechanics, cosmography, anemography, and hydrology. In the case of mathematics, however, diversity meant neither depth nor commitment. Mathematics was not a key part of the education at any given school. A student might be exposed to a particular aspect of mathematical education—typically, whatever specialty the local mathematics tutor might have possessed—but a complete education in mathematics was a low priority, and the individuals who taught mathematics were generally considered of lower status. Charles B. Schmitt concluded, "Mathematical studies occupied only a very peripheral position in the curriculum. If a dozen or more medical men were teaching at one of the larger universities at any given time, the usual complement of mathematicians was but one."[39] Mordechai Feingold's work suggests that mathematical education at the various colleges and halls was more widely available at Oxford and Cambridge, but it is worth noting that even Feingold reinforces the point that the institutional support for those who were actually hired to teach mathematics was slim well into the seventeenth century.[40] At the pinnacle of the late scholastic arts curriculum was physics, traditionally investigated through dialectical, not mathematical, methods.[41]

Thus, in the sixteenth-century university, mathematicians existed but were not key players. The universities did not grant doctoral degrees in mathematics or astronomy. The faculty entitled to teach students seeking higher degrees (law, theology, or medicine) did not include mathematicians. Mathematical instruction was for undergraduates, although there is some evidence that it entered into the education of masters students at Oxford and Cambridge.[42] If one's primary concern *was* a mathematical discipline, making a successful academic career often required a degree in one of these other, more prestigious disciplines. Copernicus studied law at Bologna and medicine at Padua, for instance.[43] University mathematicians, moreover, were expected to make themselves useful—that is, to occupy "service roles"—in their relations with the other disciplines. Astronomy could be used, for example, in service to medicine: the star charts and almanacs physicians used to understand the forces of the cosmos on the patient were calculated by mathematicians.[44] The exceptions that help prove the rule of this analysis were those mathematically inclined individuals who achieved fame not because their works were of intellectual significance, but because they did not have to count on traditional sources of academic legitimization. A mathematician *and* nobleman, Tycho Brahe (1546–1601), could stand immune to the sneers of academic institutions.[45] Galileo's status, as Biagioli has argued, was itself dependent on his skillfulness in negotiating patronage networks and making himself the object of competition in rival Italian courts. It was only at court, and not in the schools, that Galileo could be counted a philosopher.[46]

In some academic venues, however, mathematicians were making significant inroads.[47] A number of Jesuit educators were on the forefront of mathematical education. The better-known graduates of Jesuit institutions testified to this fact: Mersenne and Descartes were graduates of La Flèche, in Loire.[48] Mersenne, moreover, made key themes in the Jesuit defense of mathematics a part of his own.[49] Among the Jesuit faculty, Christopher Clavius (mathematics chair at the Collegio Romano) was a chief proponent; he campaigned to place mathematics on an equal footing with natural philosophy.[50] He was well known among mathematicians, including Hobbes.[51]

I will consider the Jesuit defense of mathematics (including elements embraced by Mersenne), and argue that Hobbes used elements of the Jesuit defense of mathematics *within* the schools as ammunition for a counterattack on behalf of mathematics from *without*. Thus, the commonalities between the two are important, but the thrust of the Jesuit defense of mathematics took a course—particularly under Clavius's student, Josephus Blancanus (Biancani)[52]—from which Hobbes departed in significant ways.

It is strange to draw parallels between Hobbes, a philosopher who fought against the schools, with persons who defended mathematics within these institutions. In spite of the important commonalities, we should not be so quick to abandon this reservation. Hobbes *was* alienated from the university milieu. Perhaps for this reason his proposed interventions into university practices were that much more sweeping. Keeping this in mind helps us make sense of his similar, but ultimately much bolder, defense of mathematics. It also helps us comprehend his willingness to use a more forceful hand in establishing the superiority of mathematicians.

First, however, I will discuss the similarities. The Jesuit defenders of mathematics made their case by arguing the excellence of their science in terms of Aristotelian notions of science.[53] This does not come as a surprise. What is surprising is that echoes of their attempt to assert the Aristotelian credentials of mathematics can be found in Hobbes's defense.

Aristotelian Standards and Mathematical Demonstration

In the mid-sixteenth century, mathematicians were drawing a critical response from the natural philosophers. A key part of their arguments focused attention on the capacity of mathematicians to make *causal* demonstrations. This challenge begins with Alessandro Piccolomini (later Pope Pius II, 1508–1578). Piccolomini did not wish to exclude mathematics from the school curriculum, but he was concerned to counter the encroachment of mathematics on the traditional provinces of the dialecticians. He did this by asserting that mathematics did not meet Aristotelian standards of a true science. Any such science had to offer causal explanations of the objects it studied, and, Piccolomini asserted, mathematicians did not do so.[54]

Particular attention in this debate fell on the distinctions Aristotle had made between syllogisms in the *Posterior Analytics* 1.13.[55] This passage was emphasized by the Jesuit natural philosopher Benedict Pereira, who is credited with offering a more philosophically rigorous version of Piccolomini's critique.[56] In the *Posterior Analytics* Aristotle calls one variety of syllogism *tou hoti* and another *tou dioti*. *Tou hoti* syllogisms assert descriptive conclusions, but Aristotle ranked them inferior to the *tou dioti* because they do not tell us *how* the thing described is caused. The superior syllogistic form, *tou dioti*, not only offers descriptive conclusions, but its middle term specifies a cause for the characteristics in the conclusion. (For those readers interested in a concrete example of the relevant syllogistic forms, I have supplied them in the notes, along with further references to these debates.)[57] True sciences, Pereira maintained, could offer *tou dioti* demonstration and not merely *tou hoti*. Proponents of mathematics put Euclid's demonstrations forward as exemplary of their practice. Pereira argued that Euclid's demonstrations were merely *hoti*, rather than *dioti*. Mathematics was not, therefore, a proper science.

The subordination of mathematics as a form of reasoning incapable of specifying causes also depended upon arguments concerning the status of the particular objects contemplated by mathematicians, and specifically whether or not mathematicians reasoned from an understanding of *essences*. Key to the traditional scholastic notion of showing causality was the ability to specify the essence of the entity studied. According to their "causal" critics, academic mathematicians did not deal with essences, but with mere quantity (continuous quantity in the case of geometry, such as lines, and discrete quantities in the case of arithmetic).[58] There was, for example, no "five" existing independently in nature; there were only five bears, five apples, or five men. Bears, apples, and men each had distinct existence and distinct essences; with reason's aid these could be grasped. They argued that judgments over quantity do not identify something with an objective reality.[59] A geometric figure, therefore, belonged to a different class of objects than a man. A man's existence was not the product of our intellect. God had created men, and according to his own ideals. Understanding that ideal, we might grasp the essential attributes of men. Using the tools of traditional dialectic, natural philosophers could understand what God had created, and reason causally from this knowledge.[60] Mathematicians did not to deal with essences but with things inessential, "accidents" in traditional scholastic terminology. Concerning the *hoti/dioti* distinction, Pereira argued that the inability to grasp essences was decisive. He wrote:

> My opinion is that the mathematical disciplines are not proper sciences.... To have a science [*scire*] is to acquire knowledge [*cognoscere*] of a thing through the cause on account of which the thing is; and science [*scientia*] is the effect of demonstration. However, demonstration (I speak of the most perfect kind of demonstration) must depend upon those things which are "per se" and proper to that which is demonstrated; indeed, those things which are accidental and in common are excluded from perfect demonstrations. But the mathematician neither considers the essence of quantity, nor treats of its affections as they flow from such essence, nor declares them by the proper causes on account of which they are in quantity, nor makes his demonstrations from proper and "per se" but from common and accidental predicates. Thus mathematical doctrine is not properly a science.[61]

This was a significant attack. It cast doubt on a claim traditionally asserted by some proponents of mathematics, though never credibly defended, that Euclid's axiomatic method of demonstration was compatible with syllogistic reasoning, that is to say, with traditional scholastic means of demonstration.[62] This claim seemed to be warranted by the fact that Aristotle frequently resorted to mathematical examples in the *Posterior Analytics*.

This was not the only claim Pereira challenged, however. By simply looking at the structure of geometrical argument and reasoning—and leaving aside questions of the inherent essential or inessential character of mathematical objects—Pereira mounted an additional challenge to the mathematician's claim to an exemplary scientific method. He offered an example of this criticism in a critique of the proof of proposition 32 in book 1 of Euclid's *Elements*. In this demonstration the interior angles of a triangle are shown to be equal to two right angles. The proof, however, involves drawing an extra line—itself not a part of the triangle—and the construction of additional triangles with this line and the sides of the original triangle. The proof offers a concrete demonstration of the proposition, but in light of its procedure Pereira could credibly claim that the correlates of a proper syllogism, specifically a causal middle term that specifies an essence, cannot be found.[63] The need to draw lines that are not a part of the triangle (i.e., auxiliary constructions) meant that the mathematician's focus was not necessarily fixed on the *object* itself. How could mathematicians reason from the essence of their objects, Pereira argued, when their proofs might require the use of figures that are not a part of their object?

Consider the answers offered by the proponents of a more mathematical school curriculum. They responded by trying to reappropriate Aristotle. They marshaled (and in some instances merely reiterated or defended preexisting) arguments designed to defend the Aristotelian standing of their discipline. Aristotle's works indeed offered opportunities for making such arguments. First, Aristotle acknowledged that mathematical reasoning yielded greater certainty than the dialectical form of reasoning. This was a critical element stressed by Clavius: "Since therefore the mathematical disciplines in fact require, delight in, and honor truth—so that they not only admit nothing that is false, but indeed also nothing that arises only with probability, and finally they admit nothing that they do not confirm and strengthen by the most certain demonstrations—there can be no doubt that they must be conceded the first place among . . . the sciences."[64]

Such claims became a key part of their strategy. They stressed the importance of *certainty itself* as a criterion for ranking different forms of scientific knowledge. They also had an answer concerning the status of mathematical objects—the entities to which they applied their reason. As noted in the introduction, many mathematical practitioners applied themselves to machinery, or to the earth itself in the case of surveying or fortification. Nevertheless, the academic mathematical elite—often fearful of social pollution from their lowly brethren—attempted to push the discussion of the character of mathematical objects in a different direction.[65]

To understand the arguments of Clavius and Blancanus concerning certainty we need to pursue an element of the critics' claims a bit further. Because the mathematicians emphasized the certainty of their form of reasoning over dialectic, one might expect the opponents to have denied them this claim. This, however, was not what occurred. Where both sides were competing to claim Aristotelian status, neither doubted Aristotle when he asserted that mathematical reason was inherently more certain than that of dialectic.[66] The ground for its disqualification, rather, was the character of the objects of pure mathematics.[67] As we shall see, the proponents of mathematics attempted to make the certainty of their reasoning serve their arguments concerning the character of the objects they considered.

These objects—the planes, lines, and figures—were perfect entities, forms that remained constant and were always in conformity with their definitions. As such, they were grasped by the intellect rather than by the senses—indeed, that is why one was said to be able to be so certain about them. Opponents such as Piccolomini were willing to grant this, and made it a part of their argument concerning the scientific inappropriateness of the mathematician's objects. As noted, a proper science dealt with something real; these figures considered by mathematicians were "unreal."

The opponents argued that the natural philosopher grasped his objects with the aid of the senses; the mathematician did not. The objects studied by the natural philosophers were less certain, and therefore less perfect, because they were in nature. Nevertheless, they maintained their superiority over the mathematicians because their reasoning was rooted in a world of real things—in fact, God's creations. For the natural philosophers, therefore, it was not simply a matter of the certainty of one's conclusions, but also a question of *what* one studied that established the proper ranking of the disciplines. The nobility of the subject—God's creation—more than made up for natural philosophy's comparative deficit of certainty.[68]

The mathematicians attempted to turn the tables by using Platonic arguments to reverse the claims concerning the "reality" of their subject.[69] While some have argued that this represents a Neoplatonic innovation in the schools, Peter Dear has argued that these arguments were already available from within school philosophy, especially Augustinian strains.[70] Whatever the source, the defenders of mathematics asserted that the objects of mathematics were real *because* they were free from the imperfections of natural things. They invested reality in the perfect, abstract, and timeless entities, and questioned the reality of things encountered with our senses in the day to day. It was precisely because they had characteristics that were unchanging, and about which one might be more certain, that they were real.[71] This argument inverted the hierarchy that privileged the traditional physics of the natural philosophers. In pursuing this shrewd effort to challenge the hierarchy, Blancanus wrote:

> Many [people] object to mathematicians that mathematical entities do not exist, except only by the intellect. However, we should know that

even if these mathematical entities do not exist in that perfection, this is merely accidental, for it is well known that both nature and art intend to imitate primarily those mathematical figures, although because of the grossness [*ruditatem*] and imperfections of sensible matter, which is incapable of receiving perfect figures, they do not achieve their end. For nature in the trunks of trees strives after the figure of cylinder, in apples and grapes after spherical or spheroid figure, in the cornea of the eye after circle, indeed, the eye itself is most spherical.[72]

Thus, the sun and the stars were spherical. So was the human eye. These things may not be perfect spheres, but this is only on account of the "coarseness of matter."[73] Nature strives to achieve the ideal forms, the perfect spheres, triangles, and other figures contemplated by the mathematician.

According to Blancanus, mathematicians were reasoning in a way that allowed them to grasp perfect forms in nature. These forms grasped by the mathematician were in the mind of the Creator: "Even though these [perfect mathematical figures] do not exist in the nature of the things, since in the mind of the Author of Nature, as well as in the human mind, their ideas do exist as the exact archetypes of all things, indeed, which are primarily intended per se, and which are [the] true entities."[74] Mathematics couldn't be excluded from the study of natural philosophy, or counted as subordinate in this endeavor. The things grasped by natural philosophers were, by comparison, "imperfect and false." Blancanus thus attempted to *reclaim* the ability to grasp essences.[75] He quotes a saying attributed to Plato by Plutarch:[76] "A triangle depicted in a chart is not a true triangle, but the true triangle is that which is in the divine mind. And from these considerations we can easily understand why Plato said that God was doing geometry [*Deum geometrizare*], that is, that just like a true geometer, God contemplates only the perfect ideas of things."[77]

The link between essences and mathematics reestablished, Blancanus could turn to the issue of the causal status of mathematical demonstrations. Whereas Piccolomini had asserted that mathematical demonstrations could not function as proper causal explanations because they did not specify essences (i.e., merely *tou hoti*), Blancanus held the contrary: "Their [mathematicians'] demonstrations in most cases show both what is the case [*quid*, i.e., *tou hoti*] and why it is the case [*propter quid*, i.e., *tou dioti*] at the same time."[78]

The preceding quotation comes from Blancanus's summation. Although I will not recount all aspects of his sprawling argument,[79] there are a number of elements that will help make clear the complex relation between Jesuit defenders of mathematics and the more aggressive course taken by Hobbes. Clavius and Blancanus were keen to defend the traditional claim that mathematics was Aristotle's own model for demonstrative reason: a claim, as noted earlier, seemingly supported by Aristotle's frequent use of mathematical examples in the *Posterior Analytics*.[80] Consider Blancanus's argument in terms of the distinction between *dioti* and *hoti* demonstrations in Pereira's attack. He bolstered his case by turning the discussion to questions of how mathematicians define their objects. The capacity to make, and reason from, precise and useful definitions was as much an issue for him as it was for Hobbes.[81] Blancanus found some Euclidian definitions exemplary. The most useful of Euclid's definitions supplied both the object's cause and its essence. It was "a momentous fact" that "geometrical as well as arithmetical definitions are entirely essential definitions, namely, definitions which explicate the whole nature [*quiddiatem*] of the thing."[82] Many mathematical definitions—although Blancanus acknowledges, not all—supply us with explanations of both *why* we call a thing what we do, but also refer us to the essential characteristics of the thing itself.

Examples of this "perfect etymology" include Euclid's definition of a square: "A square [*quadratum*] is a plane figure consisting of four [equal] straight lines and four right angles." This definition explicates not only "the concept of the name" but also "the concept of the thing at the same time." From such a definition we learn not only why it is called what is it called, but also what distinguishes it from other members of the genus of quadrilateral plane figures (such as rectangles). This, according to Blancanus, is a definition that gives us a square's "total essence."[83] Definitions such as those of a square are also causal because they show us how to construct the entity they define.[84] Not all definitions used by mathematicians had "perfect etymologies"; nor were they all causal. Euclid's definition of a line, for example, is not "perfect": "A line is so named after linen [*a lino*], as if it were a linen string; for in ancient times strings which craftsmen used for measuring were made of linen, just like nowadays they are made of hemp; but it would be ridiculous to look for this explanation in Euclid's definition, by which, however, the essence of line is made perfectly clear."[85]

This becomes the basis for Blancanus's argument concerning *dioti* and *hoti* demonstrations. It is worth quoting him at length:

> Now on the basis of what we have said about scientific definitions we should take note of a certain disparity between the ways mathematics and other sciences proceed in the cognition of their proper subjects. For in demonstrations from signs [*a signo*], from which other sciences frequently start, only the cognition of the name of the subject is required, but not the essential definition, for its essence, which is hidden, is

investigated by its accidents and its properties, from what is posterior [*a posteriori*]; and then, once the essence is detected, we return to the distinct and scientific demonstrations of the properties. However, if the perfect cognition of the object were given in the first place, as is the case with mathematical objects on account of their perfect definitions, we would proceed according to the most beautiful order of nature, from the essence of the object to the demonstration of its properties, as it happens in demonstrations from the cause [*a causa*], as are almost all geometrical and mathematical demonstrations.[86]

Thus, where definitions are causal, mathematicians offer causal demonstrations. At other times, however, mathematicians may offer causal explanations without necessarily using causal definitions, or even perfect etymologies. Finally, mathematicians might also descend to the (noncausal) demonstrative level of the practitioners of other disciplines, and merely proceed from signs.[87] Blancanus speaks of this distinction between demonstrations in terms of *a priori*, and *a posteriori*. Regarding the superior form of demonstration, he wrote: "From the premised definitions the entire nature of the subject is primarily given to us, from which, then, we always proceed from what is prior [*a priori*] to the investigation of properties."[88]

Hobbes and the Jesuit Defense Contrasted: The Ambition of an Architecton

We can now draw a number of comparisons with Hobbes. I argued in Chapter 3 that Hobbes distinguishes between disciplines that reason a priori and those that reason a posteriori. This classification was in turn based on distinctions made in terms of methods of synthesis and analysis.[89] Hobbes ranked the a priori disciplines higher because they are fundamentally compositive: they begin with parts, necessarily well defined, and work their way up to knowledge of the whole. Thus, a geometer knows the characteristics of a square on the page because he builds it himself. By contrast, the a posteriori forms of reasoning begin with some *whole*. They attempt to reconstruct the whole by working down to the level of elemental parts, and then back up again to reconstruct something that reproduces the (whole) effect first observed. Physics, according to this rubric, is a posteriori.

Hobbes and Blancanus were speaking the same language. A concern for the demonstrative status of disciplines animates both. Hobbes makes the distinction between a priori and a posteriori the distinction between those disciplines which are truly demonstrative, and those which are not: between mathematics and the science of politics on the one hand, and physics on the other.

In Blancanus's case, a key part of the argument was expressed not in the terms "a priori" and "a posteriori" but in terms of *tou dioti* and *hoti* demonstrations. Hobbes, in fact, uses a parallel terminology. He writes in *De Corpore*:

> FOR the understanding of method, it will be necessary for me to repeat the definition of philosophy, delivered above (Chap. I, art. 2.) in this manner, Philosophy is the knowledge we acquire, by true ratiocination, of appearances, or apparent effects, from the knowledge we have of some possible production or generation of the same; and of such production, as has been or may be, from the knowledge we have of the effects. METHOD, therefore, in the study of philosophy, is the shortest way of finding out effects by their known causes, or of causes by their known effects. But we are then said to know any effect, when we know that there be causes of the same, and in what subject those causes are, and in what subject they produce that effect, and in what manner they work the same. And this is the science of causes, or, as they call it, of the διότι [*dioti*]. All other science, which is called the ότι [*hoti*], is either perception by sense, or the imagination, or memory remaining after such perception....
>
> It is common to all sorts of method, to proceed from known things to unknown, and this is manifest from the cited definition of philosophy. But in knowledge by sense, the whole object is more known, than any part thereof, as when we see a man, the conception or whole idea of that man is first or more known, than the particular ideas of his being figurate, animate, and rational; that is, we first see the whole man, and take notice of his being, before we observe in him those other particulars. And therefore in any knowledge of the óti, or that any thing is [*sive quod est*], the beginning of our search is from the whole idea; and contrarily, in our knowledge of the dióti, or of the causes of any thing, that is, in the sciences, we have more knowledge of the causes of the parts than of the whole. For the cause of the whole is compounded of the causes of the parts; but it is necessary that we know the things that are to be compounded, before we can know the whole compound.[90]

For Blancanus, *hoti* is synonymous with knowledge *that* something is the case, and *dioti*, with *why* it is the case. Hobbes likewise defines *hoti* as "that so it is" and *dioti* with "why it is so."[91]

Critical differences emerge, however. Both argue that mathematics may make a priori demonstrations, but Hobbes puts greater stress on the negative implications of the new ranking between mathematics and physics. For Hobbes, it is not merely a question of what mathematics (and the science of politics) can do, but what other sciences like physics cannot do.

One way to register the difference between Hobbes and his Jesuit counterparts is not merely to compare their arguments (and how similar boasts for mathematics led in different directions), but to ask how their arguments fit within a broader institutional context. As representatives of a demeaned form of learning, what were these professors of mathematics requesting? How did they imagine themselves in relation to the professors of natural philosophy once their claims were honored? Although the Jesuit mathematicians make comparisons that favor mathematical learning over the learning of traditional natural philosophers, the texts we have been reviewing also suggest that the Jesuit mathematicians were struggling, literally, for a position at the table. Clavius's plea that professors of mathematics be allowed to attend and participate in the public defenses of students claiming doctoral degrees is illustrative of their institutional aspirations. Clavius requested that these professors be "invited to take part in formal acts in which doctors are created and public disputations held, in such a way that if he is capable he too may sometimes put forward arguments and help those who are arguing."[92] When the students see that their mathematics professors are a part of the activities considered appropriate for the most dignified, they, Clavius hoped, "will be convinced that philosophy and the mathematical sciences are connected, as they truly are; especially because pupils up to now seem almost to have despised these sciences for the simple reason that they think that they are not considered of value and are even useless, since the person who teaches them is never summoned to public acts with the other professors."[93]

Clavius and Blancanus may have claimed that mathematics deserves a higher ranking than physics within the Aristotelian hierarchy of the sciences, but the practical outcome they desired was modest. As regards their conception of the relationship between mathematical and natural philosophical learning, their ideal reveals itself as something closer to parity and mutual cooperation in a common enterprise:

> Natural philosophy without the mathematical disciplines is lame and incomplete . . . the pupils should understand that these [mathematical] sciences are useful and necessary for rightly understanding the rest of philosophy, and that they are at the same time a great ornament to all

> other arts, so that one may acquire perfect erudition; indeed these sciences and natural philosophy have so close an affinity with one another that unless they give each other mutual aid they can in no way preserve their own worth . . . . it is agreed among experts that physics cannot rightly be grasped without them; especially as regards that part which concerns the number and motion of the celestial circles ("orbes"), . . . the ebb and flow of the seas, winds, comets, the rainbow, . . . the proportions of motions.[94]

Clavius may have ranked mathematics higher than natural philosophy based on its capacity for greater certainty,[95] but he would have been happy if the natural philosophers in the Jesuit Colleges would simply refrain from ridiculing mathematics as a means of acquiring knowledge about the world: "It will also contribute much to this if the teachers of philosophy abstained from those questions which do not help in the understanding of natural things and very much detract from the authority of the mathematical disciplines in the eyes of the students, such as those in which they teach that the mathematical sciences are not sciences."[96]

As noted, Hobbes and the Jesuit defenders of mathematics give grounds for thinking of mathematics as a superior science to physics. In light of the institutional contexts just reviewed, we can now better understand the distinct ways in which they put this claim of superiority to use.[97] It is important that in the arguments of Clavius and Blancanus the task of investigating nature remains the standing goal. Investigating God's creation, and the assumption that this is the principal, and most dignified, task for a philosopher, goes unquestioned. Clavius's plea is that his discipline not be excluded from traditional scholastic philosophy. In spite of the claims to superiority based on certainty, both Clavius and Blancanus declare the worth of their discipline in terms of its capacity to fulfill the school's established goals for natural philosophy. They direct their efforts toward proving that their discipline remains true to traditional standards of philosophical accomplishment, even as they stress one standard over another to suit their purposes.

Hobbes is bolder, and this becomes visible in a number of ways. First, where Clavius asks for equal consideration for mathematical reasoning, Hobbes expects that the claim to superior certainty made by mathematical reasoning entitles it to preeminence. As he suggested in both early and later works, mathematics is not in Hobbes's conception a contributor to scholarly debate; it is the means by which scholarly debate (itself now a demeaned activity in the Hobbesian cosmos) is brought to a close. In the *Elements of Law*, he writes, famously:

> There be two sorts of men that be commonly called learned: one is that sort that proceedeth evidently from humble principles, . . . and these men are called *mathematici;* the other are they that take up maxims from their education, and from the authority of men, or of custom, and take the habitual discourse of the tongue for ratiocination; and these are called *dogmatici* . . . . those we call mathematici are absolved of the crime of breeding controversy; . . . the fault lieth altogether in the dogmatics, that is to say, those that are imperfectly learned, and with passion press to have their opinions pass everywhere for truth, without any evident demonstration either from experience, or from places of Scripture or uncontroverted interpretation.[98]

Some men have truly worthy mental possessions, others counterfeit. Where Clavius could defend mathematics as entitled to participate in scholastic debate, Hobbes emphasized mathematical certitude to such an extent that he declared it worthy of victory and demanded that others acknowledge the claim.

Second, Hobbes may have used Aristotelian distinctions of *hoti* and *dioti* to make the case for mathematics, but he largely eschews the larger Aristotelian mantle. It would be wrong to say that Hobbes made himself independent of Aristotelian learning—his continued use of the classification of demonstrative types, his reverence for Aristotelian rhetoric, for example, speak against this. However, he does not sing the praises of mathematics by trumpeting its Aristotelian credentials. He does not mention this debt, and his silence is nearly deafening when seen in terms of the evolving politics of academic disciplinary warfare.[99] Hobbes's claim was that mathematics (specifically geometry) simply was *the* model philosophy. He would displace, rather than trumpet his conformity to, Aristotelian science. This is something we can acknowledge even if in retrospect Hobbes now appears to remain quite dependent upon Aristotelian mental apparatuses,[100] and would no longer qualify as "truly mathematical" in a world whose conception of mathematicized science shunned his guidance. Thus, there is an irony to Hobbes's strategy. It uses elements of arguments developed to help preserve the Aristotelian pedigree of mathematics against the Aristotelians.[101]

Physics is not merely demoted by virtue of its uncertainty; it is also made over as the lesser image of geometry. That is, philosophy guided by Hobbes's new geometrical ideal must not only abandon its old goals of knowing nature (i.e., how God created the universe), but it must learn to borrow what it can from mathematics in order to make any contribution at all. Under Hobbes's new organization of the learned hierarchy, the old pinnacle of natural philosophy, physics, must do its best to mimic the geometer within the limits set for it by virtue of its a posteriori status. Beginning with effects, it must find the causes that could be compounded to reconstruct these entities, but it can no longer make a claim to know with certainty that it has supplied us with the actual causes that account for them. In part 4 of *De Corpore*, Hobbes introduces physics by negatively contrasting it with what he has achieved in the compositive (a priori) sciences: whereas the conclusions of the a priori sciences are demonstrable from the definitions set out from the start, in physics, he declares, we may know

> some ways and means by which [the appearance or effects of nature] may be, I do not say they are, generated. The principles, . . . upon which the following discourse depends, are not such as we ourselves make and pronounce in general terms, as definitions; but such, as being placed in things themselves by the Author of Nature, are by us observed in them; and we make use of them in single and particular, not universal propositions. Nor do they impose upon us any necessity of constituting theorems; there use being only, though not without such general propositions as have been already demonstrated, to show us the possibility of some production or generation.[102]

The claim to discern the means by which God crafted them is now removed from their reach. Thus, in directing physics to the task of reconstruction, the limited dignity that it possesses is won by way of partial imitation of the geometer's second greatest skill—re-creating. Its *raison d'etre*—to discern God's handiwork in the universe by virtue of the capacity to grasp the essences of things in nature—is in Hobbes's new order delegitimated.

The disparagement of the old natural philosophical agenda and a triumphalist approach to mathematics, and specifically geometry, as the architectonic science are the clues with which we can return to complete the comparison between Hobbes's and the Jesuit defenses of mathematics. Both Hobbes and the Jesuit mathematicians insist that mathematical demonstrations are causal, but the requirement that mathematicians work from essences is no longer a critical concern. Hobbes allows philosophers to claim knowledge of essences, but essence itself is redefined in strict materialist terms. Instead of an ideal form separate from the matter that makes up an entity, Hobbes's essence is merely the characteristic motions that we refer to when we want to distinguish a particular kind of entity.[103]

Hobbes's thoroughgoing materialism helps illustrate the point of contrast I am drawing. All is material in Hobbes's universe. Indeed, with specific reference to the "false doctrine" of abstract, or separate, essences, Hobbes writes: "The world (I mean not the earth only, that denominates the lovers of it *worldly men*, but the *universe*, that is, the *whole* mass of all things that are) is corporeal (that is to say, body) and hath the dimensions of magnitude. . . . And consequently, every part of the universe is body, and that which is not body is no part of the universe. And, because the universe is all, that which is no part of it is nothing (and consequently, nowhere)."[104] This is not only true of the things that we encounter in the world, but it is true of every part of ourselves. This includes our very thoughts.[105] There is, therefore, an important point of contrast to be made concerning the Platonic elements of the Jesuit defense of mathematics. First, we have to recognize why Hobbes's materialism means that he neither could, nor would necessarily wish to, avail himself of such an argument.[106]

As noted, these arguments—on their way to asserting that mathematics did in fact grasp essences—were an attempt to turn the intellectual status of the mathematician's objects to their advantage. Because they were free from the contaminated contributions coming in from the sense impressions—because they did not draw conceptions from the imperfect, gross matter, of imperfect nature—Blancanus maintained that the mathematicians grasped something that was also on God's mind. The figures considered by the geometer were perfect. It was their perfection that warranted Blancanus's claim that the mathematical objects existed—they were, by virtue of this perfection, more real than the objects considered by the natural philosophers. Thus, Blancanus urged scholars to follow the mathematicians and flee the imperfect and uncertain natural world for the world of more ideal imaginings. Pereira and Piccolomini urged scholars to stay rooted in the concrete world of actual matter. Hobbes employed a materialism that managed to level these distinctions by "materializing" all the components. Our thoughts, the things outside ourselves that give rise to these thoughts, all are now composed of matter in Hobbes's metaphysic. In the face of this thoroughgoing materialism, distinguishing between thoughts that are not contaminated by sense impressions, and thoughts that are, becomes impossible. Pereira's claim detaching mathematics from sense while privileging physics is likewise eviscerated.

In spite of this leveling, there remain important residual distinctions that resonate with Hobbes's thinking. All may be matter, but this does not mean that Hobbes resolves the dispute in favor of the side that calls for knowledge rooted in an attempt to grasp things in nature. The hope of championing a form of reasoning that allows one's mind to function undisturbed by the contingencies and ambiguities of sense is still very much a part of Hobbes's aspiration.[107] As we have seen, Hobbes declares that all ideas start with sense, but we give them their identity, assign them their names. What we grasp is in fact not "in nature" but is the result of our interaction (the pressing and rebounding of matter with our sense organs): the phantasms generated by this interaction are in our minds, not outside ourselves "in nature." (This is the deception of sense referred to earlier.)[108] Reason works upon these phantasms, puts language to use, combines their names into propositions, combines propositions into syllogisms, and constructs effects.

Blancanus's celebration of the immateriality of mathematical conceptions is the prelude to his further assertion that the mathematicians share conceptions of created things with God. Here again, there are elements of Hobbes's philosophy that strongly contradict this assertion. Nevertheless, I am arguing that we find the Jesuit mathematicians' boasts transformed and intensified in Hobbes's claims. First, consider the contradictions. Blancanus claims that the mathematicians, by virtue of grasping forms, grasp the thoughts in the mind of God and thus have a legitimate claim to know the order and characteristics of the world God created. Hobbes abandons this goal. I have covered some of the epistemological reasons—the deceptions of sense, his nominalism, and the rigid strictures concerning what can count as truth that goes with these. I have also mentioned the theological justifications for limiting the scope of natural philosophy. I will conclude the chapter with a more detailed discussion of the matter, exploring the links between Hobbes's insistence on these limits and what is known as the voluntarist theological tradition.

Voluntarism

Voluntarism begins as a response to what appeared to some as the excesses and implicit impiety of scholastic philosophy. All agreed that God was omnipotent. The universe, however, appeared to exhibit uniform characteristics. Indeed, the law-like characteristics were, according to some, testimony to its perfection. The task of natural philosophy was to study that order, to study God's creation. Indeed, revealing the natural order was itself a traditional source of authority. However, in asserting that nature behaved in a fashion that was uniform, that it followed the logically necessary inferences, critics of scholastic philosophy (of Thomism, in particular) suggested that this had the untoward consequence of binding God himself. Both critics and the criticized recognized that God might not merely order nature in an ordinary way, but might also do extraordinary things—miracles being among the most important, although the need to sanction the belief in miracles was by no means a constant among those who placed voluntarist limits on human knowledge. Voluntarism, therefore, was an attempt to restrain philosophical excess with theological caution. It placed limits on the human capacity to know God, to know how he operates, or to know how he created the universe, or miracles.[109]

In the seventeenth century there was no single form of voluntarism, but it was a part of the fabric of philosophical thought, including the thought of the "new scientists." We can find voluntarist views in the philosophy of Descartes[110] (who, for example, uses voluntarism as a tool in skeptically peeling back the layers of certainty that can only then be redeemed by the foundational knowledge that flows from the necessity of God's existence by virtue of his perfection),[111] and we can find members of England's Royal Society who, because of voluntarist reservations, moved further and further away from what appeared to an overanxious desire for certainty and universality in the Cartesian model of science.[112]

What is particularly interesting about Hobbes's voluntarism is that in spite of his reputation for atheism, he takes a particularly hard line in defending God's status as a being beyond human understanding. This theme is a near constant in *Anti-White*, and it extends to his more mature works, including *Leviathan, De Corpore*, and his later scientific texts. As finite creatures, there is little if anything human beings can hope to truly comprehend with regard to an infinite creature. Scripture may state things concerning God and his will, but we cannot expect that our reason will lead to an understanding of a being fundamentally unfathomable. His *power* over us justifies his rule, not our own reasoning.

For Hobbes, the exemplary case is taken from the story of Job, who received the appropriate answer from God in response to his wish to know the *reason* for his afflictions. God rejects, Hobbes notes in *Leviathan*, human reasons suggested to Job by his contemporaries, namely, that Job's sin was the reason for his suffering. Instead, God justified his afflictions "by arguments drawn from his power, such as this, 'Where wast thou, when I laid the foundations of the earth' (Job 38:4)."[113] God's ways, however, are not merely inscrutable when it comes to matters of justice. He asserts that we may know that God exists and that he is the cause of the world, both of which are "manifest" in the idea of God, but these minimal claims become a lever with which to pry up other attributes sometimes assigned to God.[114] Hobbes cautions that the names we use when we "attribute to God nothing but what is warranted by natural reason" must not contradict the honor we owe him in light of the disparity between our orders of being. Hobbes advises that we use "negative attributes (as *infinite, eternal, incomprehensible*) or superlatives (as *most high, most great*)." It is important that such terms do not "declare what he is (for that were to circumscribe him within the limits of our fancy)."[115] Thus, even the way we speak of God must signify our humility as finite creatures in face of the infinite.

What is most important for my purposes is that Hobbes uses these assertions in his attack on the traditional domain of natural philosophy. Consider what Hobbes asserts as he dictates his prohibition against bickering and disputing over God's attributes. As has been suggested by Richard Tuck, Hobbes's *Anti-White* quarantines theology, makes it nearly unassailable by philosophy by keeping their domains distinct. However, in the *Anti-White*, and in *Leviathan*, Hobbes marks off as unknowable a much larger territory than one might suspect in a thinker claiming to offer a conventional natural philosophy. Expanding a passage I quoted earlier, Hobbes writes:

> Disputing of God's nature is contrary to his honour; for it is supposed that in this natural kingdom of God, there is no other way to know anything but by natural reason, that is, *from the principles of natural science, which are so far from teaching us anything of God's nature as they cannot teach us our own nature, nor the nature of the smallest creature living*. And therefore, when men, out of the principles of natural reason, dispute of the attributes of God, they but dishonour him. . . . From the want of which consideration, have proceeded the volumes of disputation about the nature of God, that tend not to his honour, but to the honour of our own wits, and learning; and are nothing else but inconsiderate, and vain abuses of his sacred name.[116]

We should read such statements in light of Hobbes's arguments against physics as a source of authoritative, demonstrative knowledge. It is the complement of the assertions we have already reviewed concerning the limits of natural philosophical knowledge: namely, that we cannot know how God operates in the universe. We therefore should not claim that our own discoveries concerning how the things in nature *could* be created are explanations of how they were in fact created. God, by virtue of his omnipotence, might produce the things we see in nature by any means he chooses. In light of Hobbes's seeming rivalry with God, however, we can also see this use of voluntarism against the natural philosophers as a particularly resourceful piece of intellectual judo. He uses the strength of God's theological defenders as an assault on those, including the schools' very own natural philosophers, who stand in the way of the triumph of his science.

Hobbes's voluntarism is also linked to his critique of the language of scholastic natural philosophy. Why did the schools speak such nonsense? *Leviathan's* closing chapters offers three reasons. The first is captured by his well-known repetition of the ancient judge's question, "Cui bono?"[117] Hobbes accused the schools of using nonsense as a tool for pulling the wool over the people's eyes and of doing so to create a power to compete with the sovereign's.[118] Second, Hobbes suspects the schools of incompetence. The schools attempted to found a philosophy on the abuse of language. They did not begin by defining their terms. Consequently, they built their philosophy on a foundation of nonsense and were trapped in an Aristotelian haze augmented through centuries of deficient thinking.[119]

The third reason concerns an impossible goal the schools set for themselves. According to Hobbes, a key part of the problem is that the schools foolishly attempt to understand the way God himself operates in the universe. They have aspired to achieve a form of knowledge that is beyond human ken. The result is the inability to speak sensibly. Trying to understand how God works in the universe, that is to say, trying to understand the inscrutable, they fall into nonsense:

> And whereas men divide a body in their thought, by numbering parts of it, and in numbering those parts, number also the parts of the place it filled; it cannot be, but in making many parts, we make also many places of those parts; whereby there cannot be conceived in the mind of any man, more, or fewer parts, than there are places for: yet they will have us believe, that by the Almighty power of God, one body may be at one and the same time in many places; and many bodies at one and the same time in one place: as if it were an acknowledgment of the Divine Power to say, that which is, is not; or that which has been, has not been. And these are but a small part of the incongruities they are forced to, from their disputing philosophically, instead of admiring, and adoring

> of the divine and incomprehensible nature; whose attributes cannot signify what he is, but ought to signify our desire to honour him, with the best appellations we can think on. But they that venture to reason of his nature, from these attributes of honour, losing their understanding in the very first attempt, fall from one inconvenience into another, without end, and without number.[120]

Thus, Hobbes's insistence on God's inscrutability had strategic value in his war with the physics of the schools. Hobbes not only chastises the schools for their incongruities but adds an additional barb by suggesting a contrast between their impious philosophy and the orderly divisions man makes when he numbers the universe according to his own conception. In Hobbes's hands a theological position associated with humility becomes a weapon for the further demotion of physics, or against anyone who claims to know God's will, or the true natural order.

We may insert an interesting wrinkle in the commonly held view that Hobbes was an atheist. The implicit assumption of this view is that Hobbes no longer believed in the enchanted universe: all must be accounted for by a rational, mechanical, explanation. In fact, this gets important elements of Hobbes's argument wrong. In part, Hobbes defeated the forces that were declaring the existence of an enchanted universe—a universe of separate essences, such as the soul and spirits—by putting their feet to the fire of his voluntarism. The effects they try to explain, he insisted, were produced by God. For this reason they should hold their tongues concerning their causes. Hobbes was not so much trying to spread light as to insist upon the opacity of the darkness.

The effect is to redistribute learned authority. It is taken away from the disciplines that once used the wrong method—those that had attempted to overreach the human capacity to know the world. Authority is increased among the disciplines that possess the right (geometrically inspired) method. The gains go to those who, rather than claiming to know what God created, claim to know what they create themselves.

Conclusion

Finally, we can return to Blancanus's claim that the mathematician understands the order of the world, grasps the essences of things, because he shares conceptions with God. Given his strong assertion of the inscrutability of God, Hobbes did not make such a claim on his own behalf. The idea of a God who geometrizes, however, is not dead in Hobbes's thought—although the resulting transfiguration could have only aided the death of God. We cannot know how God made the world, how its operations occur, and neither can we declare general truths about the world because such claims would limit a God whom we have called omnipotent. Nevertheless, if God cannot be said to geometrize—because we cannot claim to know what God can do, or how he can do it—*we* can. That is, Hobbes doesn't entirely remove the theme of divinity from his defense of mathematics. Instead of claiming that only those with mathematical skills can know what is on God's mind, he asserts that only those with mathematical skills can reach the most dignified way of imitating God, and that is by creating themselves.

Is there a way to gauge the boldness of Hobbes's program? Even against the background of mathematically inclined scientific revolutionaries, the radicalism of Hobbes's reordering of the hierarchy and purposes of philosophy reveals itself. Consider the statement made by Galileo that asserts the relevance of mathematics to the study of the universe by comparison. (The statement was made, in fact, in anger against Clavius's successor.) Galileo's aggression, it has been suggested, may have been an indication that he was frustrated with Jesuits, who were too respectful, as mathematicians, of the domains traditionally reserved for the authoritative voice of natural philosophers:[121]

> It seems to me that I discern in Sarsi a firm belief that in philosophizing it is essential to support oneself upon the opinion of some celebrated author, as if when our minds are not wedded to the reason of some other person they ought to remain completely barren and sterile . . . . Well Sig. Sarsi, that is not the way matters stand. Philosophy is written in this grand book—I mean the universe—which stands continually open to our gaze, but it cannot be understood unless one first learns to comprehend the language and interpret the characters in which it is written. It is written in the language of mathematics, and its characters are triangles, circles, and other geometrical figures, without which it is humanly impossible to understand a single word of it; without these, one is wandering about in a dark labyrinth.[122]

We might say that Galileo's boldness appears to begin to pave a path that ran through the center of what became, for us, the "scientific revolution." He even appears to anticipate the credo of contemporary sciences with this statement. Hobbes, I've shown, was still bolder, but being bolder he is less familiar to us today than we often imagine. Beyond the basic assertions of his materialist metaphysics, he declared the grand book *illegible*.[123] Those who claimed to read the book had already proven too troublesome to trust. They claimed authority that might undermine a sovereign. By demoting physics, rather than giving it the gift of mathematical insight, Hobbes ensured that it could never claim the certainty that might allow it this authority. On the other hand, by declaring this grand book illegible he cleared a space for what he hoped would be a new way of scientific practice. Hobbes invited those who worked under the sovereign's command to pick up the writing implements—the basic matter of the universe, and his science for manipulating it. He tried to teach them how to author a book of their own. He might have considered today's mathematicized attempts to know our political natures a return to scholasticism.

6

ELOQUENCE AND THE AUDIENCE THESIS

Why is it that Hobbes's first two presentations of his political philosophy, *Elements of Law* and *De Cive*, are relatively devoid of rhetoric and *Leviathan*, his masterwork, shows such great and deliberate eloquence? We know that Hobbes said that rhetoric should be no part of philosophy.[1] Perhaps the most elegant solution to this problem would be to declare that *Elements of Law* and *De Cive* are works of philosophy and *Leviathan* is not. One could also argue that Hobbes wrote *Leviathan* as a gift to a sovereign, not as a philosophical work for the consumption of either students or fellow philosophers.

Although Hobbes did in fact write *Leviathan* as a gift to a sovereign (his critics raised the question of *which* sovereign),[2] and although Hobbes himself distinguishes between "his doctrine" and his *Leviathan*, the notion that *Leviathan* is not philosophy is unsustainable. There is too much in *Leviathan* that counts as contestable doctrine for Hobbes to maintain the distinction (and he surely would have if he had wished to). There are also differences between *Leviathan* and the earlier texts—such as the doctrine of authorization—that cannot be ignored.[3] At the very least, *Leviathan* is philosophy in spite of its eloquence, and for some interpreters (particularly those who link philosophy with grand conceptions) it is a philosophical masterpiece.[4] Indeed, for some others it is taken as Hobbes's most "mature" statement of his political philosophy.[5]

The simple solution, therefore, will not do. Hobbes's interpreters have offered a variety of alternatives. Some have suggested, not inaccurately, that the premise is false. There *are* rhetorical characteristics to be found in the earlier works, especially *De Cive*, in spite of what Hobbes claims (or seems to claim). Indeed, if Richard Tuck is correct, then *De Cive* was never meant to be widely circulated without the passages identified as most rhetorical.[6] Others have suggested that Hobbes is in essence a deceitful philosopher who uses rhetoric to mask assertions that only appear to be rationally compelling.[7] As noted, Hobbes is a prime target for a hermeneutic sneak attack, a bounty for those fighting on the side of rhetoric in the age-old battle with philosophy.

The most developed explanations, however, have come from interpreters such as David Johnston and more recently Quentin Skinner, who emphasize the differences between what they see as phases in Hobbes's thinking. These, not unlike some of the sneak-attack interpreters, begin with a conventional story. They remind us that Hobbes, although famous now for his philosophical approach to politics, began his life as a humanist. Then, as we have seen, they follow Hobbes's gossipy friend John Aubrey, who tells us that Hobbes had an epiphany when he discovered geometry at age forty (approximately 1628).[8] According to these readings, the discovery of and devotion to geometry meant the abandonment of humanism (something Aubrey does not assert). On this reading, Hobbes became confident that his particular form of new science would produce works so compelling that no one would be able to disagree with their conclusions. Why, then, does Hobbes turn back to rhetoric (*the* humanist instrument for success in persuasion) when he writes *Leviathan*?

Skinner and Johnston both think that Hobbes changed his mind. He came to the conclusion that reason alone, that is, reason unaided by the craft of rhetoric, was insufficient to accomplish his goals. The two authors differ over the motive for this change of heart—Johnston finds Hobbes's most urgent need for rhetoric in matters of religion, while Skinner finds it as a result of a diminished optimism concerning the power of reason to persuade interested men—but I will not dwell here on these differences.

I would like to put forward a third explanation. It is rooted in a theory Skinner rejects and that Johnston himself uses, but to different effect than I will. The differences in rhetoric (for there is a difference, even if we allow *De Cive*'s rhetorical characteristics to emerge) between *De Cive* and other early works, on one hand, and *Leviathan*, on the other, can be accounted for in terms of their distinct audiences. I will call this the "audience thesis." According to Johnston, Hobbes decides that the elite audiences he addressed in his earlier works were insufficient to his goals.[9] He sees in Hobbes's return to rhetoric an important lesson for those interested in the cultural transformation. Hobbes is said to have eventually realized that the only way to make an impact was to address a popular audience—a task *requiring* rhetoric.[10]

For Johnston, Hobbes was an "epic theorist."[11] He did not find that the world agreed with his theory, but became determined to make the world conform to it. To do this, he would have to modify the beliefs of those under the sway of religion. Even the rationally self-interested believer might find a good reason to incur the punishment of a sovereign if hanging over his or her head was the threat of eternal damnation. Clerics and disobedient subjects could take advantage of this priority of the eternal over the temporal and undermine the rational order Hobbes wanted to achieve. Hobbes's return to rhetoric, according to Johnston, emerges against the realization that the citizens themselves would have to be transformed.[12] For Johnston, therefore, a critical part of the rhetorical story of *Leviathan* is that he devised a theology that secretly undermines religious belief, and which particularly targets those elements of his contemporaries' faith—such as prophecy—which might create a foundation for divinely sanctioned resistance to the sovereign authority.[13]

For Skinner, by contrast, the return to rhetoric represents a transformation in Hobbes's thinking concerning the prospects of rational persuasion. The realization results in an about-face on the question of rhetoric and philosophy. On this reading, *Leviathan* is an acknowledgment that philosophical reason sometimes needs rhetoric's assistance, a great reversal of Hobbes's earlier confidence in the persuasive power of scientific reason alone.[14] Skinner is therefore unconvinced by the argument that Hobbes adopted rhetoric because he was attempting to reach a larger audience. It was not, according to Skinner, a decision to offer the elite the closed fist of dialectic while bowing to the necessity of giving the vulgar rhetoric's open palm.[15] It was, instead, a shift that acknowledged reason's limited power against passion, and even the perception of interests:

> It is doubtful, in short, whether considerations about audience go far towards explaining Hobbes's new concern in *Leviathan* to press home his scientific findings with the moving power of eloquence. Whether writing for a learned or a more popular audience, this concern remained with him throughout the latter part of his intellectual career....
> ... [W]hen we reflect on the principal reason given in *Leviathan* for insisting that the sciences are small power, and thus that their findings need to be supplemented by the force of eloquence ... Hobbes came to believe that most people are moved less by force of reason than by their perceived sense of their own self-interest. By contrast with the optimism of *The Elements* and *De Cive*, he additionally insists in *Leviathan* that, if the requirements of reason collide with people's interests, they will not only refuse to accept what reason dictates, but will do their best to dispute or suppress even the clearest scientific proofs if these seem liable to affect their interests in an adverse way.[16]

He also makes this point, in part, by referring us to the Latin edition of *Leviathan*, a text which (with its supplemental dialogues and yet more rhetorical techniques) called upon more resources from the humanist toolbox. Why attempt *popular* persuasion in the language of the elite?[17]

Skinner's conclusion against Johnston's audience thesis is convincing, but it is not strong enough to completely dismiss an audience-centered explanation for the differences between the texts. This is because mass/elite or vulgar/learned dichotomies are too simplistic for the question at hand. Furthermore, Johnston's audience thesis, while important, ignores an important possibility. The key question in the hierarchically ordered society of seventeenth-century England was the relative standing of the author to his audience. *Leviathan*, as a work addressed first to a sovereign (or a would-be sovereign, Charles II in exile), was written to the most lofty audience of all.[18]

My disagreement with Johnston and Skinner is best highlighted against a point of agreement with both. This concerns Hobbes's intent as regards the subjects of his commonwealth. Each in his own way, these authors reject the implicit view of many of Hobbes's recent interpreters, who assume that Hobbes's philosophy is rooted in fixed assumptions concerning human conduct—assumptions against which Hobbes's theory can be judged either true or false. Like Johnston and Skinner, I believe that a key part of Hobbes's project was to modify or refashion subjects. Hobbes desired to make them fitting pieces in his design for a peaceful commonwealth. Unlike Johnston, however, I maintain that the modification of subjects was a part of Hobbes's project from the start. This modification was to be effected through an education mandated by the sovereign.

For Johnston, rhetoric only becomes necessary when Hobbes determines that the gap between his theory and reality must be closed. The new religious doctrine becomes a means of closing this gap. I think that Hobbes recognized the gap from the beginning. It was in the willingness of the sovereign to mandate the teaching of his doctrines (scientific and later religious) that Hobbes sought his solution. Skinner also sees a decision to alter subjects, but discerns this much earlier in Hobbes's career (i.e., his "first phase"). According to Skinner, Hobbes's rejection of rhetoric in *Elements of Law* and *De Cive* was a direct assault on the humanist ideal of the *vir civilis*.[19] By the *vir civilis*, Skinner mostly means the man trained in eloquence to participate effectively in public deliberation—a humanist recuperation of Cicero and Quintilian's ideal of a great *public* speaker,[20] a citizen, not merely a subject. Thus, for Skinner, it is not rhetoric but science that is the driving force for modifying subjects. (It is also worth noting, however, that when rhetoric returns to Hobbes's personal repertoire, it does not similarly return to the subject's. The *vir civilis* remains dead in Hobbes's later philosophy, and instead a new ideal of eloquent style for philosophers emerges.)

Hobbes did indeed wish to alter subjects, and rhetoric was one tool among others (not least his science) for ensuring that this would happen. Hobbes did wish to change the way subjects were educated. Unlike Skinner, I do not think we can say that his antagonism for some forms of rhetoric came from *outside* humanism. Hobbes feared the power of eloquent men engaged in public speaking, especially before large assemblies. I will illustrate in Chapter 7, however, that this was a fear one could possess from *within* humanist traditions. Also unlike Skinner, I believe that Hobbes's utmost concern was in displacing the teaching of the schools—what Hobbes referred to in his nastier moments as Aristotelity[21]—rather than humanism *per se*. Unlike Johnston, I believe Hobbes was persistent in the means he adopted to achieve this goal, and in this he was not exceptional. He was following in the footsteps of some of his contemporaries; they also wished to remake human beings in accord with their political visions. Hobbes did as they did and devised a new doctrine to be taught in the schools.

This reading suggests that Hobbes had a more specific goal in using rhetoric, especially in *Leviathan*. This brings us back to the audience thesis, but now with a concrete persuasive goal in mind. For Hobbes, I would suggest, the way to ensure that something would be taught in the universities was not merely to offer it up to the public in the hopes that it would become widely read or popularly approved. Although Hobbes's critics, particularly during the Restoration (John Eachard and Clarendon, for example),[22] complained that this had in fact happened, Hobbes and many of his fellow education reformers had something very different in mind. They understood that the proper (and they hoped effective) means of ensuring that their works would be taught in the universities was by presenting them to those who possessed (or those they thought should possess) the authority to dictate what was taught (and what was not!) in the universities. For Hobbes, this was the exclusive responsibility of absolute sovereign power. The purpose of Hobbes's rhetoric was to persuade the powerful, and as we shall see, the closer to power Hobbes got the more rhetorical his texts became.

In the first part of this chapter, I provide a relatively abstract discussion of Hobbes's audience, political goals, and rhetoric in *Leviathan, Elements of Law*, and *De Cive*. Skinner argues that Hobbes's "discovery" of geometry bestowed upon him an optimism concerning the force of reason. He maintains that following this discovery, Hobbes came to the conclusion in his so-called first phase that solid philosophical reasoning did not need the assistance of eloquence. At the conclusion of the next chapter I will discuss the broader significance of my reading of Hobbes in light of this aspect of the rhetoric versus philosophy debate. In Chapter 8 I will offer a more complete approach to *Leviathan* and will illustrate how Hobbes's (and the Stuart Court's) humanist affinity for mathematics, the forms of courtly advice giving, and his educational agenda come together. We will see, moreover, that one could very well say that Hobbes did not so much "discover" geometry, but that courtly affinities for geometry (in the persons of his patrons, the Cavendish family) discovered him.

Optimism or Reason's Last Chance?

We need not be convinced that Hobbes was initially optimistic about the capacity of his contemporaries to hear or be moved by the force of reason.[23] Skinner writes as though the Hobbes of the 1640s thought he had once and for all solved the problem of making reason's voice heard above the din of controversy and passion. The dedicatory and opening chapter in *Elements of Law*, the work in which Hobbes first introduces his new civil science, admits of a different reading. In the dedicatory, Hobbes begins by assigning two kinds of learning, mathematical and dogmatical, to "the two principal parts of our nature, Reason and Passion" respectively. Mathematics is free from controversy and dispute because it deals with figures and motions only, "in which things truth and the interest of men oppose not each other." By contrast, with dogmatical learning, "there is nothing not disputable, because it compareth men, and meddleth with their right and profit; in which, as oft as reason is against a man, so oft will a man be against reason." The hope, therefore, is to "reduce this doctrine [i.e., the doctrine of justice and policy] to the rules and infallibility of reason" by putting down principles as a foundation that the passions, "not mistrusting, may not seek to displace; and afterward to build thereon the truth of cases in the law of nature (which hitherto have been built in the air) by degrees, till the whole be inexpugnable."

Skinner reads this passage as the words of a writer confident in the powers of reason and dismissive of humanist dictates concerning the need for eloquent persuasion, history, and a skeptic's understanding of the contestability of political conclusions. Hobbes does indeed suggest the superiority of his new political "Elements" to the teaching offered in history and denies the necessity of eloquence and even points to the dangers of using persuasion where real (i.e., logical) teaching is necessary. Aside from his claim to superiority over history, however, it is difficult to see why these should be seen to constitute a specific attack on humanists exclusively. Surely, Aristotle's *Nicomachean Ethics* as it was taught in the schools also taught the inherent uncertainty of political reason.[24] More to my point, it is not clear why we should not read Hobbes's *Elements of Law* as the work of a man more in despair of reason's powers. Hobbes embraces mathematics, and presents his own method, as the last great hope for reason. As I read Hobbes in these early works, his tone reflects a great deal more faith in reason (as practiced by mathematicians only) than in men. His tone resonates with a certain Platonist *ressentiment:* he is as confident in reason as he is *already* snide and bitterly resentful of the rest of humanity for its inability to grasp reason's dictates.[25] Hobbes's awareness of reason's "small power" with the multitude was not, contra Skinner, a sudden discovery brought on after the Civil War. Hobbes's expectations for reason are from the beginning paired with a sense of the thinness of most people's grasp of rational argument. If the dedicatory teeters on the edge of such a reading, then the third section of the introductory chapter ought to push it over: "If reasoning aright I win not consent (*which may very easily happen*) from them that being confident of their own knowledge weigh not what is said, the fault is not mine but theirs. For as it is my part to show my reasons, so it is theirs to bring attention."[26]

Skinner himself ignores neither these elements in Hobbes's attacks nor some of the pessimistic implications of his attack on those who would wed reason with eloquence, but he belatedly registers the tone of the philosopher's desperate frustration with his fellows.[27] He sees this frustration only in *Leviathan*, and reads the passage from the *Elements* just quoted as a conclusion that follows from his rejection of humanist expectations. On Skinner's reading, Hobbes can redirect the blame to the audience who disagrees with him because his new confidence in reason's power has allowed him to reject Cicero's counsel that the orator should make a "special effort" to win the attention and consent of the audience.[28] Of course, it seems unlikely that a humanist would never assign fault to those who fail to agree with him. It is nevertheless true that Hobbes makes no "special effort" in *Elements of Law* to win the attention and consent of the audience. I suggest he had motives other than the rejection of humanism for assigning blame and for refusing to make eloquence's "special effort."

It seems more likely that Hobbes began and ended with contempt of his fellow's capacity to hear the voice of reason. His early enthusiasm and pride centered on the notion that *he* and a few others (the true mathematicians) could make out that voice above the roar of nonsense in conflict. A writer with the confidence Skinner assigns Hobbes, someone assured of his ability to have solved the problem of making reason's voice heard, would not have thought it would "very easily happen" that right reason would not "bring attention." He would not have been so concerned that the others would not play their part and pay proper attention.[29] Ultimately, Skinner's analysis tends to blur the distinction between what Hobbes thought he accomplished in the construction of his doctrine and methods, and any claim he might make to have single-handedly achieved a practical victory over the sources of swirling confusion. This was a stubborn gap that Hobbes always recognized; it becomes obscured when Skinner writes that "Hobbes [holds in the *Elements* and much more emphatically in *De Cive*] that *ratio* possesses an inherent power to persuade and convince, and thus that the idea of a union between reason and eloquence is an irrelevance."[30]

Skinner's reading briefly considers moments in the early texts where Hobbes concedes the difficulties of making reason's voice heard. He notes that Hobbes acknowledges that persons often suffer from the "fault of the minde" called "INDOCIBILITY, or difficulty of being taught." This occurs "when men have once acquiesced in untrue opinions, and registered them as authenticall records in their minds." It then is "no lesse impossible to speak intelligibly to such men than to write legibly upon a paper already scribbled over." Skinner's assessment of Hobbes's approach to this problem is as follows:

> But Hobbes is far from regarding indocibility as an insuperable barrier to the construction of a science of politics. As he observes in the same passage, "if the mindes of men were all of white paper, they would almost equally be disposed to acknowledge whatsoever should be in right method, and right ratiocination delivered unto them." Nor is this merely a utopian prospect, for while "opinions which are gotten by Education, and in length of tyme are made habituall, cannot be taken away by force, and upon the suddaine," they can nevertheless be taken away by the same means by which they were acquired, that is, "by tyme and Education." Hobbes's highly optimistic conclusion is thus that, if the true principles of civil science were taught in the universities, we should quickly find "that younge men, who come thither voyd of prejudice, and whose mindes are yet as white paper," would readily adopt them and teach them in turn to the generality of the people.[31]

Is this "a highly optimistic conclusion"? Perhaps only in contrast with the sterner measures that Plato might endorse in light of the fact that the minds of the citizens were not like white paper. It may be optimistic to think that a mandatory education reform would produce the necessary changes in the educated, but for Hobbes the decision to forcibly uproot and replace a rotten form of education was born out of determination to meet practical challenges to the rule of reason—challenges that caused him to despair.

Hobbes was not alone in pursuing grand schemes for the reform of education, nor was he unaware of his competitors. Those in the Hartlib circle—about which more later—were submitting similarly grandiose plans based in part on the didactic enthusiasms of Comenius.[32] William Davenant, Hobbes's poet friend, would in 1654 (after he had been captured and incarcerated by English authorities) write *A Proposition for Advancement of Moralitie*. In it he proposed a scheme of using publicly funded theatrical performances (modeled on Italian comedy and bolstered by the spectacular effects Davenant had once used in court masques for Charles I)[33] to indoctrinate the common people in their duty to the state—at that time Cromwell's Protectorate. Davenant's proposition was in fact conveyed to Hartlib by Hobbes's acquaintance and fellow mathematician John Pell.[34] If Hobbes's doctrine were to be taught in the schools, it would have to receive the sovereign stamp of approval. All other doctrines that might conflict with Hobbes's (including those that threaten its basic presuppositions, such as Boylean vacuumism, i.e., anything that suggested the existence of vacuum, or of incorporeal substances) would have to count as "discourse which . . . representeth not unto us our own conceptions," thus as seditious teachings to be outlawed.

If this is optimism, it is not the type that Skinner suggests. It suggests rather that the question of who would teach, and what would be taught (particularly in the wake of Archbishop Laud's muscular interventions in the universities and the resistance with which they were met), was no small matter to Hobbes or to his contemporaries. If his remarks on teaching reflect optimism, they do so in a way that tempers this sentiment by a purposeful desire to alter what he saw as a political malady. Hobbes was confident (and remained confident) that his doctrine would form the basis of a lasting commonwealth. However, this confidence should not cloud our understanding of the anger and disgust that motivated his efforts. He justified these strong measures by emphasizing, as he does in *De Cive* (especially in the dedicatory and the preface), the miserable and dangerous character of contemporary circumstances. Not just heated oratory, but bad philosophy—an opponent Skinner's antihumanist reading tends to omit from the picture—had already scribbled over the brains of subjects. Hobbes paints a picture where halfway measures are no longer acceptable. He is boastful, but this is because his claim was to possess a solution equal to an immense problem that required the reeducation of the citizenry. There was no *volte-face* on this policy.

Politics, Education, and Eloquence for Smaller Audiences

Some of the most interesting work on eloquence in early modern Britain suggests that the goals of the *studia humanitatis* Skinner finds embodied in Cicero's civil science were not entirely compatible with the roles assumed by courtiers and others seeking favor in an autocratic society.[35] The functions traditionally assigned to rhetoric—creating citizens capable of persuading their equals in the law courts and deliberative bodies—are no longer a perfect match for those who must perform in the smaller, more exclusive arena of courtly politics (or even for those many others who had to seek favor with those who sought favor from a monarch, and so on down the line). This is not to say that eloquence was of no use in these contexts. It was considered useful, but useful because it could allow an author to ingratiate himself with a patron. The skills of the humanists were useful not merely for free citizens, but also for courtly dependents. Eloquence was necessary for a flattering description of one's patron. Moreover, the aesthetic character of one's writing or speech was itself a virtue that might be put on display when seeking favor. Eloquence took a turn toward the poetic, and the skills of the poet became a source of guidance for those who needed to ingratiate themselves with their betters, especially present and future patrons. Many of Hobbes's contemporaries did not put their eloquence to use before assemblies, but in contexts more akin to those found in Castiglione's *Book of the Courtier*, such as the smaller audience of noble patrons and the society of learned rivals who might seek a patron's favor and approval.[36]

Indeed, this raises a larger question concerning Skinner's reading of the *studia humanitatis*. While one may agree with Skinner that Hobbes's new mathematical civil science was a rejection of the model of republican citizenship (and its corresponding hatred of tyranny), one need not assume that such a rejection necessarily entailed a rejection of humanist learning or traditions. One could be sympathetic to—even complicit in the creation of—despotic regimes and remain a humanist in good standing. The Medici's immense patronage and the elaborate rational architectural plans for the Principality of Sforzinda by the Florentine Filarete (Antonio Averlino) are a reminder that while humanists may have articulated the republican sympathies of the Italian city-states, their skills also often went hand in hand with absolutism.[37] In Hobbes's lifetime he need only turn to such learned humanists as Ben Jonson or his friend and poet laureate to Charles I, William Davenant, to see that humanism by no means implied loyalty to forms of government pleasing to the critics of the Stuarts. When Charles II was restored in 1660, the iconography of his passage through a series of triumphal arches in London was itself the product of intensive humanist efforts and codified by his master of the revels John Ogilby. Ogilby's record not only describes the detail of the archways through which Charles passed, but also illustrates the precedent for their iconography with extensive humanist scholarship. From this record we know that Charles was bathed in the light of neoclassical imperial triumph. These included Virgilian celebrations in which Charles was likened at once to Aeneas and the emperor Augustus. Charles was made, among other deifications, the hero who would return the golden age after the chaos and misery brought by his republican opponents.[38]

Thus, poetic skills could allow a courtier the means by which to celebrate a patron. As regards their didactic function, such skills were cultivated in courtly contexts because they taught decorum: what could count as fitting conduct in the company of one's superiors, equals, and inferiors (and as poets took on this guiding role, they did not simply follow predetermined rules of conduct, but used their poetic skills to propagandize for or against rival ideals of "fitting" conduct at court, including that of the Crown).[39] A refined understanding of decorum was required for those who wished to better, or at least preserve, their station in an environment where rivals furiously competed to gain the good graces of select patrons.[40] Rhetoric not only made one persuasive; it made one pleasant in the company of one's superiors at a time when the norms of courtesy between the ranks made being pleasant to one's superiors necessary. I shall also briefly consider some of the trends in didactic rhetoric that Skinner overlooks when discussing *De Cive*. The two, of course, are not unrelated since a key element of the courtier's function is to render counsel, while the gentler art of instructing a sovereign is taken up in the discussion of *Leviathan*.

It is not that the more traditional rhetorical situations—such as speaking in order to move and excite a large assembly—disappeared from the scene. It should be noted, however, that Hobbes's views on those who address (or even make themselves a part of) such assemblies appear in some of his most vehement antirhetorical writings, and this is true not just in his middle period but throughout his work.[41] (The other great target is the "sophistry" of the schools.) One need not believe that Hobbes enjoyed or approved of the courtly competition for honors, but as much as Hobbes may have detested the competition for glory and recognition that courtly environments may have engendered,[42] he could not merely wish this system away.[43] He could achieve little for himself or for his program of education by pretending that the logic of patronage applied to everyone but himself. He needed to show his betters that he was worthy, and that he merited their favor. It is in this context that one must consider Hobbes's individual works in relation to their particular audiences.

Audience and Argument in the *Elements of Law*

Hobbes tells us that *Elements of Law* was written at the request of his patron, the Earl of Newcastle. As Lord Lieutenant of Nottinghamshire, a member of the Privy Council, and Governor of the Prince of Wales (later, Charles II), Newcastle's efforts at securing patronage (in part thanks to Charles's detested favorite, Buckingham) were beginning to pay off.[44] Less fortunately, his ties obliged him to the circle at court that was acting in support of the highly unpopular forced loan of 1626–27, a novel way of raising revenue practiced by Charles I as a means of meeting his pressing financial needs without having to secure the consent of the Parliament (which he had dismissed in 1626 in order to protect Buckingham from impeachment). Hobbes himself had been a part of the effort to collect the highly unpopular loan.[45] At the time that *Elements of Law* was being penned, Newcastle had reason for feeling anxious.[46] Charles I had been operating largely without Parliament, yet needed more funds as a result of the disastrous Scottish rebellion of 1638–40. A newly called Parliament (the Short Parliament of April to May of 1640) allowed many members to vent their displeasure; it would not grant the revenues Charles had requested. The Earl of Devonshire had in fact desired that Hobbes himself be elected a member of this Parliament as the representative of Derby, but the plan failed.[47] The Earl of Strafford, allied with Newcastle and a defender of the Crown's prerogative to act against Parliament in the name of *salus populi*, would not long thereafter be impeached by the Long Parliament (called in November 1640). In the meantime, those who hoped to resolve this conflict could not agree on a course of action. Newcastle and Hobbes stood firm on the absolutist position, which called for Parliament to yield, but as Hobbes petulantly records in *Behemoth*, his view was not shared even by those who found themselves allied with Charles I.[48]

Hobbes had been busy developing his new mode of reason, and with this mode his claim was to be able to defeat all other forms of discourse. In effect, we should look at Hobbes as a one-man army, a champion debater with a newly devised mode of reasoning, capable of giving combatants a logical thrashing. Hobbes was not unhappy to fashion himself in these terms. In a letter to Edmund Waller[49] in 1645 he remarks on how he spent his time while visiting his exiled patron, the third Earl of Devonshire. He notes,

I came to see my lord . . . but am no lesse in other Company than his; where I serue when I can be matched as a gladiator; My odde opinions are bayted. but [sic] I am contented with it, as beleeuing I have still the better, when a new man is sett vpon me; that knowes not my paradoxes, but is full of his owne doctrine, there is something in the disputation not vnpleasant. He thinkes he has driuen me vpon an absurdity when t'is upon some other of my tenets and so from one to another, till he wonder and exclayme and at last finds I am of the Antipodes to ye schooles. Thus I passe my time in this place.[50]

Could it be that Hobbes's patrons liked to see their fighting man put to the test?[51] It seems that Hobbes's unusual talents in debating were a source of entertainment. Court wits in the 1660s may have found him so; Aubrey's account of Hobbes in Charles II's court suggests as much. Aubrey records that they were "wont to bayte him. But he feared none of them, and would make his part good. The king would call him *the beare:* 'Here comes the beare to be bayted!'"[52] Perhaps more important for our consideration of *Elements of Law*, Hobbes's special way of reasoning (and by extension Hobbes himself) was an instrument to be used in the service of his masters. As such, we should think of Hobbes, and his *Elements*, as a new weapon in the war of words, lobbed by Newcastle at his Parliamentary opponents. Newcastle offered the Crown the services of his master of logical fencing in much the same spirit as he would later raise an army to fight on the king's behalf.[53] The *Elements* can be thought of as a demonstration project for this new weapon. The logical forks (cf. the frontispiece of *Leviathan*) were to be turned against the bumptious Parliament. Geometrical methods, already well associated with martial sciences such as fortification, ballistics, and in Newcastle's case horsemanship,[54] would now become the dreadnought of a defense of absolutism in Parliament.[55]

As Skinner and other commentators note, Hobbes does not rely on specific rhetorical techniques in this text, and even shuns them. Why is this? It is worth noting that he is not merely doing so in the context of claiming to possess political reason, but in the context of using political reason to address an assembly, namely Parliament. Rhetorical appeals in this context are the way of the enemy, and at the root of the trouble.[56] As I will argue, rhetoric at court or in the company of one's honored patrons was one thing; rhetoric in the domain of demagogues and lesser men was another. Where eloquence had become for the courtier a tool for negotiating one's way among lofty men, the use of naked logic in a parliamentary setting was less an abandonment of eloquence as a sign of the author's antagonistic intents. Hobbes's plan in the

Elements is to use the new technology of his precise logic against foes he and his party had no wish to please or appease. If logic was unpleasant by comparison with rhetoric, then so much the better. Seditious persons, Hobbes says, combine eloquence with discontent and mean judgment and intellectual capacity.[57] To this he adds:

> Eloquence is nothing else but the power of winning belief of what we say; and to that end we must have aid from the passions of the hearer. Now to demonstration and teaching of the truth, there are required long deductions, and great attention, which is unpleasant to the hearer; therefore they which seek not truth, but belief, must take another way; and not only derive what they would have to be believed, from somewhat believed already, but also by aggravations and extenuations make good and bad, right and wrong, appear great or less, according as it shall serve their turns.[58]

To return to an earlier point, a passage such as this does not bespeak optimism, but a certain political and intellectual smugness. Hobbes is putting forward a distinction: He and the party of his patrons will take the high road of reason, but most others in opposition to the monarch have taken the low road of mere eloquence. The few will hear the dictates of sound logic; the seditious among the assembly will dwell in a world of heated passion, discontent, and stupidity.

Hobbes and Newcastle therefore had no desire to be pleasant with their sovereign's opponents (and would not have encouraged pleasantries between Charles I's defenders and his opponents in Parliament). *Elements of Law* puts forward a vision of the political and intellectual world in which definition and proposition are linked to create a logically undeniable case for absolutism. The systematically constructed argument, like links in a chain, would thwart and defeat its dogmatic opponents. In this agonistic setting, there is no room for niceties, and so all rhetorical niceties are reserved for the epistle to his patron.[59]

There is, however, a fatalism that must haunt the *Elements*. The work may have circulated in manuscript form before Charles dismissed the Short Parliament, but it was not dedicated until four days after its dismissal.[60] Hobbes and Newcastle, having lost the day (or perhaps the chance to engage in the conflict for which they were preparing), could at least offer their opponents a Platonic sneer. If the Parliament did not hear the reason of their defense of absolutism, the fault lay with the Parliamentarians, and not with those who held firm to reason's dictates. The fact that they were unwilling to listen to the voice of reason could only serve to affirm the righteousness and superiority of the losers. The loss was testimony to the dogmatic forces against which they were forced into flight.

The rhetorical (or nonrhetorical) qualities of the *Elements*, therefore, are determined by its audience. Here Hobbes confronts his and Newcastle's parliamentary opponents, and perhaps more obliquely those inclined to support the Crown on grounds not in agreement with the strong absolutist line supported by Newcastle. In concluding his account of the laws of nature in the *Elements*, Hobbes writes: "The sum of virtue is to be sociable with them that will be sociable, and formidable to them that will not."[61] Here he follows his own rule. Like hostile equals in the state of nature, Hobbes uses his offensive faculties to preserve himself and his party within a logical fortress. Perhaps those at first not so inclined to follow this hard line would, upon seeing the strength of Newcastle's new weapon, run to it for protection and alliance as might frightened or hopeful individuals in the state of nature upon witnessing a champion. Newcastle himself would call for such unification behind himself and the king once the fighting had begun,[62] and there is a certain parallel with Hobbes's notions in the *Elements* as to how a first step might send frightened individuals on the way toward granting their consent and binding themselves to absolute sovereign rule.[63] Hobbes very much wished to lead such a grand unifying effort, a hope that went bitterly unrealized.[64]

Audience and Argument in *De Cive*

The situation with regard to *De Cive* is different. Here Hobbes proceeds with the task of offering lessons. In *De Cive*, Hobbes primarily[65] addresses students, young men attending the universities where his doctrine would have been—had his ambitions been achieved[66]—a mandatory part of the curriculum. What is required rhetorically of such a situation? His "Preface to the Reader" begins with a promise to teach readers their true duties as men, citizens, and Christians. One might assume that Hobbes would have little need for rhetoric in these contexts. What else could his students do but obey their master? But Hobbes does use rhetoric. Perhaps this was the mode of instruction that Hobbes most preferred.[67] It most likely reflects the fact that his ambitions were not yet achieved: *De Cive* was a civic doctrine in waiting.

His somewhat immodest preface would establish his credibility as a someone whose teachings his students should be thankful for in light of the desperate times: "Yet I have not made it [*De Cive*] out of a desire of praise: although if I had . . . but for your sakes, readers, who I persuaded myself, when you should rightly apprehend and thoroughly understand this doctrine I here present you with, would rather choose to brook with patience some inconveniences under government . . . than self-opiniatedly disturb the quiet of the public . . ." (*De Cive*, preface, 20). These remarks, and indeed the preface itself, were additions to later editions of *De Cive* (the first having been issued in a small printing in 1642, the second edition was published in 1647). These later, expanded editions of Hobbes's work also included answers to criticism and questions addressed to the first Latin edition. As Samuel Sorbière's letters testify, during this interval Hobbes was becoming more widely known in Continental circles.[68] It is therefore worth noting, in light of the expanded audience for the work (and important matters added in the preface and annotations), that Hobbes's didactic intent and tone are not merely present in the preface but were in place prior to the second edition and his newfound celebrity abroad.

For example, Hobbes sometimes employs the rhetoric of the sagacious master. He recollects his personal experience and uses it to testify for the necessity of his doctrine. Mindful of the temptations ambitious men have for republican governance, Hobbes anticipates the grievances of those who feel cheated by being excluded from public deliberations. In the context of explaining his preference for monarchy over democracy, Hobbes offers this bit of advice—not to say rhetoric—to the inevitably large number of frustrated place-seekers who complain of monarchy:

> And what grievance, if this [monarchy over democracy] be none? Ile tell you: To see his opinions whom we scorne, preferr'd before ours; to have our wisdome undervalued before our own faces; by an uncertain tryall of a littel vaine glory, to undergoe most certaine enmities (for this cannot be avoided, whether we have the better, or the worse); to hate and be hated, by disagreement of opinions; to lay open secret Counsells, and advises to all, to no purpose, and without any benefits; to neglect the affaires of our own Family: these, I say, are grievances. But to be absent from the triall of wits, although those trialls are pleasant to the Eloquent, is not therefore a grievance to them, unless we will say, that it is a grievance to valiant men to be restrained from fighting, because they delight in it.[69]

Thus Hobbes paints a picture for his students of rough days in public politics, but it is not merely in those sections where Hobbes recommends (though does not claim to demonstrate)[70] monarchy over other forms of government.

In chapter 1 of *De Cive* Hobbes engages in a series of descriptions of human conduct worthy of any humanist satirist.

Hobbes's satirical writings are not limited to the metaphors, similes, and other "mocking" tropes and figures highlighted by Skinner in *Leviathan*. We must also consider Hobbes's work in the context of the broader uses of satire employed by his contemporaries. Satire was not just the tool of those who hoped to mock their political opponents. It was also the tool for didacts and social critics, and moralists such as Ben Jonson and Bishop Joseph Hall. In these instances the attack strategy need not necessarily finger a particular opponent for ridicule. Instead, the satirist attacked vices on a level wherein specific persons remained unspecified. The sting of the attack, the laughter directed toward the ridiculous character (or characters), was to encourage the audience to correct these faults in themselves, not necessarily to convince the audience that the author's hated opponents were contemptible. (Ben Jonson often professed the first motive, but his critics and rivals attributed his satires to the second.)[71] Among those who used the techniques of satire, therefore, there were goals that certainly went beyond that of personally directed mocking and derision.[72] Moreover, they taught their audience to distance itself from the faults and vices through lavishly detailed word-pictures. Properly executed, such satire held out the promise of compelling those in the audience (at court, in the theaters, from the pulpit, or in classrooms) to become good by prodding them to distance themselves from their most tempting vices.[73]

Hall helped fostered the satiric form called the "Character" (also used by Jonson) in partial imitation of Aristotle's student Theophrastus.[74] Here pithily drawn, detailed word-pictures of vices were put before the reader: the actions of a person exemplifying the vice are compounded one with the other. Take the superstitious, and not accidentally Catholic, man: "This man dares not stiree forth til his brest be crossed, and his face sprinkled; if but an Hare crosse him the way, he retornes; or if his journey began unawares on the dismall day; or if he stumble at the threshold. If he see a Snake unkilled, he feares a mischiefe; if the salt fall towards him, he lookes pale and red, and is not quiet till one of the witers have powred win on his lappe; and when he sneezeth. . . ."[75]

The purpose was to push the reader away from vice by revealing it in its nakedness, a deciphering of troublesome attributes unseen by less discerning eyes and the less diligent conscious. "If though doe but read these . . . I have spent good houres ill; but if though shalt hence abjure those Vices; which before though thoughtest not ill-favoured, . . . or shalt hence find where thou hast any little touch of these evils, to cleare thy selfe . . . neither of us shall need to repent of our labour."⁷⁶ Hall, in fact, considered these works an efficient substitute for his sermons.⁷⁷

Hobbes uses this technique of charactery, although not in precisely the same way, in *De Cive*'s first chapter.⁷⁸ He was less hopeful for the reform of individuals, but he held out higher hopes for the possibility of the artificial man (the city or commonwealth) correcting its own faults. Thus, when Hobbes writes of the "true delights of Society unto which we are carryed by nauture," he describes this scene: "But it so happen, that being met, they passe their time in relating some Stories, and one of them begins to tell one which concerns himselfe; instantly every one of the rest most greedily desires to speak of himself too; if one relates some wonder, the rest will tell you miracles, if they have them, if not they'l feign them. Lastly, that I may say somewhat of them who pretend to wiser then others; if they meet to talk of Philosophy, look how many men, so many would be esteem'd Masteres, or else they not only love not their fellowes, but even persecute them with hatred."⁷⁹

Hobbes's remarks on why persons are anxious to be the last to leave the room ("we wound the absent") may also be added to the list. Here Hobbes does more than simply dissent from Aristotle's belief that we are born fit for political society. He also targets the dangerous flaws that he finds ineradicably seated in the vast majority. He lays them out and pushes the reader away from whatever faith he might have had that anything but fear will ensure peaceful sociability. As an empirical argument against Aristotle, these examples are not very convincing, but as a form of revealing scrutiny—typical of the aims of charactery—they aspire to something much more moving.

Audience and Argument in *Leviathan*

Finally there is *Leviathan*. Why is this text so laden with rhetorical twists, and how does Hobbes's use of rhetoric reflect the special characteristics of his audience? The most important member of *Leviathan*'s audience is the sovereign. Of course, in addressing the sovereign, Hobbes is now addressing one of his betters, and not just any better, but *the* better of all other betters (the one Hobbes would have outshine the rest like the sun outshines the stars).⁸⁰ Moreover, in this work Hobbes is not only presenting his doctrine in the best light in order to make it pleasing to those above him, but he is also making a case for his great desire to see it taught in the schools. In his conclusion, he reminds his readers of his wish: "I think it may be profitably printed, and more profitably taught in the Universities."[81] *Leviathan*, therefore, addresses those "to whom the judgment . . . belongeth."[82] Although their thoughts and desires count too, that judge is not, first and foremost, the individuals who might wish to escape the state of nature or a civil war. It is the sovereign who would be constituted and legitimized by their consent. He is not the subjects', nor Hobbes's, equal, but the power that determines what will be law and what will be taught. As the very condition that makes law and education possible, he stands above the coercive power of law and a philosopher's reason. He must, rather, be convinced to become the coercive force behind each: the power that makes the law binding and the power that will make Hobbes's constructions come true and be taught as the commonwealth's truth. *Leviathan*'s difficult task was to find the words both convincing and appropriate to making Hobbes's would-be sovereign see the worth of his doctrine and himself.

But how does one speak on behalf of a doctrine when addressing the sovereign? As in *De Cive* there is an asymmetry between the author and the audience, but in this case it runs in the opposite direction. A student may be taught a lesson; his reasoning may be put to the test, taxed; he may be cajoled and goaded. In the *Elements*, the enemy is met with Hobbes's intellectual weaponry, and so is subject to even more aggression. In *Leviathan*, Hobbes speaks to those who may approve or reject his request, and these persons are clearly under no obligation to submit to his reasoning. Moreover, attempting to force them to do so would be a tremendous breach of decorum, an act of unforgivable presumptuousness.

The sovereign (or potential sovereign) is no mere student, and cannot be addressed as such. Those responsible for safeguarding the commonwealth by ensuring that its citizens are taught the proper doctrine will want to know that the doctrine is the best available. In that it must be reasonable, its reasoning must be infallible. In that it will form the bulwark of the commonwealth's defense against seditious and dangerous views, they will want a demonstration of its strength, an illustration of its capacity to handily defeat its opponents. And, of course, it must be consistent with the commands of scripture. Here, I would suggest, are some of the critical standards by which Hobbes would have his doctrine approved and mandated at the universities.

All of these considerations must inform our sense of the rhetorical burden of *Leviathan*, but there is one more. The sovereign may have been the work's primary audience, but he was not the only audience. *Leviathan* was a public, not a private, communication to the sovereign. In reading *Leviathan* we are witnessing an author publicly addressing a sovereign. These contexts not only intensify the demands of decorum, but give the work the character of a spectacle. As a philosopher with a doctrine to defend, Hobbes may be likened to a gladiator. He must win favor by deftly sending his opponents down to defeat. Also like the gladiator, Hobbes cannot prove his merit by turning his weapon on those from whom he seeks favor. Nor can he ask his elevated audience to enter into the tussle.

This suggests a different interpretation of Hobbes's use of rhetoric than has been put forward previously. On this reading, Hobbes's views on the uses of rhetoric do not radically change, nor does his basic agenda—disciplining the commonwealth with his doctrine. What changes from the *Elements* to *De Cive*, to *Leviathan*, is the relation of Hobbes to his audience. If Hobbes does not toy with rhetoric when fighting with his equals and his inferiors in the arena of Parliament, it is because he believes his weapon of choice—his infallible logic—is the only appropriate tool for the intellectual violence he has mind. Rhetoric before (and accommodating of) an assembly (particularly one disposed toward "democratical" sentiments) is precisely the kind of the thing that he considers unacceptable. The free play of the passions cannot be permitted to those who must submit to rule. On the other hand, with those who already rule and from whom Hobbes seeks favor and to whom he defers, it is not his station to forbid them their amusements—indeed, as Aubrey's record of Charles II's remarks concerning "the beare" suggest, Hobbes sometimes *was* the king's amusement. His efforts must be devoted to demonstrating the worth of his efforts, but on the terms of those entitled to make the judgment.

If he cannot require his patron to follow his discourse and observe his triumphs as a subservient student, or opponent, he will allow himself to use eloquence in order to make his worth tangible. Here, then, is a legitimate use for the mocking tropes and other techniques, and one need not hold (as would seem suggested by Skinner's interpretation) that Hobbes would have approved of employing so many rhetorical devices under different circumstances.[83] On this reading, Hobbes's views on rhetoric remain largely unchanged and the differences that Skinner attributes to a *volte-face* in fact represent the aforementioned differences in the relation between Hobbes and his audiences.

Thus, the interpretation presented here inverts the conclusions drawn by some versions of the "audience thesis." Hobbes does not use rhetoric because he is trying to accommodate the broader audience. Quite the contrary. The loftier the primary audience, the greater the rhetorical display. Others, even many others, may observe him doing so, but his eloquence that operates in this context works contrary to the ideals of popular oratory and democratic governance. In Hobbes's hierarchical contexts, that which pleases the *patron* may augment its influence when it is also seen by many to do so, but it does not strive to please all its witnesses equally. The foremost audience, the sovereign, counts first and most. While such a work might be widely admired, Hobbes was ever mindful of who has the privilege of determining its merits. As we shall see in the treatment of *Behemoth*, eloquence might be excusable when it isn't used to excite the passions of the "democratical" masses (or to sustain a school doctrine destined to undermine the commonwealth). It is a permissible tool when it is employed for the sake of convincing those in the seats of authority to make the right doctrine the law (or the teaching) of the land.[84]

7

ALL OTHER DOCTRINES EXPLODED:
HOBBES, HISTORY, AND THE STRUGGLE OVER TEACHING

I have argued that Hobbes should be understood as having never departed from a humanist tradition in which teaching political skills through history played a prominent role. For those who have seen Hobbes's intellectual development otherwise, namely, as phased, his utilization of history could be taken as evidence of the existence of three phases. The author who began with a translation of Thucydides (and authored smaller anonymous historical works) in his early career might be said to have abandoned this first, humanist, phase for a more purely scientific phase when he wrote the *Elements of Law*. His return to history in *Behemoth* (Hobbes's account of the English Civil War, written during the Stuart Restoration) could be taken as evidence for a third phase in which he combines science and humanism.

As regards Hobbes's histories, I will make two arguments in conflict with the phased view. The first is arrayed against the view that abandoning humanism meant abandoning a view of the citizen as a man well prepared to engage in public oratory. Hobbes was from the beginning a humanist who did not ascribe to such a picture of the citizen. That is, he was already a participant in strains *within* the lettered community of Britain that had grown cynical about politics, and particularly cynical about the popular politics practiced in assemblies, notably Parliament. Indeed, the evidence presented here bolsters my earlier claim concerning Hobbes's disdain for eloquence used in the company of broader audiences. The second argument concerns *Behemoth* and his other antagonistic encounters with Presbyterians. These works provide some of the clearest evidence that Hobbes was seriously pursuing the goal of imposing his doctrine upon the schools, and that his mathematical aspirations were not a part of a scientifically neutral hiatus from political life—or humanism—but *a part of* an intensely political life. They also demonstrate that the strong antidemocratic strains were a persistent presence in his thought.

In short, the picture that I hope to present in this chapter is of Hobbes as a politically engaged pedagogue with an axe to grind over how subjects (high and low) should be educated. Hobbes's historical works, along with a polemic against Hobbes's plans for the universities, offer ample evidence for filling out this picture. Each work considered will be contextualized at some length. However, before I begin, I return to an earlier point concerning the Machiavellian sensibilities that historians (and some Hobbes scholars) see emerging when political events lead toward disillusionment.

Some British humanists of the late sixteenth and early seventeenth centuries had soured on the idealism of Ciceronian humanism that had been popular during earlier Elizabethan years. During the late Elizabethan and early Stuart years some had complained that politics had become a desperate and treacherous way of life.[1] Such shifts in fortune were echoed by a shift in the literature. Courtiers and literary patrons abjured idealistic calls to the virtuous life and grand political accomplishment. Their disaffection was accompanied by a move in the direction of authors who offered more skeptical views of human nature and the political life it fostered.

They now adopted a more suspicious style. Unless precautions were taken, they said, malice, foolishness, or some combination of these would ensure that virtuous men and their causes would suffer eventual defeat. They gave this advice to one another as courtiers, and it increasingly characterized the advice they gave to sovereigns. Although cruelty was openly lamented, kings in the early seventeenth century were advised that they would have to employ harsh methods and even trickery to keep their thrones. The ancient authors these humanists sought were chosen with the hope that they would help them prepare for a crueler world. By the beginning of the seventeenth century, Tacitus, ancient Stoics, and contemporary Neostoics such as Lipsius had won a growing following because they addressed themselves to the less dignified aspects of political life, and because they could speak to readers who felt that the reassurances of the old cosmic order were falling away.[2]

"A Discourse upon the Beginning of Tacitus"

"A Discourse upon the Beginning of Tacitus" was issued anonymously as a part of a collection of essays published in 1620 under the title *Horae Subsecivae* (Spare Time). It has been identified as Hobbes's.[3] The essay reflects the new fashion in Tacitist thought and its preoccupation with reason of state.[4] The work aspires to a Machiavellian sagacity.[5] Hobbes illustrates an unblinking admiration for the brutal accomplishments of Augustus, reservations concerning republican rule,[6] and sentiments that reflected the hardening political mentality of the age. He carefully examines, and praises for its efficacy and intelligence, Augustus's skillful conversion of a republic into a state (Hobbes says a monarchy) under his "absolute sovereignty."[7] As regards the skills and virtues necessary for political life, the idealistic humanism of republican glory is diminished and the cunning humanism of the courtly operator is acknowledged as necessary.

Noting the demise of the republic, Hobbes remarks on the new skills appropriate to Augustus's domination:

> They [Romans] find, that striving for equality, is not the best of their game, but obedience, and waiting on the command of him that had power to raise, or keep them low at his pleasure. For though other virtues, especially deep wisdom, great, and extraordinary valor, be excellent ones under any sort of government, and chiefly in a free State, (where therefore they thrive best, because they are commonly accompanied with ambition, and rewarded with honor) yet in the subject of a Monarch, obedience is the greatest virtue, and those before mentioned as they shall serve more, or less unto that, so to be had in less estimation. Therefore they now study no more the Art of commanding, which had been heretofore necessary for any Roman Gentleman, when the rule of the whole might come to all of them in their turns; but apply themselves wholly to the Arts of service; whereof obsequiousness is the chief, and is so long to be accounted laudable, as it may be distinguished from Flattery, and profitable, whilest it turn not into tediousness.[8]

Gentlemen need no longer concern themselves with ruling and being ruled in turn under this kind of regime. Judgments concerning decorum are here the more essential political skill. I argued, in Chapter 6, that such skills were put to work in *Leviathan*. In this Discourse Hobbes turns to the flaws of Agrippa (Augustus's grandchild, whom he exiled at the prompting of his conniving wife, Livia), and he notes, "He had not good education. That was the sum of all his faults."[9] A "good education," Hobbes explains, has less to do with acquiring a facility with letters (although he maintains their virtue) than with acquiring the skills necessary to handle oneself in the company of Roman power brokers:

> For where it was said, he was unfurnished of good Arts, it is not meant of letters, though that also be good in a Prince, and of ornaments the chief; for he may want these, rather than judgment, valor, or goodness of nature. But the Art that he is principally taxed to want, seems to have been the Art of conforming to times, and places, and persons, and

consists much in a temperate conversation, and ability upon just cause, to contain and dissemble his passions, and purposes; and this was then thought the chief Art of government.[10]

Decorum, not honesty, was the best policy here.

On the death of Germanicus, rumored by Tacitus to have been a murder commissioned by Tiberius (who had been forced by Augustus to adopt Germanicus, in accord with the emperor's wish to control the succession), Hobbes remarks that this element of Roman history is one "whereby [it] may be perceived in what danger an honest man stands, being near unto one that is ambitious, either before or behind him, whose nature is to destroy before him, out of hope; and behind him, out of fear."[11]

In Hobbes's reading of Tacitus, the well-prepared politico learns the importance of succession for patronage prospects. (Such thoughts might have been in the mind of Hobbes's uncle who sent him to Oxford—where he could expect to make important connections—in 1603, the same year that James I took the throne.)[12] At the same time, Hobbes's reader is taught to see public honors as a source of potential moral corruption. Commenting on the haughtiness of Tiberius, he remarks:

> Honors sometimes be of great power, to change a man's manners and behavior into the worse, because men commonly measure their own virtues, rather by acceptance that their persons find in the world, than by the judgment which their own conscience makes of them, and never do, or think they never need to examine those things in themselves. . . . Also honor many times confirms in men that intention wherewith they did those things which gained honor; which intention is as often vicious as virtuous. For there is almost no civil action, but may proceed as well from evil as from good.[13]

Hobbes lived in a world in which he suspected that public honors were often something other than a just reward for the virtuous. They could be a mask and justification for less than noble intentions.

Thucydides

Hobbes's 1628 translation of Thucydides's *Peloponnesian War* also reflects elements of this shift toward a skeptical politics.[14] In the dedicatory, as noted earlier, Hobbes informs William Cavendish[15] that in morally cloudy times, it was worth reading a historian such as Thucydides.[16] Pessimism and a warning to protect oneself from dangerous circumstances is stronger still in the essay "On the Life and History of Thucydides," which Hobbes wrote to accompany his translation. In this essay Hobbes remarks on Thucydides's wish to withdraw from the politics of democratic Athens. He takes care to approve of the historian's decision, giving particular emphasis to the travails of democratic politics: "It need not be doubted, but from such a master [Antiphon] Thucydides was sufficiently qualified to have become a great demagogue, and of great authority with the people. But it seemeth he had no desire at all to meddle in the government: because in those days it was impossible for any man to give good and profitable counsel for the commonwealth, and not incur the displeasure of the people."[17]

Thucydides knew to stay clear of democratic political life, even though it would seem that he had the skills to make himself popular with the Athenian assemblies. Extending the lesson to Hobbes's day, the right form of political education for the sons of noblemen (like Cavendish) was to stay clear of a politics dominated by Parliament. When the possibility exists of bearing the displeasure of the people, it was the duty of the tutor to teach political retreat or disengagement, while defiantly denouncing the political educations that had already corrupted political life.[18]

Hobbes also reflects on Parliament's relation to the Crown, at this time a difficult marriage. Courtiers whose policies Charles had endorsed, and who themselves had at one time enjoyed popularity with Parliament, were now finding themselves charged by that body with corruption and law-breaking. Francis Bacon and Buckingham suffered this fate. These scuffles gave rise to a debate over the forms of government. Courtiers dissatisfied with Parliament began to argue that Charles should abolish it. Malcolm Smuts has suggested that Hobbes's emphasis on the antidemocratic sentiments in Thucydides were of a piece with these antiparliamentary intents.[19]

In his attacks on the "democratical assembalie" Hobbes tends to emphasize their fickleness. He is concerned most of all with the way a crowd's erratic emotions can have disastrous effects on persons who attempt to court their favor.[20] Assemblies, he says, reward speakers because they use flattery to sway them—as was the case with Creon and the Athenian citizens in Thucydides's history. They therefore encourage demagogues rather than the men who give temperate advice. Persons who wisely counsel moderation are rejected as fools:

> For their opinion was such of their own power, and of the facility of achieving whatsoever action they undertook, that such men only swayed the assemblies, and were esteemed wise and good commonwealth's men,

as did put them upon the most dangerous and desperate enterprises. Whereas he that gave them temperate and discreet advice, was thought a coward, or not to understand, or else to malign their power. And no marvel: for much prosperity . . . maketh men in love with themselves; and it is hard for any man to love that counsel which maketh him love himself the less. And it holdeth much more in a multitude, than in one man.[21]

In his later works Hobbes often argued the converse. If assemblies tended to encourage vices in speakers, vicious speakers brought out the worst in assemblies. Individual judgment is affected in particularly damaging ways when a person is immersed in an assembly or crowd. He was particularly concerned with the capacity of demagogues to flatter and control the multitudes to suit their own good.

In *Elements of Law*, for example, he snidely describes the democratic assembly as "in effect, . . . no more than an aristocracy of orators, interrupted sometimes with the temporary monarchy of one orator" because deliberation in the contexts of an assembly will mean one superior orator (or a few) will govern because of his capacity to "sway the assembly to his own ends."[22] In *De Cive*, Hobbes answers those who make the case for the comparative superiority of governing assemblies by complaining of the abuses of monarchs. Specifically, they point to monarchs who use the public coffers to enrich their families and flattering councilors, or monarchs known to arbitrarily punish innocent subjects. His reply emphasizes that the problem is only magnified when sovereignty is held (inevitably) by demagogues in an assembly.[23]

In all his major works of political theory, Hobbes reserves a special scorn for what he saw as the typical mindlessness of the orators who excite the passions of the multitude. He employed histories and mythologies that support his views. Hobbes found in Sallust's history a model description of this misconduct in *Catiline*. Likewise in the mythology of Medea's trick on the daughters of Pelias (who were convinced they should tear their aged father to pieces in the hopes of returning him to his youth), he finds a parallel for those who fall under the spell of popular rebels.[24] In *Leviathan* Hobbes adds cautions against the proclivity of governing assemblies to be "dazzled" rather than reasoned with in receiving counsel—because there is no other way for an assembly to be given counsel but by public oratory.[25] In his discussion of counsel generally, as I have noted, Hobbes is concerned that counsel be delivered, when possible, to a sovereign in private and not in the context of an assembly, seeing also here a risk of manipulation through eloquent appeals to the passions.[26]

Returning to his analysis of Thucydides, Hobbes's prejudice against seeking to please a popular audience is pressed rather insistently in the part of *On the*

Life of and History of Thucydides that is devoted to determining Thucydides's ranking on the scale of ancient historians. Here Hobbes remarks on the evaluation of Dionysius of Halicarnassus (Greek rhetorician, d. 8 B.C.). Dionysius had proclaimed Herodotus and Thucydides *the most* eloquent historians of their distinct dialects (Ionian and Attic, respectively). Of the two, Dionysius had placed Thucydides second. According to Dionysius a history should be "grateful to such as shall read it." On this count Herodotus supersedes Thucydides, who had included a number of critical appraisals of his readers. Hobbes seizes on this and takes every opportunity to lionize Thucydides for choosing to write a history on different grounds: Thucydides's histories were less "grateful," but more honest—thereby equating Dionysius's "gratefulness" with pandering. Rather than indulge the Athenian audience's desire to see themselves praised, Thucydides taught a more valuable lesson to a people too accustomed to the flattery of public orators: "Men profit more by looking on adverse events, than on prosperity: therefore by how much men's miseries do better instruct, than their good success; by so much was Thucydides more happy in taking his argument, than Herodotus was wise in choosing his."[27]

Even in his early writings, therefore, we see Hobbes participating in a brand of humanist learning that disapproved of those who were eager to win the approval of popular audiences. The duty of a strong teacher of morals was to correct the vices of the audience, even if this meant spitting in the eyes of the public. It is not surprising that Hobbes during this time expressed his admiration for the poet and playwright Ben Jonson, whom he consulted when writing his essay on Thucydides.[28] Jonson had won an ironic popularity. His fame grew in part because he outwardly distanced himself from what he saw as the flattering and indulgent chivalric dramas of his predecessors. An inspiration to the cynical poets of the Restoration (who were also inspired by Hobbes), Jonson was smug and anxious to advertise his willingness to expose real human vices, rather than indulge the popular desire for heroics.[29]

Jonson and Hobbes were alike in that they demanded that audiences be exposed to the unattractive side of human conduct. They must be shown these things so that they may learn to avoid the vices that they witness. The historian's duty, as Hobbes himself puts it, is to record and display such events so that deeds of honor and dishonor appear plainly to those who should learn the difference. Drawing the contrast between himself and Dionysius, Hobbes writes:

> The historians that accord with his requirements will not only not profit students, but corrupt them with flattery: For he makes the scope of history, not profit by writing truth, but delight of the hearer, as if it were a song. And the argument of history, he would not by any means have

to contain the calamities and misery of his country; these he could have buried in silence: but only their glorious and splendid actions. Amongst the virtues of an historiographer, he reckons affection to his country; study to please the hearer; to write of more than his argument leads him to; and to conceal all actions that were not to the honour of his country. Most manifest vices.[30]

Hobbes's *coup de grâce* is to expose Dionysius for practicing according to the same corrupt standards he recommends to historians and educators. In a tone at once rustic and triumphant, Hobbes expounds on the glory that Dionysius might have expected when he elected to rank Herodotus over Thucydides: "What motive he had to it, I know not: but what glory he might expect by it, is easily known. For having first preferred Herodotus, his countryman, a Halicarnassian, before Thucydides, who was accounted the best; and then conceiving that his own history might perhaps be thought not inferior to that of Herodotus: by this computation he saw the honour of the best historiographer falling on himself. Wherein, in the opinion of all men, he hath misreckoned. And thus much for the objections of Denis of Halicarnasse."[31]

Behemoth

As I mentioned at the outset of this chapter, *Behemoth* was Hobbes's account and diagnosis of the English Civil War. Like the history he had written some forty years earlier, however, it was a work meant both to give an accounting of events and to be a guide to action in the present—especially on matters of how persons were to be educated. If the education reform issue most pressing at the time of his writing of his analysis of Thucydides was how young noblemen ought to approach politics in a time of conflict between the king and Parliament, the circumstances under which Hobbes composed *Behemoth* were different. Parliament was in the 1660s an advocate for revenge against those whom they held responsible for the rebellion against monarch and (the Anglican) church. And yet, as we shall see, questions of education and demagogues were as current as ever to Hobbes and to his contemporaries. Although we have no fixed date for the completion of *Behemoth*, we know that he was refused permission to publish the work in 1668.[32]

In 1660 the Stuarts were restored, although under circumstances which were bound to make many of their most loyal supporters unhappy.[33] Although the Parliament elected soon after the reintroduction of the monarchy (the Cavalier Parliament) began this period as a very strong advocate for both royal power and the restoration of the power of the Anglican Church, practical realities constrained Charles II's administration. Compromises with Presbyterians, including General Monck, who was essential to Stuart Restoration, resulted in a tense climate in which many persons associated with treachery by Royalists were able to hold positions in government and the church to which they had been appointed during the Interregnum.³⁴ The 1661 Act of Oblivion and Indemnity had been part of the Restoration settlement, prior to the election of the Cavalier Parliament, to the consternation of Royalists and loyal Anglicans, who joked that it was "an act of oblivion for his [Charles II's] friends, and indemnity for his enemies."³⁵ Of particular concern for our treatment of *Behemoth* was the fact that Presbyterians retained many positions at the pulpit, especially in London, and at the universities.³⁶ Bishop Burnet's account notes that they were making themselves popular with the people with stern oratory directed against the church and the government.³⁷ With the heated encouragement of the Cavalier Parliament a series of repressive measures were passed as regards the English clergy. This was the so-called Clarendon Code, although in some respects the restrictions were stronger than the Earl of Clarendon would have wished. He was courting moderate Presbyterians in order to preserve the uneasy consensus that had made the Restoration possible. Scottish Presbyterians were subject to more muscular persecution. One such measure against English dissenters, the "Five Mile Act," emerged, according to Burnet, in the context of the particularly difficult year of 1665. Just as Britain declared war against the Dutch (in the winter of 1664), plague hit London.

Many who could escape the plague in London did so, including Parliament. By the time of this legislation's passing it was holding its session in Oxford. London pulpits were also emptied out. Some were filled, to the further consternation of the Parliament and Anglican loyalists, with radical dissenters who preached against the "sins of the court and the ill-usage that they themselves had met with."³⁸ Their "ill-usage" was their persecution under the Act of Uniformity, which required "unfeigned assent and consent" to everything in the Book of Common Prayer (the Anglican standard), and a renunciation of the Solemn League and Covenant, the foundation of Presbyterianism.³⁹ The "Five Mile Act" was written with these ejected dissenters in mind, and it dictated that all those silenced by the Act of Uniformity had to take an oath declaring the unlawfulness of any call to arms against either the king or anyone commissioned by the king, and the unlawfulness of any call to alter either the church or the state. Those who refused this latest oath were forbidden from coming within five miles of any city, Parliament borough, or church where they had once served.[40]

Naturally, there is much else that might be mentioned within this context. A more complete picture would have to take note of the growing (and ultimately justified) suspicion of Charles II's sympathy for Catholicism (a source of anxiety for both Anglicans and Presbyterians), as well as his sympathy for a growing number of smaller sects (the Quakers, for example), who were further frightening a population desperate for peace and uniformity. Indeed, it is noteworthy that *Behemoth* was dedicated to Henry Bennet, the Earl of Arlington, Charles II's secretary of state for the south. Arlington, known to have quiet affinities for Catholicism and toleration, later withdrew his support for tolerationist policies for fear of its effect on Charles II's reign. He was also the nemesis of Hobbes's enemy, the Earl of Clarendon.[41] A full historical treatment of *Behemoth* awaits.

My goals, however, are limited. I have emphasized the continuity of Presbyterian officeholders and the Five Mile Act to illustrate that during the time of *Behemoth*'s composition, the questions of who occupied an office and how to censor the words and speech of public officers (including university faculty) were very much alive. Answering these questions will certainly be a start in understanding the political saliency of this text, and so with that goal in mind I will turn to Hobbes's account of the war.

In *Behemoth* Hobbes plainly asserts that the universities played a crucial role in fomenting the dissent that led to the war. He likens them to "Trojan horses" within the nation, and he puts the universities at the "core" of the rebellion,[42] but he begins by linking the Civil War to the misconduct of the people. They ought to have been "at his Majesty's [Charles I's] Command," but they were not. Instead, "the people were corrupted generally, and disobedient persons esteemed the best patriots." The question then arises: "But how came the people to be so corrupted? And what kind of people were they that could so seduce them?"[43]

Hobbes offers seven direct answers. To put them in brief, he lists: the Presbyterians, "the Papists," the Independents, those corrupted by democratic educations, the city of London, the ambitious and poor (either desperate for the social preferment accorded the victors or merely for wartime employment), and the ignorance of the people in general of their duty.[44] Hobbes does not accord each equal time. He passes quickly over some and subjects the Presbyterians and the "papists" to intense scrutiny. There is relatively little concerning the Independents. The Presbyterians and the democratically inclined are discussed in the same breath and the question of the people's knowledge of their duty is addressed in terms of the Presbyterian influence.

My focus will be on the Presbyterians and the universities.[45] According to Hobbes, the universities were in large measure responsible for creating and nurturing the Presbyterians. He paints them as an untrustworthy and subversive group. Presbyterians created rebellion, Hobbes maintained, by encouraging private opinions against the religious and secular authorities. They promoted these seditious doctrines because they had imbibed the poisonous Greek and Roman histories—histories Hobbes claimed were contrary to good order. Hobbes uses the same antidemocratic polemics that we saw earlier in *The Life and History of Thucydides* and which are also present in *Leviathan*.

Most scholars interested in the conflict have emphasized the differences between Presbyterian theology and the theology Hobbes defends in *Leviathan*.[46] At the core of their dispute was the question of spiritual authority, including questions of church governance. By the 1650s (if not before) Hobbes maintained a blanket opposition to any and all religious doctrines that limited the power of the sovereign over church affairs (including appointments) and religious doctrine.[47] This was the kind of doctrine that won him the hatred of both Anglicans and Presbyterians, but in *Behemoth* Hobbes focuses his attack on the Presbyterians.[48] Moreover, this attack resembles his attack on the pope and Roman Catholic theology in many respects. The two are, in fact, occasionally lumped together in *Leviathan*'s polemics.[49]

Jeffrey Collins has recently suggested that the abiding antagonisms within *Behemoth* against the Presbyterians are, in fact, a subtler and more far-reaching attack on "clericalism." That is, Hobbes was using the Presbyterians as whipping boys in an assault that reached a more potent enemy: the Anglican bishops, and their claim to a God-given authority beyond the full reach of the sovereign's power.[50] For Collins, this is further evidence of Hobbes's allegiance with Erastian strains within the English Reformation and his sympathies with Independents and Cromwellian rule. There is enough in Hobbes's written arguments against private conscience's right to political resistance to question this claim, but the mutual antagonism between Hobbes and Anglican authorities was certainly real. Collins's reading echoes their suspicions of a philosopher who fled, probably because of their ire, back to England before the Restoration. *Behemoth*'s appeal to absolutism and its dedication to a well-placed courtier with Catholic sympathies bespeak a sensibility that one may also find in Davenant's Restoration revisions of Shakespeare.[51] Those who dissent from the Anglican Church could seek the protection of an absolute sovereign. Such a sovereign might ignore alleged impiety so long as through political obedience the mortal god himself was publicly worshipped. Overlooking the sovereign's alleged impieties was also a part of the bargain. Anything else would lead to the factionalism and competition that could return the nation to civil war.[52]

In Hobbesian theology all but the sovereign are to be excluded from claiming a divine right to rule over scriptural matters. This was no small concern because it was toward scripture that radical Protestants turned to justify individual or sectarian claims to spiritual authority. Hobbes's theology allows for strictly private interpretation of scripture, but it also establishes a centralized spiritual authority in God's only chosen lieutenant on earth, the sovereign.[53]

Hobbes expected persons to wish to contemplate scripture and God's commands for themselves. He held that they may legitimately read scripture in the vernacular and devote their personal thoughts to it.[54] He set, however, severe restrictions against anyone who might claim the right or privilege to publicly teach others the meaning of scripture. All who publicly teach must derive this right from the sovereign, and they cannot teach conclusions contrary to those sanctioned by the sovereign's state church.[55] Hobbes made careful use of some of the prevalent theological notions of the day in order to establish these restrictions. As I have noted, Hobbes insisted that knowledge of God was above human capacity. Nevertheless, he was also willing to assert rules concerning what God's commands *were not*. Principally, they were not contrary to human reason: "For though there be many things in Gods Word above Reason; that is to say, which cannot by naturall reason be either demonstrated, or confuted; yet there is nothing contrary to it."[56] Human reason, moreover, dictates that one not question the word of the sovereign, and this applies to scriptural matters as well.[57]

Persons whose private convictions led them to conclusions contrary to those of the sovereign must keep these opinions to themselves; they cannot confess them publicly, let alone use them to claim spiritual authority within the state.[58] Contemporaries claiming supernatural access to God's word or will were subject to Hobbes's corrosive skepticism, a force powerful enough to eliminate the possibility of any credible claim.[59] All spiritual authority in the commonwealth flows from the sovereign office—no one, preacher, prophet, prelate, and so on, could claim the authority based on a direct grant or contact with God.[60] He made it impossible for anyone other than the sovereign to claim that God had granted him or her a right (or any form of authority) to rule over spiritual affairs.

The Presbyterians, accordingly, had violated this important rule.[61] John Wallis, a leading Presbyterian as well as the Savilian Professor of Mathematics, subscribed, for example, to the view that the powers of ordination over the ministry belonged in the hands of other pastors.[62] The Presbyterians had also sought to achieve some measure of control over the church's traditional powers of excommunication, a power exercised by the Church Courts when England was Catholic. The latter's authority had finally collapsed in the 1640s, and the Presbyterians were making a new claim to this power.[63]

What rhetorical task, therefore, did Hobbes take on in *Behemoth*? It was to persuade his audience (Arlington, but certainly Charles II as well) that they were locked in a competition with skillful and seditious enemies to achieve control over the universities and, therewith, the font of authority in England. In striving to make the case, *Behemoth* offers some of the strongest examples of Hobbes's willingness to attach strategic importance to the universities. He tells his sovereign that political education must come before one attempts to exercise power: "*A*. . . . I would have [the King] take from his enemies all hope of success, that they may not dare to trouble him in the reformation of the Universities. . . . The core of the rebellion, as you have seen by this, and read of other rebellions, are the Universities."[64] He then goes on to tell the king that he ought to use the universities to "make men know, that the people and the Church are one thing, and have but one head, the King, and that no man has title to govern under him, that has it not from him; that the King owes his crown to God only, and to no man, ecclesiastic or other."[65] *B*'s reply affirms the strategic aspects of Hobbes's message, and makes clear (again) that Hobbes was counting on a malleable, rather than a purely calculable, subject. The king is told that access to an army, to force, is not enough. Before all else, the universities need to be reformed in order to maintain peace:

> B. I think it is a very good course, and perhaps the only one that can make our peace amongst ourselves constant. For if men know not their duty, what is there that can force them to obey the laws? An army, you will say. But what shall force the army? Were not the trained bands an army?[66] Were they not the janissaries, that not very long ago slew Osman in his own palace at Constantinople? I am therefore of your opinion, both that men may be brought to a love of obedience by preachers and gentlemen that imbibe good principles in their youth at the Universities, and also that we shall never have a lasting peace, till the Universities themselves be in such manner, as you have said, reformed.[67]

Antitheatricality

Hobbes's use of the rhetoric of antitheatricality is a polemic device in *Behemoth* that is particularly worth detailed consideration for the way it connects Hobbes with a form of invective popular throughout the seventeenth century.[68]

Engaging this rhetoric, Hobbes offers a detailed analysis of the techniques the Presbyterians (and others) used to spread sedition throughout England.[69] The dialogue works to drive home the impression that the Presbyterians were masters of trickery. Hobbes has *A* uncover the deceptive means they employed to dispense their poison at the pulpit. To detect their "artifice" Hobbes instructs Charles to mind the expressions they wear, and the gestures that they perform as they make their entrance into the pulpit.[70] Readers are also advised, through *A*, to mark their pronunciation when they pray and in their sermons, so that their true intentions might be revealed.[71]

All this is typical of Renaissance antitheatrical rhetoric, and its presence here is no accident. Stage-players had become one of the more popularly dreaded social types in seventeenth-century England. What frightened Englishmen most about actors was their special ability to put on the appearance of someone else. Such fears generated an extensive antitheatrical literature. Indeed, Ben Jonson, aside from dragging the acting profession over the coals, diagnosed personal and social ills in terms of its pretense and feigning.[72] By comparing Presbyterian preachers with actors Hobbes was emphasizing the dangers they presented in a familiar way.

Popular imagination was particularly captured by the possibility that these persons would have the capacity to mimic persons of integrity or honor (or, pursuing a different kind of sham, imitating those who were truly deserving of charity). It was feared they would abuse the unsuspecting by claiming privileges and authority to which they were not entitled. Similarly, they might win undeserved trust through false promises of service to individuals or the state to gain favor or lucre.[73] Playing to such fears, Hobbes proclaims, "No tragedian in the world could have acted the part of a right godly man better than these did."[74] In a world that differentiated persons on the basis of *possessed* talents and virtues, the skill of imitating the virtuous, or the deserving, was particularly threatening.

Threats and Their Solutions

In book 4 of *Behemoth*, Hobbes takes a slightly different tack. He continues to remind Charles of the trickery of the Presbyterians,[75] yet his efforts emphasize less the deviousness of Presbyterians and insist instead on the vulnerability of Englishmen. Turning from the techniques of Presbyterian trickery, Hobbes emphasizes the potency and magnitude of the threat. He suggests that this threat requires a unique solution—the teaching of his own science of politics.

Reviewing the disastrous policies of the Rump Parliament, *B* interjects, "What silly things are the common sort of people, to be cozened as they were so grossly!" *A*'s response is quite telling of Hobbes's political purposes, and is worth quoting at length:

> What sort of people, as to this matter, are not of the common sort? The craftiest knaves of all the Rump were no wiser than the rest whom they cozened. For the most of them did believe that the same things which they imposed upon the generality, were just and reasonable; and especially the great haranguers, and such as pretended to learning. For who can be a good subject to monarchy, whose principles are taken from the enemies of monarchy, such as were Cicero, Seneca, Cato, and other politicians of Rome, and Aristotle of Athens, who seldom speak of kings but as of wolves and other ravenous beasts. You may perhaps think a man has need of nothing else to know the duty he owes to his governor, and what right he has to order him, but a good natural wit; but it is otherwise.[76]

"Good natural wit" is insufficient against the subversive temptations of democratic literature, according to this polemic. The nation therefore needs something more. It needs the training Hobbes's science of politics could deliver. It needs "a science, . . . built upon sure and clear principles, and to be learned by deep and careful study, or from masters that have deeply studied it."[77] Those who count on nature, rather than Hobbes's doctrine, are once again chided for their imprudence. Indeed, what were once in his earlier descriptions the contemptible masses with passions set aflame by conniving demagogues become, here at least, more like helpless victims powerless to resist the trickery of their eloquent deceivers unless Hobbes's science comes to their rescue. Hobbes then plays still further on these fears of corruption. Not only has England lacked the special instruction it needs to save itself from the corrupting, "democratical" doctrines promoted by the Presbyterians, but many of the pulpits that ought to have been preaching obedience were in fact preaching the very sedition the Crown needed most to combat:

> And who was there in the Parliament or in the nation, that could find out those evident principles, and derive from them the necessary rules of justice, and the necessary connexion of justice and peace? The people have one day in seven the leisure to hear instruction, and here are ministers appointed to teach them their duty. But how have those ministers

> performed their office? A great part of them, namely the Presbyterian ministers, throughout the whole war, instigated the people against the King; so did also independent and other fanatic ministers. . . . The mischief proceeded wholly from the Presbyterian preachers, who, by a long practiced histrionic faculty, preached up the rebellion powerfully.[78]

From *Behemoth* it becomes clear that Hobbes had an implicit three-step notion of how ideas are communicated to the people. The sovereign determines the doctrine to be taught at the universities. The universities teach, and thereby legitimate, compatible opinions and beliefs. Those who hold degrees, or read the works of persons with university degrees, or take training in divinity go out and, according to Hobbes, influence the views of the broader public.[79] Only this special training can help England get out from under the spell of corrupting educations—educations put forth by Presbyterians and the like. Hobbes's argument follows a straightforward logic. It is an argument about the corrupting influence of his opponents, and a proposal for an alternative political education as the antidote to the poisonous effects of their doctrine.

As the conversation over the abuses of the Presbyterian ministers continues, *B* asks "to what end" the Presbyterians pursue such actions:

> *A*. To the end that the State becoming popular, the Church might be so too, and governed by an Assembly; and by consequence (as they thought) seeing politics are subservient to religion, they might govern, and thereby satisfy not only their covetous humour with riches, but also their malice with power to undo all men that admire not their wisdom. Your calling the people silly things, obliged me by this digression to show you, that it is not want of wit, but want of the science of justice, that brought them into these troubles. . . . They wanted not wit, but the knowledge of the causes and grounds upon which one person has a right to govern, and the rest an obligation to obey; which grounds are necessary to be taught the people, who without them cannot live long in peace amongst themselves.[80]

As we saw, Hobbes's conflict with the Presbyterians was theologically substantive. I have tried to augment this view with an appreciation of Hobbes as a seventeenth-century English political participant—that is, as a polemicist/courtier who encourages the king's suspicions of his enemies—to come to a more concrete understanding of his position in this thoroughly unpleasant conflict. *A* goes so far as to claim that Presbyterian ministers bore responsibility for all the deaths in England caused by the Civil War, and that it would have been preferable had they been massacred instead. Appealing to the memory of Charles II's father, he writes: "Our late King, the best King perhaps that ever was, you know, was murdered, having been first persecuted by war, at the incitement of Presbyterian ministers; who are therefore guilty of the death of all that fell in that war; which were, I believe, in England, Scotland, and Ireland, near 100,000 persons. Had it not been much better that those seditious ministers, which were not perhaps 1000, had been all killed before they had preached? it had been (I confess) a great massacre; but the killing of 100,000 is a greater."[81] Could there be stronger evidence that Hobbes was an engaged political participant, and that his understanding of the Civil War was something other than an abstract perception about the challenges of human nature?

War Years, Education Reform, and Ward's Accusations

How aggressive was Hobbes's approach to matters of political education? One answer takes us back to the beginning of the Civil War. Earlier I mentioned Hobbes's conflict with Seth Ward and Hobbes's telling response to his accusations. As we shall see, the ambitiousness of Hobbes's education reform plans were enough to win him comparisons with some of the most radical would-be reformers of the seventeenth century. Hobbes's reply to his critics, moreover, did not pull any punches. In fact, in rejecting the description of his critics, Hobbes was willing to link his plan for an education under the sovereign's control with models of doctrinal discipline even more scandalous than his critics had imagined.

As the war between Charles I and Parliament began, censorship controls lost their effectiveness, and a flurry of publications concerning the reform of education surfaced in a newly expanded and explosive public sphere.[82] Charles Webster links the Laudian oppression with the great number and diversity of education reform schemes among oppositional Protestant sects. According to Webster, Laud created a backlash, and perhaps also a fresh precedent, in which

> all parties knew that it was necessary to control education. Accordingly the Puritans, when in power, submitted the teachers and academics as well as the ministry to religious and political tests; but the degree of positive guidance which the administration exercised was never sufficient to satisfy the educational reformers. . . . Teachers had the capacity to promote or to destroy human happiness. They were doctors of

minds (*Medicos animarum*), capable of curing the desperate ailments of the church and state. . . . The reformers believed that until parliament could be persuaded to adopt a broader definition of its educational role, it would not be able to consolidate its military victories or establish a stable puritan state.[83]

Hobbes was therefore not alone in seeking out authorities (and patrons) in order to implement educational solutions to the nation's troubles.

Some of the most noteworthy publications came from within the circle of international Protestant innovators associated with the Polish émigré Samuel Hartlib. They enjoyed a certain authority with the revolutionary parliaments and Cromwell.[84] Their schemes often entailed more comprehensive approaches to education than had been customary: not only would the traditional supervisors of the nation (teachers and ministers) be themselves supervised, but the nation itself would feel the instructive influence of state councils designed to ensure that persons employ themselves and their property in the most rational manner possible.[85]

Like Hobbes, these reformers envisioned strictly enforced doctrines to keep discipline over the nation. Hartlib's *Marcaria* was a utopian work written to promote his circle's vision of a reformed England.[86] In it a Traveller and a Scholar discuss the amazing discovery of this well-ordered and prosperous realm. The interlocutors discuss the society's various innovations, including the state's means of supplying itself with obedient divines. This discussion resonates with Hobbes's own approach:

> *Sch.* . . . But how cometh the facilitie of becoming good Divines?[87]
> *Trav.* They are all of approved abilitie in humane learning, before they take in hand that function, and they have such rules, that they need no considerable studie to accomplish all knowledge fit for Divines, by reason that there are no diversitie of opinions amongst them.
> *Sch.* How can that be?
> *Trav.* Very easily: for they have a law, that if any Divine shall publish a new opinion to the Common people, he shall be accounted a disturber of the publick peace, and shall suffere death for it.[88]

Some education reformers radically outpaced traditional humanists in pushing for useful educations. John Webster greatly deemphasized the need to teach and learn classical sources in the English language, and demanded a practical education that mixed the education of the clergy with mechanical arts, including extensive instruction in mathematical sciences.[89]

The basic assumption, however, was that the educational institutions would be used to cultivate obedient and usefully employed individuals, all within a given conception of the right social order. The reformers may have argued over varying conceptions of the improved student, varying visions of the right social order, and the appropriate persons and methods for instructing boys (and in some cases, girls) and men (and women) in practices of obedience.[90] The commonwealths imagined by the school reformers were diverse, and often utopian; these included plans for universal education, educations in horticulture, a variety of crafts (inclusive of mathematical, natural magical, and alchemical educations), and communism, according to some of their twentieth-century celebrants.[91] The basic and unquestioned assumption of these debates, however, was that schools should deliver the social discipline, whatever that discipline may be. I am not making these comparisons for the sake of wedding Hobbes to a particular religious creed, but to illustrate that for Hobbes and his contemporaries the question of education reform was often part and parcel of what it meant to have a political dispute.[92] All such political actors, including Hobbes, had their particular visions of human nature and the rightly ordered state. None of them assumed that human nature itself would generate this state. They placed the burden on themselves as educators, and on the subjects as students. Princes had to do their part and order that their doctrines be taught.

Many radical reformers met with frustration.[93] Only one radical was installed as a head of a college at Cambridge (William Dell, Caius College, Cambridge, 1649–60), and he often kept his distance from Cambridge.[94] Cromwell had reassured the universities that he would attempt to keep them functioning under his rule (in years previous Cambridge had to put a halt to instruction). Traditional annual royal celebrations and ceremonies were revived, with Cromwell playing the part of king in these affairs.[95]

The Protectorate provided a period of relative stability for Oxford and Cambridge. Within, scholars embraced an understanding of the universities as keepers of social order and tended to be very selective and suspicious when it came to the consideration of modifications.[96] Among these were a number of Hobbes's dreaded Presbyterians, including his rival, the Savilian Professor of Mathematics (and a member of the Royal Society), John Wallis.[97]

More radical thinkers were outside the universities, lobbying for further changes. Established academics at the universities made an effort to defend their institutions against such threats. As noted, one of the tracts written as a defense was *Vindiciae Academiarum*, by Seth Ward (Savilian Professor of Astronomy at Oxford) and John Wilkins[98] in 1654; it was intended as a response to John Webster's (rather extensive) critique, *Academiarum Examen* (1653).[99]

Vindiciae Academiarum is appropriately classed with a series of ongoing broadsides between Hobbes, Ward, and John Wallis (although Wallis did not help author this particular piece).[100] A great deal was at stake in these frequently vicious contests. In the conflict over the universities, while the specifics of the accusations changed, opposing sides played very heavily on linkages between moral and intellectual habits. Ward and Wilkins accuse their opponents of suffering from deficiencies either moral or intellectual, or both.[101] This was particularly the case in their assault on Webster.

Webster is charged with "ignorance of the present state of our Universities which he pretends to reform," and "ignorance in the common grounds of those Arts and Sciences which he undertakes to advance and promote."[102] Wilkins and Ward also cite his rustic rhetoric, argumentative style, and conclusions: "It is enough to nauseate and make a man sick to peruse his crude and jejune Animadversions upon *Logick, Mathematick, Physickes, Metaphysickes, &c.* with the expedients or remedyes which he proposes, wherein he has abused some good Authors, by his ill managing the notions that they have suggested to him."[103]

The most interesting item in *Vindiciae Academiarum* is an appendix associating Hobbes with the radical attack on the universities. (There is a second appendix item containing a brief attack on William Dell.) Ward and Wilkins state that they expect that Hobbes will be scornful to find himself "ranked with a Friar and Enthusiast" (namely, Dell and Webster). "The Answer to this," they wrote, "if he complaine, will be, we found him *inter Grues* [among the philosophical sect/herd], and could not without prejudice let him escape."[104] Like Webster, Hobbes is accused of not knowing what actually goes on at the universities, and with raising false, ridiculous, spiteful, and vindictive charges against the universities, the faculty, and the curriculum.

They begin by specifying Hobbes's "1. End and Design, 2. Judgement, concerning the meanes of attaining it. 3. Expectations as to the successe of his Designe, and the consequences of it."[105] Hobbes's end is that the "world" be "regulated exactly, by that modell which he there exhibits [in *Leviathan*], and that his reason should be the governing Reason of Mankind."[106] To Hobbes's judgment that "*his truth of Speculation may be converted into the utility of practice,*"[107] they respond with an accusation that he pursues "the *publicke Teaching of his Leviathan:* which he would *have protected by the exercise of entire Sovereignty.*"[108] Ward and Wilkins review the passage from chapter 30 (section 14) of *Leviathan* concerning the duty of sovereigns with regard to universities ("or is it you will undertake to teach the universities?"). Ward and Wilkins conclude, "His immediate desire and judgement is therefore, that his *Leviathan* be *by entire sovereignty imposed upon the Universities*, there to be read, and publickly taught."[109] To the last (the expectation and consequences attendant on Hobbes's possible success), they conclude that Hobbes believes that only by teaching his *Leviathan* can the universities can be made useful. Not satisfied to have his works looked upon as those of a "private author," Hobbes would have them mandated by the sovereign.[110] They make plain their view that this would be disastrous.[111]

The strategy of Ward and Wilkins (and of Wallis) was to argue that Hobbes was a philosophic megalomaniac, and an old and now incompetent man grown unaccustomed to questioning his own beliefs. He would therefore maintain his position dogmatically whenever he met opposition.[112] The fact that Hobbes had importuned the king to mandate that his doctrines be taught at the universities was taken as testimony to the truth of this characterization. In Wallis's 1662 attack, *Hobbius Heauton-timorumenos; or, A Consideration of Mr. Hobbes his Dialogues, In an Epistolary Discourse, Addressed to the Honourable Robert Boyle*, Hobbes's intentions to become "Dictator in Philosophy; Civil and Natural; in Schools and Pulpits"[113] became a part of an elaborate case against the philosopher's character:

> And to this *Fretful* Humour, (Torment enough alone) You must adde Another, as bad, which feeds it. You are therefore next to consider him, as one highly *Opinionative and Magisterial. Fansiful* in his conceptions, and deeply *Enamoured with those phantasmes*, without a Rival. He would be thought, of All that *are*, or ever *have been*, the onely *knowing* Man. And he doth not spare to professe, upon all occasions, How *incomparably* he thinks Himself to have *surpassed All*, Ancient, Modern, Schools, Divines, Heathens, Christians; How *Despicable* he thinks all Their writings, in comparison of His; and, What Hope he hath, That, *by the Sovereign command of some Absolute Prince, all other Doctrines being exploded, his new Dictates should be peremptorily imposed, to be alone taught in all Schools, and Pulpits, and universally submitted to.*[114]

Indeed, the title of this work, *Hobbius Heauton-timorumenos*, was a reference to *Heautontimorumenos* ("The Self-Tormentor"), a play adapted from Menander by Terence that portrays a very cranky old man who learns to regret tormenting the younger generation.[115]

Hobbes's response to *Vindiciae Academiarum* does nothing to refute the charge concerning the imposition of his doctrine at the universities; rather, it confirms it.[116] The reply is a major part of the sixth lesson of his *Six Lessons to* the (Savilian) *Professors of Mathematics*.[117] Responding specifically to the assertion that he wanted to have his work taught in the schools, he defends the decision to write works that promote the teaching of "civil doctrine" in the universities. He asserts that the cause of his writing *Leviathan* was his "consideration of what the ministers before, and in the beginning of, the civil war, by their preaching and writing did contribute thereunto."

> Which I saw not only to tend to the abatement of the then civil power, but also to the gaining of as much thereof as they could (as did afterwards more plainly appear) unto themselves. I saw also that those ministers, and many other gentlemen who were of their opinion, brought their doctrines against the civil power from their studies in the Universities. Seeing therefore that so much as could be contributed to the peace of our country, and the settlement of sovereign power without any army, must proceed from teaching; I had reason to wish, that civil doctrine were truly taught in the Universities. And if I had not thought that mine was such, I had never written it. . . . To me therefore that never did write anything in philosophy to show my wit, but, as I thought at least, to benefit some part or other of mankind, it was very necessary to commend my doctrine to such men as should have the power and right to regulate the Universities.[118]

The only point he contradicts is the claim that *Leviathan* would be publicly taught: "I say my doctrine; I say not my *Leviathan*. For wiser men may so digest the same doctrine as to fit it better for a public teaching."[119] Here Hobbes refers to the duty of those who must teach and preach his doctrine publicly, once they have learned it themselves in the universities.

With regard to the notion that his doctrines were in any way harmful to the commonwealth by being imposed on the universities, he responded: "You often upbraid me with thinking well of my own doctrine; and grant by consequence, that I thought this doctrine good; I desire not therefore that anything should be imposed upon them, but what (at least in my opinion) was good both for the Commonwealth and them. Nay more, I would have the state make use of them to uphold civil power, as the Pope did to uphold the ecclesiastical."[120]

In fact, Hobbes seemed at times a very attractive figure to those who wished to appeal to civil powers in order to put down powerful religious establishments, and this appeal pulled in both anti-Presbyterian Independents in England and Catholic anti-Jesuits in France. This may explain why Hobbes was admired and at times courted by both Henry Stubbe[121] and François du Verdus.[122]

Conclusion

Hobbes belongs to that small club of individuals who managed to effect within their persons a curious combination of rigorous modern philosophical thought and thorough political engagement. In this chapter and the previous I have drawn out the thick connections between political life and Hobbes's decisions as a writer. He had a philosophical doctrine to promote, defend, and (as I suggested) even take into a political battle. It is because of this curious combination that the question of rhetoric also proves interesting when studying Hobbes's work. As noted, the relationship between humanism's foremost political instrument—rhetoric—and philosophical reason has been so influential that it has supplied the framework in which interpreters have marked what they see as key transitions in Hobbes's thought and career. In Hobbes, the *political* philosopher, we have found a microcosm of a particularly modern predicament: can reason alone—abstract, precise, and demanding—be made to work in the messy domains of political life? In finding a Hobbes who goes through phases—one who begins within the humanist tradition, who then departs from it to pursue a mathematical philosophy (including a mathematical political doctrine), and then turns back into a philosopher who implicitly understands the hubris of his assumption concerning the power of reason in the political domain—interpreters such as Skinner and others have found a valuable lesson for those engaged in politics who seem overconfident in their assumptions concerning reason in the political realm.

I have been arguing throughout this book for a different reading of Hobbes. Although I would not wish to suggest that everything Hobbes thought flowed naturally from his humanism—we must give him credit for his individual intelligence, imagination, and daring on both counts—I have assembled evidence that Hobbes in no way had to *depart* from humanism to adapt a mathematically inspired way of thinking. We should think of Hobbes as an intellect exposed to a number of influences simultaneously, and from the very start of his career. These include humanism, and (as I have noted in this chapter) especially the strand of early modern British humanism that had become disillusioned with political life in general, and with popular parliamentary politics in particular. He was also exposed to scholasticism and Aristotelianism, against which he staged his own mathematical rebellion, one that illustrated a residual dependency on Aristotelian approaches to philosophical reasoning. Finally, Hobbes was exposed early on to mathematical thought. As illustrated in Chapter 2, this enthusiasm for mathematical learning drew support from some (although not all) humanist educators who saw in mathematics an example of clarity and useful learning with which to scold the practices and habits of the schools. As I shall discuss in Chapter 8, the enthusiasm for things mathematical was further bolstered in the Stuart Court. We should see the rhetorical characteristics—the humanism of the early modern British court—and mathematics as coming together in *Leviathan*.

What, then, of the larger lessons to be drawn concerning reason and rhetoric, or reason and humanist political engagement? In spite of the disagreement I have with the traditional "phased" views of Hobbes's career, I believe that Hobbes still, and perhaps now more than ever, can be usefully viewed as a scholar whose work is a microcosm of the problems we face today in trying to negotiate the relations between reason and politics. For if Hobbes was not so very far removed from political life when he turned to mathematics—if he was not optimistic and naïve but politically seasoned and capable when he turned to mathematics—then the lesson of Hobbes's career suggests something different. In the argument presented here, Hobbes emerges not as a philosopher who thought he could do without the skills of the politically engaged, but as a figure who understood that turning to mathematics in defense of his absolutist doctrine was politically suited to the goals he and his patrons were seeking. In short, we cannot see Hobbes's contemporary critics as having simply launched an assault on an arrogant philosopher who hungered for recognition. He was not seeking to recruit sovereign assistance for the sake of merely forcing fellow academics to accept his views, or to increase his fame. Those who see Hobbes's polemics with his fellow mathematicians (and other learned rivals) as nothing more than a rough, seventeenth-century version of contemporary academic dispute miss what was at stake. Hobbes was very blunt about why he thought reason needed to win the day. It needed the coercive force of the state. Rhetoric was for Hobbes a key means of securing this force. Today, for us, Hobbes must therefore be a negative exemplar. As we shall see, reason itself was more than a little subject to the temptations of pride.

It should also be noted that the phased views of Hobbes (as well as those that turn Hobbes into the object of a hermeneutic sneak attack) also fit neatly into a number of critical narratives (some postmodern) that emphasize the paucity of political awareness characteristic of the moderns and modern political thinkers. While I have sympathy with the spirit of some of these critiques, I have put forward a reappraisal of Hobbes that contradicts some of their basic assumptions.

8

THE HUMANIST FACE OF HOBBES'S MATHEMATICS, PART 2:
LEVIATHAN AND THE MAKING OF A MASQUE-TEXT

Thus far, I have discussed Hobbes's enthusiasm for mathematics largely in terms of his relationships to humanist educators and fellow mathematicians. I also noted that Hobbes's thoroughgoing materialism was central to his positions in these debates. What I have not done is show how Hobbes's humanism and his materialism, in the broadest sense, come together. This chapter will be focused on various aspects of what I have called the "high culture" of mathematics in the seventeenth century.

Among Hobbes's papers at Chatsworth there are sketch plans for two gardens (figs. 2 and 3) and a fortress (fig. 4).[1] These designs are typical of the high mathematical culture. What is particularly noteworthy about all three of these designs is that each involves a combination of circles, or (as in figure 3) semicircles, enclosed within squares. The angle formed by the battlements of the fortress (fig. 4), although not fully represented, forms a square enclosing the fortress's circular walls, a point illustrated by the dotted line on the original connecting the sides of two of the battlements.[2] Hobbes had attempted, and of course failed, to square the circle. These rudimentary sketches in his possession were likely preliminary designs to memorialize what might have been. They were to memorialize what would have been a crowning mathematical accomplishment. That Hobbes kept such sketches, perhaps even made them himself, can be no more than a probable sign of his participation in the culture that I describe. The best evidence of Hobbes's connection to, indeed his participation in, the high culture of mathematical enthusiasm is to be found in his published texts. In *Leviathan* Hobbes makes his greatest appeal to the passion for practical mathematics that already existed in the Stuart Court. Nevertheless, rough drawings that may seem to be little more than humiliating reminders of an impossible aspiration suggest how Hobbes, or his patrons, might have wanted his accomplishment recognized. Mere agreement that he had in fact squared the circle may not have been enough. Within a culture in which his patrons, the Crown, and many gentlemen had long since developed

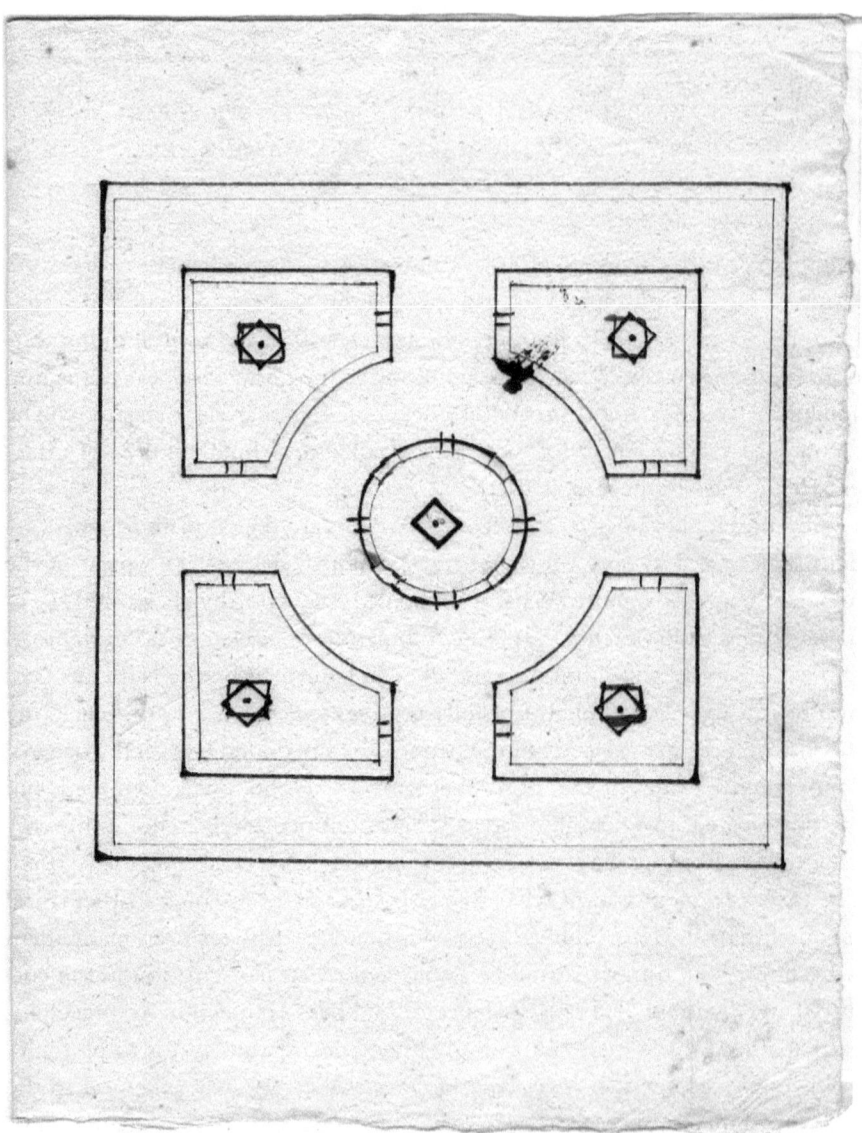

Fig. 2 Sketch plan for a garden. © Devonshire Collection, Chatsworth. Reproduced by permission of Chatsworth Settlement Trustees.

Fig. 3 Sketch plan for a garden. © Devonshire Collection, Chatsworth. Reproduced by permission of Chatsworth Settlement Trustees.

Fig. 4   Sketch plan for a fortress. © Devonshire Collection, Chatsworth. Reproduced by permission of Chatsworth Settlement Trustees.

a connoisseur's sensibility for the magnificent things produced by practical mathematicians, Hobbes's designs for the memorials would have been especially apt. They would be a material, practical mathematical expression of his skills as a geometer. For Hobbes geometry is ineradicably bodily; it was simply the most precise way to manipulate matter. In these memorials matter itself—whether fortress walls or hedgerows—would be made to give ostentatious testimony to his status as its master-manipulator.

Following a discussion of the assumptions that have traditionally concealed the connections between Hobbes and the high culture of mathematics, I describe Hobbes's relation to the mathematical interests of his patrons (especially William Newcastle) and to his patron's patrons (and eventually his own), the kings Charles I and Charles II. I discuss the artisans and humanists who actually helped nobles (and would-be gentlemen) associate themselves with mathematical ways. Gentlemen and noblemen wished to possess the virtues associated with mathematical learning and the material fruits of this learning. This analysis leads to a comparison between the court masque, where the high culture of mathematical learning reached its apogee, and *Leviathan*, which we can see as a masque-text.

Background Practices: Architecture, Art, Patronage, and Competitive Mathematical Learning

Let me return to the comparison of Mulcaster and Hobbes given above at the close of Chapter 2. Both embraced mathematics as an element of a proposed plan for education reform. Mulcaster gave mathematics an equal place with the other learned disciplines: his plan included a distinct school for mathematics, as it did for the more conventional subjects, such as grammar. By contrast, Hobbes put all his eggs in one basket. He made geometry his absolute standard: other disciplines would have to do what they could to emulate the practices of geometry and would be measured against its successes. Hobbes, moreover, promised to accomplish greater things with mathematical reason—things Mulcaster would have found overambitious, inappropriate, and even impious. Mulcaster counseled mathematicians to follow nature; Hobbes exhorted them to be creators, competitors with nature.

As we move from elite humanist pedagogues of the prior century to the seventeenth century's producers and consumers of mathematical learning and practices, the question becomes: What did the mathematically trained student do with his skills? Why did he value these skills, and how do these valuations coincide with Hobbes's understanding of the fruits of mathematical learning? As with other aspects of education in the Renaissance and early modern period, perceptions of social standing influenced what persons did with learning, *how* they found it useful, and the way they chose to associate themselves with it. One could choose to *be mathematical* in Hobbes's age, but what it meant to make mathematical ways an element of one's identity involved a complex set of considerations linked to a social hierarchy.[3]

With the exception of Mulcaster (who approved of expanding mathematical training to tradesmen), the humanists reviewed in Chapter 2 took it for granted that their arguments in favor of mathematical learning made the case for giving *gentlemen* a mathematical education. It was possible, even beneficial, they claimed, for gentlemen to acquire mathematical habits of mind. As noted in our discussions of Vives, Ascham, and Mulcaster, this position was not universally held. Some educators feared that the mathematically trained head might become argumentative or lost in the clouds of abstraction—skills not suited to those who, especially at court, must maintain pleasing conversation and cordial relations. Hobbes himself was criticized for failing on this score, even by those who favored mathematical education.[4]

In spite of the reputation his critics helped create for him as an ungentlemanly debater, genteel uses for mathematics are distinctly relevant to Hobbes's affinity for the subject. If Hobbes has not been associated with these uses in the twentieth century, it is not because of the efforts of his seventeenth-century critics, but because of the assumptions of conventional views of his career that persist today.

Reason, Passion, Mathematics, and Modernity

Many political theorists discuss Hobbes's mathematical proclivities within a framework that associates him with the cold hard rationalism of modern social science. On such a view, mathematics would seem the route to a passionless, calculating, and impersonal modality of life and thought. Hobbes in particular has been understood as the champion of life-numbing mathematical reason over passion. At the risk of repetition, it is worth returning to what Hobbes tells his patron in the dedication to the *Elements of Law*:

> From the two principal parts of our nature, Reason and Passion, have proceeded two kinds of learning, mathematical and dogmatical. The former is free from controversies and dispute, because it consisteth in comparing figures and motion only; in which things truth and the interest

of men oppose not each other. But in the later there is nothing not disputable, because it compareth men, and meddleth with their right and profit; in which, as oft as reason is against a man, so oft will a man be against reason. And from hence it cometh, that they that have written of justice and policy in general, do all invade each other, and themselves, with contradiction. To reduce this doctrine to the rules and infallibility of reason, there is no way, but first to put such principles down for a foundation, as passion not mistrusting, may not seek to displace; and afterward to build thereon the truth of cases in the law of nature (which hitherto have been built in the air) by degrees, till the whole be inexpugnable. Now (my Lord) the principles fit for such a foundation, are those which I have heretofore acquainted your Lordship withal in private discourse, and which by your command I have here put into method.[5]

In spite of the expectations this passage might create, Hobbes's works as a whole illustrate both the difficulties of excluding the passions, as well as a program to recruit, rather than exclude, passion where necessary, advantageous, or—as I hope to show—already at work in reason's gratifying image of itself.

Of course, the passions are never entirely banished from the practices of those who claim to fight on the side of reason over passion. Philo-sophy is itself a profession of love, and Plato's philosophers are as much in love with the life spent in contemplation of the forms, as they detest the life among unphilosophical men. Allegedly dispassionate reason, moreover, is often found playing the part of hero and savior, or the insulted and aggrieved victim. Although Hobbes did not attempt to entice his students by following Plato in encouraging love of a transcendent ideal, even he makes a very straightforward attempt to recruit defectors from among the politically disruptive passions to his side of the conflict. Hobbes sought the assistance of fear, of a violent death in particular, rather than fight a polarized battle between (his) reason and all the other passions (of others).[6] The aspiration for a foundation that the passions do not *mistrust*, therefore, did not necessarily exclude the possibility of a foundation that certain passions might embrace. Curiosity, the desire (i.e., passion) to know causes, is another important example. Hobbes found in curiosity an avenue to philosophical inquiry. Curiosity is one of the things that distinguishes human beings from beasts, distinguishes wiser persons or peoples from their opposites, and begets the search for causes of things that includes the search for first causes.[7]

With Hobbes (as with Plato), the most interesting rapprochement with the passions is the one least expected—the use and appeal to passions that seem hypocritical in the face of the forthright denunciations, in the name of reason, of passionate persons and those who play upon passions. Rather than seek Hobbes's concessions to passion, we can also discern his own passions at work as he promoted and defended his program to institute a new political doctrine. Hobbes's confident ways allow us to witness another manner in which passions find their way back into the realm of reason. Hobbes's words and actions testify that there are passions to acquire reason (aside from a simple love of wisdom), to associate oneself with reason, to deny the reasoning power of one's opponents where competition is involved, and a passion to reap the benefits promised by the exercise of reason. Reason and pride are hard to disentangle.

Hobbes understood this, although better in others than in himself. He is at his best when he describes intellectual arrogance and competition. He illustrates his talents in defense of his assertion of our inherent intellectual equality (i.e., habits of mind not cultivated through science):

> That which may perhaps make such equality incredible is but a vain conceit of one's own wisdom, which almost all men think they have in a greater degree than the vulgar; that is, than all men but themselves, and a few others, whom by fame, or for concurring with themselves they approve. For such is the nature of men, that howsoever they may acknowledge many others to be more witty, or more eloquent, or more learned; yet they will hardly believe there be many so wise as themselves: For they see their own wit at hand, and other men's at a distance. But this proveth rather that men are in that point equal, than unequal. For there is not ordinarily a greater sign of the equal distribution of anything than that every man is contented with his share.[8]

In spite of the seeming promise quoted from *Elements of Law*, Hobbes was clearly not immune to passion, and least of all to the passion for intellectual distinction. Hobbes indulges one of reason's most potent temptations. He uses reason, passionately, as a weapon against chaos and disorder. Hobbes (as we shall see, not unlike his contemporaries who celebrated Stuart sovereignty on the terms of a traditional telos) pitted reason against the chaos of conflicting political factions and their opinions.

Hobbes shared with these contemporaries a common hope that reason could force a peaceful silence. Reason, particularly mathematical reason, and the desire for peace and quiet in a bloody age were intimately wed in their aspirations. We might call this the passion for the final word. Hobbes certainly participated in this kind of competition, but given his context it is equally important to see the connection he (and others) made between someone who could have the last word and the peace and quiet they collectively sought. Hobbes's particularly forceful conceptions of reason harmonized with the allure of absolutism.

A parallel exists between Hobbes's views on patronage within the absolutist system and his concept of intellectual recognition. All men are equal in that each is satisfied with his share, but all will also be made intellectual equals in the commonwealth. This will occur in the same way that the absolutist sovereign makes all men competing for patronage equal. The sovereign must outshine all the others the way the sun outshines and obscures the stars during the daytime (*Lev.*, 18.19). So too, all claims to the great prize of intellectual accomplishment, assent, in a commonwealth must be equally subordinate to the expression of the sovereign's judgments. The universities, the source of all intellectual distinction and opinions, therefore had to be converted from seats of sedition into obedient students of Hobbes's doctrine (*Lev.*, 30.14; see also 20.3 in the Latin edition). Of course, insofar as the sovereign adopted Hobbes's reason for his own, making it the state's official doctrine, Hobbes could claim intellectual kudos. For Hobbes, reason held out the promise of quieting his bumptious contemporaries, of ending the din of babbling competitors in the quest for honor. If reason needed eloquence, as I noted earlier, it was not to persuade the many, but to persuade the state's most powerful actor to impose reason's dictates upon the many.

These passions, a part of reason's vanity, were already cultivated in the absolutist court. They were passions that had a prior attachment to mathematical learning, understood as a prized possession and an attribute of character and identity. I will illustrate this in the comparison of *Leviathan* and the masques of the Stuart Court. I will begin, however, with some of the more straightforward passions for mathematical reason that Hobbes shared with his contemporaries (including humanists). "Right and profit," to return to the terms of Hobbes's dedicatory to *Elements of Law*, also prove central concerns among those who chose to pursue mathematical learning in the Renaissance and early modern period.

Hobbes and Burckhardt's Humanism

In Chapter 3 I argued that Hobbes was satisfied with a science that did not do what most of us associate with contemporary social science: speak truths about the world, and, in particular, truths predictive of human behavior. I argued that, for Hobbes, there were other criteria for success: knowing what we make ourselves. As noted, he announces his success in meeting these criteria when he tells his readers that he will teach philosophers how to imitate God.

We can link these boasts to strands within the culture of humanism that Burckhardt identifies with the rise of the individual.[9] Burckhardt's exemplars cultivated mathematical learning that led to the construction of magnificent buildings, arts that would allow persons to control the symbols by which they, or their patrons, represented their power. They celebrated, and sought to stand as exemplars of, human virtue, accomplishment, and dignity through the tastes they cultivated, the people with whom they associated, the things they accumulated, the buildings they constructed, and the talents they developed.

Burckhardt's account of Leone Battista Alberti is to the point:

> In three things he desired to appear faultless to others, in walking, in riding, and in speaking. He learned music without a master, and yet his compositions were admired by professional judges. Under the pressure of poverty he studied both civil and canonical law . . . till exhaustion brought on a severe illness. [At age twenty-four] he set to work at physics and mathematics. And all the while he acquired every sort of accomplishment and dexterity, cross-examining artists, scholars, and artisans of all descriptions, down to the cobblers, about the secrets and peculiarities of their craft. Painting and modeling, . . . [he] held every human achievement which followed the laws of beauty for something almost divine. To all this must be added his literary works, . . . on art, . . . architecture, . . . Latin prose . . . ; elegies, eclogues, and humorous dinner-speeches . . . various moral, philosophical, and historical works; and . . . poems.[10]

Alberti reaped the rewards of cultivating a knowledge of practical mathematics, most notably knowledge of classical architectural forms. His success became a standard for others to follow. His *Ten Books on Architecture* were a critical contribution to the recovery of Roman architectural forms; in this work Alberti re-presented the architectural writings of Vitruvius.[11] In the *Ten Books* Alberti addresses himself to the well-off amateur, the dilettante, the potential patron. Alberti supplies an exemplary instance of one of the "commodious" uses for mathematical knowledge. In a culture where vast expenditures could be seen as not a vice but a virtue in princes and aristocrats, Alberti taught the wealthy to advertise their power and magnanimity through the creation of structures with proportions and ornaments that echo classical doctrines of a harmoniously constructed universe.

This is part of what Hobbes has in mind when he reminds readers of the "incommodities of war" and the state of nature, where there is "no navigation, . . . no commodious building, no instruments of moving and removing such things as require much force, no knowledge of the face of the earth" in the life so famously described as "solitary, poor, nasty, brutish, and short" (*Lev.*, 18.9). These were the advantageous uses of the earthly technologies associated with mathematical practice. It is of a piece with his general praise of mathematical learning: his appreciation of mathematical instruments, of the mathematician's assistance to navigators and architects, and of the capacity, through practical math-ematical learning, of "moving ponderous bodies."[12] Although no Vitruvian, Hobbes, like Alberti, had an affinity for mathematics that focused on the feats of engineering and architecture that were sometimes practical, sometimes magnificent, and often attempted to serve both ideals at once.

The humanists who argued the glory of *homo faber* could point with pride to mathematicians like Archytas, who is said to have crafted a mechanical bird that actually flew. Such a deed meant, they boasted, that men with such skills could duplicate some of the most impressive elements of God's handiwork. Pythagoras had won admiration for mathematical learning by having designed remarkable war machines for the defense of Syracuse.[13] As I suggested earlier, the requirement that sciences describe the actual world, in the context where these serve as models for exemplary mathematical service, need not figure so prominently.[14] The ability to associate his philosophy with the mathematical ways, the possessed virtues, of those who produce such material commodities might have supplied Hobbes with justification enough. The pleasures of reaping the fruits of mathematical learning (including the promise of peace imposed by the force of its reason) gave Hobbes and his patrons sufficient reasons for their pursuit.

MATHEMATICS DISCOVERS HOBBES

What was Hobbes's relationship to the glorified practical applications of mathematical learning? As noted, in his verse autobiography Hobbes associates himself—from his student days, prior to his so-called discovery of geometry—with practical applications, especially in geography, navigation, mapping, and astronomy. He preferred these to the practices of scholastic philosophy:

> . . . more pleasant studies I then sought,
> Which I was formerly, tho' not well, taught.
> My fancy and my mind divert I do,

> With maps celestial and terrestrial too.
> Rejoice t'accompany Sol cloath'd with rays,
> Know by what art he measures all our days;
> How Drake and Cavendish a girdle made
> Quite round the world, what climates they survey'd;
> And strive to find the smaller cells of men.
> And painted monsters in their unkown den.
> Nay, there's a fullness in geography.[15]

The autobiography does not exhaust Hobbes's connections to practical mathematics. As I noted in Chapter 2, he was obviously proud of having produced his own map of Greece to accompany his translation of Thucydides. Most important, Hobbes's key patrons had strong interests in mathematics and had connections to the culture of practical mathematics that predated their acquaintance with Hobbes. William Cavendish, Earl of Newcastle (1593–1676)—to whom Hobbes dedicated the *Elements of Law*—was an enthusiastic patron of practical mathematical artisanship. It is true that his brother Charles in particular cultivated interests in philosophical and experimental topics, allowing Hobbes to gain exposure to the intellectual communities of France and England (including Mersenne, Walter Warner, and others),[16] but there is no reason to assume that Hobbes's mathematical interests did not also extend to the less theoretically advanced curiosities of the family.

A key component in the education of many young noblemen was a tour abroad. Both William and Charles were taken on tour by Sir Henry Wotton in 1612 (Wotton was on a mission to Savoy to negotiate a marriage between Prince Henry and the Infanta Maria of Savoy).[17] He was eloquent and learned, and was appointed ambassador to Venice and later provost of Eton College (Francis Bacon was the losing competitor for this position). He was also one of the leading voices in gentlemanly mathematical concerns. His *Elements of Architecture* (1624) was instrumental in shifting English architectural style away from the Gothic extravagance of the Elizabethan period toward (the cleaner, more harmonious) neoclassical Vitruvian/Palladian style. Wotton was, in effect, a seventeenth-century English Alberti.[18] Like their Italian counterparts, Englishmen already knew that great buildings functioned as monuments to those who commissioned them: Wotton and James I's architect Inigo Jones (Ben Jonson's collaborator and eventual rival) taught them to refigure these monuments along neoclassical lines.

The rule that governed human conduct and eloquence, decorum, also ruled the construction of magnificent architecture: the work had to be appropriate.

Great men had to be represented by great buildings. What Wotton (and Jones) did was redefine what might count as fitting the dignity of a patron and/or prince. They were also responsible for elevating the status of the individuals who could bring these artifices into being. Prior to the late Elizabethan and early Stuart periods, persons who executed the designs of great houses were on the lower rung of the English hierarchy. They were regarded with those who worked with their hands, not with their minds. Their names went unrecorded, and throughout the seventeenth-century "mechanic" was often used as a term of derision. Nevertheless, as practitioners such as Jones and mathematical gentlemen like Wotton were making their names—and as Hobbes was maturing—a new figure, "the architect," emerged from the crowd of demeaned artisans. The architect became known as the individual who could give material manifestations to the ideals, and increasingly complex self-conceptions, of the noble selves whose castles, halls, lodges, and churches they were designing. These Renaissance influences were a late arrival in England: under the parsimony of Elizabeth's reign, state-sponsored extravagance—including the mathematically assisted kind that had established itself in Italy years before—was kept in check.[19]

In spite of these checks, the Cavendish family had in fact been disposed toward the glorious uses of practical mathematics early in this transformative period, even before their engagements with Wotton. Bess of Hardwick, the matron of the generation that had given birth to Hobbes's patrons, commissioned Hardwick Hall and Chatsworth, two Derbyshire exemplars of ostentatious Elizabethan architecture. They included a sophisticated feature made possible by the application of practical mathematics: through clever surveying and hydraulic engineering the castles had "running water" from a diverted stream channeled through the house.[20] These were the "high-tech" homes of the English Renaissance. Hardwick Hall was so pompous that in later years it inspired complaints of prodigality.[21] As a tutor to the cousins of the Earl of Newcastle (i.e., the succeeding Earls of Devonshire, also named William Cavendish), Hobbes followed the families as they spent part of the year in each of these homes,[22] and he eulogized the family and the practical mathematical accomplishments that were a part of these castles in his poem, *De Mirabilibus Pecci* (1627).[23] As noted, we think of Hobbes as having "discovered" mathematics, but in light of the Cavendish's family's prior interest in the practical arts of mathematically crafted spectacles, it can be said that the high culture of mathematics discovered Hobbes in 1608 when he was first hired as a tutor.

The Earl of Newcastle (1592–1676) followed Bess's example and also took on ambitious architectural projects. He augmented his inherited properties of

Bolsover and Welbeck, and even drew some of his own architectural plans.[24] As his career in the court of Charles I advanced, he built a home in the (then) London suburb of Clerkenwell (a mile and a half from Whitehall); when in London, as he often was, Hobbes lived in this home.[25] Newcastle also remained closely associated with the chief figures of the plastic arts. While in exile, Hobbes's patron was forced to "economize": in Antwerp, he purchased the home that had belonged to Rubens—now the Rubens museum.[26] Although Newcastle followed the family tradition of magnificent buildings and ostentatious show, he was also doing no less than cultivating the habits and interests that facilitated friendship, patronage, and notoriety.[27] Mathematics was also utilized with Newcastle's other interests: music and horsemanship.[28]

These contexts must be kept in mind when we consider the meaning of Hobbes's self-identification as an "able architect," or when he speaks of the "commodities" (including architecture) associated with mathematical learning. Calling himself an "able architect" suggests an identity more closely linked with the profession than we might expect. In this context, an "able architect" is someone with more than just a complex plan; it connotes an individual capable of designing a grand edifice, something in the (then relatively new) English fashion of using practical mathematics to impress.

A Discourse of Rome: Practical Mathematics and Patronage

A Discourse of Rome, argued by its recent editors Noel Reynolds and Arlene Saxenhouse to be a work by Hobbes, reflects this milieu. It speaks to the mores of an (increasingly reflexive) English gentlemanly culture that was in the process of making the connoisseurship of art and architecture a part of a young nobleman's education. This work dwells on the monuments and various edifices of Rome, and offers a defense for the Christian appreciation of pagan accomplishments.[29] It praises architecture and building as an appropriate "recreative" for gentlemen and offers a useful articulation of how the expectation of decorum in architecture functioned to encourage the building of monumental structures:

> I know few recreatives that possess us more, than the humor of building, in respect they both satisfy our own present invention, and serve to our posterity, as perpetual remembrances, and memorials of their progenitors, adding present content to ourselves, perpetuating reputation in the world, remaining as living Monuments of our magnificence, and beneficent expressions of our greatness.

> And although munificence in this kind, be by many esteemed superfluous, I rather hold it convenient, so it be of our abundance, and diminish nothing of the competency of our estates. . . .
>
> First, this Art of Architecture is honorable in all men's esteem, and profitable to ourselves. Next, it keeps us busied in thought, and action, and so diverts us from delights more dangerous. Then upon occasion it enables us in the use of fortifications. Fourthly, it gives a kind of extraordinary delight to ourselves, when we see those things, which before we had but formed a conceit, made visible. Next, it is an addition of repute to the City where we live. And lastly, it makes a man's fame to spread both at home, and abroad.[30]

Mathematical practices, as described here, offer gentlemen a chance at immortality.

The Cavendish family was not alone in cultivating an interest in the utilization of glorious practical mathematics. During the Stuart regime ambitious families had additional reasons for pursuing the ostentatious display of a cultivated knowledge of mathematics. After the long and prudently parsimonious dry spell under Elizabeth,[31] the Stuart Courts were aggressively patronizing artisans who produced the ostentatious commodities associated with mathematical learning.[32] James himself singled out mathematical education as a necessary part of his son's education in *Basilicon Doron*.[33]

As Hobbes was entering the political scene, James I and Charles I's courts had already used their patronage to make prominent a number of individuals who were synonymous with conspicuous uses of mathematical learning.[34] Portraits of the two kings were commissioned from artists who understood and exploited the techniques of perspective line drawing, Rubens and his student Van Dyck. As was the case with neoclassical architecture, their techniques introduced fashions in the representations of sovereignty to England that were already established on the Continent. Newcastle's friend, Rubens, used these techniques to offer monarchs and noblemen representations of themselves that put forward new, often very subtle, articulations of their dignity. In portraiture, the techniques of perspective line drawing were used to allow the sovereign's face to gaze out beyond the picture. That crafted gaze might interrogate the viewer. The painter might use perspective to assign the viewer a subordinate place in relation to the sovereign or noble subject by virtue of painting his subject from the perspective of eyes gazing upward.[35] Rubens painted James I in the center of the ceiling of Whitehall Chapel as God; James in this image thus becomes the ordering presence of a universe made harmonious by his rule.

Inigo Jones used mathematical skill to insinuate himself into court society. Jones was appointed Surveyor of the King's Works in 1615 and held the position until the Civil War. He worked as an architect and designed the scenes for the masques and entertainments performed at court. Jones employed Vitruvian principles in what he designed, two examples being the façade of St. Paul's Cathedral and the Banqueting House at Whitehall Palace.[36]

I wish to briefly expand on the Vitruvian influence, for it will offer a point of contrast when we turn to *Leviathan*. As a Vitruvian, Jones's underlying philosophy of architecture was posited on Platonic and Pythagorean assumptions. The universe was created by God in accordance with a set of universal proportions—mathematical relations between numbers that were also the basis for musical harmony.[37] Jones asserted that a structure that conformed to these harmonious principles operated on men's minds as a civilizing force. A building or perfectly proportioned scene used in a court masque could by its very presence serve as an inspiration. It functioned metonymically: at once an instance of divine, civilizing harmonies, and as a way to associate the rule of the sovereign with the establishment of a divinely sanctioned harmony and order. According to Jones's Neoplatonic vision, persons who take in such a view would be encouraged to follow the dictates of reason, to take their place as a part of a harmonious whole, and to eschew the disordering and chaotic impulses of unruly passions.[38] Jones's interpretation of Stonehenge reflected this philosophy of artisanship. According to Jones, the Romans had placed these (he insisted, harmoniously arranged) stones to create a temple to Coelus in the Tuscan style. Its purpose was to act as a civilizing force on the barbaric Britons.[39]

> You cannot but remember, in what manner the ancient Inhabitants of this Island lived, before reduced to Civility by the *Romans*, . . . how they were first instructed by them, in several *Arts* and *Sciences*, whereof the *Britains* wholly ignorant, before the *Romans* Arrived here, and teaching them. . . . doubtless it appears to you, as in Truth it [Stonehenge] is, a work built with much *Art, Order,* and *Proportion.* . . . For, where *Art* is not, nothing can be performed by *Art.* . . .
>
> *Stone-Henge* [was] anciently a *Temple*, dedicated to *Coelus*, built by the *Romans*; . . . the more to civilize the Natives, introduce the *Art* of Building amongst them, . . . by stupendious and prodigious Works, to eternize the Memory of their high Minds to succeeding Ages.[40]

Finally, mathematical knowledge was not merely the property of artisans like Jones; it had become a part of the royal curriculum. James I and Charles I were particularly proud of their knowledge of mathematics. It had become a part of the royal curriculum. Salomon de Caus presented Prince Henry (James's first son, d. 1613) with designs later published as *Les Raisons des forces Mouvantes*.[41] This work included discussions of natural philosophy and mechanical inventions. De Caus organized his views of natural forces axiomatically, in imitation of the geometer's mode of reasoning. From these axioms (in fact they proceeded on the basis of Aristotelian assumptions concerning the basic elements of the universe) he derived plans for the construction of both simple and elaborate mechanisms, machines designed to tap the powers of nature. These included pumps that would use the power of the sun to move water through fountains or animate elaborate statuary.[42]

Charles I fashioned himself an expert in the commodities produced by mathematical artisans. He is said to have invented a primitive slide rule.[43] His biographer, William Perringchief, wrote: "He could judge of fortifications. . . . He had excellent skill in the building of guns [and] ships. . . . He understood and was pleased with the making of clocks and watches . . . he delighted to talk to all kinds of artists, and he did sometimes say, he thought he could get his living . . . by any trade he knew of, except the making of hangings [tapestries]: although of these he understood much and greatly delighted in them."[44] A mathematically inclined king was an encouragement to others to take up mathematically learned habits and to associate themselves with its commodities.[45] For Newcastle, mathematical learning was therefore not only a part of his family's tradition; it was also a part of a useful strategy to secure patronage. Thanks to this interest, he and the monarch had a common appreciation for the ideals of learnedness. His mathematical interests gave him the opportunity to become more familiar and friendly with Charles I. After several extravagant displays of his hospitality in the form of financially ruinous parties and entertainments to accommodate Charles on his travels ("progresses") through the kingdom in 1633 and again in 1634[46] (entertainments which, notably, were scripted by his friend Ben Jonson, and may have included a small role for Hobbes himself),[47] Newcastle finally succeeded. After a long and impatient wait, his gifts to the monarch were repaid: he was awarded the title of tutor to Prince Charles (i.e., the future Charles II) in 1638.[48]

This context gives us a framework for understanding Hobbes's patronage relations to the Cavendish clan. Hobbes not only served their interests by seeing their children educated, advising in their business and financial affairs, and assisting Charles Cavendish in the construction of his own mathematical curiosities; he also was an asset in the family's bid for royal patronage. As a mathematically learned man, his allegiance to the family testified to this family's capacity to serve as worthy educators to the king's children. Hobbes's position as mathematics instructor to Prince Charles, therefore, was not merely his accomplishment, but was likely the logical extension of the rewards—and service due—to the Crown as a part of Newcastle's office as tutor to Charles I's son.[49] We ought to see Hobbes's very presence and dependence on the Cavendish family as a part of the larger strategy to put the family's learnedness on display[50]—a strategy that had long been linked to the ostentatious use of mathematical virtuosity. (Whether Hobbes ultimately served their ends because of his association with political and theologically scandalous views is an important but separate issue.)

BEN JONSON AND INIGO JONES: MATHEMATICAL LEARNING AND DISTINCTION

Jonson and Jones engaged in one of the better known intellectual duels among early seventeenth-century men of letters. The conflict between the two has been discussed at length by others, and this is not the place to try to significantly deepen our understanding of it.[51] I wish, rather, to use elements of the conflict (largely Jonson's concerns) to open a window on mathematics and the intricacies of competitive learnedness in the absolutist court that will illuminate Hobbes's work.

Jonson and Jones had collaborated on masques for James I and for Charles I. With Charles's reign, however, Jonson fell out of favor, and an ongoing rivalry between the two blossomed into public vitriol.[52] Jonson attacked Jones for the theatricality of his manners and accused him of using his equally flamboyant architectural skills to upstage Jonson's own prose. Jones, he argued, was succeeding on the basis of a corrupted learning, a "shop-philosophy." The success of Jones's work represented the dawning of a "money-gett, Mechanick-Age!"[53] From Jonson's point of view, the spectacular show and "motions" of Jones's stage machinery undermined the didactic aspects of the masque.[54] Those who worked with words, according to Jonson, had to be ranked higher than those who worked with machinery, props, costumes, and stage scenery. He was, in short, appealing to the Platonic prejudices of the mind over the body. Jones would have none of it. He credibly asserted that his stage constructions *were* didactic, and Platonic in their own right. Indeed, in spite of this conflict, the two for many years did in fact teach their audiences together.[55]

Given the specific attacks on Jones as an overambitious architect, one might assume that Jonson was voicing his disagreement with practical mathematics *per se:* a humanist angered by being displaced by a mathematical show-off. Jonson's polemics, however, were a straightforward condemnation of neither mathematical learning nor architecture. In fact, Jonson had studied classical architectural techniques very carefully, and he kept company at Gresham College with some of the mathematics teachers of London.[56] He was familiar with the mathematical knowledge that Jones had used to make his name.[57] Vitruvian aesthetics called for well-ordered compositions, generally. The rules might be applied to buildings, but also, according to Jonson, to poems and to persons.

These aesthetics informed some of Jonson's work, but in spite of his admiration for the philosophy of classical architecture, he was unwilling to allow an architect (Jones) to play the architecton in their collaborative efforts. That is, he dissented from Jones's implicit claim to take charge (and center stage), and moreover to supervise Jonson's own work. Jones had the more expansive view of the architect's office, and the two quarreled over its proper scope and authority. In the course of this conflict Jonson renamed Jones "Dominus Do-All."[58] Jonson was equally capable of claiming a mathematically learned upper hand: he criticized Jones for having deviated from Vitruvian norms, which in Jonson's view dictated a more limited role for the architect than Jones had assumed for himself.[59] Ultimately, Jones was triumphant. Jonson remained out of favor while Jones continued to produce court masques with the collaboration of other poets. Newcastle remained allied with Jonson, and the Entertainments at Welbeck and Bolsover, written by Jonson, were an attempt at rehabilitation.[60]

Jonson blended his typically humanist concern for the connection between a person's language and character with the Vitruvian ethos of harmony. If Vitruvius had inspired Italian Renaissance thinkers such as Da Vinci to present, in his famous "Vitruvian Man," an embodied microcosm of the harmonious proportions of the universe, Jonson appropriated this topos for the realm of words.[61] How persons used words—how they spoke and how they wrote— were indicative of the virtues they possessed. Dignified persons used dignified language, and dignified language shared in the universal harmonies that Vitruvius and his followers tried to make their guide in building.[62] Jonson wrote: "*Language* most shows a man: speake that I may see thee ... No glasse renders a man's forme, or likenesse, so true as his speech. Nay, it is likened to a man; and as we consider feature, and composition in a man; so words in Language: in the greatnesse, aptnesse, sound, structure and harmony of it."[63] Vitruvian themes, blended with the connection between words and ways, emerge in this piece of praise of James I:

> Read him as you would doe the booke
> Of all perfection, and but looke
>   What his proportions be;

No measure that is thence contriv'd,
Or any motion thence deriv'd,
But is pure harmonie.[64]

The expectation of decorum—that what one does must be fitting to oneself—made possible a certain metonymic free play. Decorous acts of one kind became the medium for gauging the successes and failures of others, and were each understood as expressive of a self's claim on a particular form of virtuosity. Jonson brought this comparative logic to bear on acts of creation. Writing itself could be compared to the activity of architecture; a poet builds a poem just as an architect does his buildings.[65] The poet must lay each word carefully and methodically and according to principles of good order: "The congruent, and harmonious fitting of parts in a sentence, hath almost the fastening, and force of knitting, and connexion: As in stones well squar'd, which will rise strong a great way without mortar."[66] Residuals of this understanding also guided Hobbes's expectations concerning proper philosophical method. Hobbes knits with efficient causes but, with characteristic boldness, eschews appeals to the universe's grand harmonies.[67] Jonson and Hobbes, nevertheless, have something in common in addition to the preference for systematic construction. Hobbes also argues from the presupposition that a particular kind of man, a man educated in a specific learned skill, will make his skills—the virtues he possesses—manifest in the way he handles and uses the language. We, today, have not yet given up these habits. We still draw distinctions rooted in language use. They follow wherever there is inequality, but within the preliberal worlds governed by norms of patronage, appetites and aptitudes for claiming distinction were cultivated with a different intensity.

Jonson is most revealing of the social complexities that attended mathematical learning when he casts suspicion on would-be gentlemen who would make a false show of mathematical learning to insinuate themselves into court society.[68] One of Jonson's early plays, *Every Man in His Humour* (first performed by the Chamberlain's Men, Shakespeare's company, in 1589) has such a character. His name is Bobadill, and he personifies the ambitions of those who hoped to parlay bogus mathematical skills into royal patronage.[69] He believes he has found a mathematical vocabulary well suited to his ploy to pass himself off as a great soldier and a great gentleman.

Bobadill announces his plan to impress the Crown in Act 4:

> . . . I would vnder-take (vpon this poore head, and life) for the publique benefit of the state, not only to spare the intire liues of her subjects in

generall, but to saue the one halfe, nay, three parts of her yeerely charge, in holding warre, and against what enemie soever. And how would I doe it, think you? . . .

Why thus, sir. I would select nineteene, more, to my selfe, throughout the land; gentelmen . . . and I would teach these nineteene, the speciall rules, as your *Punto*, your *Reuerso*, your *Stoccata* . . . This done, say the enemie were fortie thousand strong, we twentie would come into the field, the tenth of *March*, or thereabouts; and wee would challenge twentie of the enemie; they could not, in their honour, refuse vs, well, wee would kill them: challenge twentie more, kill them, twentie more, kill them; twentie more, kill them too; and thus, would wee kill, euery man, his twentie a day, that's twentie score; twentie score, that's two hundreth; two hundreth a day, fiue dayes a thousand; fortie thousand, fortie times fiue, fiue times fortie, two hundreth dayes kill them all vp, by computatation.[70]

Jonson's parody of the mathematical soldier makes clear—in a way that no explanation can—that persons in the seventeenth century (and late sixteenth century) fashioned themselves with mathematics. Dressing oneself up in the trappings of mathematical skills useful to the state and linked with its glory was one way to "dress for success." This helps explain why so many mathematical instruments for sale in London shops were well-polished gems that never saw the field.[71] Moreover, Jonson's Bobadill illustrates that the dynamics of competitive mathematical self-fashioning had already grown quite complex.[72]

Jonson insisted that his audience learn to look upon so-called mathematical practitioners with a discerning eye. It was not simply a matter of whether a gentleman was mathematical or not, but *what kind* of mathematics he professed to know, and whether he truly understood the practices he claimed to have mastered. The same kind of discernment that had become the basis for the distinction between good poets and bad would also be applied to mathematics. As Bobadill ticks off his calculations, Jonson has us discover a blustery fool whose empty head hides behind a mathematical façade.[73] False claims to mathematical virtues are made to reveal themselves in the act of promising royalty the impossible. Later in his career, Jonson would submit Jones to the same treatment in the character of Coronell Vitruvius.[74]

Although there is no simple correspondence between Jonson's and Hobbes's notions of mathematical learning, I want to suggest that Hobbes and many of his contemporaries took their claim to mathematical learning seriously in much the same spirit. Hobbes, famously, is satisfied with citizens who keep their rebellious thoughts to themselves while professing an outward loyalty to the sovereign, but as we have seen, he is no less willing than Jonson to charge the politically or intellectually disobedient with fraud, fakery, opportunism, or incompetence.

We already saw an example of this in Hobbes's accusations against Presbyterians in *Behemoth* and in the *Six Lessons*, and we will see this is true as well in the mathematical context of his attacks on John Wallis. Hobbes and Jonson converge at precisely the point where we are most blind to the passionate character of Hobbes's investment in mathematical learning. Most important for our purposes, Jonson illustrates that mathematical skills were not just disembodied techniques, but the possessed virtues that allowed for performances by specific persons, and that these performances—the words they spoke, and the actions they took—were constitutive of claims to a particular kind of identity. Hobbes associated his own particular vision of mathematical practices with an identity, that of a proper geometer. It was an identity he was willing to fight to protect. High stakes were attached: Hobbes's claim to serve the sovereign hinged upon this image and the kind of virtuous service he could provide. It is worth noting that Hobbes, in spite of his reputation as a poor mathematician today, was successful enough in defending his reputation after his conflict with John Wallis that one practical mathematician published his work in translation during the Restoration.

Venterus Mandey, a mathematics teacher—and peddler of his own instruction books—published his English translations of two of Hobbes's Latin mathematical works of 1671 and 1674, *Rosetum Geometricum* and *Principia et Problemata aliquot geometrica*, in 1682. He included Wallis's criticisms of Hobbes's claims, and Hobbes's criticism of Wallis's remarks in turn. Mandey himself offers no comment on the dispute. The translations were made a part of his *Mellificium Mensionis; or, The Marrow of Measuring*, a book that offered basic geometry as well as mathematical instruction especially for "Glaziers, Painters, Plasterers, Masons, Joyners, Carpenters, and Surveyors" among others.[75] Before returning to this topic of how and why a mathematical reputation mattered to Hobbes, I want to review a final instance in which competitive claims to possess such mathematical ways became a matter of distinction.

Bobadill, the mathematically fraudulent soldier, suggests another element of Hobbes's context where the association between mathematics and men's "right and profit" asserted itself. Hobbes lived while England was attempting to bring itself even with the new technologies of warfare and fortification already employed on the Continent.[76] When Hobbes was young, London was already filled with ambitious mathematicians and instrument makers.[77] They promised a variety of commodious innovations, to include instruments to improve the aim of artillery pieces, better tools and techniques for navigation and surveying, and mathematical skills for the ordering and managing of troops.[78] England's Ordnance Office began under Henry VIII, and continued to play a prominent role in the seventeenth century.[79] Under the Crown's authority, it distributed the machinery of warfare and employed engineers and mathematicians with the aim of improving the nation's technological prowess in the military arts. Pedagogues also took part in serving up England's mathematical smorgasbord.[80] One, Thomas Hood, taught courses commissioned by prominent Londoners. They produced books promising to teach men how to become ideal captains and expert gunners. They also promised to teach men to become shrewd businessmen.[81] Hobbes's Restoration translator, Mandey, was carrying on this tradition.

The enthusiasm for mathematics did not exclude gentlemen, but—as Jonson suggests with Bobadill—not all who sought to associate themselves with mathematical learning were necessarily gentry. For some, mathematical skills, or at least the outward appearance of having mastered the mathematical skills associated with a martial or naval life, might have looked like a route to gentility, a way of climbing the social latter. Scholars who have studied the highly ornamented mathematical instruments of the seventeenth century have assumed that the mathematical practitioners who made these instruments were hoping to appeal to the gentry. This seems likely, but the market for such instruments may have also been the London parvenu.

The constellation of courtly mathematics, parvenus, and poetic skill perhaps come together in a unique way in the person of Hobbes's friend William Davenant. The author of *Gondibert*, which included a scholarly preface addressed to Hobbes—and to which Hobbes supplied a complimentary reply—launched his career at court from humble beginnings and won favor prior to the Civil War through his collaboration with Jones in most of the court masques performed before Charles I and Queen Henrietta Maria. Once the war had broken out, Hobbes's patron Newcastle was made a general of the king's Northern army. At the request of the queen, Davenant was made his ordnance officer, a position requiring practical skills in mathematics.[82] To the surprise of historians, Davenant (attacked by his critics, Royalist or otherwise, for every flaw) was never criticized for his performance in this role. He was even rewarded by Charles II for his services.[83] I have discussed Hobbes's relationship with Davenant elsewhere,[84] but there can be little doubt that Hobbes was immersed in the high culture of mathematics and those who sought to take part in it.

Leviathan as the Sovereign's Mathematical Self

In Chapter 3 I discussed Hobbes's insistence on our inability to know God. There is a remarkable passage in *Leviathan*, written as an assault on those who claim knowledge of God, which brings together many of the themes thus far discussed. Beginning with a comment on the logical contradictions implied by the doctrine of God's omnipresence (and in particular the paradoxical presence of Christ in the sacrament) Hobbes launches a larger attack:

> They will have us believe that by the Almighty power of God one body may be at one and the same time in many places . . . as if it were an acknowledgement of the Divine Power to say: that which is, is not; or that which has been, has not been.
>
> And these are but a small part of the incongruities they are forced to, from their disputing philosophically, instead of admiring, and adoring of the divine and incomprehensible nature; whose attributes cannot signify what he is, but ought to signify our desire to honour him, with the best appellations we can think on. But they that venture to reason of his nature, from these attributes of honour, losing their understanding in the very first attempt, fall from one inconvenience into another, without end, and without number; in the same manner, as when a man ignorant of the ceremonies of court, coming into the presence of a greater person than he is used to speak to, and stumbling at his entrance, to save himself from falling, lets slip his cloak; to recover his cloak, lets fall his hat; and with one disorder after another, discovers his astonishment and rusticity.[85]

Here, in part, is an example of how Hobbes solves the rhetorical problem I referred to in Chapter 6. As a book designed to instruct a sovereign, *Leviathan* must take on a complicated task. Equals can be assaulted with logic, but sovereigns cannot be treated like equals. They can, and are here, treated to the delights of watching Hobbes ridicule his philosophical and theological opponents. In this quotation, moreover, the ridicule refers us back to the decorum of the absolutist court. Hobbes references a clumsy performance in front of a "greater person," but the subtext of the passage in full would have put contemporary readers in mind of the absolutist court. How to conduct oneself in the presence of God was becoming the model, in the Stuart Court as in others in the seventeenth century, for how to conduct oneself in the presence of the monarch. A part of the message this passage conveys is that Hobbes, unlike his incompetent rivals, knew how to conduct himself in front of gods, immortal and mortal.

In the introduction I claimed that we had to understand Hobbes's writings and *Leviathan* in particular as works that might not be for us. Our democratic prejudices tell us that what we read is there to persuade *us*. Hobbes operated in a world in which such democratic prejudices were not operating. Moreover, to the extent that their precursors were making themselves felt as a challenge to central authority, we have seen evidence that Hobbes was struggling against them. This claim might meet an objection. Thomas Hobbes was a consent theorist. If a consent theorist's work is not designed to persuade potential political subjects (or citizens) to give their consent, then (one might demand to know) for whom does he write?

I am not arguing that Hobbes had nothing to say in *Leviathan* to those whose consent was required. As noted earlier, Hobbes needs persons who are convinced that they must satisfy an unmet need for peace by finding a sovereign. They can no longer be convinced that nature or God will deliver them from misery and death without radical human intervention. These themes are only reinforced in *Leviathan*, but if the work's primary audience member is the potential sovereign himself (or itself), then there is an answer to this objection. *Leviathan* is a mirror for a sovereign who must be taught to *accept* the consent of the people, as well as the teaching of the doctrine (i.e., Hobbes's own) that shows them why they should consent to being ruled. Monarchs were already portraying themselves as analogous to God. *Leviathan*, I will show, is the text that allows them to perpetuate this self-image while placing their rule on a new footing. Masques were the most elaborate and dramatic form of the mirror for princes genre. Understanding *Leviathan* as a masque-text, and in light of the complexities of masque presentation, will also help show how Hobbes tried to negotiate several difficult tasks at once. In *Leviathan* he attempts to convince a sovereign already accustomed to seeing his image in God affirmed afresh, and to do so in way that both complimented the Crown and trumpeted his own accomplishments.

Court Masques

Court masques have been described as little more than the festive, lunatic propaganda characteristic of a court known for its bloated, decadent, and lascivious entertainments. More considered investigations of masques as complex pageants of dance, costume, spoken word, and scenery reveal that they have more to offer than fodder for whiggish condemnations of royal excess.[86]

Undoubtedly, there were many elements of excess. The expression of Stuart sovereign prerogative sometimes did, because it knew it could, take a turn toward what others found unappealing. Ambassadors sometimes reported, particularly during James I's reign, stories of obscenely expensive costumes, spattered by the mess created by drunken courtiers and monarchs.[87] Masques were, indeed, entertainments, but they were composed with purposes larger than mere indulgence in mind.

They were grand ceremonies staged on behalf of the monarch. In the seventeenth century Stuart kings, with the sophisticated assistance of poets like Jonson and Davenant and practical mathematicians like Jones, used masques to give expression to visions of their sovereign rule. The structure of the masque and the relation between what happened on stage and in the audience made the masque a drama in which sovereignty was literally enacted. This was never more so than under the rule of Charles I, whose own sense of decorum (and disgust with the excesses of his father's court) caused him to devote serious attention to his masques.[88] Moreover, their authors took the "mirroring" element of this tradition seriously. Mirrors for princes were didactic works.[89] They presented the sovereign, and their audiences, with an image of him- or herself. These were idealized images, and as such, images that reflected particular ideals. The Crown and courtiers had a hand in shaping these ideals, but so did the poets and Jones.

The genre is not a widely familiar form of performance today. Perhaps the best-known masque is the disrupted one Prospero crafts as a wedding gift for Miranda and Ferdinand in Act 4 of *The Tempest*.[90] The masque's origins have been traced to the Tudors.[91] These performances began as musical entertainment with dancing in Henry VIII's court.[92] Although masques utilized some of the most sophisticated tools of stagecraft, it is important to understand that although they were scripted, had characters, and were performed in costume, they were not plays.

The first contrast must be drawn in terms of performance space. Theaters had recently become the institutionalized venue for public plays.[93] The masque, by contrast, typically took place at court, often at the Banqueting House at Whitehall, which James I had commissioned Inigo Jones to rebuild. The specific costumes, scenery, and temporary stages for each occasion were also designed by Jones.[94]

Masques and plays were intended for and performed before different audiences.[95] Public theaters such as the Globe and the Swan were open to anyone who could purchase a ticket. As best as we can tell from limited historical records, the typical English Renaissance theater's ticketing practices echoed an economic and social hierarchy: the groundlings stood at the base of the stage;

those who could afford to pay more sat in covered seats that ringed the stage and ground. Compared with the court masque, however, the public theater was a relatively democratic space.[96] The members of the audience at a masque were the Crown's invited guests. Furthermore, they were seated according to their host's plan, and where they were seated was an issue. Status was measured by proximity to the Crown.[97]

The idea that linked status and relative proximity to the Crown was hardly new; seating at meals, for example, linked honor with relative proximity. However, the fruits of practical mathematics in seventeenth-century England—the use of perspective lines in the design of the stage and seating, in particular—made nearness to the Crown at a masque something beyond the ordinary.[98] Jones's designs ensured that it was not merely physical proximity that privileged a seat near the Crown. Sitting in the best seats meant that one witnessed a performance from a perspective very close to that of the sovereign.

One reason this made a difference was that the seventeenth-century masque stage, unlike its counterpart, the Renaissance theater stage, was designed for what we would call "special effects." Public theater productions could avail themselves of sheet-metal thunder and trap doors, but the masque was a much more elaborate spectacle. Unique stages were designed for particular masques. Screens behind masque stages allowed for changes of scenery. Jones used perspective line techniques to create the illusion of depth—illusions best realized from the perspective of the sovereign's seat. Jones also devised mechanical devices above and below the stage that allowed persons (typically costumed as gods) seated on clouds or in chariots to float down from above. Mountains or castles might be seen to arise from below.[99]

In the midst of this the Crown occupied a place that was distinguished along several dimensions. By design it was the one perfect perspective on the action and scenery. Here mathematics and absolutist ideology were made to work hand in hand. The designer of the masque stage and seating was following the rule of decorum. The Crown ruled by divine right, was a human divinity, and therefore ought to have a God's-eye perspective on stage. Geometrical perspective techniques engineered the perfectly commanding view.[100] The further one sat from the Crown's commanding view, the less dazzling the spectacle on the stage might appear. To see what the monarch saw—from one's *proper*, that is to say, assigned position—was a sign to oneself and testimony to others of your share in his or her divinity.[101] But the sovereign's eyes were not the sole concern. In fact, the sovereign not only had to have the best view of the stage, but the masque's seating designs ensured that the sovereign was visible to all the guests.

The practical mathematical management of vision, including the godlike perspective of the sovereign, had an important correlate within the dramatic structure of the masque. Again the relationship between what happened on stage and what happened in the audience was very much unlike a traditional play. Playgoers traditionally sit passively and watch a spectacle. The proscenium arch, an innovation Jones himself introduced to the English stage, has become a barrier between the playgoing audience and the players. We are said to suspend disbelief and pretend that the world behind the arch is not taking place in our here and now. Unlike the audience at a theater, the audience at a masque shared the same cooperative space and time as the players making these representations.[102] Moreover, the masque audience—and most especially the sovereign—was not only part of the spectacle, but the spectacle's raison d'être.

Although masques varied from one performance to the next, they existed to introduce a series of problems on stage for which the only solution is the sovereign's intervention from the audience. A masque was a way to present chaos which the sovereign, or possibly the sovereign's consort, brings to order through the exercise of virtue. The king or queen's role in some instances involved stepping out of the audience and on to the stage in the Elizabethan and Caroline masques. (James was not willing to take the stage. Elizabeth, Charles I, and Queen Henrietta Maria, who commissioned her own masques, were.)[103] In some masques, the Crown's seat was itself a part of the stage.[104] As Stephen Orgel has noted, in a court masque, "the noble spectator watched what he became."[105]

What was communicated, and to whom, and how did the noble spectator see what he would become? *The* audience member, as I have noted, was the sovereign. What of the others? Orgel notes that at a masque, "There were, properly speaking, two audiences and two spectacles. The primary audience was the monarch, and the performance was directed explicitly at him. . . . At these performances what the rest of the spectators watched was not a play but the [monarch] at a play, and their response would have been not simply to the drama, but to the drama and its primary audience, the royal spectator."[106] Thus, the proscenium arch was not the barrier it would become for the traditional playgoing audience. Rather, it communicated a lesson that allowed it to stand as an entranceway to a new instantiation of the monarchy's self.[107] The performance on stage enacted a re-presentation of the monarch's self *to himself*. Potentially, he was to become—during the unfolding performance—what his masque makers would have him be.[108]

Given these stakes, masque makers often found themselves taking instruction from the king or queen. Thus, a part of what the other spectators witnessed in a masque performance was an expression of how the monarch himself would be known.[109] In *The Tempest*, Prospero is the author of his own masque, and the spectacle is an expression of his power and dominion as he would have his guests know it.¹¹⁰ (This makes the disruption by Caliban's conspiracy, the memory of which prompts Prospero to call off the masque before its completion, all the more meaningful.) In the actual performance and production of masques, the Ariels were Jonson, Jones, and (following Jonson's fall from favor) other inventors such as Hobbes's friend William Davenant.¹¹¹ The sovereign's self-representation was necessarily mediated through their services and their willfulness as artists and clients with pedagogical intent.

The sovereign's propaganda purposes and the inventor's didactic intent might exist in tension. On the other hand, the genre's didacticism meant that those who wrote masques also undertook to offer the sovereign a better vision of himself—an exemplary self whose deeds and dignity offered a pattern for behavior. One might delight the sovereign with an image of himself somewhat different from the self that first sat in the seat of honor, not simply because the masque presented, as it did in any case, an idealization of the sovereign power, but through the variations and modification that a skillfully executed masque could suggest.¹¹² The opportunity to teach and counsel (as with traditional mirrors for princes) emerged in the course of the masque's progression from antimasque, to the masque, and finally, to the revels.

The antimasque was the chaotic moment. Typically following a scene in which an initial order is presented, the antimasque introduces forces of disturbance. These disruptive forces are put on display through dance, costume, and the speech of a representative character, sometimes a pantheistic god of ill repute, such as Momus.¹¹³ In *The Golden Age Restored*, the antimasque is summoned by the Golden Age's naturally deficient counterpart, "*Iron Age.*" The personator of the Iron Age calls out the disruptive forces, costumed antimasquers themselves personating vices dancing on stage to cacophonous music:

> Rise, rise then up, thou grandame vice
> Of all my issue, Avarice,
> Bring with thee Fraud and Slander,
> Corruption with the golden hands,
> Or any subtler ill that stands
>   To be a more commander.
> Thy boys, Ambition, Pride and Scorn,
> Force, Rapine, and thy babe last born,
> Smooth Treachery, call hither,
> Arm Folly forth, and Ignorance,
> And teach them all our pyrrhic dance.¹¹⁴

The masque follows the antimasque (although some performances had a sequence of antimasque scenes). Here the monarch intervenes. He either steps across from one side of the proscenium arch to take the stage, or gestures from his seat of honor. It is the moment when the performance represents for all gathered the sovereign's extraordinary power to alter the world by his will. Chaos and disruption is then typically displaced by peace, calm, and order. Storm clouds give way to golden rays. In *The Golden Age Restored*, Pallas Athena, Jove's (and therefore James's) agent, enters the stage. She shows her shield and thereby restores the order of the Golden Age. At this moment the performers personating vices of the Iron Age freeze. Pallas Athena has turned them to stone. This act clears the way for the rule of Jove, whom Jonson associates with James I himself.[115] In the concluding moment, the revels, masquers pick partners from the audience and execute an orderly dance.

The king has literally called the tune, and it is the role of the courtiers in the revels to dance to it. Their doing so at once affirms, conforms, and creates the order he has, in godlike fashion, just commanded into being. The masque as a form began in the sixteenth century as little more than a dance performance/entertainment, and the conflict between the antimasque and the masque and revels was a conflict between styles of dance, one performed by the forces of chaos, the other (brought about through the monarch's presence or participation) of order.[116] In all cases, however, the sovereign's participation meant that the masque expressed not just order, but a particular expression of order *coming into being* though the sovereign's intervention.

Seventeenth-century masques had a topical quality. Author and architect attempted to present disruptions on stage that reflected contemporary challenges to the monarch. In the context of absolutist pretensions, the difficulties of addressing contemporaneous threats to the sovereign's rule were real.[117] How a disruption was presented, how it was figured as a particular set of faults and troubles, and the presentation of the sovereign as the counterforce and remedy were each a matter of political expression.[118] They suggested to the sovereign, and to his guests, a way of seeing the troubles, and a way of understanding how the sovereign could or should correct them.

One of Jonson's longer and more complex masques, *Hymenaei, or the Solemnities of Masque and Barriers at a Marriage*,[119] illustrates some of the characteristics I have described and contrasts nicely with what we can think of as the masque-like characteristics of *Leviathan*. In this performance the antimasquers emerge from a tremendous globe, figured as a microcosm, to disrupt a marriage ceremony. Out of a globe eight costumed men emerge accompanied by music Jonson calls "contentious." These eight represent the four humors and the four affections.[120] Swords drawn, they surround an altar at center stage and "disturb the ceremony."[121] A plea is made for "a power like reason" to come from the microcosm to counter their "untempered humours" and "wild affections" by "instruct[ing] their darkness, make them know and see / In wronging these, they have rebelled against you."[122] "Reason" emerges, "personated" in the language common to Jonson and Hobbes, by a costumed woman.[123] She is a mathematical figure. Jonson describes her: "Hereat Reason, seated in the top of the globe (as in the brain, or highest part of man), figured in a venerable personage, her hair white and trailing to her waist, crowned with lights, her garments blue and semined with stars, girded unto her with a white bend filled with arithmetical figures, in one hand bearing a lamp, in the other a bright sword."[124] Responding to the plea, Reason stifles the disorder.

Hymenaei presented James I with at least two idealized images of himself. First, it magnified an element of Jacobean propaganda. James I associated himself with peace and concord, and in particular the concord between England and Scotland—the two nations brought together through his kingship. To express this association, he linked himself with the peace and concord of an idealized conception of marriage. In him, the two kingdoms are brought into union.[125] Later, he would attempt to use the marriages of his own children to make Britain the broker of a peace between Spain and Protestant Europe. What we know of these efforts at national, international, or even courtly matrimonial bliss—including the wedding that this masque celebrated between Frances Howard (from a pro-Spanish Catholic family) and the Earl of Essex—was that they sometimes ended in disaster. Most commentaries on this masque have focused on these very badly botched elements of Jacobean statesmanship.[126] James's difficulty in uniting kingdoms, notably the unwillingness of Englishmen to accept Scottish influences at court, was represented as unruly passions contained by Reason's command (that is to say, the command of James I's reason).

However, if *Hymenaei* figured James and his queen as the ideals of matrimonial concord, it also presented James with an image of himself that emphasized his scholarly interests. Reason, notably, comes out of the microcosm to defend James's matrimonial utopia. Moreover, *Hymenaei* is an exceedingly learned text, including extensive scholarly notes by Jonson on his and Jones's sources for the symbolism. What emerges in the masque propaganda, as well as in his addresses to Parliament, is that James I fashioned himself as a philosopher-king (the same could be said of Charles I).[127]

Reason's comportment is particularly interesting for our purposes. She does battle with the humors and affections, but Jonson's Reason is clearly not devoid of passion herself. Rather, Jonson gives Reason all the pride and rectitude of a piqued noble. We should not read this as an attempt at irony, but as the articulation of how both Jonson and indeed James hoped the *force* of reason itself would be felt. Reason is here portrayed as rightfully angry and affronted by the disruption; she demands that the world and the ceremony be put right again. Reason barks: "Forebear your rude attempt! What ignorance / Could yield you so profane as to advance / One thought in act against these mysteries."[128] They sheathe their swords, and the business of ranking and ordering the ceremonies begins; then Reason speaks in praise of union. Later, after Juno has descended from the clouds to the stage, Reason is assisted by "Order" (another personation), whose costume is "painted full of arithmetical and geometrical figures . . . and in his hand a geometrical staff."[129] Order leads figures signifying the "virtues of the dames" "to their places."

In *Hymenaei*, therefore, mathematical learning is a part of the spectacle on multiple levels. Made in collaboration with Jones, we can expect that the performance space bore the stamp of his perspectival designs, and that Jones's mechanical devices were an element in the masque's construction (i.e., in the mechanics of the globe and the lowering of Juno to the stage). As the masque progresses, Union and unity are celebrated with mathematical Neoplatonic mysteries. Divinity is associated with unity, and unity with Union (i.e., marriage) and Juno (or *Unio*, as Jonson styles her name). Thus the couple, marriage itself (an act whereby two are made one), and James are wrapped in the mysteries of divine forces of the universe, and made the symbol of divine harmonies and a symbol of James's divine right.[130] Reason describes the accomplishment of the well-ordered marriage scene:

> Such was the gold chain let down from heaven,
>   And not those links more even
> Than these, so sweetly tempered, so combined
>   By Union, and refined.
> Here no contention, envy, grief, deceit,
>   Fear, jealously have weight,
> But all is peace and love and faith and bliss:
>   What harmony like this? . . .
> Now no affections rage nor humours swell,
>   But all composèd dwell.[131]

In Hobbes, there would be no golden chains let down from heaven, but (as before) the way Hobbes introduces the world in which these chains are replaced did not depart from the norms and habits of address in which they were.

Leviathan as Masque-Text

One function of Hobbes's *Leviathan* is to present the sovereign with an image of himself. He offers the sovereign a complex self-image—one that includes his subjects—and we can better understand these complexities through a comparison to masque representation.[132] Insofar as the Leviathan is composed of all the subjects, the monster-state on the frontispiece is their own portrait. Insofar as the Leviathan cannot come into being until the would-be subjects promise one another to transfer their right of self-protection to a sovereign power that represents them, the image in the mirror is also that of the sovereign himself. The sovereign who represents the multitudes, in Hobbes's words, "personates" *them*.[133]

Tracy Strong has commented on the curious reading of "Nosce te ipsum" in *Leviathan*'s introduction. Hobbes does not make the standard translation, "Know thyself." Rather, he uses the phrase "Read thyself." On Strong's interpretation, this suggests that *Leviathan* might be read as a work of Protestant civic scripture. The citizens must read themselves in the text, and become that which they read.[134] This is not all the introduction suggests. It concludes:

> But let one man read another by his actions never so perfectly, it serves him only with his acquaintance, which are but few. He that is to govern a whole nation must read in himself, not this or that particular man, but mankind, which though it be hard to do, harder than to learn any language or science, yet when I shall have set down my own reading orderly and perspicuously, the pains left another will be only to consider if he also must not find the same in himself. For this kind of doctrine admitteth no other demonstration.[135]

Leviathan as an image of its readers has a nested character. The order of the whole repeats itself on the level of individual parts. Thus, when all individual readers are unified as the Leviathan, they can all be said, in some capacity, to "govern a whole nation." Here then is what Strong has identified as the democratic element in Hobbes's thought. What I am suggesting is that before that unity is achieved, Hobbes is counting on a prior, considerably less democratic, moment that forms and solidifies the whole. In that moment, the individual who is to become the sovereign must read in himself a whole nation. *Leviathan*, therefore, presents that whole national self to the (would-be Hobbesian) sovereign. That sovereign self is to become the Leviathan and at the same time their personator. He is also the artificial man's (mortal) soul.[136] Thus, the sovereign—at first Charles II, but perhaps also Cromwell if Hobbes's Royalist critics were correct—must read in himself every man, and the book that teaches him to see himself as a nation is *Leviathan*, the book that bears his name.

I took note earlier of Stephen Orgel's observation that the masque audience witnessed two performances: they witnessed the performers on stage, but also (and primarily) the king witnessing and finally participating in the masque performance. *Leviathan* was a text presented to a sovereign. That sovereign was, in fact, Parliament (Hobbes returned to England in February 1652; Cromwell's Protectorate was decreed on December 16, 1653; it is noteworthy that Cromwell did have masques performed for him),[137] but we know that Hobbes attempted to deliver a handwritten, vellum-bound copy of the book to Charles, but was not long thereafter blocked from seeing him by his enemies, who were already surrounding the new king in Henrietta Maria's exiled court in France.[138]

Leviathan was a book for sovereign eyes, and like the masque a mirror. Like the mirror of the masque, however, others were to witness the sovereign's seeing himself in this mirror, and as a part of the experience also find themselves reflected in it (in subordinate positions). *Leviathan* was a self that contains themselves, neatly ordered and dutiful as the frontispiece suggests. Hobbes presents the sovereign with a reflection that is also the image of his subjects assembling themselves from chaos into his well-ordered self, his well-ordered commonwealth.

What specifically did Hobbes ask his audience(s) to see in this masque-text? The golden age, as Hobbes noted in *De Cive*, is gone. Harmonious nature is revealed as an illusion. The dangerous man not yet fit for society is the problem, the antimasque, and the authorization of the sovereign is the masque, the establishment of a new order. Hobbes's theatrical language, his account of personation, is not in the least out of place. In the context of absolutism it too abides by the rules of decorum. The sovereign becomes the new subjects' collective representative. The sovereign walks on stage, and as he does, he is at once the ordering presence that assembles the multitude. He becomes the person of that multitude whose members have contracted with one another to author (i.e., authorize) his person, and own his actions.

It is, as always, a matter of instruction. The would-be representative is made the actual sovereign through the covenant made by the would-be subjects. When the covenant is spoken, the representer *is* the sovereign, made a mortal god, and the covenanters are made his subjects, the assembled elements of his self:

> The only way to erect such a common power as may be able to defend them . . . from foreigners and the injuries of one another . . . [that] they may nourish themselves and live contentedly, is to confer all their power and strength upon one man, or upon one assembly of men, that may reduce all their wills, by plurality of voices, unto one will, which is as much to say, to appoint one man or assembly of men to bear their person, and every one to own and acknowledge himself to be author of whatsoever he that so beareth their person shall act, or cause to be acted, in those things that concern the common peace and safety, and therein to submit their wills, every one to his will, and their judgments, to his judgment. This is more than consent, or concord; it is real unity of them all, in one and the same person, made by covenant of every man with every man, . . . as if every man should say to every man I authorize and give up my right of governing myself to this man, or to this assembly of men, on this condition, that thou give up thy right to him, and authorize all his actions in like manner. . . . the multitude so united in one person is called a COMMONWEALTH, in Latin CIVITAS. This is the generation of that great LEVIATHAN, or rather (to speak more reverently) of that *Mortal God* to which under the *Immortal God*, our peace and defence. . . . he that carrieth this person is called SOVEREIGN, and said to have *Sovereign Power;* and every besides, his SUBJECT.[139]

It is, arguably, the most fictive moment in *Leviathan*. Having described the state of nature, which he acknowledges may have never existed,[140] he now dramatizes the creation of the mortal god by showing us how that unity is created through a second fiction subsequent to the first. The Leviathan is created when it is "as if" every man should speak his authorization. In this most fictive moment, however, the covenanters *make true* the sovereign, and the sovereign in turn exercises his authorizing power to assert the veracity of the creation. He does not ensure its historical accuracy, but affirms that the image (i.e., the Leviathan) is, in fact, himself as he would be known. He becomes the soul that imparts motion to parts of the body politic.[141] *Leviathan* and the masques of Jones and Jonson, and later Jones and Davenant—with whom Hobbes was discussing poetry while writing *Leviathan*[142]—also have this in common: the self presented to the royal audience is a self crafted by the hand of a mathematically learned artificer.

In that he promises a godlike sovereign, was Hobbes following in the footsteps of those helping sustain the ideology of rule by mysterious divine right? Quite the opposite. Whereas Jonson speaks of heavenly golden chains, Hobbes knits his own from causes. Hobbes's audacity is therefore best discerned at the moment where he diverges from a common theme of sovereign divinity. Hobbes's sovereign is taught that his godlike qualities are not a gift from above, but from below. Consenting individuals (suddenly made subjects by their consent) make him a deity by authorizing his absolute rule. Thus, the sovereign not only should find every man in himself, but Hobbes's masque *dictates* that he find every man in the commonwealth in himself. Hobbes shows the sovereign that he can be a god by virtue of ruling by his doctrine. The subjects make him the mortal god. It was this critical shift in the means of legitimating the sovereign that so irritated the loyalists.[143]

Although Hobbes grants his sovereign absolute rule over his subjects—makes him a god—he does so in a way that echoes a claim made by revolutionaries. The Crown's parliamentary opponents argued that the source of the sovereign's power was the people's consent, and allowed that persons, and indeed the commonwealth as a whole, could rightly resist a king who threatened their self-preservation, or who went beyond the prescribed limits of a covenant that had been the basis for their consent. From this they concluded that the people (or more specifically, their representatives in Parliament) were entitled to resist the Crown. Hobbes, however, denies that consent driven by the need for self-preservation entitles persons to remove their authorization, and also differs as to who could count as the commonwealth's representative. From the Royalist perspective, the very mention of consent rather than legitimation from a higher source was starting down the road to sedition. Many held to the claim of divine sanction of the Crown's rule, and attacked Hobbes for deviating from this standard.[144] During the Restoration he was painted by his Royalist critics as one of the world's great immoralists for refusing to recognize an earthly authority higher than the king.[145]

As one explores these contrasts, one also finds that the two ways of deifying the sovereign correspond to two ways for the sovereign to *be* mathematical. Here again the important distinction between imitating the divine as creator, and imitating creations (see Chapter 3), reasserts itself. According to divine right kingship, the king himself is endowed with special characteristics from God that entitle him to rule over his subjects. The sovereign is thus made godlike in his masque representation by Jonson and Jones, by virtue of *echoing* the principles used in the creation of the universe by its maker. The Stuart monarchs were told by their masque makers—or they told their guests and subjects through their masque makers—that they were the living embodiments of the divine harmonies that governed the universe. When they were not casting themselves as God himself, they could at least be his pantheistic equivalent.

They deserved to rule because they participated in this form of perfection, and by implication (and by dramatic representation on the masque stage) they could rule by the force of their example.[146] Harmony, the reason and principle of the world, would emanate from their persons to the state—hence the associations between James and proportion and measure in Jonson's poem. His harmonious attributes were testimony to the Platonically inflected divine sanction behind his rule. A nation that made him its measure would find itself a world where dissension, troubles, and chaos would be purged, and as Reason declares in the masque, a world where "all composèd dwell."

There could be nothing further from Hobbes than a reason that defends mysteries, as Jonson's Reason does. Having left the Golden Age in the past, Hobbes declares that the days when sovereigns can defend themselves or justify their rule in terms of mysteries are over. Hobbes's scornful account of the absurdities of ancient religions reads in places like a catalogue of the personations used in the Jonsonian/Jonesian masque to celebrate the mysterious powers of the monarch. There is little, he notes, that they did not declare "a god or devil, or by their poets feigned to be inanimated, inhabited, possessed by some spirit or other."[147] One could use these mysteries to make persons obedient long ago, relying on their "ignorance of causes," and so it was possible to "obtrude on their ignorance, instead of second causes, a kind of second and ministerial gods: ascribing the cause of fecundity to *Venus;* the cause of arts, to *Apollo;* of subtlety and craft, to *Mercury;* of tempests and storms to *Aeolus.*"[148] According to Hobbes, the "first founders, and legislators of commonwealths among the Gentiles" were able to hold people in an ignorant obedience and peace by "in all places [having] taken care; first, to imprint in their minds a belief, that those precepts which they gave concerning religion might not be thought to proceed from their own device, but from the dictates of some god, or other spirit (or else that they themselves were of a higher nature than mere mortals, that their laws might the more easily be received)."[149] It is not that Hobbes thought poets like Jonson or his royal patrons were believers in these myths, but he was (nonetheless) calling for an end to the appeal to any form of mysterious legitimation. Hobbes's sovereign is not a god because of any relationship he might have with or to divine harmonies of the universe.[150]

Hobbes was not telling the sovereign to conform to the principles of an order which he reads in nature. As noted, God and God's way of ordering the universe are pushed out of reach by Hobbes's voluntarist theology. Likewise, the conduct of the Hobbesian sovereign is visible to the law or moral censure of the subjects. The high demands of conformity with heavenly virtues, at least as a matter of sovereign legitimacy, no longer apply. Hobbes instructs his sovereign that he is to become like a god through construction. He is to be engineered, to be made by the authorizing citizens. Instead of being mathematical because he is an exemplar of divine harmonies, Hobbes's sovereign is mathematical because he is a precisely constructed artifice, like a well-made building. He is mathematical in that he is the product of technique, rather than in the mysterious sense evoked in the Neoplatonic themes employed by Jonson and Jones. He is material, rather than spiritual. He is man-made, and also the last word on the morals of his commonwealth. With no higher standard against which to measure this sovereign, Hobbes was predictably criticized not just by Parliamentary partisans but also by the defenders of the Anglican Church (such as Clarendon and Bishop Bramhall), who believed that such external, natural, standards were necessary if one was to distinguish a good and just monarch from a tyrant. One need not be a seventeenth-century republican to insist on the use of the word "tyrant," which Hobbes associated with sedition.

There is a relevant story that reflects Charles I's mathematical interests. He attended a mass where angels were made to appear to raise the host from the altar. Following the ceremony, Charles leaped up to try to examine the machine that had created the illusion.[151] One could say that Hobbes tried to effect a selective displacement by appealing to the Stuart's curiosity. Instead of putting the machinery behind a mystery, he insisted on purging all mystery and putting the machinery on stage. The machinery was, however, definitively put on stage. Hobbes wished for his sovereign, and the doctrine that crafts this mortal god, to be admired as something magnificent in and of itself. He understood absolutist tastes and made them a part of his accomplishment. Rather than use something man-made to imitate sacred mysteries put forward to legitimate rule by divine right, Hobbes erects a magnificent artifice that asserts that men made their legitimate sovereign for themselves.

A key part of the image's suasiveness is its way of being mathematical. It shows itself as a piece of precise engineering, of being well-crafted, unified, and solid by virtue of its design. *Leviathan* was an idealized commonwealth for a sovereign who admired the well-executed and the mathematically ingenious artifice. Hobbes's Reason was not the mysterious force that Jonson's was, but some of reason's tasks remain the same. Reason must use its power to impose order, peace, and quiet where there was once disorder. The appeal to support the king because he embodied divine harmony had failed. We can think of Hobbes's political philosophy as an attempt to build a sovereign body out of sterner stuff.

While earlier masque makers turned the Stuart kings into pagan gods with particular attributes, Hobbes turns the sovereign into the Judeo-Christian god. He is above their legal scrutiny, but he is entitled to direct their actions as he sees fit. It is his might, rather than his example, that Hobbes emphasizes as the power that gives order to the commonwealth. He is the unquestionable ground of the law that is also outside the law.

The philosophers are promised in *De Corpore* that they will be made capable of using Hobbes's philosophy to imitate God as a creator, but in *Leviathan* the sovereign is promised that he is to be made into the mortal god. The sovereign becomes the creator that philosophy crafts. *Leviathan* teaches the sovereign to see himself as the bringer of order, as the mortal version of the Grand Geometer.[152]

9

CONCLUSION

My intention throughout this book has been to pull Hobbes away from his scientific admirers and to move him too close for comfort to the antifoundational critics who disparage the aspirations attributed to him by his scientific admirers. Thoughtful antifoundational political theory is mindful not only of the unexamined presuppositions that guide and inform others, but acknowledges its own. Bringing Hobbes a bit closer will help with the latter, and so I will conclude by indicating where I think his example could inspire introspection. Along the way, I will also locate my reading of Hobbes in relation to the tradition within political theory that has tried to pull him from scientific admirers in the past.

An Audience Denied

In light of the previous chapter it is now possible to expand upon the idea of *Leviathan* as a gift, and how this gift bespoke Hobbes's failed political efforts within the patronage system. In this specific context, Hobbes can be said to have failed because as a gift (like Newcastle's grand parties for Charles I discussed in Chapter 8), *Leviathan* was something given with an eye to receiving something in return.[1]

We know of Hobbes's efforts from Edward Hyde (the Earl of Clarendon), his adversary within the exiled Royalist community. His, and others', accounts of the matter and the existence of a handwritten vellum copy indicate that Hobbes delivered *Leviathan* to his math student, Charles II.[2] In the context of court culture, or in any relationship between persons ranked within the patronage economy of the seventeenth century, gifts were no simple affair. Hobbes has been associated with the beginnings of modern free-market forms of exchange. This is in no small part because Hobbes was a theorist of contracts, and not least because the social contract is formed between equals in the state of nature. He also uses the language of "price" in a way that some associate with the free market's tendency to commodify its world. This focus may lead us to overlook the fact that Hobbes retained the extraordinarily subtle knowledge of the complexity of gift exchanges characteristic of earlier premarket, hierarchical ages.[3]

On the part of the gift-giver, there was an expectation that the item given be something worthy, both of the receiver and of the giver him- or herself. A bad gift was an insult. It was either too little from you, or not good enough for him or her. Daring to give a gift to the king was therefore all the more challenging. Decorum indicated that it had to be the best one could provide. A king commanded something magnificent. On the other hand, those whose gifts the king accepted (for bad gifts, or gifts from a bad source, could be refused) were rewarded. They were recognized as being capable of providing something praiseworthy. Moreover, within the logic of the gift, the receipt of a gift created an obligation on the part of the one who received it.[4] Something had to be given in return. An absolutist sovereign, immune from the rules binding others, might be free to ignore the expectation of reciprocity, but decorum indicated that the great person's return gift should exceed the original offering in the same way that the great person exceeded the person who initiated the exchange.

Hobbes was well aware of how gifts raised questions of status. He noted, for example, how a disproportionate benefit from a person one considered an equal could be seen as a challenge. It could become a source of animosity, whereas a benefit exchanged with an equal or a recognized superior would be something different. As he tells us in *Leviathan:* "To have received from one to whom we think ourselves equal, greater benefits than there is hope to requite, disposeth to counterfeit love, but really secret hatred; and puts a man into the estate of a desperate debtor. . . . For benefits oblige, and obligation is thralldom; and unrequitable obligation, perpetual thralldom. . . . [However,] to receive benefits, though from an equal or inferior, as long as there is hope of requital, disposeth to love; for in the intention of the receiver, the obligation is of aid and service mutual."[5] A happy rivalry may come about, notes Hobbes, "the most noble and profitable contention possible," when each side in this exchange wishes to exceed the other "in benefiting." In such a circumstance, "the victor is pleased with his victory, and the other revenged by confessing it."[6]

What did Hobbes wish in return for his gift to Charles? He made it clear:

> I think it may be profitably printed, and more profitably taught in the Universities (in case they also think so, to whom the judgment of the same belongeth). For seeing the Universities are the fountains of civil

and moral doctrine, from whence preachers and gentry, drawing such water as they find, use to sprinkle the same (both from the pulpit and in their conversation) upon the people, there ought certainly to be great care taken to have it pure, both from the venom of heathen politicians and from the incantation of deceiving spirits. And by that means the most men, knowing their duties, will be the less subject to serve the ambition of a few discontented persons in their purposes against the state, and be the less grieved with the contributions necessary for their peace and defense[7]

In light of what Hobbes was asking in return for his gift it is no wonder that Clarendon made a point of censuring the work.[8] Instead of the reward Hobbes requested, Clarendon seemed satisfied that Hobbes received the just deserts due one who had delivered a very bad gift. The exiled king's gift, "engrossed in Vellum, in a marvelous fair hand," was in fact an immoral and scandalous doctrine. Hobbes's reward came in the form of the agents of "the Justice" seeking his apprehension.[9] He was, quite literally, denied his audience.[10]

It is noteworthy that Hobbes was keeping company or corresponding with a number of poets, including the poet laureate William Davenant, while composing *Leviathan*.[11] As a masque maker, a poet such as Davenant was well practiced in the crafting of eloquent gifts that presented the king with an image of himself. As a masque-text, *Leviathan* took a form Stuart kings had grown accustomed to, and so we can (as I argued in Chapter 8) see Hobbes's presentation of his philosophy in this form as an attempt to dress his doctrine in the clothes most fitting to a court appearance. In electing to write *Leviathan* in the way that he did (and the other texts in their ways) Hobbes was exercising judgment as he himself defined it: a capacity to discern and distinguish, a skill necessary to philosophers, but also appropriate to anyone who must distinguish "persons, places, and seasons."[12]

With *Leviathan*, Hobbes was not only following a norm of courtly address. He was giving the king his advice in a mirror, and showing him how magnificent he would be if he were to accept it as his image. The message to Charles, as noted, was: make my doctrine the doctrine of the state, and you will become this mortal god whose construction I have explained and justified in the text. In short, read yourself in this book and your subjects will do likewise. The Stuart monarchy had used the language of god-imitation to announce legitimate rule by divine right. Hobbes masterfully substituted his own doctrine of sovereignty established by consent, promising Charles that he would remain a god on earth, if on different terms.

Had Hobbes been successful, courtly decorum would not have been his only defense for his eloquence. At the point where Hobbes's counsel became the sovereign's command, his eloquence—now converted into the sovereign's own eloquence—would be beyond reproach, immune by virtue of being the sovereign's. It would also have been in accord with Hobbes's own guidance concerning another appropriate use for eloquence: "Where a man may lawfully command, as a father in a family, or a leader in an army, his exhortations and dehortations are not only lawful, but also necessary and laudable. But then they are no more counsels, but commands, which, when they are for execution of sour labour, sometimes necessity (and always humanity) requireth to be sweetened in the delivery by encouragement, and in the tune and phrase of counsel, rather than in harsher language of command."[13]

As it happened, *Leviathan* was a text all dressed up and with no place to go but back to Britain. There it did become a popular book. From this we need not conclude that the work's foremost audience was the public itself, or that it was written as a simple work of popular oratory. As noted, the masque-like structure of its presentation suggests a more complicated form of eloquent persuasion. Hobbes clearly wished for *Leviathan* to be printed, but printed under the protection of a sovereign. We may speculate that Hobbes also imagined that his *Leviathan* (had it received that protection from Charles) would have functioned as a kind of promissory note from the exiled Stuart king to his future (or at least potential) subjects. In a less speculative vein we may say that Hobbes authored a book fit for a monarch that spoke to the relationship between a sovereign and the people, and it drew the attention of many in Britain. As a wider seventeenth-century audience read the book, like the persons sitting near to the monarchy in a masque audience, they would learn to see themselves as the orderly part of an absolutist artifice. In its moment of creation, Hobbes's artificial man would be made by the people, and, at once, recognized as the sovereign's self.

Today's Audience

I stated in the introduction that I hoped to make Hobbes doubly untimely. He would be pulled away from his scientific admirers and brought too close for comfort to the antifoundational critics least sympathetic to these admirers and the Hobbes they praise. I have argued that Hobbes is *not* many of the things that both sides have either said he is, or have implicitly accepted as true. In accord with the approach of antifoundationalism, I have tried to show how contemporary assumptions have tended to conceal the aspects of Hobbes I have described. These assumptions have also, in some instances, led readers to attribute motives and purposes to him that he did not share with contemporary social scientists and philosophers.

Here is a very brief summary. He did not, I argued, hold his philosophy to a correspondence theory of truth. Hobbes was not only *not* claiming to use his science to reveal a true natural order, or true natural causes, but he made it a matter of human responsibility to create and replace the old theological or natural order with a constructed one. The contingent character of the world is something antifoundationalist political philosophers insist upon as a counterattack upon the confident discoveries of Enlightenment thought. The world's contingency was in fact the condition of Hobbes's claim to take on and meet the aforementioned responsibility. Hobbes's own metaphysical assumptions were not robustly defended in his philosophy, but posited and also appealed to as a part of his own largely antimetaphysical program. He was not interested in making mathematics contribute to what had been natural philosophy's goal in revealing the world. He expected natural philosophy to recognize, and subordinate itself to, a new intellectual hierarchy in which physics borrowed its diminished dignity by imitating the mathematical mind's second-best accomplishment, re-creating nature's effects. Mathematics, specifically geometry, held first place because it created, and could, like God, create originally. He did not claim to, nor did he in fact, work by rationality alone. He sought the cooperation of the passions, especially fear. He did not fight the traditional fight between philosophy and rhetoric. We need not go looking for a covert use of rhetoric as his philosophy's secret weapon, or as a sign that he changed his mind. His use and criticism of rhetoric were largely consistent with his own understanding of its appropriate practice.

In the introduction I mentioned that Hobbes's claim to imitate God was nothing new to his interpreters, nor was the tradition within political theory of pulling Hobbes away from his scientific admirers. I noted that this reading can be thought of as an extension of this approach. Like Sheldon Wolin, therefore, I have argued that on his own terms, Hobbes ought to be exempted from the expectations of empirical social sciences.[14] Like Strauss, I have argued that Hobbes's humanism is central to what he was doing from the start.[15] Like James and Jacobson, I think Hobbes undertook to rival God in what he was doing.[16] Like Schmitt, I recognize that, as a secularized god, Hobbes's sovereign acts with impunity while all others are constrained by the regular order of the laws he makes binding.[17] Like all of the foregoing, I consider Hobbes's rejection of the telos sustained by his predecessors as critical. While retaining more of the past than we have acknowledged, it is still fair to say that Hobbes employed the tools of that past to transform his world and culture in a revolutionary way.

Unlike all of the foregoing, however, I have not conceded Hobbes's scientific territory to his more modern admirers. The view of Hobbes's career as having a single phase, one in which his humanism and his affinity for mathematics go together, allows us to reunite elements of his thought that (these) twentieth-century perspectives have divided. The claim to imitate God, and to craft a mortal god, goes hand in hand with his claim to think and construct like a geometer. Of these authors, Wolin is the most resistant to conceding this territory to Hobbes's scientific admirers, but because he subscribed to the phased view of Hobbes he gave up too much of the struggle before it started.[18] I also have tried to supply a historical context in which the poetic, for Wolin "epical," aspects of Hobbes's work can be connected to concrete modes of political participation and practical goals in the patronage economy.

In more recent years, political theory has wondered less how it can meet the (Wolinian) demands of "Great Political Theory" and worried more about how our culture, our political philosophies, and our persuasions have perpetuated unexamined foundational assumptions which do harm. Concepts that have become a part of our political woodwork—such as pluralism, the autonomous self, and most important for our purposes, consent and sovereignty—are being reworked and challenged. The hope is that the foundational assumptions that have been associated with these harms may either be stricken or at least embraced much more tentatively and in a more reflective manner.

This approach in political theory has been aptly described by Stephen White as political theory's "ontological turn," and by William Connolly as a part of the practice of "ontopolitical interpretation."[19] I hope that my reading of Hobbes makes the case for a historically comparative ontopolitical approach. In the contexts of late modernity, especially in the contexts of the social sciences, one of the most urgent tasks of political theory has been to convince the self-declared inheritors of the scientific revolution that they too must be concerned with the ontopolitical dimensions of their work. As Connolly has noted, there is a widespread sense that "with the (purported) demise in modern philosophy of Aristotelian teleology and Christian doctrines of creation, the human sciences have finally moved into position to take the world as it is."[20] Whereas the old teleological visions of the world make explicit claims concerning human beings and their place within an order of being generally, contemporary moderns have thought themselves somehow past the need for considering what now seem merely speculative, and therefore dispensable, considerations. They are mistaken; the ontopolitical dimensions remain whether or not they are acknowledged.

We know that Hobbes was a part of the effort to discredit the old teleological doctrines. I have also hoped to show how much Hobbes remained a part of the past that we think he left behind. As regards the social and civic sciences of today, Connolly and others (myself included) are concerned to renew interest in and attention to their ontopolitical dimensions. Following Foucault, we can show how unexamined assumptions about human being can "contain dangerous demands and expectations" for those who must live within the confines of these rubrics.[21] These frameworks normalize subjects, just as prior expectations concerning the sciences struggle to convert Hobbes into something which his works defy.[22] Needless to say, the normalization of subjects today under later regimes of truth is a more morally pressing concern than how we interpret Hobbes. My own reading of Hobbes may not, on some views, follow Foucault far enough in that it retains the category of "author" and concerns itself with this author's intents.[23]

As I noted, however, antifoundational critics wish to examine their own fundamental assumptions. Where should they look and why? The modus operandi of antifoundational criticism is to dig up, interrogate, and show the self-subverting aspects of our concepts. They highlight the harms and contradictions fostered by (either implicit or explicit) strong ontological commitments and draw our attention to the inevitable violence that occurs as insufficiently reflexive ideals and ideologies lead their subscribers to try to close the gap between the protean world and their rigid concepts. For Connolly, the view from this position leads the way toward an ethos mindful of these harms and determined to minimize them.[24]

This reading of Hobbes does not amount to, nor does it wish to be, a "knockdown argument" against Connolly's position, but it can raise a question I hope will be helpful. Can those who grant the contingencies of the ontopolitical perspective be counted on to adopt his, or a like-minded, ethos? The struggle against strong foundations and the resistance to violence have been paired habitually in recent years by political philosophers. But a will to do violence and to seek coercive authorities need not spring from a strongly held metaphysical (or foundational) belief or commitment. Hobbes was a robustly antimetaphysical thinker and yet a staunch defender of a violent sovereign. His mortal god was the counterpart to the God of the Old Testament. It may be enough to show those who already intend to live by flawed but nevertheless commendably humane standards that violence is the result of their unexamined concepts. They grow ashamed. The admirable audacity of contemporary ontopolitical perspectives makes them grow ashamed.

Hobbes, like Machiavelli before him, embraced a different form of ontopolitical audacity. The implicit expectation of today's antifoundational detective work is that exposure is a prelude to diminution. That is, revealing these acts of violence—showing that "natural" categories are arbitrarily imposed, and in some cases the product of a potent yet latent will to mastery—will likely result in a certain chastening. Others, it is hoped, would be moved to resist what they might have otherwise thought of as harmless, or as things too obscure and technical to be worthy of attention.

Not unlike antifoundationalists today, Hobbes's audacity was in part grounded in a devotion to pulling down the strong ontological commitments that were beginning to crumble. He did not, contrary to customary readings of his place in early modern science, claim to replace them with a new set of assumptions rooted in a firmer grasp of the world's permanent foundations. For Connolly, the new threat to coexistence is fundamentalism, understood as the urge to protect fundamentals, and to do so by defining "every carrier of critique or destabilization as an enemy marked by exactly those defects, weaknesses, corruptions and naïvetés you are under an absolute imperative to eliminate."[25] Hobbes was an absolutist, but this was not his absolutism. Not only did he pull down old foundations; his politics, while dictatorial in matters of political education, should not be mistaken for a rallying cry to prop up a new dogmatic alternative. His absolutism appeals to those who have grown tired of the "jostling" brought about, in large part, by rival dogmatists. Their claim to transcendent truths is what he hopes to undermine, and yet the appeal to a well-*constructed* order is precisely the hope to deliver the world from the violent competition of doctrines. His sovereign is the supremely violent substitute for the (allegedly) all-powerful Judeo-Christian God, who has failed to redress the misery begotten by his fractious followers.

Dogmatists excuse and mask the arbitrary nature of their violence in the name of mysterious and unquestionable moral foundations. Hobbes offers an open justification for the sovereign's overwhelming violent power, the quest for peace. Against the dogmatists of his own day, he deploys intellectual judo. The God with whom they each claimed to be allied was also said to be so superior to man as to be inscrutable. Hobbes rigorously insisted upon the inscrutability of God to deny anyone but the sovereign the capacity to claim divine justification.

Hobbes and today's antifoundationalist thinkers therefore have something in common. They wish to put out the flames spread by foundationalist conflicts. Connolly hopes to do so by using his antifoundationalist practices to diminish their confidence. He pours water on the flames by showing them the way their assumptions are subject to challenge. Hobbes fights the fires with explosives. His inclination was to use the dynamite of his own supremely confident antifoundationism and the power of a sovereign to suck up all the available fuel. Their theological and ontological foundations would be displaced. His fundamentals do not claim to be grounded in a mysterious ultimate reality, but in the protection and promotion of an overwhelming force.

Hobbes's ontopolitical audacity (not unlike Machiavelli's) would not have been shamed by those who might demand that it confess its violent origins.[26] Challenges to his (alleged) scientific detachment or objectivity would be similarly unimpressive to one whose goal was to create order out of chaos. As a practitioner of maker's knowledge, Hobbes would have felt the challenge of one who could suggest that his constructions were poorly built. This would not have come in the form of a claim that he failed to grasp the processes of nature, but that his method of manipulating matter, his "architectural skill," was somehow incompetent. Someone who could suggest that Hobbes did not possess the constructive skills he claimed was a threat. This was the challenge John Wallis posed in his refutation of Hobbes's attempt to square the circle (and their ongoing conflicts), and it is why the stakes that attached to their conflict were centered in claims to an identity. Who truly possessed the talents to call themselves a geometer? I discuss this conflict in the appendix.

I wish to return to Connolly's critique of consent theory, but before doing so I will expand a bit on how Hobbes can help us see the limits of antifoundational critiques inspired by Richard Rorty's work, which focus their efforts on challenging epistemological claims.

The Limits of the Epistemological Critique

Protesting the ontological indeterminacy of either the world or politics, I have argued, is no way to catch Hobbes unawares.[27] Hobbes's solution to the problems of an ontologically indeterminate universe was never a willingness to look harder for the one foundation not yet shaken by skepticism—nor was it to introduce that foundation surreptitiously. Rather, having realized the social contingencies upon which any foundational claim rests, Hobbes set to work in crafting a political and intellectual commonwealth that protected its foundations by force.[28]

In this regard, the interpretation of Hobbes that I have presented does not fit the accepted critical narrative of the early modern period that now informs antifoundational thought. It has been customary to note that seventeenth-century new science emerged in the midst of a crisis. However, the approach to this tends to veer too quickly in its attention from political and social problems to problems of a more epistemological nature. Following the lead of Richard Rorty, and the Rortian reading of John Dewey, Stephen Toulmin's *Cosmopolis* is illustrative of this approach.[29]

Toulmin details the upheavals of the seventeenth century and writes of a political context that fits Donne's lament, "'Tis all in pieces, all coherence gone."[30] He also points to the terrible social uncertainties (resulting from the murder of Henry IV in France, and from the Thirty Years' War) that made the moderate skepticism of Descartes's predecessors seem inappropriate. According to Toulmin, this context created a heartfelt demand for a form of knowledge that could assert and defend absolute certainty. He writes:

> In the conditions of the time, then, the issues of certainty, rational consensus, and necessity, which the 16th-century skeptics had left as a challenge to philosophy, were far more than matters of theoretical taste or opinion. . . . People at large were left in bewilderment, sensing that matters were now out of hand. . . . It is with these circumstances in mind that we can understand why the Quest for Certainty developed the appeal it did, from the 1630s on. The shift within philosophy, away from practical issues to an exclusive concern with the theoretical—by which local, particular, timely, and oral issues surrendered their centrality to issues that were ubiquitous, universal, timeless, and written—was no quirk of Descartes. All the protagonists of modern philosophy promoted theory, devalued practice, and insisted equally on the need to find foundations for knowledge that were clear, distinct, and certain. Facing dogmatic claims by rival theologians, it was hard for onlookers of goodwill to restrict themselves to the cool modesty of an Erasmus or a Montaigne. . . . All along, of course—if Dewey and Rorty are right—this was too much to expect. No set of "clear and distinct ideas" could ever be found. . . . Given the historical situation of Europe in the 1630s and '40s, however, to suggest that the rationalist experiment was never worth making would be to betray a lack of sensitivity.[31]

It is precisely because Toulmin is correct about the social and political contexts that he should have reassessed the Rortian view of the Quest for Certainty.

Hobbes was not searching for a foundation, but announcing its constitution. Rather than a *quest*, it was a requirement. Or, being a requirement, it could no longer be a *quest*. The question of the dubiousness of seventeenth-century epistemology should, in the case of Hobbes, be considered secondary to the larger question of what he and his contemporaries were demanding politically (inside and outside the academy). Hobbes was willing to *make* truths in the political realm. He did not answer the urgency of a chaotic situation with a search for foundations deemed unshakable through natural or theological necessity, but with a construction project that would build and defend truths with the force of an absolute sovereign.

Hoping to make sovereignty itself his foundation (the first mover[32] of his political and philosophical doctrines), Hobbes promises to play the role of "able architect" and build a philosophy and a state that would stand firmly upon it. Hobbes's solution to political and philosophical chaos was to use the authority of the state to stamp an order upon it. His boast was to have devised an order (social and intellectual) that exemplified the virtues embodied in the ways of geometers—clarity, precision, and a capacity for building something solid, certain, and even magnificent. The first and last word on contentious subjects was something Hobbes thought should be reserved for a sovereign; his claim was to allow the sovereign to build an artifice rooted in this authority that would be well ordered and lasting. Why did Hobbes think such an enterprise might be appealing to his contemporaries?

Hobbes had an awareness of how periods of crisis and confusion were likely to make absolutist governments look comparatively attractive. "A Discourse upon the Beginnings of Tacitus" speaks directly to this sensibility. In noting the final success of Augustus over Republican Rome, the Discourse reads, "After the violent storms of civil wars, succeeds now the calm of Augustus's government. For it fares with the body of a whole State, as it does with the body of one man, that when a Fever has spent the matter, and bilious humor, whereby itself was nourished, the body comes afterwards to a moderate temperature."[33]

Historians John Morrill and J. D. Walter conclude that there was a discrepancy between the expectations of propertied contemporaries prior to the revolution and what actually happened during the English Civil War. Preexisting social and economic tensions were indeed made worse, but for our purposes it is noteworthy that many experienced a "moral panic" and were expecting a "popular explosion, fear of which ran like a red thread through the political history of the period."[34]

Following Charles I's execution in 1649, the Royalist propagandist publisher Richard Royston (who also published *Philosophical Rudiments*, the English translation of *De Cive*, in 1651 with an illustration of "Religion" personated by a figure resembling Charles I)[35] published *Eikon Basilike, The Pourtraicture of His Sacred Majestie in his solitudes and sufferings*, the rhetorical masterpiece by Charles I and his ghostwriter John Gauden.[36] Proclaiming his own martyrdom, with references likening it to Christ's,[37] Charles I's posthumous book uses imagery that decries his enemies for creating chaos and sets the stage (literally) for the return to order upon a Stuart restoration. The book includes what purports to be Charles I's reaction to his difficulties with the Long Parliament and his fleeing Whitehall Palace and London at the start of the conflict:

> As it is one of the most convincing Arguments that there is a God, while his power lets bounds to the raging Sea; so its no lesse, that he restraines the madnesse of the people. Nor doth any thing portend more Gods displeasure against a Nation, then when he suffers the confluence and clamours of the vulgar, to passe all boundaries of Lawes, and reverence to Authority. . . .
>
> Nor was this a short fit or two of shaking, as an ague, but a quotidian feaver, alwaies encreasing to higher inflammations, impatient of any mitigation, restraint, or remission.[38]

Finding fault with the "Demagogues and Patrones of Tumults," Charles observes, "it is no strange thing for the Sea to rage, when strong winds blow upon it; so neither for Multitudes to become insolent, when they have Men of some reputation for parts and piety to set them on."[39] The Stuarts, their earliest supporters, and the many more who were shocked by the king's execution came to see the politics of the unruly masses as dangerous and life-threatening. Fear, the passion Hobbes had always been willing to make an ally to his philosophy, was an opening to absolutism.

When Charles II returned to an uneasy Restoration compromise, Royalists saluted him as Augustus fighting back the forces of chaos personated by "Rebellion" and "Confusion," an accomplishment they proclaimed the fulfillment of "God's justice."[40] Hobbes used very similar language to describe the "tumults" of rebellion in *Leviathan*. Ancient histories that celebrated republican victories over tyrants were likened to the bite of a dog with rabies:

> Their venom . . . I will not doubt to compare to the biting of a mad dog, which is a disease the physicians call *hydrophobia*, or *fear of water*. For as he that is so bitten has a continual torment of thirst, and yet abhorreth water, and is in such an estate as if the poison endeavored to convert him

into a dog, so when a monarchy is once bitten to the quick by those democratical writers that continually snarl at his estate, it wanteth nothing more than a strong monarch, which nevertheless out of a certain *tyrannophobia* (or fear of being strongly governed), when they have him, abhor him.[41]

He was particularly colorful in his description of the madness of a multitude when it is led by persons claiming divine inspiration. Although the madness may not be easily visible in a single person, Hobbes notes,

> when many of them conspire together, the rage of the whole multitude is visible enough. . . . For as in the midst of the sea, though a man perceive no sound of that part of the water next him, yet he is well assured that part contributes as much to the roaring of the sea as any other part of the same quantity, so also, though we perceive no great unquieteness in one or two men, yet we may be well assured that their singular passions are parts of the seditious roaring of a troubled nation.[42]

Hobbes scandalized many of his contemporaries because he sought a human cure for such diseases. Where others found in their efforts at restoration a sign of divine justice, Hobbes found the solution in the discovery of the right method of building a commonwealth. Mathematically skillful persons could build solid edifices, and they could chart the seas. As Britain's circumstances made absolutism increasingly tempting, Hobbes put himself forward as the one to supply the designs for order and peace. It was a promise he made by referencing the ill consequences of using the wrong method:

> For men, as they become at least weary of irregular jostling and hewing one another, and desire with all their hearts to conform themselves into one firm and lasting edifice, so for want, both of the art of making fit laws to square their actions by, and also of humility and patience to suffer the rude and cumbersome points of their present greatness to be taken off, they cannot, without the help of a very able architect, be compiled into any other than a crazy building, such as, hardly lasting out their own time, must assuredly fall upon the heads of their posterity.[43]

While his contemporaries were making their own efforts and searching for (and claiming) divine sanction for the order they would restore, Hobbes's plan for the construction of a mortal god emerged, to use an anachronistic phrase, as one of the world's most profound attempts to "do it yourself." His contemporaries picked up on this audacity. It is why a Restoration critic such as John Eachard mocked Hobbes as a philosophical Bobadill by having his "bookseller" preface his work with his own set of impossible mathematical promises.[44] Nor, given Hobbes's poetically trained sense of eloquence, is it surprising that among his admirers and detractors the poets were particularly attuned to his claim to a philosophy that would teach men to build in a way that rivaled God. Abraham Cowley, an admirer, wrote:

> Vast *Bodies* of *Philosophie*
> I oft have seen, and read,
> But all are *Bodies Dead;*
> Or *Bodies* by *Art fashioned;*
> I never yet the *Living Soul* could see,
>   But in thy *Books* and *Thee.*
>   'Tis onely *God* can know
> Whether the fair *Idea* thou dost show
> Agree intirely with his *own* or no.
>   This I dare boldly tell,
> 'Tis so *like* Truth 'twill serve our turn as well.[45]

If Cowley's praise is for Hobbes's capacity to re-create nature by his own means, an anonymous critic of both Hobbes and Cowley was willing to chastise the philosopher for his bolder forms of building:

>   Good Men his Knavery spie:
> His Books contain some Truths, and many a Lie,
> Some Truths *well known, but strange* Impiety.
> . . . .
> What's Nature but the Ordinary way
> Wherein our Good Creator doth display
> His *Power,* and *Wisdom* in the things he *made*
> For his own *Goodness* sake? Man's not a *Shade,*
> But *utter Darkness,* whilst he *acts alone,*
> Whilst his works are *not natures;* but *his own.*
> What! *Hobbes,* and *Nature* thus to *parallel!*
> What's this but to *confront* Bright *Heaven* with *Hell!*
> So doth the Poets wit suit with this *Theme:*
> He that will *Hobbes* Applaud must first *Blaspheme.*

> He brings those *Wares*, which he shall never sell
> To any, but those darkn'ed Souls, which *lie*, where *Adam fell*.
> The Power of Earthly Princes he doth *foolishly pretend*
> 	By his fictitious Loyalty t'extend
> To larger measures; gives to Kings what due to God
> Thus what he seems to make *more great*, he really makes *none:*
> For sure on Earth there is *No Monarchy*,
> If it consist in ABSOLUTE *Sovereignty*.
> The King of Kings commands us to obey our King,
> By *cheerful* Doing, or by *quiet* Suffering:
> He that the Power of Kings would have much higher
> His King Dishonours, and his GOD he doth Despise:[46]

Hobbes's response to political and intellectual chaos was to build an order by his own means, and to his critics this looked very much like inviting kings to play at being God. Such critics had a better idea of Hobbes's ambitions than many of his admirers or critics today. It is in light of Hobbes's response to a world that he understood to be contingent and in flux that we perhaps need to reevaluate the assumption that has animated many critical accounts of modern rationality.

Some have seen the solution to the problems attributed to foundationalism in a form of therapy for what has been called "Cartesian anxieties."[47] Such (Rortian) therapy is intended to teach persons not to search for solid foundations by showing, in part, that we already do well every day without them (and would do better still upon this realization). Against this possibility we might say that there are also "Hobbesian anxieties" with which we must contend. These do not manifest themselves in a desire to establish rational and grounded knowledge of the world without. Thus, releasing persons like Hobbes from these "Cartesian anxieties" may likewise release them for other fears that may, under certain circumstances, generate an overwhelming desire for peace, quiet, and order. (Fundamentalism, another threat, seethes with anger over the threatened loss of order, which it will restore dogmatically.) "Hobbesian" anxieties are driven by the more immediate and pressing fear of political and social disorder. Hobbes found the problem and solution in philosophy, but even in his solution he did not find it necessary to claim a definitive knowledge of the natural world, or to deny in any way the idea of the world as something constructed. On the contrary, it was against the background of a constructed world that Hobbes's claims were so bold: he promised to show his audiences how they too might build out of chaos. Hobbes may be said to build his machine-state mathematically, but it is not the kind of (more modern) machine which he expects to fuel by some regular power rooted in knowledge of nature's ordinary courses. It is not, notably, a machine fueled by "human egoism." As we have shown, Hobbes does not seek comfort in finding nature's seemingly regular patterns. Finally, Hobbes and his seventeenth-century contemporaries illustrate that a belief in the world's contingency does not always produce an impulse to loosen the hold of political authority. Perhaps it is naïve to hope that it will do so today.

Consenting to Absolutism

I have covered some of the reasons why Hobbes thought his contemporaries might find his absolutism an attractive option. I will now bring this reading of Hobbes to a close with a comparison of Hobbes's appeal for absolutist sovereignty and the hopes implicit in a recent challenge to concepts of sovereignty and consent. William Connolly has made the case that the persistent gap between "the actual practices" of states and the images of the integral, unified states these concepts beget is a space filled with unacknowledged violence. Connolly's goal, in accord with the aforementioned strategy of forcing those who work by these concepts to see and acknowledge this violence, is to reveal how the gaps are generative of a detrimental form of politics. He calls this the politics of homesickness.

The homesick mourn the loss of the state that has somehow lost control over itself, over its distinct and identifiable place. It is a longing to return to a state that never was. Homesickness thereby begets actions and modes of thought that try to close the gaps, and "whenever these stopgap concepts become installed in cultural self-understanding they conceal a series of cruelties, dangers, and violences in the present that need to be addressed."[48] If we reveal the cruelties and violence, we will be on our way, Connolly hopes, toward a more cosmopolitan, multidimensional imagination of how to *be* democratic. Instead of "yearning for a settled politics of place," we can disrupt the experience of sovereignty and reconceive political self-rule in a way less complicit with these harms.

Connolly's analysis draws upon and expands the scope of an essay, from 1957, by Paul Ricoeur, "The Political Paradox." This was a response to the Soviet Union having thwarted an attempt by Hungary to defect from the Warsaw Pact in 1956 by bombing and sending in tanks and troops to put down its resistance. The event, Ricoeur maintained, illustrated a permanent characteristic of politics that had a significance that went beyond immediate historical events.[49] Ricoeur noted that the paradox shows itself most clearly in Rousseau's *Social Contract;* Connolly seconds and augments this claim. A simple historical objection to the idea of a social contract demands to know: did a social contract actually ever take place? Ricoeur converts the simple objection into a more profound observation: "One might object that this pact has not taken place. Precisely. It is of the nature of political consent, which gives rise to the unity of the human community organized and oriented by the State, to be able to be recovered only in an act which has not taken place, in a contract which has not been contracted, in an implicit and tacit pact which appears only in political awareness, in retrospection, and in reflection."[50]

Those who idealize democratic sovereignty, Connolly maintains, must find something to trouble their ideals in this assertion. It shows that built within the structure of sovereignty there are fictions that, when exposed, must compromise the integrity that these idealists imagine. Connolly bolsters this point by drawing further on Rousseau's *Social Contract*. Here Rousseau first acknowledges that consent occurs in an act that has not taken place: "In order for an emerging people to appreciate the healthy maxims of politics, and follow the fundamental rules of statecraft, the effect would have to become the cause; the social spirit, which should be the result of the institution, would have to preside over the founding of the institution itself; and men would have to be prior to the laws what they ought to become by means of the laws."[51]

Persons without the state, the "emerging people," would have to possess the social spirit that state laws themselves were supposed to generate. This is the paradox of founding, and Connolly goes on to note that if Rousseau acknowledges the paradox, his next move is to "conceal the legacy of this paradox." Rousseau's wise legislator conceals the paradox by recourse to religion. He puts the laws in the mouths of the immortals, because "emerging people" lack the prudence to come to these conclusions on their own. They will obey without having to be convinced, but not, Connolly insists, without being coerced. Rousseau's general will "artfully conceals" the violence necessary to sustaining the "regulative ideal" of a free, unconditioned, political will.[52] Coercion is concealed, for example, in the way that Rousseau naturalizes the subordination of women to the authority of men, and of us all to the unified authority of the family.[53]

Connolly's treatment of Rousseau's *Social Contract* quoted here passes over the legislator's use of religion in the Founding, but the appeal to the supernatural that Rousseau references is nicely contrasted with the creation of

Hobbes's mortal god. Although Hobbes does not reference a precise parallel, it is worth noting that he considers the "golden age" when sovereignty could be exercised without scrutiny—because human wisdom was disguised behind divinities—had passed. This suggests the larger challenge to perspectives that think they will check violence by bringing it into the light of day.

Hobbes's mortal god is not intended as a disguise. *Leviathan* stages its creation and makes it an eminently visible act. As I have noted, Hobbes's greatest audacity consisted in what he refused to hide, and it is why later natural law theorists were anxious to bury him in the same way that earlier generations sought to bury Machiavelli. States, as the paradox of politics would seem to suggest, require miracles to get started. They must be exempt from the rules of causality, like a First Mover. Hobbes's sovereign does not hide the paradox, or undertake to disguise the violence (or the threat of violence) involved in a founding. Like Pomponazzi and Hill's miracles, he was open to declaring these things within the orbit of human capacity.[54]

Hobbes may therefore serve as a reminder of an ordinary, but disappointing, state of affairs. In spite of all the harms that must be unearthed by the concepts that do, indeed, mask them, there is a more dispiriting possibility to consider. The appeal of what Ricoeur called the "evil linked to the essence of politics"—the problem posed by the successful use of lawless power, the not yet but soon to be legitimated power that founds states—needs even more attention than either Ricoeur[55] or Connolly grants it. Each is dedicated to undoing the forgetfulness that covers over, that legitimates, lawless power after the fact with the cover of legal legitimacy. This is a worthwhile venture, but the careful skills cultivated for the sake of offering these reminders have developed alongside their own form of forgetfulness. Because violence is often hidden, it is comforting to think that an unmasking of the concepts that help conceal it will be enough to at least motivate persons to abandon or modify their thinking so as to avoid the sin of violence. Let's hope this works, but the practice of revealing the connection between metaphysics and violence is prone to forget that there were (and one must know still are) circumstances and sentiments, such as Hobbes's, which make the appeal to a miraculous violent founding appealing.

Because Hobbes was well aware of the paradox of politics, he insisted that human beings were not "born fit" but had to be "made fit" for life together. This is why his foremost audience member was the sovereign who might ensure they had the instruction that bolstered that rule. But these are not subjects who ignore the violence of the sovereign; they openly enable it. They seek to augment the sovereign's power to threaten those who they believe threaten them. They do not do so out of a fidelity to transcendent moral standards, but because they are convinced those standards are no longer available. Their fear, in combination with Hobbes's guidance, makes them ready to settle for something less. This is the popular audience Hobbes sought to, at once, appeal to and sustain through state indoctrination. I noted that we, today, are not Hobbes's audience. In recent years, one might have thought that we had become so. If we are to avoid this outward affinity for violence, we will need to do more than engage in antimetaphysical detective work. Not all who are aware of the paradox of politics will be scandalized by it.

APPENDIX

WHO IS A GEOMETER?
WALLIS, ALGEBRA, AND A HUMANIST DEFENSE OF MATHEMATICAL PRACTICE

I have argued against the view that Hobbes's turn to mathematics and geometry was a turn away from humanism. I have also argued that Hobbes's affinity for mathematics bears the marks of the humanist culture. Hobbes and the humanist educators that preceded him admired the same things in the mathematically trained mind. Finally, I have shown how Hobbes's promotion of his mathematically inspired philosophy also bears the marks of what I have called the mathematical "high culture" of the Stuart Court. But how deeply enmeshed is Hobbes's humanism within his mathematics? Here I will offer evidence that his humanism—the practices, habits, and framework in which Hobbes understood his claim to intellectual mastery—is thoroughly woven into his concept of mathematics.

Although I will not offer a comprehensive treatment of Hobbes's mathematics, I can make this point in light of a key part of the controversy in which Hobbes defended his conception of mathematics and attacked that of his opponent, John Wallis. Inevitably, this will also raise the larger question of the relationship of Hobbes's mathematics to his politics generally. More might be said in linking Hobbes's promotion of what he claimed was an infallible philosophical method, and his preference for absolutist government, but in this appendix I will limit my treatment to the more immediate political considerations that attended the Hobbes-Wallis conflict.

Until recent efforts by historians of mathematics, there has been little to supersede George Croom Robertson's account of it. That has now changed.[1] Among most mathematically centered commentary, however, reflections on the politics of the conflict have been relatively slim. Douglas Jesseph has recently pursued these matters in greater detail, but he has also insisted upon a relatively bright line between the political and mathematical disputes between Hobbes and Wallis.[2] I have already commented on Jesseph's approach in Chapter 5, and here again it seems to me that the evidence Jesseph discusses undermines his claim to a firm distinction. Consideration of the question of

Hobbes's conflict with Wallis from the point of view of humanism will further reinforce the case. (Unlike Jesseph I will not attempt to settle the question of Hobbes's atheism, an issue raised by Wallis's attack.)

I shall first describe the crux of the key element of their conflict, the dispute over the merits of algebra. Then, after a discussion of the political contexts (some of which I have already described in Chapter 7), I will illustrate that this debate between Hobbes and Wallis was also, and at once, a debate over who was entitled to call himself a proper geometer. Moreover, in taking on this characteristic of a debate over an office or title, Hobbes pursued his side of the argument in a framework provided to him by his humanist contemporaries and predecessors.

The Problem with Algebra

Wallis was a strong advocate of algebraic methods in geometry, and has been understood as a pioneer. The enthusiasm for algebraic technique was something he shared with Descartes—although Wallis was loath to give Descartes credit for the development of algebraic techniques.[3] Algebra, as developed by Descartes and also practiced by Wallis, entailed the reduction of all geometrical entities to a single unit, the line. Algebraic technique, moreover, violated the guiding principles of Hobbes's practice (principles I described in Chapters 3 and 5). It did not start with elemental parts and work its way up to the construction of figures. It did not proceed one carefully placed step at a time. Indeed, from the point of view of Hobbes and those who favored more traditional geometrical practices (such as Newton's teacher, Isaac Barrow), the audacity of early modern algebra was signaled at the very start of Descartes's *La Geometrie*.[4] His work did not begin with postulates, axioms, or definitions. Rather, he began with a reductive assertion that he claimed would facilitate the creation of a much more useful, and universalizable, mode of reasoning. He was not interested in studying and defining given figures. Rather, he proposed that mathematicians reduce and redescribe all figures in terms of a given (arbitrarily chosen) basic unit:

> Any problem in geometry can easily be reduced to such terms that a knowledge of the lengths of certain straight lines is sufficient for its construction. Just as arithmetic consists of only four or five operations, namely, addition, subtraction, multiplication, division, and the extraction of roots, which may be considered a kind of division, so in geometry, to

find required lines it is merely necessary to add or subtract other lines; or else, taking one line which I shall call unity in order to relate it as closely as possible to numbers, and which can in general be chosen arbitrarily, and having given two other lines, to find a fourth line which shall be to one of the given lines as the other is to unity (which is the same as multiplication); or, again, to find a fourth line which is to one of the given lines as unity is to the other (which is equivalent to division) . . . and I shall not hesitate to introduce these arithmetical terms into geometry.[5]

That unit having been specified, the quantities associated with figures could be transferred into an equivalent language of numbers and symbols. Thus, a line might be called a, two lines multiplied by one another, i.e., a square, renamed a^2; a circle with a radius of three, for example, could be represented by the equation $x^2 + y^2 = 9$. Those promoting algebra gave the mathematician permission to translate the figures used in geometry into a language of symbols, directing the attention of his reason to these instead of actual figures on the page.[6] This meant that instead of thinking of compounding lines with one another to create figures up to three dimensions, the algebraic program dictated that when we add lines to lines we simply get more lines. The square, a^2, therefore may be converted to a single value, commensurable with a single line b. (A 5 by 5 unit square was equal to 5^2, which was equal to a 25-unit line.) This line may be added to, subtracted from, multiplied, or divided. As a conceptual ground for this approach Descartes declared that between geometry and arithmetic, arithmetic was the prior science. One could, therefore, legitimately reduce geometrical operations to mathematical ones, and practically speaking this was done by virtue of the reduction of all to a single arbitrary unit.

Finally, one of the most threatening elements of the algebraicization of geometry from Hobbes's point of view becomes clear when we identify Descartes's innovation by its synonym, *analytic geometry*. *Analytic geometry* was indeed analytic, in that instead of instructing the mathematician to work his way up from particular definitions or axioms, he was instructed to begin with the equation that described the figure he wanted to study.[7] Through the addition and subtraction of other figures or lines, the individual values of the variables might be determined. That is, the analytic geometrician worked from the top down, beginning with the completed "figure" and ending his calculations with a conclusion that specified the value of a variable that expressed the quantity sought for in terms of the universal unit.[8]

As far as Hobbes was concerned, Wallis and Descartes were taking mathematics in the wrong direction in every sense. Instead of working up from well-defined terms, they were working down from symbols. Instead of teaching generative practices as he believed they ought to be—starting with the posited ground and moving up—they were oriented first toward the dissecting of assumed forms:[9]

> The rule, both in Mr. Ougthred, and in Des Cartes, is this: "When a problem or question is propounded, suppose the thing required done, and then using a fit ratiocination, put A or some other vowel for the magnitude sought." How is a man the better for this rule without another rule, how to know when the ratiocination is fit? There may therefore be in this kind of analysis more or less natural prudence, according as the analyst is more or less wise, or as one man in choosing of the unknown quantity with which he will begin, or in choosing the way of the consequences which he will draw from the hypothesis, may have better luck than another. But this is nothing to art.[10]

Hobbes insisted, moreover, that geometers were meant to create and reason over the actual figures on the page, and to define their terms according to the motions that created these figures. Both Hobbes's ideal geometer and Wallis's algebraicized geometer worked with names, broadly construed, but for Hobbes there was a critical difference. While proper geometers maintained a close connection between their terms and the matter in motion on the page, the techniques of algebra made for a greater gap between matter and the symbols with which one performed one's calculations.[11] On these grounds, he opposed the shift away from matter to a further removed symbolic realm by the algebraic practitioners.[12] While proponents of using algebra in geometry argued that they had devised a convenient shorthand for the long processes of geometrical reasoning, Hobbes argued that the translation to symbols could only cloud the mathematician's reason. The mathematician would have to translate back from the symbols into words and then from the words to the geometric figures, a "double labour." This was another reason why the proponents of algebra were corrupting proper philosophical practice. Hobbes continued his critique: "I shall also add, that symbols, though they shorten the writing, yet they do not make the reader understand it sooner than if it were written in words. For the conception of the lines and figures (without which a man learneth nothing) must proceed from words either spoken or thought upon. So that there is a double labour of the mind, one to reduce your symbols to words, which are also symbols, another to attend to the ideas which they signify."[13]

Such objections overlap with elements of what has been described as the conservative reaction to analytic geometry, such as that offered by Barrow.[14] In some respects, however, the word "conservative" does not fit Hobbes.[15] Hobbes, as we have noted, celebrated Euclid and ancient geometry, but he was not interested in merely preserving either against the assaults of analytic geometers. Rather, he hoped to improve upon ancient geometry, and sought to use it as a model for other sciences. He wanted to export the practices of geometry that he thought applicable to philosophy in general.[16] A key example concerns the use of definitions, and can be illustrated by referring back to Blancanus's (see Chapter 5) view on Euclid. Blancanus noted that some of Euclid's definitions were "causal"; they not only named a thing, but also explained how that thing might be created. Not all definitions, however, were causal; some merely specified essences. Hobbes argues that whenever possible, we ought to use definitions that specify the cause of the thing defined, and this is a standard that he applies not only to geometry, but to philosophy in general.[17] The practices that Hobbes wants to import from geometry to the other disciplines are first, therefore, filtered through his own refinements. Of course, not all sciences (as we have noted, not natural philosophy) will be able to produce the kind of demonstrative certainty that we see in geometry. Hobbes's scrutiny, however, is not limited to natural philosophers. Although he praises Euclid, there are moments where Hobbes suggests that Euclid slipped from a standard of diligent practice. These are mistakes that needed to be reformed. At other moments Hobbes maintains that Euclid's statements are ambiguous—although probably in line with his own views.

These concerns emerge in his conflicts with Wallis over how geometers should define their basic terms (e.g., points, lines, and planes). The definitions had to reflect the fact that these were—in keeping with Hobbes's view—referring to the sense impressions created by actual matter. On this point, he fought vehemently against Wallis; he characterized him as lax and undisciplined in his use of definitions. We see this element of the conflict emerge in their arguments over the proper way to define a line. Hobbes objected to Euclid's definition: "A line is length which hath no breadth," but this definition received a mild objection. "If candidly interpreted," Hobbes suggested, the definition was "sound enough, though not rigorously so."[18] He was not willing to count on candor—and he goes out of his way to state that he counted on Wallis to use anything but candor. To ensure the integrity of geometry against bad practitioners like Wallis, Hobbes put forward a new definition and insisted that it become the new standard: "*A line is a body whose length is considered without its breadth.*"[19] Importantly, a line *is* a body, but a body whose breadth we choose not to consider. Against Euclid's definition he was particularly concerned with the fact that persons were drawing the inference that a line is something with no breadth at all—a mere abstraction.[20] This was not only absurd, but entirely disconnected from matter. The specter of "incorporeal substances" lurked behind this way of practicing geometry—the ramifications of which I will deal with momentarily. Hobbes notes Wallis's contentment with the incorporeal conception of a line,[21] and answers that a line must be defined as he defines it, by means of its generation: "I say, to me, howsoever, it may be to others, it was fit to define a line by motion. For the generation of a line is the motion that describes it. And having defined philosophy in the beginning, to be the knowledge of the properties from the generation, it was fit to define it by its generation."[22]

These issues are quite important to Hobbes's geometry, and to his conception of philosophy as a whole. These disagreements also reflect, as I have illustrated, the connection between his insistence that geometers reason over words that describe matter in motion,[23] and the great stress he put upon generation over analysis. If geometers merely reasoned over words detached from matter, he asserted, then the claim that we can demonstrate what we *make ourselves* both loses its connection to substances we can move, manipulate, and compound into the effects we desire and disconnects geometry from the concrete sense of engaging in acts of construction. Wallis, pursuing a program of mathematics that relied on the abstraction of all quantity into number (i.e., algebra), was pushing in the opposite direction. Moreover, if the geometer risks the further removal of his reasoning from matter, motion, and generation, then his contribution might be no better than those of wrangling, useless schoolmen, and Hobbes had denounced their morass of ambiguous terms as leading to pointless and boisterous squabbles and dangerous doctrines. These points have been reviewed in the recent literature.[24] Beyond this, however, there is an element to these debates which commentators have passed over.

Hobbes's debates with Wallis were over something larger than technique, narrowly defined. These debates also concerned the question of the geometer's identity, and therewith the characteristics and virtues appropriate to those who called themselves geometers. Hobbes scholars have noted the sometimes vindictive elements of the debate. Rogow notes, for example, that the conflict had descended to the point where Hobbes referred to Wallis's mathematics as "all Error and Railing, that is *stinking wind*, such as a Jade [a horse] lets flie when he is too hard girt upon a full belly."[25] Wallis had referred to one of Hobbes's books as a "shitten piece."[26] The remarks certainly illustrate Rogow's point concerning the low-flying nature of this debate, but the insults also have a substantive connection. Hobbes's suggestion that his algebraic opponent was "windy" was a rude metaphor for the way his terms had detached themselves from matter.[27] Wallis's retort similarly transposed the terms of the debate.

More important, their eager attempts to denigrate their opponent's character and competence have a political significance and help reveal the connections between Hobbes's mathematics and his humanism. We can see this through a closer look at Hobbes's *Six Lessons to the Professors of Mathematics*.[28] As I noted in Chapter 7, the second professor was Seth Ward, coauthor (with John Wilkins) of *Vindiciae Academiarum* (1654), a vehement defense of the universities against their attackers, including Hobbes, whom he accused of knowing neither geometry nor the state of the discipline as it was practiced at Oxford.[29]

What is the connection to humanism and to larger political issues? Douglas Jesseph has rightly argued that the philosopher fought so vehemently and persistently against Wallis because Hobbes's approach to geometry was the cornerstone of his approach to philosophy as a whole. Delegitimation of this part suggested good reason for delegitimation of the whole.[30] Because this is correct, however, I find Jesseph's additional conclusion that the charges of political intrigue and disloyalty traded between the two "function as a side issue in the dispute rather than a focal point."[31]

As I have noted, Hobbes placed particular emphasis on the connection between good language (i.e., the proper use and handling of language) and good philosophy. He connected bad philosophy with the careless use of language, but in other instances with a malevolent or at least a selfish desire to deceive. The practice of making the connection between language and character (as I noted in Chapter 8) was very much at home within humanism. Indeed, the humanist Ben Jonson taught his contemporaries to thicken the nexus between language and character by teaching them to investigate abuses of language in his characters. Their flaws and vices—just as the king's, or another poet's, virtues—were revealed in their words ("Speak that I may see thee").[32] Furthermore, I have argued that Hobbes's primary political goal was to see his doctrine taught in the universities by sovereign mandate (and conversely, to see the doctrine of his rivals—and no doubt the rivals themselves—purged from the universities). This suggests that attacks on loyalty and political intrigue were in fact central to the debate between Hobbes and Wallis. This is not to suggest that the opposite of Jesseph's claim is correct (that is, that it was not about mathematics, but merely a political battle). In fact, humanism, mathematics, and education politics come together in the *Six Lessons* and other works where Hobbes makes it clear that he is not merely questioning whether his opponents hold correct views on specific mathematical matters, but whether they possess the intellectual skills that might entitle them to be called geometers at all.

Who Is a Geometer?

Hobbes begins the *Six Lessons*, true to form, by defining his terms and principles: "I SUPPOSE, most egregious professors, you know already that by geometry, though the word import no more but the measuring of land, is understood no less the measuring of all other quantity than that of bodies. And though the definition of geometry serve not for proof, nor enter into any geometrical demonstration, yet for understanding of the principles of the science, and for a rule to judge by, who is a geometer, and who is not, I hold it necessary to begin therewith."[33] Indeed, the question of *who can, or should, count as a geometer* is Hobbes's constant refrain throughout the *Six Lessons*.[34] Focusing on Wallis's attack on his attempt to square the circle,[35] Hobbes took note of one quip attacking his way of defining a line for being irregular: "To this definition you say, first, 'what mathematician did ever thus define a line or length?'" He replies: "Whether you call in others for help or testimony, *it is not done like a geometrician*; for they use not to prove their conclusions by witnesses, but rely upon the strength of their own reason" (my emphasis).[36] Hobbes was, however, unwilling to hold himself to the "no witness" standard when it came time to assess Wallis's qualifications as a geometer. He cites the authority of distinguished geometers, gathering their testimony to make the case for the propriety of his method and the inadequacies of his opponent's.[37]

His first witness is Euclid. Although Hobbes was not content with all of Euclid's geometry, his reservations did not prevent him from claiming the glorious mantle of ancient learning—itself a habit of humanist polemics. He goes to some lengths to suggest that he was closer to Euclidean practice than Wallis. For example, concerning Euclid's (fourteenth) definition of "figure" in the *Elements*, Hobbes praises Euclid's definition and equates it with the phrase: "A figure is quantity every way determined." He then adds a double insult: "This definition of Euclid cannot therefore possibly be embraced by you that carry double, namely, mathematics and theology. For if you reject it, you will be cast out of all mathematic schools; and if you maintain it, from the society of all school-divines, and lose the thanks of the favour you have shown (you the astronomer) to Bishop Bramhall."[38]

Another interesting witness in Hobbes's trial of Wallis's identity is Henry Savile himself, whose memory he evoked against the Savilian professor.³⁹ Simultaneously, Hobbes claimed that his geometry had solved problems ("moles" on the body of geometry) that Savile had uncovered.⁴⁰

There should be no question that Hobbes thought himself more deserving of the office and the honor than Wallis. Making light of one of Wallis's critical comments on his work in the *Six Lessons*, Hobbes quips: "If your founder [i.e., Savile] should see this, or the like objections of yours, he would think his money ill bestowed."⁴¹ In a later work, ΣΤΙΓΜΑΙ, . . . *or* MARKS *of the Absurd Geometry, Rural Language, Scottish Church Politics, and Barbarisms of John Wallis* . . . Hobbes takes up a charge from *Vindiciae Academiarum* that he was unaware of the progress of mathematics at Oxford:

> But lest you should be thought to grant me anything, you say, you the astronomer, "geometry hath now so much place in the universities, that when Mr. Hobbes shall have published his philosophical and geometrical pieces, you assure yourself you shall be able to find a greater number in the university who will understand as much, or more, of them than he desired they should," &c. But though this be true of the now, yet it maketh nothing against my then. I know well enough that Sir Henry Savile's lectures were founded and endowed since. Did I deny then that there were in Oxford many good geometricians? But I deny now, that either of you is of the number. For my philosophical and geometrical pieces are published, and you have understood only so much in them, as all men will easily see by your objections to them, and by your own published geometry, that neither of you understand anything either in philosophy or in geometry. And yet you would have those books of yours to stand for an argument, and to be an index of the philosophy and geometry to be found in the universities. Which is a greater injury and disgrace to them, than any words of mine, though interpreted by yourselves.⁴²

The circumstances suggest why he might have felt compelled to make this point in public, and with so much anger. The "Epistle Dedicatory" to the *Six Lessons* is dated June 10, 1656; ΣΤΙΓΜΑΙ was published in 1657. By this time Hobbes had already returned from France after being driven out by his enemies in the exiled court.⁴³ Wallis was also (as noted in Chapter 7) a prominent Presbyterian, a member of the Westminster assembly of divines (established by Charles I's Parliamentary nemesis Pym in 1643) that had instituted a new religious order for the Commonwealth. Hobbes had reason to look upon Wallis with bitterness, some envy, and spite. Had all worked as Hobbes had hoped, the Stuarts would still rule. Persons like himself, who stood to defend

Charles against Parliament, would have been rewarded for their loyalty. Hobbes might have been made the Savilian Professor of Geometry. Now Charles I was dead, and the post was occupied by a person who had taken the other side and who had also been anxious to show the errors in Hobbes's attempts to square the circle. Furthermore, as Jesseph notes (following Aubrey and Wood), Wallis obtained his Savilian professorship under dubious circumstances. Not only had he been appointed by a revolutionary Parliament, he also held other positions simultaneously (Keeper of the Archives or Antiquary, a position denied to Richard Zouch, for his Royalist sympathies), a violation of the Savilian statutes, according to Hobbes's friends Aubrey and Henry Stubbe.[44] Indeed, an extract of a letter from Stubbe is appended to the ΣΤΙΓΜΑΙ. It is a defense of Hobbes and a lengthy attack on Wallis concerning their disputed points on Latin and Greek usage, grammar, and entomology.[45]

Following the restoration of Charles II, Wallis was permitted to keep his position and remained a prominent figure in the universities and the Royal Society. Ward was in fact removed from Oxford, but landed another plum; he was appointed chaplain at Westminster.[46] This could have only further infuriated Hobbes. It might also explain why Hobbes continued to attack Wallis for such a long period of time—he did not bother to respond to many of his critics.[47] One of his later attacks, posing as an anonymous letter to Wallis from a defender of Hobbes, *Considerations upon the Reputation, Loyalty, Manners, and Religion of Thomas Hobbes of Malmesbury* (1662),[48] should be seen in the context of works written by returning Royalists. As noted in Chapter 5, many returning supporters of the king and the Anglican Church were never completely satisfied with the arrangements necessary to the Stuart Restoration. It had been restored by a coalition that included Presbyterians and former supporters of the revolution. The Earl of Clarendon was leading the Court in a policy of unification and compromise; this meant that Charles II was not able to rectify all the grievances among the Royalists—some of whom had had their property confiscated by their enemies. Their frustrations sometimes made it into print. They wrote angry apologies for themselves, recounting their loyalty and sacrifice and bitterly complaining of the advantages enjoyed by those who had sided with the king's enemies.[49] Hobbes's *Considerations* can be seen as a part of this growing genre. Hobbes had to face the double difficulty of making plain his own complaints against his critics (including Wallis), while defending himself from Anglican loyalists who were so deeply offended by his religious doctrines. As Jesseph notes, Wallis took full advantage of Hobbes's potential difficulties and accused him of atheism, of defying the Anglican Church, and of having written *Leviathan* for Cromwell.[50]

We should also connect Hobbes's attacks with his larger project for the reform of university philosophy. He wanted to see his doctrine taught in the schools, and he argued that his doctrine would cure the commonwealth of its illnesses. Hobbes had held up a particular vision of the geometer as the exemplar others would have to follow. The success of Wallis's algebraic method was a threat to that vision of the geometer, and therewith to Hobbes's claim to know what was best for the universities to teach.

As noted, Hobbes associated the geometer with proper philosophic method. Painstaking and well-regulated in his thinking, the geometer worked from the ground up, from basic definitions and principles to the construction of a desired effect. These were the practices Hobbes referred to when describing those who bore the "infallible signs of teaching exactly and without error."[51] Furthermore, and in contrast with their counterparts in traditional moral, political, or natural philosophy, Hobbes insisted that the geometer's teachings and conclusions were infallible. He pushed this vision of the geometer's distinctiveness by offering a brash mapping of the academic terrain, one that codified the mathematician's position at the pinnacle of the academic hierarchy while reducing the status of disciplines such as physics.

The greater significance of Wallis's challenge begins to emerge in the context of these claims. The fact that there could be a conflict between geometers—worse yet, one in which Hobbes himself was a target—was, in and of itself, a threat to his boasts concerning the extraordinary status of geometry. Hobbes's claims concerning geometry were either going to force him, or his opponents, into a corner.

Given these boasts and expectations, we can see why Hobbes was so heavily invested in, and so determined to protect, his vision of the geometer. His geometer followed the correct methods, and Hobbes had previously drawn invidious contrasts between these sound ways and those who had ruined philosophy. In chapter 5 of *Leviathan*, for example, he wrote, "There can be nothing so absurd, but may be found in the books of philosophers. And the reason is manifest. For there is not one of them that begins his ratiocination from the definitions, or explications of the names they are to use; which is a method that hath been used only in geometry; whose conclusions have thereby been made indisputable."[52] The right method uses definitions, defines in terms of matter, and supplies us with a means of generation. The geometer's way is, for Hobbes, the perfect contrast with the chaos one might witness among disputing scholastics. It was also going to be the talent that would cure England of the chaos fostered by factions, each working according to its own religious and civil doctrines. Wallis was not, of course, a scholastic, but Hobbes painted him in the same colors because the potential for ambiguity and bad habits was, as far as he was concerned, being introduced all over again by the practitioners of algebra. They were allowing equivocal symbols to contaminate the singular practice that he had held up as the new model of philosophical excellence.

Thus the debate over mathematical method was itself centrally concerned for Hobbes with matters of character and identity, features he linked to the *habitus* of the geometer. Hobbes had made *his* particular vision of the geometer an exemplar that he now felt the need to protect against Wallis's algebraic approach. As noted, Hobbes held that persons did not only depart from the proper practices of philosophical language out of carelessness, but also out of malevolence, greed, wickedness, and assorted other human deficiencies more culpable than mere error. In *Leviathan*, for example, Hobbes describes school philosophy in terms of a grand plan on the part of the pope to ensure that the vast domains under papal control would remain obedient to the Vatican. He was ready to use the same set of polemical tools to cast suspicions on those who had sided against Charles I, and especially against the learned representatives of Presbyterianism such as Wallis.

In *Leviathan* Hobbes paints a picture of the schools as a confused mass, a "Kingdom of Darkness"—dark by virtue of its malevolence, but also by the ignorance of many who had no means of seeing through the trickery of their deceivers. Concerning their absurd words Hobbes remarks: "When men speak such words, as put together, have in them no signification at all; but are fallen upon by some, through misunderstanding of the words they have received, and repeat by rote; by others from intention to deceive by obscurity. And this is incident to none but those, that converse in questions of matters incomprehensible, as the School-men; or in questions of abstruse philosophy. The common sort of men seldom speak insignificantly, and are therefore, by those other egregious persons counted idiots."[53]

The attack on Wallis demonstrates an anxiousness not merely to reveal his deficiencies as a philosopher by measuring him against the standards of proper Hobbesian philosophical language; he even invites readers to scrutinize Wallis's language for more basic moral and social deficiencies. Turning to Wallis in the ΣΤΙΓΜΑΙ, Hobbes quotes the scurrilous language of his opponent, inviting readers to discern the flaws of his character:

> Consider also these words of yours: *"It is to be hoped that in time you may come to learn the language, for you be come to great A already."* And presently after, *"were I great A, before I would be willing to be so used, I should wish myself little a a hundred times."* Sir, you are a doctor of divinity and

a professor of geometry, but do not deceive yourself, this does not pass for wit in these parts, no, nor generally at Oxford; I have acquaintance there that will blush at the reading it.[54]

The precursors for such attacks on intellect and character can be found among Hobbes's humanist contemporaries. In the section that follows the similarities will be shown as we place Hobbes's further criticisms side by side with humanist polemics of a similar nature.

Common Themes in the Defense of Philosophic and Poetic Identities: Jonson, Burton, and Hobbes

I have been arguing that Hobbes thought of his method of philosophy, not merely in terms of the conclusions it could reach, but also in terms of the persons it could produce. I have argued, in short, that Hobbes's science must be understood as a possession manifest in practice (see Chapter 2). As such, his science dictated the practices with language, the practice that philosophers would need to possess, to perform the tasks he associated with their role, or "office." Those who in fact possessed those skills would deserve the name "philosophers," and the others would be condemned as impostors. Therefore what was at stake in his debate with Wallis was more than a matter of how to perform mathematical calculations, or even where mathematical learning might best be applied. For Hobbes and Wallis the debate also concerned a claim to an identity. It hinged on Hobbes's capacity to establish his way as *the* way for philosophers. They should seek to possess the same intellectual virtues that he did.

In pursuing a debate such as this Hobbes found himself on ground already familiar to humanist polemicists. We can, in fact, find common elements in Hobbes's attack on Wallis and Ben Jonson's attack on rival poets. Furthermore, as we shall see in the brief example from Robert Burton, Hobbes was not the only one to question identities in the name of defending mathematical practice.

I noted in Chapter 8 that Ben Jonson had taken on a twofold task in defending poetry. Poetry had to be defended as a worthwhile endeavor against those who condemned it generally, but Jonson also made himself the arbiter of who should count as a true poet (or playwright, since these were the same thing for Jonson). Poetry's name had been dragged through the mud because some so-called poets were deficient practitioners of the art. Placing himself in the position of master-practitioner and judge of other poets,[55] Jonson frequently lamented the state to which poetry had been reduced by these practitioners (particularly those who pandered to the low tastes of the popular audience): "Nothing in our Age, I have observ'd, is more preposterous, then the *running judgements* upon Poetry, and Poets; when wee shall heare those things commended, and cry'd up for the best writings, which a man would scarce vouchsafe, to wrap any wholesome drug in; hee would never light his Tobacco with them. . . . Yet their vices have not hurt them; Nay, a great many they have profited; for they have beene lov'd for nothing else. And this false opinion growes strong against the best men: if once it take root with the Ignorant."[56] Poetry itself was still a noble thing with lofty goals.[57] Its true form was not vicious, but the impostors who posed as poets were. In a brief jibe at his competition, and not unlike Hobbes's scoffing remarks above, Jonson writes:

> To Play-wright
> Play-wright me reades, and still my verses damnes,
> He sayes, I want the tongue of Epigrammes;
> I haue no salt: no bawdrie he doth meane.
> For wittie, in his language, is obscene.
> Play-wright, I loath to haue thy manners knowne
> In my chast booke: professe them in thine owne.[58]

Jonson maintained that his flawed competitors were not fit to be called poets. They were "poetasters," and insofar as they were known as poets the practice itself was debased and in need of rehabilitation by its true practitioners.[59]

The offenses committed by bad poets and the offenses of bad geometers are distinct and offend against different standards of virtuous performance (although in the case of the Presbyterian Wallis, Hobbes had the opportunity to associate him with the vice of playing on popular base passions—see Chapter 7). Nevertheless, the mode of defense against these vices is drawn from the same humanist reservoir. Hobbes thus defends the matter of his ideal vision of geometry by insisting upon the distinction between the practice as it is, and as it ought to be. In the preface to *De Principiis et Ratiocinatione Geometrarum*[60] he claims: "It is against geometricians [geometras], dear reader, not against geometry that I write. That very method is the way of navigation, of architecture, painting, computation, and finally (the noblest of all sciences) the mother of physics, and is that which is raised up as equal to the greatest praise."[61]

Such humanist defenses of learned disciplines predictably lead to a preoccupation with unmasking counterfeit worthies. This was a kind of courtly preoccupation (which, again, Ben Jonson encouraged and refined),[62] but it was a habit of thought and accusation that spread beyond courtly confines. The competition for honors and office was fierce in England. In this climate, some of the nation's most prominent scholarly humanists participated in, and even encouraged, this sensibility.[63] Robert Burton is an important example. The author of *Anatomy of Melancholy*, he also wrote *Philosophaster*, a play performed at Oxford university.[64] Doubly interesting for our purposes, Burton was also among those humanists who pursued mathematics in a serious way. His concern for the discipline (as well a desire to make himself the arbiter of the integrity of other learned disciplines in the schools) reveals itself in the play.

The play is set in an Italian town that wishes to start a university. The town lets it be known that they are looking for scholars of high repute, and that they have the money to make it worth their while. What they attract, however, are "philosophasters," make-believe scholars, con-men who do their best to fake their way into distinguished chairs. A band of these imposters arrives in town, and their leader is (the wonderfully named) Polupragmaticus. The play begins as he gives his instructions to his accomplices, including the one intending to pose as a mathematician, Lodovicus Pantometer:

> POL. Come, get ready, quickly I say. Bring the tunics, togas, beards, clothes and habits.
> LOD. Are you sure that this is the day of admission?
> POL. More than sure. Today at the tenth hour the duke will be here and also the students to be admitted to the university. You take these books, you these instruments. You will pretend to mathematics, you philosophy, you medicine, and I just knowledge in general.
> LOD. But where do we get this knowledge?
> POL. Stupid. Just take this book. Learn from it certain sesquipedalian words.
> LOD. But how will I be able to use these words or this art?
> POL. How? Like this. If you are at table or in conversation, take a square or a book. If one side is longer, say that it is a rectangular parallelogram, say a rhombus or rhomboid. If it is multilateral and regular, call it a polygon. Othewise, a trapezoid.
> LOD. I'm to say that?
> POL. Cut a slice of bread in the form of an icosahendron: say it is a cone, a cylinder, a prism, or a parallelepiped. Having this compass always close by, you will describe some geometric figures. You will show how to make a pyramid in a given cube, an octahedron from the given pyramid, and from the octahedron a decahedron, tetrahedron, or hexahedron. . . .

POL. After that, you will talk about algorisms and algebra, or about contracted numbers, surds [e.g. roots], subsolids, about zenzic root, the zenzizenic root—and things of that sort.[65]

As with Jonson, Burton reveals his frauds by asking the audience to listen to their speech. The counterfeiter may sound like the real thing, but *Philosophaster* teaches its audience that fakers only mimic the sounds they hear from true practitioners. Unmask them and they show themselves to be full of nonsense. They do not know the meanings of the words they speak, and when we allow them to pass, they bring down the practice, discredit their pretended profession, and become a source of pervasive corruption.

How does this relate to Hobbes's opposition to Wallis? Wallis was not a counterfeit mathematician. It is too crude to assert that Hobbes thought of Wallis as nothing more than a sham like Lodovicus Pantometer. However, Hobbes was invested in a particular vision of the geometer and his practice. For promoting a form of mathematical practice that deviated from his ideal, Hobbes did his best to persuade his readers that Wallis ought to be dismissed in much the same way that Burton would have us dismiss Lodovicus Pantometer—as a pretender to learning, a corrupter of education, a philosophaster.

There is a second parallel between Hobbes and these figures. Hobbes shares an understanding of what a misguided, corrupt, and corrupting education looks like. There is an intense focus on language, and the deficient practitioners are either fooled or attempt to fool others by speaking words that they do not understand. In this context, Hobbes looked upon the habits of the geometer as a form of intellectual and political salvation. The cure for the swirling nonsense of the corrupters and the corrupted was to institute new practices modeled after the practices of geometers.[66] The trend toward algebraic techniques in geometry spelled disaster for Hobbes. He had hoped to reform the habits of speakers and writers on the model of *his* geometer's practices. Wallis's mathematics was to Hobbes an infection of philosophical incautiousness injected directly into the heart of the architectonic practice Hobbes was defending. It would have robbed his architectonic science of its certainty, and instead of teaching generation it would have been reduced to an analytic art. Moreover, the very identity "geometer" that Hobbes had hoped to promote, teach, and defend was put at risk.

In conclusion, we can see that Hobbes's preoccupation with who is entitled to claim the identity of the true geometer was more than a question of mathematical theory. It was also a question of political practice. For Hobbes, Wallis represented the unjustified success of a faction following the Restoration that had betrayed the Crown, and of a man who had attacked his competency personally. He had profited when, according to Hobbes, he deserved to be punished. (For his part, Wallis encouraged others to think much the same of Hobbes.) Important for our purposes, Hobbes's arguments turn on a question of worthiness or due, and in making these arguments we can see that Hobbes seamlessly wove his writings concerning the use and abuse of mathematics and language into a humanist framework concerning corruption and fraudulence already available to him. One might be tempted to conclude that Hobbes was doing nothing more than making use of the rhetorical tools available to him. On such a reading one could speak of a purely mathematical component of his thought, one separable from his humanism or his politics. Hobbes's emphasis on personal character, however, suggests otherwise.

Hobbes's emphasis on the practices of the proper geometer, the contrasts he drew between his (honest and precise) methods and those of his rivals, push toward a different conclusion. For Hobbes, *doing* geometry or philosophy was not merely a matter of specific techniques, but also a matter of *being* a geometer or philosopher. Working within the framework already established by humanist understandings of what it was to be a master—a person in full possession—of a learned discipline, Hobbes was just as concerned with establishing his authority over *who* the geometer or philosopher should, or shouldn't, be. From the evidence reviewed in Chapter 7 it is also clear that many persons wished to be known as mathematical in their ways and accomplishments.[67] Situated within the "office"-centered humanist culture of his contemporaries, it should come as no surprise that questions of intellectual practice, identity, and character were inextricably linked in his thought. These preoccupations did not hit a boundary when Hobbes became interested in mathematics; they were carried through. Hobbes's humanism, his mathematics, and his politics were similarly intermingled.

NOTES

In citing works in the notes, authors' surnames and short titles have generally been used. The following works are cited only by short title or abbreviation.

Anti-White	Thomas Hobbes. *Thomas White's "De Mundo" Examined*. Translated by Harold Whitmore Jones. Bradford: Bradford University Press, 1976. This work is cited by chapter and section.
CM	Ben Jonson. *Ben Jonson: The Complete Masques*. Edited by Stephen Orgel. New Haven: Yale University Press, 1969.
Dec. Phys.	Thomas Hobbes. *Decameron Physiologicum; or, Ten Dialogues in Natural Philosophy*. In *EW*, vol. 7.
De Cive	Thomas Hobbes. *De Cive: The English Version* [*Philosophical Rudiments Concerning Government and Society*]. Edited by Howard Warrender. Oxford: Oxford University Press, 1983. This work is cited by chapter and paragraph.
De Corpore	This short title will be used to refer to both Hobbes's work in Latin titled *Elementorum philosophiae sectio prima De corpore*, which can be found in *OP*, vol. 1, pt. 4, and the English translation, *The Elements of Philosophy, The First Section, Concerning Body*, which can be found in *EW*, vol. 1. All quotations in English are from *EW*. Unless otherwise indicated, all references are to chapter and article.
De Homine	Thomas Hobbes. *De Homine*. Translated by Charles Wood, T. S. K. Scott-Craig, and Bernard Gert. In *Man and Citizen: "De Homine" and "De Cive" by Thomas Hobbes*, edited by Bernard Gert. New York: Anchor Books, 1972. All quotations in English are from this edition. Unless otherwise indicated, all references are to chapter and section.
EL	Thomas Hobbes. *The Elements of Law, Natural and Politic*. Edited by Ferdinand Tönnies. Cambridge: Cambridge University Press, 1928. All references are to part, chapter, and section.
EW	Thomas Hobbes. *The English Works of Thomas Hobbes of Malmesbury*. Edited by William Molesworth. 11 vols. London: John Bohn, 1839–45.
Lev.	Thomas Hobbes. *Leviathan*. With selected variants from the Latin edition of 1668. Edited by Edwin Curley. Indianapolis: Hackett, 1994. Unless otherwise indicated, all references are to chapter and paragraph.
ODNB	*Oxford Dictionary of National Biography*.
OP	Thomas Hobbes. *Opera Philosophica quae Latine scripsit omnia*. Edited by William Molesworth. 5 vols. London: John Bohn, 1839–45. All references are to volume and page number of this edition.
Six Lessons	Thomas Hobbes. *Six Lessons to the Professors of Mathematics, one of Geometry, the other of Astronomy, in the Chairs set up by the Noble and Learned Sire Henry Savile, in the University of Oxford*. In *EW*, vol. 7. This work is cited by lesson and by the page number in *EW*, vol. 7.

Chapter 1

1. Some important attempts to reappropriate Hobbes from his early twentieth-century admirers—in the nineteenth century he was largely left to the authoritarian wings of utilitarianism—are Strauss, *Political Philosophy of Hobbes;* Oakeshott, "Introduction to *Leviathan*"; and Wolin, *Hobbes and the Epic Tradition of Political Theory.* For an interesting discussion of Hobbes among the utilitarians, including Molesworth, see Francis, "Nineteenth-Century Theory."
2. De Tocqueville, *Democracy in America,* 12.
3. Robert Filmer's objections to Hobbes might be Exhibit A in the case for this reading. See *Observations Concerning the Originall of Government, upon Mr Hobs "Leviathan," Mr Milton against Salmasias, H. Grotius "De Jure Belli,"* in Filmer, *Patriarchia and Other Works,* 184–97.
4. De Tocqueville, *Democracy in America,* 503–4.
5. *Lev.,* 18.19.
6. De Tocqueville, *Democracy in America,* 60, 252.
7. *Lev.,* 17.13.
8. For a recent work that bolsters and defends the Anglican Church's assault upon Hobbes for challenging its authority, see Collins, *Allegiance of Thomas Hobbes.*
9. Kahan, *Aristocratic Liberalism,* 164.
10. De Tocqueville wrote to reassure his aristocratic audience that *all* need not be lost, even if much would be. The hunger for equality he posited would always be satisfied. If not in the right way, he warned that it would be satisfied in wrong and more dangerous ways. A tyrannous majority of America's middling culture, or the next egalitarian system, could and would surpass the tyranny of the old absolutists. Both de Tocqueville and his fearful audience believed that equality's march would ultimately diminish the role and authority of the aristocracy, as well as the intermediary institutions between the people and the exercise of sovereign power. To survive with liberty intact, democracies would have to cultivate their own substitutes. Such a feeling fuels the urgency of de Tocqueville's plea, in the second part of *Democracy in America,* for the formation of associations in democracy and his insistence, in *The Old Regime and the French Revolution,* that centralization in France was first the work of absolutists, not the Revolution.
11. Straussian esoteric readings, often undemocratic, can give us a taste of this offense, but I am not arguing an esoteric reading of Hobbes. Esoteric texts in the Straussian mold try to hide differences from an audience thought unsuited. "They" are either deemed not yet, or never, ready to fully understand or appreciate the philosopher's unconventional truth. The message is therefore deemed too dangerous to the author, to society, or both to allow it to become public. See Strauss, *Persecution and the Art of Writing.* Writers who addressed audiences already presumed unequal in matters of power and social station by high and low alike openly recognize (and function within) a system of public distinctions. Rediscovering these distinctions is not (as it is with Strauss) an invitation to learn a secret, but an invitation to take seriously the differences between what it might mean to offer up a political philosophy today to the general or academic audience and what it could have meant in the seventeenth century.
12. Gadamer, *Truth and Method,* 296.
13. Nietzsche, *Untimely Meditations,* 60.
14. See Walzer's observations on Hobbes scholarship in "Good Aristocrats/Bad Aristocrats," 41–53.
15. A dispute this book will not try to resolve is the one between revisionists, who find within divine right theorists (including James I) a consensus on the existence of limits to the powers of the monarch, and Johann Sommerville, who has argued that those who claimed an immediate sanction for royal power were in fact as "absolutist" in their thinking as any of the more conventionally recognized absolutists on the Continent. What is clear, however, is that Hobbes was promoting a contentious claim concerning sovereign legitimacy. On the question of divine right, see Figgis, *Divine Right of Kings;* Burgess, "Divine Right of Kings Reconsidered,"

837–61; Russell, "Divine Rights," 101–20; and Sommerville, "English and European Political Ideals," 168–94.

16. Including Schmitt's approach in *Political Theology*.

17. See, especially, Schmitt, *Concept of the Political*.

18. Schmitt's later and sustained work on Hobbes declares his *Leviathan* a failure as a myth or symbol. I have no desire to turn *Leviathan* into what Schmitt wished it had been—a myth that could have successfully defended overwhelming state power. Moreover, I find many of the terms of Schmitt's criticism of this failure execrable. That said, Schmitt's vision of Hobbes's failure can be rebutted. It is precisely because his science is not neutral, because the building of mechanisms meant something profoundly different to Hobbes than it meant to Schmitt, that Schmitt's understanding of Hobbes falls short. Schmitt, *The Leviathan in the State Theory*, esp. 65–87.

19. Martin, *Francis Bacon*.

20. Jardine, *Francis Bacon;* Spragens, *Politics of Motion;* Leijenhorst, *Mechanisation of Aristotelianism*. All three argue dependencies upon a spurned Aristotle.

21. For a new and provocative reading that distances Hobbes from Descartes by investigating the former's thoroughgoing materialism, see Frost, *Lessons from a Materialist Thinker*.

22. Hobbes, it could be argued, began with a world already in pieces (or going to pieces), and claimed to know a way to rebuild it. Compare this claim to his views of the seditious. He compares those who would destroy standing governments to the daughters of Pelias (king of Thessaly), who, upon the conniving Medea's advice, chopped up and boiled their father with herbs, falsely expecting him to return alive and renewed in his youth. *De Cive*, 12.13; *EL*, 2.8.15; *Lev.*, 30.7.

23. In a lesser-known piece, D. G. James makes much of the notion and comes close to my reading, but refuses to consider the radical possibilities for Hobbes's science. For James, ultimately, the division between Hobbes's humanism and his science must remain strong. James, *Life of Reason*, 1–62.

24. His friend John Aubrey is the source for this claim. See Aubrey, *"Brief Lives,"* 1:321–403, esp. 332.

25. See, notably, Johnston, *Rhetoric of Leviathan*, and Skinner, *Reason and Rhetoric*.

26. The boundaries around the concept of "humanism" have been the subject of debate. I will be linking Hobbes to the more capacious conceptions of humanism, such as Eugenio Garin's, that link its practices not only with the *vita activa*, but with philosophically salient contributions. For a useful review of humanism's various conceptions, see Celenza, *Lost Italian Renaissance*. The connections to Garin's work will become clear.

27. I use the term "artifice" as Hobbes did, to mean "clever or artful skill" or "ingenious device."

Chapter 2

1. See, for example, Peters, *Hobbes*, 13–52, esp. 19–22 and 45–52, and MacPherson, "Introduction," 16–20. Both authors record this temptation, and note that Hobbes's transition cannot plausibly be considered entire in this moment—these observations are testimony to the strength of the temptation. More important for our purposes, they both see the beginnings of a critical break from humanist practice. Strauss argues that Hobbes's turn to Euclid obscures the prior and most critical moment of his philosophy. Nevertheless, even Strauss considers the discovery of Euclid a significant development in Hobbes's work. Without abandoning his thesis concerning the genesis of Hobbes's thought, he writes of a radical departure in method. Hobbes thus joins the bandwagon of the scientific revolutionaries, but this movement is given an autonomy in Strauss's early reading that manages to reinforce its distinctiveness. For Strauss, Hobbes's science is the building that hides the earlier moral decision at its foundation. See Strauss,

Political Philosophy of Hobbes. Spragens, *Politics of Motion*, esp. 60–74 and 144–46, on geometric/ mechanical perspectives, is another complicated case. Borrowing from Kuhn, Spragens argues that Hobbes is a part of a change in scientific paradigms. Spragens describes Hobbes's world as supplanting Aristotle's, and yet also argues that Hobbes's science sustains and transfigures a number of Aristotelian concepts. Spragens associates these alterations with the concepts that he takes to be the driving force behind the scientific revolution: new and radical ways of understanding motion. The commonalties with Aristotle become the backdrop for an argument—based on the significant departures that Spragens links with the change in paradigms—that works harder than most to link Hobbes to a scientific revolution.

2. Aubrey, "*Brief Lives*," 1:332.

3. Several typical humanist sources describe Pythagoras's "discovery" of the truth of what we now call the Pythagorean Theorem and then repeat the report, attributed to "the logician" Apollodorus by Diogenes, that he sacrificed a hecatomb (a hundred oxen) in thanks to the gods. See Diogenes, *Lives* 8.12; also see Vitruvius, bk. 9, preface, and Cicero, *De natura deorum* 3.88, who has doubts about the act of sacrifice. Proclus's commentary on Euclid's forty-seventh proposition also mentions a sacrifice.

4. In his *Verse Autobiography*, Hobbes records that after learning logic, "My fancy and my mind divert I do,/With maps celestial and terrestrial too./Rejoice t'accompany Sol cloath'd with rays,/Know by what art he measures all our days;/How Drake and Cavendish a girdle made/ Quite round the world, what climates they survey'd;/And strive to find the smaller cells of men./And painted monsters in their unknown den./Nay, there's a fullness in geography;/For Nature e'r abhor'd vacuity." Hobbes, *Verse Autobiography*, ll. 55–64.

5. Hobbes, "To the Readers," x.

6. Ibid., x–xi. Hobbes here notes that he has not merely gathered the places and locations as he could from historical sources, but has compiled an accompanying index, "to shew you that I have not played the mountebank in it, putting down exactly some few of the principal, and the rest at adventure, without care and without reason, I have joined with the map [this] index, that pointeth to the authors which will justify me where I differ from others."

7. Turner, "Literature and Mapping"; Cormack, "Good Fences."

8. See Helgerson, *Forms of Nationhood*, 107–47. Surveying a broader field than mere cartography, Helgerson closes his book with observations on Hobbes largely unrelated to specifically cartographic topics. See also Conley, *Self-Made Map*, and Smith, *Cartographic Imagination*. Unlike, say, Smith, this account will draw its subject not toward a world to which he is already said to belong—the world of objectivity ushered in by this understanding of cartography's impact— but towards the residual humanist's understanding of mathematics as a virtue practiced by a not yet objectified person.

9. Gordon, "Introduction," vii. Peacham, *Complete Gentleman*, chaps. 7–9, specifically recommends mathematical education.

10. Skinner (in *Reason and Rhetoric*) sees three phases, as does Johnston, *Rhetoric of Leviathan*, although the latter sees Hobbes's second phase as a lapse in a humanistic concern with the "transmission of ideas" combined with an enthusiasm for science and geometric (axiomatic) reasoning presumed missing from his humanist phase. Johnston, *Rhetoric of Leviathan*, 22–25. In Skinner's account Hobbes is first a humanist. In the second he rejects humanism, and in the third (which includes his authorship of *Leviathan*) he returns to effect a synthesis of his rhetorical and scientific approaches to political philosophy. In Johnston's view, Hobbes's use of religion also helps mark a boundary between the second and third phases. These approaches make rhetoric the centerpiece, which raises the issue of whether Hobbes, in his so-called scientific phase, had to rely on rhetoric.

11. See Chapter 3, and Peters, *Hobbes*, esp. 20–21, 24, and 43–74.

12. See Strauss, *Political Philosophy of Hobbes*, and note 1. Also see Skinner, *Reason and Rhetoric*. Skinner adds to our understanding of the context in which Hobbes took an interest in mathematics. He notes flaws in Aubrey's dating, and points to other important contexts. These include

his contacts with Charles Cavendish and William Cavendish, the Earl of Newcastle. In *Reason and Rhetoric*, 250–57, he stresses the contact with Mersenne. Nevertheless, Skinner holds to the old tradition of Hobbes scholarship, and pairs an affinity for mathematics with Hobbes's alleged departure from and abandonment of humanism.

13. Strauss, *Political Philosophy of Hobbes*, 95–107; Skinner, *Reason and Rhetoric*, 250–57.

14. Strauss, *Political Philosophy of Hobbes*, 27–29, 109–28. Strauss asserts that Hobbes's "epoch-making" innovation, his decision to put rights before moral laws (assumed immutable and discoverable by reason by those on the former side of the ancients/moderns divide) is masked by his mathematical method and cannot be derived from it. Thus Strauss sees decisions made in the humanist phase of Hobbes's career as fundamental to all his subsequent work. Defending this reading requires, nevertheless, that Hobbes make at least a conspicuous change in method, and Strauss does indeed maintain that Hobbes took a path that obscures, and even risks, the moral root of his own thinking, threatening a complete collapse into relativist skepticism. See ibid., esp. 155, 164. Strauss thus challenges conventional views of the importance of Hobbes's move toward a technical science of politics, but his thesis concerning the masking of the genesis of his philosophy leaves him invested in a narrative of a transition from one phase to another.

15. Skinner, *Reason and Rhetoric*, 347–56, 427.

16. Kahn, *Rhetoric, Prudence, and Skepticism*.

17. Hobbes, *Ad nobilissimum dominum*. This work must also be seen in light of Hobbes's affinity for geometry. It is a work of a branch of geometry, chorography. See Cormack, "Good Fences."

18. Hobbes, *Thucydides*.

19. Noel Malcolm has noted an ambiguity in the historical record, and suggests that Hobbes might have entered Magdalen as early as age thirteen. Malcolm, "Summary Biography," 13–44, n. 9.

20. Aubrey, "*Brief Lives*," 1:328–29.

21. Hobbes, "To the Readers," viii–ix.

22. Ibid., v–vi.

23. Hobbes, "Of the Life and History of Thucydides," in *EW*, 8:xiii–xxxii.

24. For interpretation in the broad context of contemporary European history, see Scott, *England's Troubles*, pt. 1, esp. 58–68, and Sommerville, *Thomas Hobbes*, 9–10.

25. Hobbes, "To the Readers."

26. Hobbes notably devotes no small effort at the start of his essay on Thucydides to demonstrating Thucydides's connections to Thracian royalty. See Hobbes, "Of the Life and History of Thucydides," in *EW*, 8:xiii–xxxii.

27. Aubrey, "*Brief Lives*," 1:347.

28. Hobbes, "Of the Life and History of Thucydides," in *EW*, 8:iv.

29. Johnston, *Rhetoric of Leviathan*, chaps. 1 and 3.

30. If Helgerson is correct, then the cartographic sensibilities, while remaining absolutist in ideology, were arrayed against the Stuarts in works of Elizabethan nostalgia. See Helgerson, *Forms of Nationhood*.

31. Skinner, *Reason and Rhetoric*, pt. 1.

32. Ibid.; Copenhaver and Schmitt, *Renaissance Philosophy*, 214–17, 223–25. Kennedy, in *Quintilian* and in *Classical Rhetoric*, 198–207, discusses both how early antischolastics such as Valla and Erasmus used Quintilian in their efforts to subsume dialectic within the rhetorical tradition and the enduring role of Quintilian, in spite of authors like George of Trebizond, who put themselves forward as his competition.

33. Quintilian, *Institutio oratoria* 1.10.3–5.

34. Quintilian wanted to reclaim philosophy itself for the orator. See *Institutio oratoria* 1.10.11 and bk. 1, preface, 10–20. See also Kennedy, *Classical Rhetoric*, 198–207.

35. *EL*, 1.8.2.

36. Dear, *Mersenne*, 80–200. On the fifteenth- and sixteenth-century connections between piety, mathematics—both the scholar's and the artisan's—and the search for commonalities

between divine and human minds, see also the discussions of Nicolas of Cusa in Debus, "Mathematics and Nature"; Watts, *Nicolas Cusanus*, esp. 61–66, 72–73, and 87–152; and Long, "Power, Patronage, and the Authorship of *Ars*."

Mersenne was a Jesuit-trained friar of the Minim order who lived in the Annunciation Convent in Paris. He had studied with Descartes and became the center of the scientific republic of letters. Hobbes wrote with great appreciation for Mersenne personally and for his note among thinkers and credits him with his initial standing in the community of philosophers. Hobbes, *Verse Autobiography*, ll. 132–36, 175–88. On Mersenne, see Dear, *Mersenne*.

37. He does, however, pepper his argument with concrete examples of geometric know-how, particularly in the detection of falsehoods (e.g., an equal perimeter length between two pieces of land does not imply that the two are equal in area. Mindful of this, an orator could challenge someone who argued that some island is very large because it took a very long time to circumnavigate its coastline). Referring again to geometry's use in astronomy, Quintilian notes that Pericles was able to dispel the panic among Athenians caused by an eclipse of the sun: "If Nicias had known this when he commanded in Sicily, he would not have shared the terror of his men nor lost the finest army that Athens ever placed in the field." Although "we are not concerned with the uses of geometry in war," he nevertheless mentions Archimedes's famous accomplishment: [He] "single handed[ly] succeeded in appreciably prolonging the resistance of Syracuse when it was besieged." *Institutio oratoria* 1.10.48.

38. This was an association that was quite common and most likely rooted in the fact that so many of Aristotle's examples in sound logic make use of mathematical examples. This became a key point for defenders of mathematics, especially in settings (such as the Jesuit colleges) where Aristotelian science remained the standard by which certainty was judged. See Mancosu, *Philosophy of Mathematics*, who rightly makes the point that the inertia of Aristotelian standards of deductive certainty carries right through to the seventeenth century, including Hobbes's own understanding of what makes mathematics certain.

39. Quintilian, *Institutio oratoria* 1.10.36–39.

40. See Rose, *Italian Renaissance of Mathematics*.

41. Kristeller, *Renaissance Thought*, 92–119. For a more recent treatment, see Rummel, *Humanist-Scholastic Debate*.

42. This name reflected national pride—Quintilian was born in Spain—but it was also meant to suggest the potency of his influence on his contemporaries throughout Europe and England. Vives, *De tradendis disciplinis*, cii.

43. He was also charged with designing the education of Princess Mary. He secured the patronage of Lord Mountjoy, and was already well established with More (and Erasmus). Wolsey helped Vives obtain a university lectureship in rhetoric. He was expelled when he supported Catherine of Aragon as Henry pursued divorce. See Watson's introductory essay in Vives, *De tradendis disciplinis*, lxxiii–lxxxii.

44. Feingold's brief mention of Vives's reservations concerning mathematics, in my view, downplays the more positive aspects of Vives's perspective. That Vives recommends mathematics "only . . . in so far as [it is] applicable to practical, everyday problems," for example, should not count as a form of humanist dismissal. Feingold, *Mathematician's Apprenticeship*, 29. Rather, it was in keeping with the humanist affirmation of the need for practically useful education—especially since Vives applauds the usefulness of mathematical learning.

45. Vives, *De tradendis disciplinis*, 201.

46. Ibid., 202.

47. Ibid., 204.

48. Rudolph Agricola, cited in Gilbert, *Renaissance Concepts of Method*, 84n. For a discussion that illustrates the commonalities of Agricola's and Vives's attacks on scholastics, although not with regard to mathematics, see Rummel, *Humanist-Scholastic Debate*, 153–92.

49. Gilbert, *Renaissance Concepts of Method*, 84.

50. Vives, *De tradendis disciplinis*, 202.

51. Ascham, *The Scholemaster*, 14–15.

52. On the fear of scholarly preoccupations, and the popular notion of the ill-mannered scholar generally, see Shapin, "'A Scholar and a Gentleman.'"

53. Shapin, *Social History of Truth*. For later examples, see Tenison, *The Creed of Mr. Hobbes Examined*, and Tenison's student, Eachard, *Mr. Hobbs's State of Nature Considered* and *Some Opinions of Mr. Hobbs Considered*.

54. Vives, *De tradendis disciplinis*, 203.

55. Ibid., 204.

56. "Only let pupils practice pure and good music which, after the Pythagorean mode, soothes, recreates, and restores to itself the wearied mind of the student; then let it lead back to tranquility and tractability all the wild and fierce parts of the student's nature." Ibid., 205.

57. Ibid.

58. Ibid., 206.

59. Mulcaster, *Positions*, 241. For the tirade directed at Ascham, see *Positions*, 244.

60. Ibid., 243. Mulcaster was in residence at Kings College, Cambridge, from 1548 to 1550, entering as a "King's scholar." See DeMolen, *Richard Mulcaster*, 4.

61. Mulcaster, *Positions*, 243.

62. Ibid., 241. He writes, "One disgrace them with contempt, and the other make them contemptible" (242).

63. Ibid., 245.

64. Ibid., 242, also makes reference to Plato's entrance test.

65. Ibid., 245–46.

66. Ibid., 243.

67. Buckley, *Arithmetica memorativa*. Buckley was also a mathematical instrument maker. The *Dictionary of National Biography* notes that Buckley constructed a mathematical quadrant designed by Cheke as a gift for Henry VIII, among other instruments.

68. Mulcaster, *Positions*, 243–44. It is noteworthy that Xenophon's Socrates, unlike Plato's, is *not* a partisan of lofty, philosophic geometry, but is instead a very strong proponent of practical mathematics. He even speaks in opposition to astronomy and theoretical mathematics on grounds that such studies serve no useful purpose. See Xenophon, *Memorabilia* 4.7. Reijer Hooykaas has linked Peter Ramus's celebration of practical mathematics—over against the high theoretical practices of many of his academic contemporaries—with Xenophon's Socrates. See Hooykaas, *Humanisme, science et réforme*, 20–23 and 59–62.

69. Feingold, *Mathematician's Apprenticeship*, 29–31; Schmitt, "Science in the Italian Universities"; Shapin, "'A Scholar and a Gentleman'"; Biagioli, "Social Status."

70. Mulcaster, *Positions*, 244.

71. Ibid. Mulcaster was more daring, moreover, in allowing gentlemen to learn skills that might—in the eyes of earlier humanists such as Elyot—cause them to risk contamination by engaging in practices more typically associated with the lower orders. See Barker, "Introduction," xxii.

72. Feingold, *Mathematician's Apprenticeship*, 190–213; Turner, "Mathematical Instruments," 51–88.

73. Although it goes beyond the scope of this study, Hobbes could be usefully compared to earlier Italian Renaissance figures (such as Lorenzo Valla—an influence on Vives) who also had affinities for mathematics, nominalism, and voluntarist attacks on scholastic natural philosophy. See Trinkaus, "Humanism and Science," and Rose, *Italian Renaissance of Mathematics*, esp. 5–25.

74. *Lev.*, 3.3.

75. Ibid.

76. Charles I, *Eikon Basilike*. On *Eikon Basilike*, see Potter, *Secret Rites and Secret Writing*, 160–65, 169–87. On the early Royalist associations between Charles I's sufferings and those of Christ, see Ashton, *Counter-Revolution*, 207, 212.

77. *Lev.*, 3.3.

78. On the particular value of our passions in bringing order to our thoughts, see Barnouw, "Hobbes's Causal Account," 115–30.

79. *Lev.*, 4.12.

80. Ibid., 4.13.

81. Ibid., 46.10.

82. Ibid.

83. See, notably, Biagioli, *Galileo, Courtier*; Blair and Grafton, "Reassessing Humanism and Science," 535–40; Cochrane, "Science and Humanism," 1039–57; and Garin, *Science and Civil Life*.

84. Mulcaster, *The First Part of the Elementary*.

85. Ibid., 28.

86. Ibid.

87. Ibid., 28–30. The distinction between the mere cultivation of these skills and their further refinement and perfection is on Mulcaster's terms the distinction between educational efforts he qualifies as natural and those he describes as artificial.

88. Ibid., 28.

89. *Lev.*, 5.19.

90. It is also what unites him with some of the (more contemporary) mathematical humanists of the seventeenth-century English court, such as Inigo Jones. I make these comparisons, and further contrasts, in Chapter 8.

Chapter 3

1. *De Corpore*, "Author's Epistle to the Reader," xiii.

2. For an important exception, see Jacobson, *Pride and Solace*, 51–92. See also Schmitt, *The Leviathan in the State Theory*, esp. 31–37.

3. See, for example, Kavka, *Hobbesian Moral and Political Theory*, 29–51; Watkins, *Hobbes's System of Ideas*, esp. 72–74; Hampton, *Hobbes and the Social Contract Tradition*, 11; and McNeilly, *The Anatomy of Leviathan*, esp. 76–77, 83. For Kavka's disagreements over the issue of egoism with McNeilly (and Gert), see Kavka, *Hobbesian Moral and Political Theory*, 44–51.

4. *Lev.*, 13.9.

5. *De Cive*, 3.9.

6. *Lev.*, 30.6. See also *EL*, 2.9.8: "There is no doubt, if the true doctrine concerning the law of nature, and the properties of a body politic, and the nature of law in general, were perspicuously set down, and taught in the Universities, but that young men, who come thither void of prejudice, and whose minds are yet as white paper, capable of any instruction, would more easily receive the same, and afterward teach it to the people, both in books and otherwise, than now they do the contrary." Note that in quoting parallel passages from Hobbes's early and late philosophy, I do not suggest that his philosophy remained static. Clearly, however, there were continuities. I think that his grand educational agenda, his hope to see his doctrine taught by sovereign mandate, was one of them. It is also possible to read changes (between early and later texts) as indicative of shifts in his philosophy when they might be better explained as changes in Hobbes's audience. On this and the educational agenda, see Miller and Strong, "Meanings and Contexts."

7. I use "nominalism" in a narrow, perhaps anachronistic, sense. Earlier nominalists (especially Ockham) had a larger agenda, which may have overlapped with certain aspects of Hobbes's. A more complete look at Hobbes and philosophical language would also have to consider the possible influences of Mersenne's aspiration for the creation of a universal language. The notion of a language suited to speaking philosophical truths clearly has resonance. Moreover, because Mersenne fell into the camp that argued that the universal language would have to be

created—he held that all languages were—rather than discovered, there are affinities with the constructivist elements of what I am calling Hobbes's nominalism.

8. Hobbes does speak of the experience of words, that is to say, customary words and phrases, as well as experience of sensations and so the distinction between experience of fact and sensation on the one hand and the experience of speech on the other must be made. See, for example, *EL*, 1.4.11.

9. Ibid., sec. 10; *Lev.*, 3.7–10. Prudence is foresight based on past experience; specifically, experiences in which we learn to associate sensations and conceptions that occur together.

10. For a defense of the lower faculties, and in particular the connection between Hobbes's reason and experience in curiosity, see Barnouw, "Hobbes's Psychology of Thought."

11. It also follows from this that Hobbes does not base his science on assertions of fact. There is something Hobbes calls "knowledge of fact" (*De Homine*, 10.5), but the mere existence of this category within Hobbes's thought does not mean that he used matters of fact as a ground for his science. To assume that he wished to do so is to make the kind of whiggish leap contested here. Such a leap would also have to contend both with the work of Shapin and Schaffer in *Leviathan and the Air-Pump*, and—in the context of his science of politics—with the straightforward statement at the close of *Leviathan*, "The matters in question are not of fact, but of right, wherein there is no place of witnessing." *Lev.*, "A Review and Conclusion," 15. Establishing matters of fact was precisely the kind of contentious business that Hobbes sought to avoid by resorting to a mathematically inspired science. Its certainty was meant to be unpolluted by disputes over matters of fact.

12. *Lev.*, 3.9; *EL*, 1.6.4.

13. *Lev.*, 3.3.

14. Ibid., 3.2–5; on curiosity, see Barnouw, "Hobbes's Psychology of Thought."

15. *Lev.*, 3.11.

16. *EL*, 1.4.11.

17. *Lev.*, 4.1.

18. Ibid.

19. *De Corpore*, 2.2; *Lev.*, 4.3 and 4.9.

20. Miller and Strong, "Meanings and Contexts."

21. *Lev.*, 4.3.

22. Ibid.

23. *De Corpore*, 3.8.

24. *Lev.*, 4.4, 12–13, 20–21, and 24; *Lev.*, 5.5–19; *EL*, 1.5.6–8 and 13–14; *EL*, 1.6.3.

25. *De Homine*, 10.3. Hobbes also mentions in this chapter the capacity to lie and the layer upon layer of habitual self- and collective deception that occurs in the schools. Again, Hobbes notes that the human being is the only animal that can deceive itself. In *Leviathan* he finds "those men that take their instruction from the authority of books, and not from their own meditation, to be as much below the condition of ignorant men as those endued with true science are above it. For between true science and erroneous doctrines, ignorance is in the middle. Natural sense and imagination are not subject to absurdity. Nature itself cannot err; and as men abound in copiousness of language, so they become more wise, or more mad, than ordinary. Nor is it impossible without letters for man to become either excellently wise, or (unless his memory be hurt by disease or ill constitution of organs) excellently foolish. For words are wise men's counters, they do but reckon by them; but they are the money of fools, that value them by the authority of an Aristotle, a Cicero, or a Thomas, or any other doctor whatsoever, if but a man." *Lev.*, 4.13.

26. *De Corpore*, 3.8.

27. *Lev.*, 4.3.

28. Ibid.

29. See *De Corpore*, 6.13–15, for a complete list of the strictures on how to form definitions. Hobbes states that accidents are best defined by examples, rather than definitions, but

nevertheless defines "accident" as "the manner by which any body is conceived; which is all one as if they should say, an accident is that faculty of any body, by which it works in us a conception of itself." *De Corpore*, 8.2. As an example, take hardness. The accident of hardness is properly attributed to a body (it has the accident of hardness, or its mode of motion qualifies as "hard") when "no part gives place, but when the whole gives place." Ibid. Hobbes's accidents can be thought of as characteristics that attend to bodies—at root, how they move. One can see how these characteristics would make a different kind of impression on the organs of sense than a body with the accident of "softness." With the exception of a few global accidents, like extension (because there is no body without extension), accidents occur in particular combinations to yield up impressions of the particular kinds of phantasms.

30. *Lev.*, 5.4. See also *Lev.*, 4.13.

31. Ibid., 5.1.

32. For Hobbes's account of the arithmetic of phantasms, see *De Corpore*, 1.3. Only in speech, however, can we begin to address causes. This is because in speech we may create abstract names, including those that identify characteristics or "accidents" of bodies. Thus, man is defined by Hobbes as a rational, animate creature. Being rational is an accident that defines the matter that is brought together under the name "man" and is a cause in accordance with Hobbes's understanding of causality. All that can be explained causally in Hobbes's philosophy is explained by the concatenation of accidents. Such accidents are the necessary causes of a particular named entity.

33. *De Corpore*, 3.3.

34. *Lev.*, 5.17.

35. The status of mathematics and mathematicians in relation to natural philosophy in the sixteenth and seventeenth centuries was a part of, by this time, a long-standing controversy in the schools. Hobbes's defense was bolder than most because of his willingness to put creation so much further above any other goal—including that of modeling reality. The conflict and the progress of mathematicians in making encroachments into the territory of natural philosophy has been approached from a variety of perspectives. Some of the more important works include Dear, *Discipline and Experience* and *Mersenne*; Mancosu, "Aristotelian Logic and Euclidean Mathematics," in which Mancosu briefly discusses Hobbes's conflict with Wallis; Shapin and Schaffer, *Leviathan and the Air-Pump*; Jardine, *Birth of History*; Westman, "Astronomer's Role," 105–47; and Crombie, "Mathematics and Platonism."

36. *Lev.*, 4.12.

37. Hobbes was not the only one in England at this time to make this claim. See, for example, the preface to Hylles, *The Arte of Vulgar Arithmeticke*, Biii.

38. *Lev.*, 4.1.

39. *Lev.*, 4.2; *De Corpore*, 2.4.

40. *De Corpore*, 3.1. See also *Lev.*, 4.11–12, and *EL*, 1.5.10.

41. *De Corpore*, 3.2.

42. Ibid., 3.7.

43. On the growing popularity of sense as a criterion for acceptable knowledge, see Shapiro, *Probability and Certainty*. Also see Shapin and Schaffer, *Leviathan and the Air-Pump*.

44. *De Corpore*, 3.8.

45. Ibid., 3.7. Also see 3.10: "Truth adheres not to things, but to speech only, for some truths are eternal; for it will be eternally true, if man, then living creature; but that any man, or living creature, should exist eternally, is not necessary." This assertion is explained by the fact that Hobbes defines "living creature" as one of the accidents that are necessary to "man"; in his terminology, a cause of man. Thus, it is true that "man" entails the notion of "living creature," but it could be that men, and all living creatures, will one day be gone. Nonetheless, the formal truth that "man" is a "living creature" will nonetheless remain true. In *Lev.*, 4.11, Hobbes writes: "For True and False are attributes of Speech, not of Things. And where Speech is not, there is neither Truth nor Falsehood."

46. These questions are asked, for example, in McNeilly, *The Anatomy of Leviathan*, 65, 186–91, 250–54. The expectation is that Hobbes either must have, did, or should have made empirical reality the standard against which his philosophy should be judged. It can be found in some of the most influential philosophical interpretations of Hobbes's work in last fifty years: see, for example, Watkins, *Hobbes's System of Ideas*, esp. 72–74, and Kavka, *Hobbesian Moral and Political Theory*, 6–11. See my discussion in Chapter 1.

47. See Gadamer, *Truth and Method*, esp. 265–379. Searching for Hobbes's own satisfactions is also in the spirit of Oakeshott's reading. See Oakeshott, "Introduction to *Leviathan*." See, however, the criticisms of Oakeshott's reading later in this chapter.

48. *De Corpore*, 6.1.

49. *Lev.*, 7.3. This statement also gestures toward Hobbes's nominalism, a topic I take up later in this chapter.

50. Oakeshott, *Rationalism in Politics*, 237; *De Corpore*, 6.1 and 25.1.

51. Tönnies, *On Social Ideas and Ideologies*, 34–35.

52. For a parallel rejection (although not of Tönnies specifically, in this instance), see the important treatment of questions of verification in Brandt, *Thomas Hobbes' Mechanical Conception of Nature*, esp. 193–204.

53. See esp. *EL*, 1.2.4–10, and *Lev.*, 1.4–5.

54. *Lev.*, 1.4–5.

55. On prudence's status as knowledge, and specifically in contrast to the knowledge established by reason (the only form of reason which can be called "true" because it takes the form of knowledge of the consequences of words), see *Lev.*, 3.7, where prudence is defined as "applying the sequels of actions past to the actions that are present; which with most certainty is done by him who has most experience, but not with certainty enough [in the Latin edition, "complete certainty"]. And though it be called prudence when the event answereth our expectation, yet in its own nature it is but presumption." It is presumption, Hobbes tells us, because foresight of things to come in nature can only be had by him who makes these things come about, i.e., supernaturally. See also *Lev.*, 5.17 (on prudence's mere knowledge of fact), and *EL*, 1.4.10–11.

56. A slight clarification must be added to this point. Although Hobbes defines reason as "reckoning (that is, adding and subtracting) of the consequences of general names agreed upon for the marking and signifying of our thoughts" in *Lev.*, 5.2, in the prior section (5.1) he links reasoning's business of adding and subtracting to "all manner of things that can be added together and taken one out of another." This would therefore seem to include things other than words. Hobbes notes that arithmeticians add and subtract numbers, and geometricians add and subtract lines, figures, angles, and so on. (See also *Lev.*, 2.4.) Does this open up the possibility that Hobbesian reason concerns itself with making claims about empirical reality? Even if we ignore Hobbes's contradictions (see also *De Homine*, 10.3, in which numbers are counted as a part of speech), it is difficult to see how it could when Hobbes defines truth strictly in linguistic terms. (See *Lev.*, 4.11–12.)

57. *Lev.*, 9.1. The Latin edition maintains the distinction between knowledge of fact and knowledge of consequences. It should be noted that Hobbes is not fully consistent with himself on the organization of the sciences. As Sorell notes in "Hobbes's Scheme of the Sciences," the organization changes in *De Corpore*, 1.9. Even here, however, Hobbes maintains the boundary between knowledge derived from experience and philosophical knowledge. See *De Corpore*, 1.8: "It [philosophy] excludes *history*, as well *natural* and *political*, thought most useful (nay necessary) to philosophy; because such knowledge is but experience, or authority, and not ratiocination." How such histories are useful to philosophy may be a subject for debate; however, it is clear that one thing knowledge of fact cannot do is either establish or disconfirm philosophical truths. This has been a matter of grave disappointment to those who see Hobbes as a forerunner of modern hypothesis-testing science. See Brandt, *Thomas Hobbes' Mechanical Conception of Nature*, and Wallace, *Causality and Scientific Explanation*, 17–29.

58. Hobbes, "To the King," in *Seven Philosophical Problems*, 3, in *EW*, vol. 7. For discussions of related Renaissance theology in the context of science, including voluntarism, see Oakley, "The Absolute and Ordained Power of God and King" and "The Absolute and Ordained Power of God in Sixteenth- and Seventeenth-Century Theology," 437–39; Malet, "Isaac Barrow"; Shapin, "Robert Boyle and Mathematics"; Funkenstein, *Theology and the Scientific Imagination*; Oakley, *Omnipotence, Covenant, and Order*; Shapiro, *Probability and Certainty*; and Klaaren, *Religious Origins of Modern Science*.

59. *Lev.*, 31.14–28. Oakeshott notes the connection with the Scotist tradition. Oakeshott, *Rationalism in Politics*, 245 n. 37. For a discussion of the similarities between the limits Hobbes places on our knowledge of God and specific assertions and arguments of Calvinist and medieval traditions, see Martinich, *Two Gods of Leviathan*, 185–219.

60. Hobbes wrote, "For though there be many things in God's Word above Reason; that is to say, which cannot by naturall reason be either demonstrated, or confuted; yet there is nothing contrary to it." *Lev.*, 32.2. Hobbes gives reason a "veto power" over what God's Word might mean. He nevertheless arrives at the same destination concerning the relation of reason to revelation. See also Johnston's discussion in *Rhetoric of Leviathan*, 138–39. Hobbes's originality lay not in claiming that scripture's meaning is not inconsistent with human reason. It is, rather, in the particulars of what he claimed right reason to have in fact dictated, namely, his own doctrine concerning a subject's obedience. See also Springborg, "*Leviathan* and the Problem of Ecclesiastical Authority," and Mulligan, "'Reason.'"

61. Consider, for example, Hobbes's objections to Descartes's *Meditations*, "The Third Set of Objections with the Author's Reply," particularly objections IX, X, and XI. Descartes, *Oeuvres*, 7:171–96. See Pacchi, "Hobbes and the Problem of God," which, in particular on its reflections on Hobbes's *Anti-White*, illustrates how far Hobbes was willing to go to limit our knowledge of God. Pacchi sees Hobbes's God as a "supposition never verified." He also asserts that Hobbes's God is "the highest sanction of the validity and coherence of the mechanical order of the material universe." Ibid., 182–83. I agree with Pacchi that God is the "last hypothetical term of human reasoning" (that is to say, the unquestioned cause that must initiate all others to follow), but in so far as this "validity" is extended to claims to know with certainty how the natural universe was in fact created, I think Hobbes's voluntarism contradicts such a conclusion.

62. Oakeshott, *Rationalism in Politics*, 243–44.

63. The phrase is Oakeshott's. See ibid., 245.

64. On this, see my article "Oakeshott's Hobbes and the Fear of Political Rationalism."

65. "The system of Hobbes's philosophy lies in his conception of the nature of philosophical knowledge, and not in any doctrine about the world. And the inspiration of his philosophy is the intention to be guided by reason and to reject all other guides: this is the thread, the hidden thought, that gives it coherence, distinguishing it from Faith, 'Science' and Experience. It remains to guard against a possible error. The lineage of Hobbes's rationalism lies, not (like that of Spinoza or even Descartes) in the great Platonic-Christian tradition, but in the skeptical, late scholastic tradition. He does not normally speak of Reason, the divine illumination of the mind that unites man with God; he speaks of reasoning." Oakeshott, *Rationalism in Politics*, 245.

66. *De Corpore*, 1.6.

67. Hobbes, "To the King," in *Seven Philosophical Problems*, 3–4, in *EW*, vol. 7. The practical expectations that Hobbes creates for his philosophy do, however, necessitate a subtle distinction: the distinction between truth claims which assert that something exists in a particular way in the world (which, as I have indicated, his philosophy does not make) and things that must exist in order for his philosophy to fulfill its practical functions. His philosophy may not speak truths about the world, but to be practical it must speak truths that can guide us in concrete practices of construction. This requires that at least one thing about the world be assumed: that it is composed of bodies. "Body" is one of the things to which Hobbes attributes an independent existence. *De Corpore*, 8.1. This is not a conclusion of Hobbes's philosophy, but a starting presupposition, an axiom—just as geometry has axioms. In order for Hobbes's philosophy to function

in a practical way, the world must be full of matter (and have no vacuums). He was a plenist. See Shapin and Schaffer, *Leviathan and the Air-Pump*.

There are also some interesting and important parallels between Hobbes's practical boasts (it's good enough if we can make it ourselves) and the constellation of doctrines and arguments that historians of science have called "probabilism." Perhaps most noteworthy are the parallels with Mersenne (who was instrumental in helping Hobbes establish his reputation) and other Jesuit defenders of mathematics in the schools. On Mersenne and the other Jesuit partisans of mathematics within the schools, see Dear, *Mersenne*, 42–47. See also Dear's discussion of the Augustinian strains in Mersenne's arguments against skeptics and Descartes in ibid., 48–116. Using Augustine as a tenuous supplement to the Thomistic orthodoxy, Mersenne asserts the possibility of divine illumination, particularly through the practice of mathematical reasoning. Unlike Hobbes, Mersenne asserts the conformity of rational ideas to the real world by calling on Augustinian claims linking rational faculties with divine illumination. See also Schaffer, "Wallification," and Shapiro, *Probability and Certainty*. For a useful treatment of Hobbes that speaks against his assimilation into the probabilist camp, see Kahn, *Rhetoric, Prudence, and Skepticism*. In demanding and claiming certainty, Hobbes parts company with those who embraced and cultivated probabilism (such as the members of the Royal Society described in Shapiro, *Probability and Certainty*, who sought a middle ground between knowledge and opinion as previously defined in the schools). Moreover, Hobbes's nominalism means that they are much more invested in achieving empirically testable, probable, truths, whereas Hobbes was not. The greatest overlap occurs with regard to the claim to deliver practical knowledge in the form of instructions in how to manipulate matter in motion. On probabilism, see Shapiro, ibid., and Hacking, *Emergence of Probability*, 1–48.

68. "And supposing some motion for the cause of your phenomenon, try, if by evident consequence, without contradiction to any other manifest truth or experiment, you can derive the cause you seek for from your supposition. If you can, it is all that is expected, as to that one question, from philosophy. For there is no effect in nature which the Author of nature cannot bring to pass by more ways than one." *Dec. Phys.*, chap. 2, in *EW*, 7:88.

69. *De Corpore*, 1.6.

70. Ibid.

71. See the discussion of "maker's knowledge" in Pérez-Ramos, "Francis Bacon and Man's Two-Faced Kingdom" and *Francis Bacon's Idea of Science*, and Child, "Making and Knowing." Child, however, shies away from more interesting conclusions concerning Hobbes's civil science. See also Funkenstein, *Theology and the Scientific Imagination*, esp. 290–345. Although not discussing maker's knowledge, Norman Jacobson's reading of Hobbes in *Pride and Solace* makes light of the godlike claims that Hobbes makes for his philosophy. I find that Jacobson's assertions are in many respects similar to my own conclusions, although his study and mine have different purposes.

72. Sorell suggests, in "Hobbes's Scheme of the Sciences," that Hobbes's various classifications of the sciences are not consistent. *Leviathan* seems to divide up the sciences in a different way than is suggested, for example, in *De Corpore*. Perhaps the most important of these inconsistencies concerns the uncertain status of the sciences that concern the passions, including ethics. One suspects that this debate will continue. I would point out that the distinction that I am referring to is between works. Needless to say, I am not claiming that the division between a priori and a posteriori sciences is the only basis for Hobbes's classification, I am merely claiming that his decision to divide the sciences along these lines is indicative of his concern.

73. *De Homine*, 10.5.

74. Ibid., 10.5. See also *De Corpore*, 30.15.

75. *De Corpore*, "The Author's Epistle to the Reader," xiii–xiv; *Lev.*, "Introduction," 1.

76. Nicolaus of Cusa, *Idiota de mente*, 51. (Also see Clyde Lee Miller's translation of *Idiota de mente*, 45.) On this passage, see especially the analysis of Watts, *Nicolas Cusanus*, esp. 133–233, and 91–94. The commonalities between Hobbes and Cusanus are significant and worthy of

further exploration on several points. These include: man's capacity to imitate God and, in this context, the relative dignity of original creation and the imitation of divinely produced effects; the link between God's world-creative Word and mind, and our own words and minds. Finally, the two can be compared with regard to the doctrine that makes measure the common feature of both human and divine thought. My study is limited and does not allow for sufficient comparison on all these points.

77. See the works by Oakley and Funkenstein cited in note 58.

78. See also *De Corpore*, 6.1, on the distinction between the "science of causes" and all other sciences (*dioti* as opposed to *oti*).

79. *De Homine*, 10.5.

80. Ibid.

81. Ibid. The concept of a "mixed" form of mathematics occurs in Aristotle, *Posterior Analytics* 1.7 and *Metaphysics* 13.3 (esp. 1078a, 14–17). Aristotle, however, did not classify physics as a "mixed" science; for Aristotle it was an autonomous discipline. Hobbes, by defining physics as a mixed form of mathematical science, makes a characteristically brash move. He subordinates physics to mathematics in a way that flouts the Aristotelian tradition. For a new and excellent discussion of the (often more cautious and politic) encroachments of mathematics on physics in the Renaissance, see Dear, *Discipline and Experience; Mersenne*, 63–70; and "Jesuit Mathematical Science." Hobbes's brash use of the notion of mixed mathematics should be contrasted in particular to that of the Jesuit professor of mathematics Christopher Clavius.

82. *De Corpore*, 6.4. Also see the remarks on analysis in 6.1, 9, and 10.

83. Ibid., 6.6 and 6.12. See also the remarks on synthesis in 6.1, 9, and 10.

84. As Sacksteder has also pointed out, this means that the distinction between sciences like geometry and sciences like physics is one of perfect or imperfect convertibility. In geometry one may either use resolution or composition and precisely retrace one's steps up or down the chain of deductions. By contrast, if one begins (as in physics) with a whole and resolves the parts, there is no guarantee of the necessity of the resolutive steps (i.e., going down). As he notes, we cannot reduce natural phenomena without remainder—something that can be done in the case of geometrical figures. Because we are unconcerned with the actual processes of production, it matters very little how one resolves a whole in physics, so long as it is resolved into its most basic elements; we then begin to synthesize the effect by our own means. As a knowledge of the real world, it could only be hypothetical, and (as I have shown) Hobbes urges us to be unconcerned with this. It is the pragmatic criterion of producing effects that most concerns him, so much so that we miss Hobbes's point if we say that his accomplishments in physics are "only" hypothetical. In emphasizing this "limitation" we fail to understand the practical trajectory of Hobbes's (more practically oriented) goals. Sacksteder, "Three Diverse Sciences."

85. *De Homine*, 10.5; *De Corpore*, 6.12. Hobbes asserts, that is, that demonstration is strictly a matter of synthesis (or composition). It does not entail the resolving (or analytic) steps with which one begins in "mixed" sciences such as physics.

86. Jesuit mathematicians used the distinction, for example, in the sixteenth and seventeenth centuries, as they struggled to establish the legitimacy of mathematics in the schools. I discuss Hobbes's relation to this debate elsewhere. See, however, Mancosu, *Philosophy of Mathematics*, 1–33, and see especially Biancani, *De Mathematicarum Natura*, chap. 1, and Mancosu, "Aristotelian Logic and Euclidean Mathematics." For a contextually richer treatment of this struggle, see Dear, "Jesuit Mathematical Science," *Mersenne*, and *Discipline and Experience*. See also Jesseph, "Hobbes and Mathematical Method." Jesseph helps us understand how arguments based on this distinction also inform the opposition of mathematical conservatives such as Hobbes (and Isaac Barrow) to analytic geometry. For a review and a new analysis of Hobbes's method among political theorists, see Hanson, "The Meaning of 'Demonstration' in Hobbes's Science." I come to very different conclusions than Hanson, who, it seems to me, ignores key differences between Hobbes and Descartes on the worthiness of analytic methods.

87. "It is better to know how we can best use present causes than to know the irrevocable past, whatsoever its nature." *De Homine*, 10.4.

88. This is not to deny that analytic methods cannot be used among those who are called upon to live in Hobbes's state. See, for example, *De Corpore*, 6.7, and the discussion in Sorell, *Hobbes*, 7–13. As I noted, all of Hobbes's sciences entail a combination of resolution and composition (analytic and synthetic reasoning). The critical point, however, is that civil philosophy (like other a priori sciences) begins with construction.

89. "When a man reasoneth, he does nothing else but conceive a sum total from additions of parcels, or conceive a remainder from subtraction of one sum from another.... For as arithmeticians teach to add and subtract in numbers, so the geometricians teach the same in lines, figures, (solid and superficial), angles, proportions, times, degrees of swiftness, force, power, and the like; ... Writers of politics add together pactions to find men's duties; and lawyers, laws and facts, to find what is right and wrong in the actions of private men." *Lev.*, 5.1.

90. *De Homine*, 10.5.

91. *Lev.*, "Introduction," 1.

92. For example, in Barber, *Strong Democracy*, 32–33.

93. *Lev.*, "Introduction," 1.

94. This series of analogous relationships may suggest an irreverent possibility. Our creation (the commonwealth) exceeds ourselves (man). Does God's creation (man) exceed Him? This raises an issue that preoccupies a number of Hobbes scholars: was Hobbes an atheist? In my view, this question becomes interesting when it suggests a place for Hobbes in the process Weber described as the disenchantment of the world. Instead of asking whether Hobbes fits with a contemporary understanding of atheism (which, too often, is the question), I think it is more fruitful to ask how Hobbes's plan to turn man into an equivalent, if not a superior, leads toward the diminution of God's place in the universe. This would also have the advantage of achieving a closer fit with the conceptions of atheism that informed Hobbes's accusers. Mintz, *The Hunting of Leviathan*, 39–40. A reading that would preserve the traditional hierarchy between God and his creation, however, is also possible. Imperfect man uses his most perfect, most divine, faculty—his reason—to overcome his imperfection by creating something better than himself.

95. Blumenberg, *The Legitimacy of the Modern Age*, 63–75, 115–20, 184, 457–81.

Chapter 4

1. Foucault, *The Order of Things*.

2. Machiavelli, *The Prince*, chaps. 18–19; Erasmus, *Education of a Christian Prince*, esp. 22, 26–27, 36–41; *De Cive*, dedicatory.

3. *De Cive*, preface, 2. The cloudy beginnings of civil science are further related by Hobbes through reference to ancient mythology, and in such a way as to equate his accomplishment with aggressive sexual victory, not unlike Machiavelli's approach to Fortuna. The end of the golden age of peace began when "Saturn was expelled [not unlike Charles I!] and the doctrine started up that one could take up arms against kings. This ... the ancients ... aptly symbolized.... They say that when Ixion was invited by Jupiter to a banquet, he fell in love with Juno herself and harassed her. In place of the Goddess, a cloud was offered to him in the form of Juno. From the cloud were born the Centaurs, partly human in nature, partly horses, a belligerent and restless race. Change the names, and it is as if they had said that private men, summoned to the Councils on the highest questions of state, attempted to subject Justice, sister and wife of sovereign Power, to their own understanding, but, embracing a false and empty semblance of her like a cloud, have generated the ambivalent dogmas of the moral philosophers, partly correct and attractive, partly brutal and irrational, the cause of all quarrels and killing. Since such opinions arise every day, anyone who dispels these clouds," as Hobbes claims to do by showing that justice and injustice, good and evil, are matters for the commonwealth to decide on its own, "he will ... reveal the

royal road to peace and the dark and shadowy ways of sedition." *De Cive*, preface, 7–8. Hobbes, by the terms of this metaphor, casts himself as the one man who might accomplish what Ixion and the moral philosophers failed to do. Instead of yielding a creature half-beast and half-human, he would produce one half-god and half-human. Triumph over Juno, moreover, could be suggestive of a triumph over nature itself.

4. Hooker, *Of the Laws of Ecclesiastical Polity*, bk. 1, chap. 5, sec. 1.

5. Ibid., sec. 3.

6. He cites Aristotle's *De anima* 2.4. Here Aristotle justifies the telos revealed by reproduction. It gives us our imperfect share in divine eternity.

7. Among the most instructive is Charles Trinkaus's work. Trinkaus tends to believe in the ultimate piety of his ambitious humanists while also recognizing the trajectory that leads toward God's replacement. See Trinkaus, "Marsilio Ficino and the Ideal of Human Autonomy." Garin is bolder, and more politically centered, in his studies than Trinkaus in asserting the independence of humanist thought. See also Cassirer, *The Individual and the Cosmos*.

8. Extensive discussions of the theme of divine imitation among Italian Renaissance humanists can be found in Trinkaus, *In Our Image and Likeness*.

9. I quote Trinkaus's translation in ibid., 247. The original is Manetti, *De dignitate et excellentia homini*, fol. 27v–8r.

10. Ibid. Trinkaus notes parallels in 1 *Corinthians*, 3:9–12, 22, 33, and Cicero, *De natura deorum* 2.60: "The human race has dominion over all the products of the earth. We enjoy the treasures of plains and mountains; ours are the streams, ours the lakes; we cultivate the fruits and plant trees; we give fertility to the soil by works of irrigation; we restrain, straighten or divert our streams—in short, with our hands we set about the fashioning of another nature, as it were, within the bounds and precincts of the one we have." Trinkaus's translation of *De natura deorum*, in *In Our Image and Likeness*, 247–48.

11. Augustine, *City of God* 5.2.18, as noted by Trinkaus, in *In Our Image and Likeness*, 248.

12. To be sure, a key element of Ficino's argument hinges on the immortality of the human soul—a doctrine in direct contradiction with Hobbes's mortalism. It must be noted, therefore, that my argument is not that Hobbes and these writers were in agreement, but that notions of man as a creator were available to writers in the seventeenth century and that these help us better understand Hobbes's claims concerning the imitation of the divine.

13. Ficino, *Theologia Platonica de Immortalitate animorum*, 2.224–25 (bk. 8, chap. 3); quoted in translation in Trinkaus, *In Our Image and Likeness*, 482–84.

14. Rossi, *Francis Bacon*.

15. Hine, *Marin Mersenne*, 165–76. As Hine points out, strict naturalism excludes belief in all supernatural events. It was on this basis that Mersenne condemned naturalists as atheists, since naturalism did not leave room for belief in miracles.

16. See Pine, *Pietro Pomponazzi*; Hine, *Marin Mersenne*; Kraye, "Philosophy of the Italian Renaissance"; and Douglas, *Philosophy and Psychology of Pietro Pomponazzi*, 270–303. For an interpretation that deemphasizes the irreligious potential of Pomponazzi, see Kristeller, *Eight Philosophers*, 72–90. Unlike many scholars interested in the occult forces in the Renaissance, Pomponazzi was an Aristotelian. This need not preclude views contrary to what we think of as the scholastic tradition. For an influential reassessment of Renaissance Aristotelianism, see Schmitt, *Aristotle and the Renaissance*.

17. See Hine, *Marin Mersenne*.

18. Hill, *A briefe and pleasaunt treatise*. Hill's work was republished in the sixteenth and seventeenth centuries, and reprinted in 1974. I have used text and images from the 1650 edition of Thomas Hill's *Naturall and Artificiall Conclusions*. Following Trevor Hall (1972), the British Library catalog notes that evidence exists that the work may have been published as early as 1567. It also states in the 1586 edition that the text is a "compilation of translated material from a number of earlier writers, most notably Girolamo Cardano (1501–1576)." The polymath Cardano's interests in astrology overlapped with those of Pomponazzi. Cardano received a medical degree from

Padua in the year of Pomponazzi's death; he was also elected rector there. Moreover, the secret of walking on water was taken without attribution by Hill from Cardano. See *Les Livres*, 432B (from chap. 8 of *De la Subtilité*, "On Marvelous Inventions"). What is remarkable, even in what would have been seen as a somewhat crass book of secrets like Hill's, is that he dispenses with the exercises in excuse-making for bringing such scandalous (and, Cardano knew, therefore tempting) knowledge to light.

19. Hill, *A briefe and pleasaunt treatise*, 48–49. Timbrels were one-sided drums, not unlike tambourines. To turn water into wine, see ibid., 20.

20. The last two editions attribute authorship not to Hill but to Saint Albertus Magnus (d. 1280).

21. See Helgerson, *Self-Crowned Laureates*. Attacks on poetry from Puritan quarters are discussed in Agnew, *Worlds Apart*. Views on the court poet's motives are developed in Javitch, *Poetry and Courtliness* and "Il Cortegiano." For more complex views, working from, yet critical of, Javitch, see Whigham, *Ambition and Privilege*, and Montrose, "Of Gentlemen and Shepherds." See also Sharpe, *Criticism and Compliment*.

22. Puttenham, *Arte of English Poesie*, 3.

23. Both Puttenham and Sidney take the suggestion from etymology, deriving the English *poet* from the Greek *poiein*, "to make." Puttenham, *Arte of English Poesie*, 3; Sidney, *Defense of Poesy*, 212–50; on "making," see 215. Note that Sidney also goes out of his way to temper the boastfulness of the claim: ". . . maker: which name, how high and incomparable a title it is, I had rather were known by marking the scope of other sciences than by any partial allegation." It must also be noted that Sidney, although concerned to defend the science of poetry, was an aristocrat and not a professional poet in the sense that later seventeenth-century poets such as Jonson were.

24. Sidney, *Defense of Poesy*, 216.

25. In *Anti-White*, chap. 1, secs. 2 and 3, Hobbes distances the philosopher from the poet. He does so, however, in terms of the way the two practices express themselves.

26. Girard, *Violence and the Sacred*.

27. Ibid., chap. 6, esp. 151–53.

28. Garin, *Science and Civil Life*, 13.

29. Ibid.

30. Ibid.

31. Toulmin, *Cosmopolis*, 66–70.

32. Toulmin's referents are Rorty, *Philosophy and the Mirror of Nature*, and Dewey, *The Quest for Certainty*.

33. *Lev.*, 31.41.

34. Ibid., 13.10.

35. *De Cive*, preface, 11; *De Cive*, 1.2.

36. In *Elements of Law*, Hobbes makes fewer such appeals directly to the audience, but does makes appeals to history (*EL*, 1.14.12) and speaks of death as "that terrible enemy of nature," from which we expect pain and a loss of all power (1.14.6).

37. *Lev.*, 11.2–3, 24–25, and 9; *De Cive*, preface; *Lev.*, 13.3, 6–7.

38. *Lev.*, 31.33. See also his discussion of miracles. Hobbes notes that we can no more know how regular processes in nature, such as the fossilization of wood, are effected than we can know how God might have turned man into stone or a pillar. *Lev.*, 37.3.

39. Hobbes will allow that he will not speak of the felicity of the afterlife, a gesture which at once feigns reverence but which has the immediate effect of cordoning off the boundaries of the thoroughly human world.

40. *Lev.*, 6.58.

41. Ibid., 18.15.

42. Ibid., 17.13, 18.3.

43. Schmitt, *Political Theology*; Schmitt, *The Leviathan in the State Theory*; Agamben, *Homo Sacer*, 35–38, 104–11.

44. Schmitt's crusade was against much of the Enlightenment, and in particular Enlightenment liberalism. His politics were inspired by nineteenth-century reactionaries and the search for new forms of unified authority to replace the old. He was deeply mindful of the loss of the unified church-monarchical states, and their replacement with political ideals of a more abstract, universalistic form. He was particularly critical of the liberal commitments to constitutionalism, the rule of law, free speech, popular rule, and the concomitant belief that states could be neutral with regard to fundamental value commitments. A conservative, Schmitt wrote in part to avenge the loss of these strong states. With the demise of the Weimar Republic, he became a Nazi. His theoretical efforts on behalf of that regime did not yield the results he had hoped for. In his intellectual struggles, he at first thought he had found an ally in Hobbes. His early admiration for Hobbes is recorded in *Political Theology*, esp. 33–35, 47–48, 52, and *Concept of the Political*, 65–67, where he groups Hobbes with sobering thinkers such as Machiavelli who might awaken those under the spell of liberalism to the possibility of real existential threats to the state, and the concrete (decisionalist) means to cope with them. Liberals might allow a conflict of (mere) competitors (incorrectly miscasting political conflicts as if they were not fundamentally different from economic ones) to operate within a pluralist society. What they missed, particularly in the demise of the Weimar Republic, was the possibility that the political parties and other forces active in Germany at the time of his writing were, in some cases, not competitors but enemies unwilling to work within the confines of a constitutional order. Schmitt considered it characteristic of liberalism to either ignore, evade, or conceal enmities and the very possibility of the enemy. Hobbes, he thought, knew they were there. Against enemies, a state sovereign was entitled to decide upon the exception: to go outside the boundaries of the ordinary lawful order which he warrants with his power, and to exercise extraordinary, extralegal, measures. The sovereign could exceed the limits imposed by law and expose enemies (domestic or foreign) to the more aggressive measures permitted in the state of nature. Schmitt, *Political Theology*. After his experiences with and among the Nazis, he would emphasize what he described as fissures in Hobbes's state, openings that would be exploited (notably by Jewish thinkers) to destroy the unity of the modern state from within. Schmitt, *The Leviathan in the State Theory*, esp. 55–57. This reassessment of Hobbes can be attributed, in part, to Leo Strauss's perhaps embarrassing critique of Schmitt's earlier work, wherein he not only recollects the liberalism inherent in Hobbes's philosophy, but also suggests that Schmitt himself remained dependent upon liberal habits of thought in his plea to revive an awareness of the necessary belligerence of "the political." Strauss, "Notes on Carl Schmitt." Schmitt's later work gives greater emphasis to the liberal aspects and precursors within Hobbes's work and presents Hobbes as partially culpable for the failure of modern states to unify. He is particularly focused on Hobbes's position that sovereigns, as heads of state churches, might be indifferent to the inner conscience of subjects so long as they outwardly profess obedience to the state-mandated faith and to the sovereign. Schmitt, *The Leviathan in the State Theory*, 55–64, 69–74.

45. Schmitt was not the only early twentieth-century reader, however, to highlight this aspect. See his discussion of Joseph Vialatoux's *La cité de Hobbes; Théorie de l'État totalitaire, Essai sur la conception naturaliste de la civilization*, in "The State as Mechanism," 76 n. 7, and appendix, 92–93.

46. Schmitt's awareness of these elements received a goad from Strauss, "Notes on Carl Schmitt," but as we shall see, there were elements of Hobbes's political and intellectual tool box which Schmitt considered suspect from his earlier writings, notably *Political Theology*. The case for Strauss's impact is made in Meier, *Carl Schmitt and Leo Strauss*. Schmitt himself writes of the additional lessons he took from Ferdinand Tönnies, a common influence on both Schmitt and Strauss. Schmitt, *The Leviathan in the State Theory*, esp. 67–68.

47. See note 44 for the broader contexts of this element of Schmitt's thought. See Strong, "Carl Schmitt and Thomas Hobbes," for a discussion of Schmitt's "new twist" on old-fashioned anti-Semitism.

48. Schmitt's sources in Hobbes are *An Answer to a Book Published by Dr. Bramhall . . . Called the Catching of Leviathan*, in *EW*, 4:279–408, published in 1682, and *Leviathan*, chap. 42. He does not cite specific pages (in either source), but does refer to the "lip service" confessions offered

to state authorities by nonbelievers. See *Lev.*, 42.11. Also see 42.79: "In sum he [the sovereign] hath supreme power in all causes, as well ecclesiastical as civil—as far as concerneth actions and words, for those only are known, any may be accused. And of those which cannot be accused, there is not judge at all but God, that knoweth the heart."

49. Schmitt, *The Leviathan in the State Theory*, 55–63, quotation from 57.

50. As a description of Descartes's thinking, Schmitt's stress on the singularity of Descartes's rational God can strike one as superfluous. It was not as if Descartes were combating polytheistic scholastic doctrines. His great stress on this unified rationality of this era's thought reflects in part his own decisionalist agenda. I will not attempt to critique Schmitt's brief pronouncements on Descartes or their sources.

51. Schmitt, *Political Theology*, 47.

52. Heidegger, *Being and Time*, 43–47, 71–72, 122–34.

53. Schmitt, *Political Theology*, 47.

54. Ibid., 5–7.

55. Ibid., 31–35, 5–15. See also his emphasis on the enemy in Schmitt, *Concept of the Political*, and Strauss's analysis, "Notes on Carl Schmitt." See also Bauman's description of Schmitt's project, in Bauman, "Seeking in Modern Athens."

56. Schmitt, *Political Theology*, 36.

57. This is a crucial element in Agamben's *Homo Sacer*; he refers to it as a "zone of indistinction," an "anomie," or a void. Following what he argues is Walter Benjamin's critique of Schmitt, the exception has become the rule in the modern state. See Agamben, *Homo Sacer*, 35–38, and *State of Exception*.

58. Schmitt, *The Leviathan in the State Theory*, 33–34; *Lev.*, 17.13.

59. These fables become a point of departure for Derrida in *Rogues* and his seminars in 2001 and 2002. See also Derrida, *The Beast and the Sovereign*, and Marin, *Food for Thought*.

60. Schmitt, "The State as Mechanism," 49.

61. Agamben, *Homo Sacer*, 35–38.

62. "Hobbes remained personalistic and postulated an ultimate concrete deciding instance . . . and heightened his state, the Leviathan, into an immense person and thus point-blank straight into mythology. This he did despite his nominalism and natural-scientific approach and his reduction of the individual to the atom." Schmitt, *Political Theology*, 47. "It is striking that one of the most consequential representatives of this abstract scientific orientation of the seventeenth century became so personalistic. . . . But juristic thought in those days had not yet become so overpowered by the natural sciences that he, in the intensity of his scientific approach, should unsuspectingly have overlooked the specific reality of legal life inherent in the legal form. . . . What matters for the reality of legal life is who decides." Ibid., 34.

63. Ibid., 48.

64. Ibid., 52.

65. Schmitt, "The State as Mechanism."

66. Schmitt, *The Leviathan in the State Theory*, 37; Heidegger, *Being and Time*, 43–47, 71–73, 122–34. Although Heidegger does not speak of machinery here, he does emphasize the way Descartes's philosophy "obliterates" distinctions between the being of Dasein and other entities, esp. between extended substance (or "Thinghood"), human beings, and the creator god of Christian theology. For Heidegger, the notion that the human being is created in the image of God remains a cause of philosophy's forgetfulness of being. *Being and Time*, 73–75, 126. It is also noteworthy that Heidegger insists that Descartes's decision to know being mathematically is not the cause but the symptom of a prior mistaken belief in the "self-evident" substantial character of being, that it is something merely "present-at-hand" (128–29).

67. Schmitt, "The State as Mechanism," 32.

68. Heidegger, *Being and Time*. The reference is to the later Enlightenment thinker Julien Offray de La Mettrie, author of *L'Homme Machine*, who is said to have moved forward with the vision of man that Hobbes and Descartes foster.

69. Ibid., 67. See also Schmitt, "The State as Mechanism," esp. 98–100.

70. *De Cive*, 1.2.

71. This point has been made before, in a variety of ways, in Johnston, *Rhetoric of Leviathan*; Thomas, "Social Origins"; and Strauss, *Political Philosophy of Hobbes*.

72. *Lev.*, 30.5–6, 30.14.

73. Ibid., 29.1.

74. Ibid.

75. Tuck, *Philosophy and Government*, 319–45. See especially the discussion of Hobbes's time as Charles II's mathematics tutor. Hobbes was not always in good graces during the period of Charles II's exile, however, or later, during the Restoration. Opponents in Parliament threatened to have him condemned as a heretic. This, however, should not be taken as a sign of his political marginalization. Arguably, the attacks upon Hobbes during this period ought to be understood as testimony to his importance. Who would bother to attack someone who didn't count? Signs that Hobbes may have counted include the fact that he was living in London at this time and was in close contact with and supported (although never unequivocally) by important courtiers. *Behemoth* is dedicated to the Baron of Arlington, a member of the clique that took control over the court following Clarendon's ouster. Clarendon had taken some pride in helping diminish Hobbes's access to the Crown during exile. Aubrey's account of Hobbes's rehabilitation is also noteworthy. He claims to have arranged for Hobbes (in 1660) to stand at the street corner as the recently restored Charles II passed by in his coach. Charles's recognition of Hobbes and the subsequent audience while the king sat for his portrait (by Cowper) may seem demeaning by contemporary standards, but by the standards of court society, Hobbes had achieved (in fact recovered) a remarkably high degree of access. His mere presence at court would have made him one of the most notable philosophers, let alone individuals, in the nation. Aubrey, "*Brief Lives*," 1:339–41. Aubrey's account of Hobbes's access as well as his conflicts at court seem indicative of the tenor of the period:

> About a weeke after [the "chance" encounter in the street] he had orall conference with his majesty at Mr. S. Cowper's, where, as he sate for his picture, he was diverted by Mr. Hobbes's pleasant discourse. Here his majestie's favours were redintegrated to him, and order was given that he should have free accesse to his majesty, who was always much delighted in his witt and smart repartees.
>
> The witts at Court were wont to bayte him. But he feared none of them, and would make his part good. . . . from 1660 till the time he last went into Derbyshire, he spent most of him in London at his lord's (little Salisbury-howse; then Queen Street; lastly, Newport-house). (Ibid., 340–41)

76. In *Basilicon Doron*, James teaches his son that he must imitate God. This is the argument presented in sonnet form, which follows the dedication:

> God giues not Kings the stile of *Gods* in vaine,
> For on his Throne his Scepter doe they swey:
> And as their subiects ought them to obey,
> So Kings should feare and serue their God againe:
> If then ye would enioy a happie raigne,
> Obserue the Statutes of your heauenly King,
> And from his Law, make all your Lawes to spring:
> Since his Lieutenant here ye should remaine,
> Reward the iust, be stedfast, true, and plaine,
> Represse the proud, maintayning aye the right,
> Walke alwayes so, as euer in his sight,
> Who guardes the godly, plaguing the prophane:
> And so ye shall in Princely vertues shine,
> Resembling right your mightie King Diuine.
>
> (pp. 1–2)

77. For parallels between Hobbes and Stuart absolutism, see Sommerville, *Thomas Hobbes*, 96, 103, 114–15, 123. Hobbes goes unmentioned in Oakley's "Jacobean Political Theology," but given the connections in Oakley between the absolute and ordinary powers of God (and later of popes, and then kings), and the development of "reason of state" in early modernity, the parallels could be further developed using the power to create as a starting point. Oakley, "The Absolute and Ordained Power of God in Sixteenth- and Seventeenth-Century Theology" and "The Absolute and Ordained Power of God and King in the Sixteenth and Seventeenth Centuries."

78. King James VI and I Stuart, *Basilicon Doron*, in Stuart, *Political Writings*, 13.

79. See, for example, Stuart, *Political Writings*, 62–84 (*The Trew Law of Free Monarchies*) and 179–249 (*A Speech to the Lords and commons of the parliament at White-Hall . . . XXI of March, Anno 1609; A Speech in the Starre-Chamber, the XX of Jvne, Anno 1616; A Meditation Vpon the 27. 28. 29. Verses of the XXVII Chapter of Saint Matthew or A Paterne for a Kings Inavgvration* [Dec. 29, 1619]).

80. Writing to Elizabeth: "But you (Madame) my most Honored and Gracious: if I should seeme to offer you this my deuise for a discipline and not a delight, I might well be reputed, of all others the most arrogant and iniurious: your selfe being alreadie, of any that I know in our time, the most excellent Poet. Forsooth by your Princely purse fauours and countenance, making in maner what ye list, the poore man rich, the lewd well learned, the coward couragious, and vile both noble and valiant. Then for imitation no less, your person as most cunning counterfaiter liuely representing Venus in countenance, in life Diana, Pallas for gouernement, and Iuno in all honour and regall magnificence." Puttenham, *Arte of English Poesie*, 4–5.

81. *Lev.*, 30.7–13, 30.14.

Chapter 5

1. "Architecton" suggests a master over *productive* practices, and so the term is particularly apt, considering the importance of generation to Hobbes's picture of the ideal science. For some reflections on architectonics, and the competition between architectons, see McKeon, "Uses of Rhetoric," esp. 1–12. It is important to point out, however, that geometry is not logically prior to, or the condition of, all the other sciences. The discipline that *is* prior to all other sciences and the condition for them is *philosophia prima*, or "first philosophy." This is not, however, a science that specifies particular causes and effects, but one that defines the most basic terms (such as "cause" and "effect") that other sciences (mathematics and physics) must use. First philosophy is not, therefore, productive or generative, but the condition for sciences that are either generative, or regenerative. Furthermore, first philosophy does not produce demonstrations; rather, its role in laying down unquestionable definitions makes it the condition for demonstrative science. Further investigations of Hobbes's understanding of first philosophy should lead to a more sophisticated understanding of his foundationalism. See Zarka, "First Philosophy," 62–85; *Anti-White*, chap. 1, sec. 1; *Lev.*, 46.14; *De Corpore*, 6.17; and *Six Lessons*, lesson 2, in *EW*, 7:222, 226. What one does with causes, effects, and definitions, the means of controlling motions, and the demonstrative (or nondemonstrative) status of the conclusions of a particular science are measured against the achievements of the geometrician's practices. Hobbes suggests as much when he speaks of geometry as a model for the other sciences: "So much of geometry is no part of philosophy, which seeketh the proper passions of all things in the generation of the things themselves." *Six Lessons*, lesson 1, in *EW*, 7:205. That is, the practices of the geometrician are not *merely* a part of philosophy, but an exemplar for many of the other parts. They are not, however, as Sacksteder (in "Hobbes: Geometrical Objects" and "Three Diverse Sciences") has argued, identical with the practices of the geometrician. Hobbes's ranking of the disciplines does not amount to a complete homogenization. Indeed, the distinctions between the disciplines have to remain for there to be a ranking at all. As we have been emphasizing, geometricians are able to use the methods of synthesis and analysis in a way that distinguishes them from natural philosophers, and yet because all sciences (according to Hobbes) make use of synthesis and analysis, a hierarchy emerges in terms of demonstrative certainty achieved by these

methods. Geometry and the other a priori practices emerge at the top of this hierarchy. It is in this common currency of the uses of synthesis and analysis that the other disciplines are measured against the geometrician's.

2. Aubrey, "*Brief Lives*," 1:331. Sorell has noted similarities (and some contrasts) with Bacon, as well as some fundamental inconsistencies between the organization of the sciences as it is presented in *De Corpore* (and in the preface to *De Cive*) on the one hand, and in *Leviathan* on the other. Sorell, "Hobbes's Scheme of the Sciences." Sorell, *Hobbes*, 6, 24–28, makes helpful observations concerning the independence of civil science from physics. Sorell suggests that one way to understand Hobbes's discussion of the order of the sciences is to see it as a recommendation that a student master one discipline before learning the next. In essence, I am arguing that Hobbes would have all sciences past his first philosophy depend upon geometry as a matter of pedagogical priority. Because Hobbes, and not nature itself, builds the commonwealth, this pedagogical priority is the only kind of dependence we should expect in his philosophy.

3. Gaukroger, "Descartes' Project for a Mathematical Physics." As Gaukroger notes, Aristotle's insistence on a homogeneity between the principles of inquiry and the subject under consideration meant that mathematics was by definition ruled out of physical inquiry: "Physics is concerned with those things that change and have an independent existence, mathematics with those things that do not change and have no independent existence" (97). As will become clear, there is a distinction to be made between what Aristotle argues on this subject and what Aristotelian scholars are willing to claim.

4. See ibid. and Gaukroger, *Descartes: An Intellectual Biography*, on influences on Descartes.

5. See, for example, Tönnies, *On Social Ideas and Ideologies*.

6. *Anti-White*, chap. 1, sec. 1.

7. See ibid., chap. 2, secs. 1 and 8, on exemplary use of definitions and geometrical care with language; see chap. 4, sec. 1, on how Hobbes redefines "perception" in a way that suits his nominalism; see chap. 9, sec. 16, for his attack on school metaphysics in the name of real *philosophia prima*, and mathematically guided reasoning; see chap. 14, sec. 1, and chap. 26, sec. 2, for more on Hobbes's nominalism; and see chap. 23, sec. 1, for Hobbes's opinion on the superiority of mathematical method over the other branches of philosophy. Moreover, as regards specific natural philosophical arguments, Hobbes is quite willing in this work to tear down the arguments of White and other natural philosophers (or, in many cases, White's arguments against rival natural philosophers), but is often (although not entirely) careful to assert the conjectural character of the natural philosophical enterprise as a whole. He often demurs rather than offer up natural philosophical explanations himself; see, for example, *Anti-White*, chap. 8, sec. 1 (on the formation and nature of comets), chap. 10, sec. 11 (on gravity), chap. 11, sec. 1 (on magnets), chap. 16, secs. 2 and 3 (on tides), and chap. 24, sec. 1 (the moon).

8. *Dec. Phys.*, chaps. 1 and 2, in *EW*, 7:69–88.

9. Ibid., chap. 1, in *EW*, 7:72.

10. Ibid., 72–73. Hobbes asserts that some few "effects of nature, especially concerning the heavens" have been assigned "rational causes"—notice that he does not say natural causes. Acknowledging the accomplishments of ancient astronomers, he then writes:

> B. . . . yet what is that to the numberless and quotidian phenomena of nature? Who is there amongst them or their successors, that has satisfied you with the cause of gravity, heat, cold, light, sense, colour, noise, rain, snow, frost, . . . and a thousand other things which a few men's lives are too short to go through, and which you and other curious spirits admire (as quotidian as they are), and fain would know the causes of them, but shall not find them in the books of naturalists; and when you ask what are the causes of any of them, of a philosopher now, he will put you off with mere words; which words, examined to the bottom signify not a jot . . . as are intrinsical quality, occult quality, sympathy, antipathy, antiperistasis. . . . Which pass well enough with those that care not much for such wisdom, though wise enough in their own ways; but will not pass with

you that ask not simply what is the cause, but in what manner it comes about that such effects are produced.

That is cozening. What need had they of that? When began they thus to play the charlatans?

11. Ibid., 74–76.
12. Ibid., 76–78.
13. Ibid., 78.
14. Ibid. Asked further why the schools bothered to "assign any cause at all, seeing that they could not show the effect was to follow from it," interlocutor B finds a political motive: "The Schools, as I said, were erected by the Pope and Emperor, but directed by the Pope only, to answer and confute the heresies of the philosophers. Would you have them then betray their profession and authority, that is to say, their livelihood, by confessing their ignorance? Or rather uphold the same, by putting for causes, strange and unintelligible words, which might serve well enough not only to satisfy the people whom they relied on, but also to trouble the philosophers themselves to find a fault in."
15. Hobbes uses this argument quite often in his combat with Boyle over the vacuum pump experiments. Shapin and Schaffer, *Leviathan and the Air-Pump; Dec. Phys.*, chap. 3, in *EW*, 7:89–95.
16. *Dec. Phys.*, chap. 1, in *EW*, 7:79–80. He also writes: "Your desire, you say, is to know the causes of the effects or phenomena of nature; and you confess they are fancies, and, consequently, that they are in yourself; so that the causes you seek for only are without you, and now you would know how those external bodies work upon you to produce those phenomena." Ibid., chap. 2, in *EW*, 7:82. See also *De Corpore*, 7.1: "If we do but observe diligently what it is we do when we consider and reason, we shall find, that though all things be still remaining in the world, yet we compute nothing but our own phantasms."
17. *Dec. Phys.*, chap. 2, in *EW*, 7:84.
18. *De Corpore*, 26.1.
19. Ibid.
20. He then goes to work against Lucretian defenses for vacuum. This is another instance of Hobbes clearing the ground (attacking assumptions contrary to those fundamental to his reinvention of the sciences). *De Corpore*, 26.3.
21. *De Homine*, 10.4–5.
22. *De Cive*, dedicatory.
23. *Lev.*, 46.11. See also *Lev.*, 46.1.
24. Jesseph, *Squaring the Circle*, 341. The quotation from Wallis is from *Elenchus Geometricae Hobbinae*, 108.
25. Jesseph, *Squaring the Circle*, 343.
26. Ibid., 77.
27. Ibid., 132–34.
28. Ibid., 135.
29. [Ward], *Vindiciae Academiarum*. This work was published anonomously; however, the Dictionary of National Biography attributes the body to Ward and the preface to Wilkins. See Jesseph, *Squaring the Circle*, 67 n. 16.
30. Jesseph, *Squaring the Circle*, 67; Malcolm, "Hobbes and the Royal Society," 54.
31. Jesseph, *Squaring the Circle*, 68–69. Ward wrote: "I have heard that M. *Hobbs* hath given out, that he hath found the solution of some Problemes, amounting to no lesse then the Quadrature of the Circle, when we shall be made happy with the sight of those labours, I shall fall in with those that speake loudest in his praise, in the meane time I cannot dissemble my feare, that his Geometricall designe (as to those high pieces) may prove answerable to a late Opticall designe of his, of casting Coinicall glasses in a mould, then which there could not be any thing attempted, lesse becoming such a man, as he doth apprehend himselfe to be." [Ward], *Vindiciae Academiarum*, 57.

32. *Lev.*, 46.13; quoted in [Ward], *Vindiciae Academiarum*, 58.
33. [Ward], *Vindiciae Academiarum*, 58–59.
34. Malcolm, "Hobbes and the Royal Society."
35. Feingold, *Mathematician's Apprenticeship*, 1, 86–88.
36. The relevant works here are White, *Chrysaspis, seu, Scriptorum suorum*; the anonymous work, *Querela geometrica*; and White, *Chrysaspis to Querela*. On White's thought, see Southgate, "*Covetous of Truth*," "'Cauterising the Tumor of Pyrrhonism,'" and "Blackloism and Tradition." For a reading which suggests that Hobbes and White shared not just intellectual but also political interests, see Collins, *Allegiance of Thomas Hobbes*.
37. The case for differentiating Italian mathematicians according to social status, not just in the universities, but at court, and among those who worked as practitioners in practical fields such as surveying and hydrology has been made by Biagioli, "Social Status." It is only against this differentiation, he argues, that efforts to unify mathematicians under the banner of the superior certainty of their collective endeavors can be appreciated in its full significance.
38. Schmitt, "Science in the Italian Universities," esp. 35–56; Jardine, *Birth of History*, 225; Feingold, *Mathematician's Apprenticeship*; Westman, "Astronomer's Role." Biagioli discusses the status of mathematicians in *Galileo, Courtier* and "Social Status." For a recent discussion of mathematical educations in Jesuit institutions, see Gaukroger, *Descartes: An Intellectual Biography*, 51–67, and Dear, *Discipline and Experience*, 32–62. For an alternative reading—one focused more on texts than institutional contexts—see Wallace, *Causality and Scientific Explanation*.
39. Schmitt, "Science in the Italian Universities," 44.
40. Feingold, *Mathematician's Apprenticeship*, 29–41, 168.
41. Ong, *Ramus, Method, and the Decay of Dialogue*, 142–45.
42. Feingold, *Mathematician's Apprenticeship*, 41–43.
43. Westman, "Astronomer's Role," 117.
44. Ibid., 120.
45. Ibid.; Jardine, *Birth of History*.
46. Biagioli, "Social Status"; Biagioli, *Galileo, Courtier*.
47. Wallace, *Galileo and His Sources*, 139–41. Feingold, *Mathematician's Apprenticeship*, 55–82, discusses the mathematical (although sometimes broadly styled "scientific") interests of many persons at Oxford and Cambridge. It is important to note that many of these individuals were in positions at the universities that allowed them sufficient range to pursue their mathematical learning while also performing the offices of appointments not strictly associated with teaching mathematics, notably college heads, and others (fellows or some with church or medical careers) who potentially could have served the important, but wide-ranging, role of tutor. Not all mathematicians in Europe, however, were willing to so assert themselves, and this likely reflects the range and diversity of mathematicians along the social spectrum. Mathematicians nearer to the bottom did not wish to take on the scions of the universities. For this stratum, occupying subordinate positions in the university would have been a welcome elevation, even as their established counterparts found these demeaning. See Biagioli, "Social Status."
48. On Descartes's connection to Jesuit mathematics, and sources of these interests outside his Jesuit education (e.g., connections to Isaac Beeckman), see Gaukroger, *Descartes: An Intellectual Biography*.
49. Dear, *Mersenne*.
50. Dear, "Jesuit Mathematical Science"; Dear, *Mersenne*, 37–39; Dear, *Discipline and Experience*, 32–62; Wallace, *Galileo and His Sources*, 136–41.
51. See especially Hobbes, "Contra Geometras," the preface to *De Principiis et Ratiocinatione Geometrarum*, in *OP*, 4:389–90. See also *OP*, 4:135, 162–65, and 264–65. Hobbes was respectful toward Clavius, but he did not consider him beyond criticism. See *Dec. Phys.*, chap. 9, in *EW*, 7:162, and *Six Lessons*, lesson 3, in *EW*, 7:235, 244, 247, and 257–60, esp. 258: "I confess I agree not in all points with Peletarius, nor in all points with Clavius. It does not thence follow

that I agree not with the truth. I am not, as you [Wallis], of any faction, neither in geometry nor in politics. If I think that you, or Peletarius, or Clavius, or Euclid, have erred, or been too obscure, I see no cause for which I ought to dissemble it." See also *Six Lessons*, lesson 3, in *EW*, 7:262, 264, and lesson 4, in *EW*, 7:273, 291. Hobbes's critic, John Wallis, suggested that Hobbes was mistaken concerning the nature of numbers, and that his error reflected his use of Clavius's edition of Euclid, which designates numbers differently than the Greek edition. Wallis, *Hobbius Heauton-timorumenos*, 23–24. There are related discussions and criticism of Clavius's definitions and reasoning in Hobbes's *Anti-White*, chap. 23. Feingold, *Mathematician's Apprenticeship*, 56, 66, 67, 71, 110, 117, 173, 215, notes the familiarity with Clavius in England.

52. For background, see Wallace, *Galileo and His Sources*, 126–48; Dear, "Jesuit Mathematical Science," *Mersenne*, and *Discipline and Experience*; Mancosu, "Aristotelian Logic and Euclidean Mathematics"; Gilbert, *Renaissance Concepts of Method*, 86–92; Biagioli, *Galileo, Courtier*, 205–6, 218–27; Crombie, "Mathematics and Platonism"; and Jardine, *Birth of History*, 225–57, and "Epistemology of the Sciences."

53. As is made clear in treatments such as Gaukroger, *Descartes: Philosophy, Mathematics, and Physics*, Aristotle's formal exclusion of mathematics from the study of physical phenomena did not mean that schoolmen did not draw on other parts of the corpus to draw support for the mathematical study of these phenomena.

54. This challenge was offered in 1547 in a treatise entitled *Commentarium de Certitudine Mathematicarum Disciplinarum*. As Mancosu notes, Piccolomini's argument contains the assertion that mathematical demonstrations—while reaching a superior degree of certainty to physical demonstrations—did not meet the very highest standards of demonstration. They were not "the most powerful demonstrations" (*demonstratio potissima*). Such demonstrations had to be causal (and, Piccolomini argued, the first premises had to be universal, prior to, and better known than the conclusions). The middle terms had to form the definition of a property, be unique, and function as the proximate causes of the conclusion. On this debate, see Mancosu, *Philosophy of Mathematics*, esp. 12–13, and Jardine, "Epistemology of the Sciences."

55. For a summary introduction, see Jardine, "Epistemology of the Sciences," esp. 693–97. For a more complete bibliography, see note 57 and Mancosu, *Philosophy of Mathematics*, 213–14 n. 6.

56. Benedict Pereira, *De communibus omnium rerum naturalium et affectionibus*, 1562. While Pereira does indeed defend the traditional superiority of natural philosophy over mathematics, it must also be noted that he was not of one mind with all of his Jesuit colleges. See Jardine, "Epistemology of the Sciences."

57. See *Posterior Analytics* 1.13. Using Aristotle's examples, consider the following:

The planets do not twinkle.
What does not twinkle is near the earth.
Therefore, the planets are near the earth.

This syllogism illustrates what Aristotle calls a demonstration *tou hoti*, or what was often called *demonstratio quia*, or demonstration of the fact (here, the fact that the planets are near the earth). He distinguished it from a demonstration that also offered causes, or a *tou dioti*, also known as *demonstratio propter quid*, or demonstration from the reasoned fact. The elements of the foregoing syllogism can be rearranged to conform with this higher standard, thus:

What is near the earth does not twinkle.
The planets are near the earth.
Therefore, the planets do not twinkle.

In this syllogism the middle term (the planets are near the earth) is the cause; it yields more than a description of a fact. It is the cause that accounts for the conclusion. That is, the planets do not twinkle *because they are near the earth*.

For a fuller explanation, including a brief discussion of a finer distinction in demonstrative technique (*potissima* demonstrations, argued as distinct and superior species by Averroes), see Wallace, *Galileo and His Sources*, 116–17; Mancosu, *Philosophy of Mathematics*, 1–33, and "Aristotelian Logic and Euclidean Mathematics"; Jardine, "Epistemology of the Sciences"; and Dear, *Discipline and Experience*, 26–31. As Mancosu points out, however, the key elements of the debate hinge on the causal status of mathematical demonstrations, a debate that made the *dioti/hoti* distinction the crucial one.

Readers familiar with the debates over the continuity of the sciences between the medieval and modern age will find the discussion of *hoti* and *dioti* forms of demonstration familiar. Let me make clear, therefore, that I am by no means making an argument for such continuity. In the past, connections have in fact been made by Watkins, *Hobbes's System of Ideas*, esp. 27–81, connections that relied heavily on the conclusions by Randall, now criticized. See Jardine, "Epistemology of the Sciences," and Hanson, "The Meaning of 'Demonstration' in Hobbes's Science." Hanson voices and reinforces a number of sound criticisms of Randall's thesis and its inheritors in Hobbes studies. He also rightly notes that Hobbes's interpreters have not adequately understood what it meant for Hobbes's science to be geometrical. I disagree, however, with Hanson's assertions concerning the question of the applicability of mathematics to the material world (there was *nothing but* matter for Hobbes) and Hanson's claim that Hobbes found this solution by adopting something akin to a counterfactual form of demonstration. I will not try to explain these disagreements in detail here, but will note I do not think his view takes the differences between Hobbes and Descartes (particularly over analytic methods) seriously enough. The same could be said with regard to Hobbes's emphasis on the superiority of generative sciences and his voluntarism. Nor do I think one need hold that Hobbes had a "modern sense of deduction" to disagree with Hanson's positive thesis; it seems to me that Hanson relies too heavily on the disassociation.

58. Dear, *Mersenne*, 64–66.

59. Ibid., 64–65, notes that continuous quantity was said to depend upon discrete quantity—for the very idea of continuity is itself a continuity of discrete entities—and this in turn was dependent upon unity. Those discrete quantities, in other words, had to be composed of units. Both Mersenne and the opponents of mathematics could agree on this. They differed, however, over how to interpret this dependence on unity. The Jesuit dialectician Pedro da Fonseca argued that it was not a real being, but a mere *ens rationalis*; this was a crucial element in the argument made in the *Coimbrum Commentaries*. Thus, a group of five entities might be seen as two groups; one of three and of two, or four and one, and so on. This depended on how we choose to apprehend them; the mere fact that it was our choice was grounds for disqualification because the mathematical object, it was argued, did not rely on the independent source, God's creative will.

60. Thus if we know that an essential attribute of men is that they are reasoning creatures, we can form a syllogism that reveals cause, such as the following: Socrates is a man. Men are capable of reasoning. Socrates, therefore, is capable of reasoning. Socrates can reason because he is a man; the middle term gives us the cause for this conclusion. The cause here is final, not efficient.

61. *De communibus omnuim rerum naturalium preincipiis et affectionibus*, 24–25; translated and quoted in Mancosu, *Philosophy of Mathematics*, 13.

62. Gilbert, *Renaissance Concepts of Method*, 86–92.

63. Mancosu, *Philosophy of Mathematics*, 10–14.

64. Clavius, "In disciplinas mathematicus prolegomena," in *Opera mathematica*, vol. 1; cited in Dear, *Discipline and Experience*, 38.

65. Biagioli, "Social Status," offers a highly detailed account of the social status of Italian mathematicians that illustrates these distinctions. For a contending view, see Long, "Power, Patronage, and the Authorship of Ars." John Dee was an English mathematician—tutor to Queen Elizabeth—who feared that these earthly, that is to say, seemingly lowly, mathematical vocations would contaminate mathematics as a learned subject. See Dee, *Mathematicall Praeface*.

66. See, for example, Wallace, *Galileo and His Sources*, 131–32, on Paulus Valla and his plagiarist Ludovico Carbone at the Collegio Romana, and Aristotle, *Prior Analytics* 57b 4; *Posterior Analytics* 77a 26–35, 77b 30, 78a 11, 79a 7; and *Nicomachean Ethics*, 1142a 11–30.

67. Jardine, "Epistemology of the Sciences."

68. Wallace, *Galileo and His Sources*.

69. Dear, *Discipline and Experience*, 38–39; Dear, *Mersenne*, 65–70; Dear, "Jesuit Mathematical Science."

70. Dear, *Mersenne*, 67; Crombie, "Mathematics and Platonism."

71. Dee, *Mathematicall Praeface*, sig. a.iij: "And for vs, Christen men, a thousand thousand mo occasions are, to haue nede of the help of *Megethologicall* [i.e., geometrical] Contemplations: whereby to trayne our Imaginations and Myndees, by litle and litle, to forsake and abandon, the grosse and corruptible Obiectes, of our vtward senses: and to apprehend, by sure doctrine demonstratiue, Things Mathematicall."

72. Biancani, *De Mathematicarum Natura*, 180.

73. Ibid.

74. Ibid.

75. Ibid., 181–84. Here Blancanus builds on the initial link between the perfect status of mathematical objects. Mathematicians, he argues, grasp essences and do so in the most scientific way because they give definitions that not only describe mathematical objects but also supply their causes. This, in fact, is an argument that asserts that mathematical demonstrations are *potissima*.

76. Plutarch, "Table Talk," vii.

77. Biancani, *De Mathematicarum Natura*, 181.

78. Ibid., 206.

79. Blancanus's argument also employed a large selection of citations. He was determined to defeat Piccolomini on traditional scholastic grounds—by the authorities on mathematics and philosophy. Aristotle, Proclus (Euclid's ancient commentator), Plato, and others are brought to the side of mathematics in this dispute. Ibid., 186.

80. Aristotle, Blancanus wrote, "appears to do nothing else," in the *Analytics*, "but to delineate the idea of perfect demonstrations on the basis of geometrical demonstrations." Ibid., 185. He points to a number of instances. The first is in the *Posterior Analytics* 1.23: in this section Aristotle warns that two things may have a common attribute, but we ought not necessarily assume that these attributes are essential. He offers an example where the attributes are in fact essential. Both isosceles and scalene triangles, Aristotle notes, have the attribute of having interior angles equal to two right angles. This attribute belongs to triangles *qua* triangles. Aristotle proceeds to emphasize the need to ensure the commensurability of middle terms with the predicate (for example, the middle term "all men are mortal" and the predicate "Socrates is a man" are commensurate because both speak of men). For Blancanus, however, the key point is that Aristotle *uses* a mathematical example (a story about triangles) to explain the characteristics of an essential attribute. "As you see, Aristotle explicitly asserts that the demonstration by which the geometer shows that the triangle has three angles equal to two right angles proceeds from what are first, immediate, per se, and insofar as it is what it is: and by no means from what are incidental." Ibid.

81. See, for example, *Lev.*, 4.12–13, 5.7, 34.1, and 46.14, and *De Corpore*, 6.13, where Hobbes writes: "The reason why I say that the cause and generation of such things, as have any cause or generation, ought to enter into their definitions, is this. The end of science is the demonstration of the causes and generations of things; which if they be not in the definitions, they cannot be found in the conclusion of the first syllogism, that is made from those definitions; and if they be not in the first conclusion, they will not be found in any further conclusion deduced from that; and, therefore, by proceeding in this manner, we shall never come to science; which is against the scope and intention of demonstration." See also *De Corpore*, 6.14–17.

82. Biancani, *De Mathematicarum Natura*, 181.

83. Ibid., 181–82. He adds: "For as soon as we learn that a square consists of the said things, the soul does not desire to learn anything more about its essence, but comes to rest, whence it is obvious that this definition is of the best kind."

84. Ibid., 183–84.

85. Ibid., 182.

86. Ibid., 184.

87. Because Blancanus is anxious to associate other disciplines with proof from signs, it is not entirely clear from this quotation that he believes that mathematicians also sometimes descend to this level, but in fact he did. In the appendix, where the causal status of Euclid's demonstrations is reviewed, he notes that the second demonstration of the first book of *Elements* (where Euclid shows two lines are equal, because they are equal to a third) is "not from a cause but from a sign [*a signo*]." Ibid., 208. There are numerous other examples.

88. Ibid., 184.

89. This is, in fact, a distinction with ancient origins. For a detailed discussion of the meaning of these terms in Pappus, see Hintikka and Remes, *Method of Analysis*. For Hobbes's classification of sciences according to their different uses of the methods of analysis and synthesis, see also Sacksteder, "Three Diverse Sciences," and Hanson, "The Meaning of 'Demonstration' in Hobbes's Science." It must be emphasized that this was not a simple dichotomy where a priori sciences use synthesis and a posteriori sciences use analysis, for in fact all the sciences ranked within Hobbes's schema may use both. Rather, the key question is how one might start one's reasoning. If, as in geometry, or the science of politics (according to Hobbes), one *can* begin with elemental parts and work up to a completed whole, the steps along the way are convertible. If, however, as Sackstedter points out, one must begin with observed effects and work one's way down to causes, there is always the risk that some element of the actual cause may be left out. There are, as he puts it, remainders that may go unspecified in the sciences Hobbes calls a posteriori. Among the a priori, there are no remainders because we construct the artifices ourselves. Hintikka and Remes argue, in the case of Pappus's work, against oversimplified understandings of the method of analysis.

90. *De Corpore*, 6.1–2. In his "Translator's Commentary," in *Computatio Sive Logica/Logic*, Aloysius Martinich points to the need for a consistent translation in order to preserve Hobbes's repeated use of Aristotle's *hoti/dioti* distinction; Martinich makes the argument in the context of a discussion that emphasizes the Paduan connection to Hobbes's thought first put forward by John Randall, in *The School of Padua and the Emergence of Modern Science*. (*Computatio Sive Logica/Logic* is the same work that Molesworth identifies as chapter 1 of *De Corpore*.)

91. *De Corpore*, 26.11. It should be of interest that the English translation does not match the Latin edition. See *OP*, 1.361–62, where he does not refer to *dioti* and *hoti*. Hobbes, nevertheless, holds to the division we are referring to. He states that investigations of the universe (in this case astronomy) achieve knowledge not of causes but of "substitutes": "quorum phaenomena etsi non oriantur a causis quas supposui." See also, *Mathematicae Hodiernae*, bk. 1, in *OP*, 4.38–39, 42–43.

92. Clavius, "Modus quo disciplinae mathematicae in scholis Societatus possent promoveri"; quoted in Crombie, "Mathematics and Platonism."

93. Ibid.

94. Ibid.

95. Clavius's argument is echoed in Blancanus. See for example, the discussion of Plato in Biancani, *De Mathematicarum Natura*, 197–99. Clavius's classification, however, plays on the question of the homogeneity of the sciences. One of Aristotle's general rules is that each science begins with its own unique set of first premises. Not all forms of reasoning (like politics and mathematics) share the same levels of certainty. There is, therefore, a general prohibition against attempting to use the principles and practices of one science as a basis for drawing conclusions in another. The rule of homogeneity, therefore, requires that the principles of a science concern the same genus as its objects; in this way one can ensure a deductive link between them. Disciplines

such as astronomy and music, however, were well-known violations of the rule. They used the premises of pure mathematics to reason over celestial motions or sounds. What pleased Clavius was that Aristotle made a special exception for these forms of mixed mathematics, calling them sciences subordinate to the higher discipline. See *Posterior Analytics* 1.7 and *Metaphysics* 13.3 (esp. 1078a 14–17), and he included among these sciences the last half of the quadrivium (which not only meant astronomy and music, but was also understood to include geography and mechanics). As Dear notes, "The very attempt to fit the applied disciplines into a general model for a science made clear Aristotle's acceptance of the scientific status of all the mathematical disciplines." Dear, "Jesuit Mathematical Science," 38. This cleared the way for two important aspects of his argument. First, he located mathematics between metaphysics (the contemplation of pure forms) and physics (the contemplation of natural things). This is the point that echoes in Blancanus. However, as Dear points out, making Aristotle's exception the basis for his argument allowed Clavius to duck the task of having to argue the causality of mathematical demonstrations (the task that Blancanus explicitly takes up).

96. Clavius, "Modus quo disciplinae mathematicae in scholis Societatus possent promoveri"; quoted in Crombie, "Mathematics and Platonism."

97. The boundaries between the proper provinces of mathematics and physics were in flux. It appears that Galileo, for example, was more interested in furthering mathematics at the expense of physics than some of his Jesuit counterparts. See Dear, "Jesuit Mathematical Science" and *Discipline and Experience*.

98. *EL*, 1.13.4.

99. Hobbes's silence points to what is useful in Mancosu's approach, but it also points to its limits. He is correct when he asserts that we cannot understand seventeenth-century mathematics without making ourselves familiar with the *Quaestio* and the attempt to assert the Aristotelian credentials of mathematics. This means that the public abandonment and denunciation of Aristotle by figures like Hobbes can be misleading, but it does not make these renunciations less interesting or significant. Rather, they become that much more interesting.

100. Leijenhorst, *Mechanisation of Aristotelianism*.

101. There is evidence that Hobbes was content to use Aristotle against Aristotelians in other contexts as well. In *Dec. Phys.*, chap. 1, in *EW*, 7:71–72, Hobbes praises Aristotle as one of the few who pursues knowledge in a proper philosophical spirit. He is held distinct from those who merely pursue learning as a means to "maintain themselves or gain preferment" and therefore do not truly think through their doctrines but instead acquiesce, "in the authority of those authors whom they have heard commended." Nevertheless, when an interlocutor in these dialogues asks if he must read Aristotle to study natural philosophy, he is told that it is not necessary.

102. *De Corpore*, 25.1.

103. *De Corpore*, 8.23 and 10.7; *Six Lessons*, lesson 1, in *EW*, 7:218–21. Criticisms of separate essences are in *Lev.*, 46.15–21, and Hobbes, *Behemoth*, 42.

104. *Lev.*, 46.15.

105. Ibid., 1.4–5 and chap. 2 in its entirety. See also *EL*, pt. 1, chap. 2, esp. sec. 10, which illustrates the link between his materialism, his understanding of sense, and in particular what he calls the "deception of sense." For detailed studies of Hobbes's materialism, see Brandt, *Thomas Hobbes' Mechanical Conception of Nature*; Mintz, *The Hunting of Leviathan*, 63–109; and Shapin and Schaffer, *Leviathan and the Air-Pump*, 80–154.

106. Mersenne also made use of arguments that connected the thoughts in the mind of the geometrician with the thought in the mind of God. On this, see Dear, *Mersenne*, esp. 48–79, who also argues that this is best seen as a form of Platonism long since available to the schools through Augustine—which helps us make sense of Mersenne's vehement opposition to Neoplatonists such as Robert Fludd. He also notes that Mersenne limits the scope of the natural philosophers' knowledge through voluntarist reservations (see ibid., 48–54). I will not draw conclusions concerning the relation between Hobbes and Mersenne here. Against the temptation to find continuity, see ibid., 238; here, Dear's arguments work equally well against any attempt to claim an

internal continuity (*pace* Randall or Crombie) between Hobbes and the Jesuit mathematicians I discuss. What does seem certain, however, is that understanding the Jesuit mathematicians can help us understand Hobbes. One need not assert a continuity in order to put this kind of contextual knowledge to use.

107. See Tuck, *Philosophy and Government*.

108. "Whatsoever accidents or qualities our senses make us think there be in the world, they are not there, but are seemings and apparitions only. The things that really are in the world without us, are those motions by which these seemings are caused. And this is the great deception of sense, which also is by sense, to be corrected. For as sense telleth me, when I see directly, that the colour seemeth to be in that object; so also sense telleth me, when I see by reflection, that colour is not in the object." *EL*, 1.2.10.

109. On Hobbes's voluntarism, see Zarka, "First Philosophy"; Martinich, *Two Gods of Leviathan*; Pacchi, "Hobbes and the Problem of God." On voluntarism in broader scientific contexts, see Osler, *Divine Will and Mechanical Philosophy*, 15–35. Some additional complexities concerning the relation between miracles and efforts to establish truths about the ordinary course of nature are considered in Dear, "Miracles, Experiments, and the Ordinary Course of Nature," 663–83. See also Malet, "Isaac Barrow"; Shapin, "Robert Boyle and Mathematics"; Shapin, *Social History of Truth*, 231–32 n. 65; Funkenstein, *Theology and the Scientific Imagination*; Oakley, *Omnipotence, Covenant, and Order*; Shapiro, *Probability and Certainty*; and Klaaren, *Religious Origins of Modern Science*.

110. For recent discussions, see Beyssade, "On the Idea of God." Also see Hatfield, "Reason, Nature, and God in Descartes," and Gaukroger, *Descartes: An Intellectual Biography*, 203–10.

111. In a useful contrast with Hobbes, Descartes in the *Principles of Philosophy* takes care to use voluntarism to unhinge the grounds for certainty in mathematics. He states that one reason we may doubt the demonstrations of mathematics just as much as we doubt the thoughts suggested to us by sense is that "we have been told that God who created us can do all that He desires" and so may have created us "in such a way that we shall always be deceived" (part 1, principle 5). He later rejects this suggestion, however, as being incompatible with God's perfection (part 1, principles 29 and 30), but at least a part of what Descartes is doing is insisting that even the seemingly most certain truth, aside from our own existence, cannot be known without doubt until we first find grounding in the existence we can uniquely attribute to God by virtue of his perfection (part 1, principles 13–15). Even then, we must acknowledge that God is so perfect an entity that we, in our imperfections, cannot possibly know him in the way that a maker knows his own machine. Rather, it is by a "natural light" which permits us to consider what flows as a consequence of his perfection, but which does not allow us, finite creatures, to know "His infinite perfections" (part 1, principles 17–19). Moreover, Descartes asserts a prohibition on allowing our investigations of nature to trump what "God reveals to us or to others certain things concerning Himself" (notably, theological assertions such as the Trinity or the "mysteries of the incarnation"). As we shall see, Hobbes also declares a prohibition on philosophical encroachment on sacred truths, but unlike Descartes he does not lift the skeptical doubt from our capacity to know what God created or how he created it. Instead, in making geometry his model science he counsels us to remain content with not knowing the workings of nature, but knowing what we make ourselves. Perhaps more like Hobbes, Descartes uses voluntarism to deny a more traditional goal of scholastic knowledge: knowledge of final causes in natural things. For Descartes, however, God does permit us knowledge of his efficient causes of these things (part 1, principle 28). Descartes, *The Principles of Philosophy*, in *Philosophical Works*, 1:220, 231–32, 224–25, 230–31.

112. Shapiro, *Probability and Certainty*. Shapin has argued that Boyle's experimental philosophy put itself forward as a more moderate, modest, way of investigating the order of nature. It did not claim universal laws; most notably, "Boyle's Law" was not declared a law by Boyle, but only became declared as such when it crossed the channel to France where claims concerning the order of nature were still being made with greater confidence than they were in England.

There, however, pious caution was also blended with a concern for the decorum of a scientific community and a desire to avoid the disputation that emerges when members measure their success in terms of unqualified, general, conclusions concerning the natural order. Shapin, *Social History of Truth*, 310–54.

113. *Lev.*, 31.6.

114. Ibid., 31.14–15. From these follow prohibitions against those who make other attributions, including attributions used by philosophers, such as the notion that God is eternal, or that he is finite, that he has "ease" from his care of mankind, that "attribute *figure* to him," or those who "conceive and imagine (or have an *idea* of) him in our mind; for whatsoever we conceive is finite." The list goes on. See ibid., 31.16–27.

115. Ibid., 31.28.

116. Ibid., 31.33; my emphasis.

117. Ibid., 47.1. See also Curley's translation of chapter 47 of the Latin *Leviathan* as well as Curley's note 2 to the translation.

118. "For who will endeavour to obey the laws, if he expect obedience to be poured or blown into him? Or who will not obey a priest, that can make God, rather than his sovereign, nay than God himself? Or who, that is in fear of ghosts, will not bear great respect to those that can make the holy water, that drives them from him? And this shall suffice for an example of the errors, which are brought into the Church, from the entities and essences of Aristotle" *Lev.*, 46.18.

119. This becomes a particularly interesting criticism when we consider what Hobbes has to say concerning the role of first philosophy. Central to the schools' mistake is the way that they define *their* "philosophia prima." Whereas Hobbes declares that it is up to men to determine for themselves the meanings of the terms that form the foundations of their philosophical knowledge, the schools choose instead to adopt a metaphysics that they take to be an explanation of the supernatural: "Now to descend to the particular tenets of vain philosophy, derived to the Universities, and thence into the Church, partly from Aristotle, partly from blindness of understanding; I shall first consider their principles. There is a certain philosophia prima, on which all other philosophy ought to depend; and consisteth principally, in right limiting of the significations of such appellations, or names, as are of all others the most universal: which limitations serve to avoid ambiguity, and equivocation in reasoning; and are commonly called definitions; such as are the definitions of body, time, place, matter, form, essence, subject, substance, accident, power, act, finite, infinite, quantity, quality, motion, action, passion, and divers others, necessary to the explaining of a man's conceptions concerning the nature and generation of bodies. The explication (that is, the settling of the meaning) of which, and the like terms, is commonly in the Schools called metaphysics; as being a part of the philosophy of Aristotle, which hath that for title. But it is in another sense; for there it signifieth as much, as books written, or placed after his natural philosophy: but the schools take them for books of supernatural philosophy: for the word metaphysics will bear both these senses. And indeed that which is there written, is for the most part so far from the possibility of being understood, and so repugnant to natural reason, that whosoever thinketh there is any thing to be understood by it, must needs think it supernatural." *Lev.*, 46.14.

120. Ibid., 46.23.

121. Dear, "Jesuit Mathematical Science," 162–63. For a different reading, see Biagioli, *Galileo, Courtier*, 306–7.

122. Galileo, *The Assayer*, 183–84. Sarsi was a pseudonym for Orazio Grassi, who assumed the mathematics chair at the Collegio Romano after Clavius.

123. Descartes's God did not write an illegible book. See the discussion in Chapter 4 and note 111 in this chapter. Descartes's claims concerning God, and creation's legibility, account for Hobbes's needling Descartes in his objections to the *Meditations*. Hence his voluntarist assaults on Descartes's "idea" of God, his demonstration of God's creation, and even on the notion of a God who can't deceive. Descartes, *The Philosophical Works of Descartes*, 2:66–74, 77–78 (objections V, VII, IX–XI, XV, and "Final Objection").

Chapter 6

1. See, for example, in Hobbes, *Anti-White*, chap. 9, sec. 10; *EL*, 1.5.14 and 1.13.3–4; *De Cive*, 12.12; and *Lev.*, 5.14.

2. Edward Hyde, the Earl of Clarendon and Hobbes's great critic, suggested that the sovereign Hobbes had most in mind was not Charles II, but Oliver Cromwell. Of course, Clarendon was the same individual who claims to have helped drive Hobbes from Paris for having presented such a dangerous philosophy to Charles II. Clarendon was writing after he himself had been cast out of Charles II's court by enemies that he associated with Hobbes. See Clarendon, *Brief View and Survey*, esp. 8–9, 60, 115, 141, 177, 188, 192. Collins, *Allegiance of Thomas Hobbes*, is in essence an affirmation of the accusations of Hobbes's Anglican critics.

3. See my "Uniqueness of *Leviathan*," 75–103.

4. Oakeshott, "Introduction to *Leviathan*."

5. Notably by Gauthier, *Logic of Leviathan*, and, for different reasons, by Quentin Skinner.

6. Tuck, "Introduction," viii–xxxiii, esp. xiii–xiv; Skinner, *Reason and Rhetoric*, 376–81; who asserts that the change in Hobbes's attitude toward eloquence took place between the 1642 and 1647 editions of *De Cive*. If the 1642 edition was never intended for wide distribution, we may be unable to infer a significant shift in attitude.

7. Kahn, *Rhetoric, Prudence, and Skepticism*.

8. Skinner casts some small doubt on Aubrey's account, suggesting that it was more likely that Hobbes's interests in mathematics (especially geometry) began in 1629 and in France, where Hobbes first reports looking at Euclid. He also notes the possible influence of the scientific activities of the Cavendish family at Welbeck Abbey. Nevertheless, the idea that Hobbes had come across something new and earth-shaking is affirmed. Skinner, *Reason and Rhetoric*, 250–51.

9. Johnston, *Rhetoric of Leviathan*, esp. 71–77.

10. Ibid., 66–91. Furthermore, Hobbes is also said not to have at first realized the immense barriers to his theory.

11. Wolin, *Hobbes and the Epic Tradition of Political Theory*.

12. Johnston, *Rhetoric of Leviathan*, 92–218.

13. Ibid., 134–84.

14. Skinner, *Reason and Rhetoric*, 347–56, 427.

15. Ibid., 426–27.

16. Ibid., 427. Skinner also suggests the possibility of influences on Hobbes during the period when he changed his mind. These include French theorists of reason of state—who were particularly mindful of the gap that could emerge between interests and reason—and William Davenant. Acknowledging that these are somewhat speculative, however, Skinner thinks that "it was in consequence of the brooding in the 1640s about the causes of the English civil war that he felt obliged to reconsider his views about the place of rhetoric in public debate." Ibid., 427–31.

17. Ibid., 426.

18. I will return in this section to a detailed discussion of the relationship between Hobbes and his audiences in each of the three texts and address further complexities attending to *Leviathan*'s audience in Chapter 8. Prior to this, in Chapter 7, I will consider Hobbes's key historical works, his translation of Thucydides, "On the Life and History of Thucydides," which accompanied the translation), and *Behemoth*, as well as some of his other encounters with Presbyterian opponents.

19. Skinner, *Reason and Rhetoric*, 284–93.

20. Ibid., 66–110.

21. *Lev.*, 46.13.

22. Eachard, *Mr. Hobbs's State of Nature Considered*, 183, 187; Eachard, *Some Opinions of Mr. Hobbs Considered*, 17; Clarendon, *Brief View*.

23. Skinner, *Reason and Rhetoric*, 298–301. Some of the arguments that follow are drawn from Miller and Strong, "Meanings and Contexts." Thanks to Tracy Strong for permission to use them.

24. Case, *Speculum moralium quaestionum*, 259–60.

25. This snobbery was turned into an art form by Ben Jonson, whom Hobbes much admired and whom he consulted in his translation of Thucydides. Cf. Hobbes's comments on Thucydides: "It need not be doubted, but from such a master Thucydides was sufficiently qualified to have become a great demagogue, and of great authority with the people. But it seemeth he had no desire at all to meddle in the government: *because in those days it was impossible for any man to give good and profitable counsel for the commonwealth, and not incur the displeasure of the people . . . he that gave them temperate and discreet advice, was thought a coward, or not to understand, or else to malign their power . . . it is hard for any man to love that counsel which maketh him love himself the less.*" Hobbes, "Of the Life and History of Thucydides" (Grene), 571.

26. *EL*, 1.1.3; italics added.

27. Skinner, *Reason and Rhetoric*, 274, 282–84.

28. Ibid., 300.

29. Nor would he have written as Hobbes wrote in the dedicatory to *De Cive*: "I have long been of the opinion that there was never an exceptional notion that found favour with the people nor a wisdom above the common level that could be appreciated by the average man; for either they do not understand it, or in understanding it, they bring it down to their own level." *De Cive*, dedicatory, 3. Here I have used Silverthorn's translation.

30. Ibid., 302.

31. Skinner, *Reason and Rhetoric*, 301.

32. Webster, *Samuel Hartlib and the Advancement of Learning*, 1–72.

33. Nor was this the last time Davenant promised that his theatrical productions could supply a source of political education. See my "Two Deaths of Lady Macduff."

34. Jacob and Raylor, "Opera and Obedience." See 241–50 for the text of the *Proposition* itself. Jacob and Raylor's wide-ranging analysis is interesting and provocative—suggesting, for example, connections between Davenant's argument for this project and the poet's own selective misreading of Hobbes's understanding of the passions. Those concerned with the issues of rhetoric, education, passions, and interests, and Hobbes's relation to these issues, will find this analysis of Hobbes, Davenant, and the Cavendish circle of interest. I thank Patricia Springborg for bringing this to my attention.

35. Javitch, *Poetry and Courtliness* and "Il Cortegiano"; Whigham, *Ambition and Privilege*. Skinner uses both sources. Another classic in this genre is Montrose, "Of Gentlemen and Shepherds." These authors are not, of course, in complete agreement. Following Javitch's analysis of Puttenham, Whigham and Montrose argue that the guidance Puttenham was offering was not simply analogous to courtly conduct but also a medium of courtly assertion. As the author of a defense of poetry dedicated to Queen Elizabeth, Puttenham was not only reading the rules of courtly behavior, he was rewriting them in order to suit his own needs and was cautiously criticizing elements of court life.

36. Castiglione, *Book of the Courtier*, 15–17.

37. Garin, *Science and Civil Life*, 21–48, esp. 40–45. For scholars of the Renaissance, this raises the question of the long-term influence of Baron's *Crisis of the Early Italian Renaissance*. See the discussion in Celenza, *Lost Italian Renaissance*.

38. Ogilby, *The Entertainment of His Most Excellent Majestie*, esp. 26–28, 40–42. See also the introduction to this edition by Ronald Knowles.

39. Sharpe, *Criticism and Compliment*.

40. In his discussion of decorum, Skinner cites one of the principal figures who make such points, Javitch, yet he does not engage Javitch's challenge to continuity between classical rhetoric and the rhetorical skills required in these new circumstances. Skinner, *Reason and Rhetoric*, 193. Puttenham, a key exemplar of the new, more courtly rhetoric, is of course mentioned throughout Skinner's work; in connection with decorum, Skinner notes that Puttenham "insists on the value of 'ornament' as a means of making the truth more attractive, and underlines the alleged parallel with the artful enhancement of feminine beauty in a manner evidently designed to appeal

particularly to his courtly audience" (196). Nevertheless, Skinner does not connect the concern with ornament with the pleasure demanded by those who have favor to dispense. Thus, the absence of eloquence in this context could represent an affront, something Skinner does not take into account when discussing Spencer's reading of *King Lear*. Ibid., 197–98.

41. For example, *Lev.*, 19.5 and 25.15.

42. Much of what Hobbes has to say concerning vainglory and pride appears in the context of his discussions of the state of nature, the laws of nature, or in his decrying of the vainglorious men who turn to assemblies in order to satisfy their hunger for power and recognition. Nevertheless, he also connects the destructiveness of these passions with those who seek honors and offices from the sovereign authority. See, for example, *Lev.*, 18.15–19, 27.13–17, and 11.3 and 7. Note that in chapter 18 Hobbes recommends a strong-willed sovereign to prevent the facetiousness of the prideful contenders for favor, but he does not do away with a system of titles of honor, or appointments. In a passage revisionist historians might approve of, Hobbes finds a key source of outwardly republican forms of sedition in the designs of frustrated seekers of royal patronage. Those who find themselves "postponed to those in honour . . . think themselves regarded but as slaves." Those who wish to have monarchy changed into democracy in fact claim "no more [than] the sovereign should take notice of his ability . . . and put him in employment and place . . . rather than others that deserve less." *EL*, 2.8.3.

43. For some recent (by no means comprehensive) discussions of patronage relations and courtly address in the Stuart era, see Peck, *Court Patronage*; Seaward, *Cavalier Parliament*; Cust, *Forced Loans*; Smuts, *Court Culture*; Sharpe, *Criticism and Compliment*; Hirst, *Authority and Conflict*; Marcus, *Politics of Mirth*; and Fletcher, "Honor, Reputation, and Local Officeholding." Patronage has proven a critical issue among revisionst and what may be called postrevisionist historians. These sources, combined with the works on courtly poetry just mentioned, represent a variety of different views. Compare the frameworks in approaching patronage in Russell, *Parliaments and English Politics*, and Stone, *Crisis in the Aristocracy*. Within Hobbes scholarship, the classic work associating the philosopher with reformist sentiments among the aristocracy concerned with the competition over honors is Thomas, "Social Origins." See also Zagorin, "Clarendon and Hobbes," and Wood, "Thomas Hobbes."

44. Cust, *Forced Loans*, 197–98; Trease, *Portrait of a Cavalier*.

45. Sommerville, *Thomas Hobbes*.

46. In fact, Hobbes did not complete *Elements of Law* until five days after Parliament had already been dismissed. Nevertheless, according to Hobbes, drafts were circulating before the dissolution of Parliament.

47. Sommerville, *Thomas Hobbes*; Tuck, *Philosophy and Government*, 313–14.

48. Hobbes, *Behemoth*, 33, 114–15.

49. On Waller, see Malcolm, *Correspondence*, 2:913–14. Waller's loyalties, like Davenant's, were flexible in way that Hobbes could approve. He had been among the first spokesmen for the grievances of the Commons, but turned in opposition away from its more extreme proposals—such as the abolition of the episcopacy. As the war began, he was on the king's side, and in May 1643 he and his brother-in-law (Nathaniel Tomkins) were involved in a botched plot to take London for the king. Unlike his brother-in-law, Waller saved himself, eloquently pleading his own case; he was imprisoned in the Tower, and released into exile in November 1644. In Thomas Hobbes to Edmund Waller, July 29/August 8, 1645, Letter 39, in Malcolm, *Correspondence*, 1:124, Hobbes reports that he had been attending to the education of Waller's son Robert and a nephew (Malcolm speculates Tomkins's son). Waller's reputation for eloquence was well known, and he remained a constant (if not always public) admirer of Hobbes. Hobbes expresses his delight at the thought that Waller had at one time considered translating *De Cive* into English.

50. Thomas Hobbes to Edmund Waller, July 29/August 8, 1645, Letter 39, in Malcolm, *Correspondence*, 1:124.

51. Biagioli, *Galileo, Courtier*, on the uses of "fighting men" in the context of scientific debate. Cf. Bourdieu, "Sentiment of Honor," 191–241, upon whom Biagioli draws.

52. Aubrey, "*Brief Lives,*" 1:340.

53. Trease, *Portrait of a Cavalier,* 54–55.

54. The work referred to is *Considerations touching the facility or Difficulty of the Motions of a Horse on Streight Lines, & Circular.* The editor, Arthur Strong, attributes the work to Hobbes. Noel Malcolm attributes it to Robert Payne, Newcastle's chaplain. Malcolm, *Correspondence,* 2:813–14, 872–77. Skinner, *Reason and Rhetoric,* 251n, seconds Malcolm.

55. For a recent review of mathematical professions during the Renaissance in Italy, see Biagioli, "Social Status," 41–95. Galileo taught at an Italian military academy.

56. See esp. *EL,* 2.8.13–15.

57. Ibid., sec. 12. Here Hobbes uses Catiline as the exemplar of this combination of characteristics. Ibid., sec. 13.

58. Ibid., sec. 14.

59. "For myself, I desire no greater honour than I enjoy already in your Lordship's known favour; unless it be that you would be pleased, in continuance thereof, to give me more exercise in your commands; which, as I am bound by your many great favours, I shall obey." *EL,* "Epistle Dedicatory."

60. See Sommerville, *Thomas Hobbes,* xii–xiii, 17–19, for the chronology.

61. *EL,* 1.17.15.

62. In his counter-declaration to Lord Fairfax's 1642 call for the men of York to defend the Parliamentary cause against Newcastle's army, the Earl of Newcastle wrote: "The Lord *Fairfax* requires all Parties to appear [i.e., to marshal forces against Newcastle's monarchical army], and I Command them all upon their Allegiance to stay at home. . . . It were a more conscionable and discreet part of them, to repair all as one unanimous body to the Sovereign's Standard, and drive out these Incendiaries from among them, who have been the true authors of all the pressing grievances and miseries of this Country." Cavendish, *A Declaration.*

63. *EL,* 1.19.3 and 4.

64. Although, as Skinner himself so forcefully argued in earlier works, Hobbes was not without his admirers. See Skinner, "Thomas Hobbes and His Disciples in France and England," "The Ideological Context," and "Conquest and Consent."

65. Of course, in the dedicatory to William Cavendish he has a different audience. It is worth noting the deferential tone that Hobbes assumes in this rhetorical situation. Hobbes was once the second Earl of Devonshire's tutor, but now, as his secretary and more properly his servant, Hobbes invites his patron to censure his errors.

66. Although it is *De Cive* that is to teach the students, Hobbes's wish to see his doctrines taught is made clear in the earlier text. See *EL,* 2.9.8.

67. *Lev.,* 25.9, on the gentler ways of giving commands.

68. Thomas Hobbes to Samuel Sorbière, May 6/16, 1646, and Sorbière to Hobbes, May 11/21, 1646, Letters 40 and 41, in Malcolm, *Correspondence,* 1:125–30.

69. *De Cive,* 10.9.

70. Skinner makes note (in *Reason and Rhetoric,* 261) of the special, nondemonstrative status of chapter 10 of *De Cive,* yet can only see this as evidence that the philosopher was on the warpath against prudence. Since passages such as the one quoted from *De Cive,* 10.9, work in a way complementary to the lessons he claims to demonstrate, they suggest that Skinner is mistaken. It is difficult to see why we should not conclude that Hobbes was willing to forge an alliance between reason and rhetoric (when addressing the appropriate audiences) sooner than Skinner would allow.

71. See the Epistle and Prologue to Jonson, *Volpone,* 27–37. Jonson articulates the strategy: if the audience were to laugh at these faults, exemplified by the persons put on display, they would be forced to measure themselves against the elevated moral individual that could rightfully look down in scorn and laugh at the vices put up for ridicule.

72. Skinner's analysis of laughter's connection with scorn aptly illustrates a key part of this dynamic. See Skinner, *Reason and Rhetoric,* 198–204. Much of what Skinner reviews could very

well support an argument linking laughter with satiric moral correction (see the brief remark on Burton on page 204 of *Reason and Rhetoric*). Skinner's own analysis, however, very quickly heads in the direction of showing its applications as a "lethal weapon of debate," a way of pouring derision on particular opponents.

73. Jonson, *Discoveries*, ll. 2334–39, in *Ben Jonson*, 8:634. He writes in this section: "The person offended hath no reason to be offended with the writer, but with himself; and so declare that property to belong to him, which was so spoken of all men, as it could be no man's several, but his that would willfully and desperately claim it."

74. Bishop Hall was a moderate Puritan, an unyielding persecutor of vice and proponent of virtue, but still a supporter of the episcopacy. For Hall's fame and influence as a satirist, see McCabe, *Joseph Hall*, and Boyce, *Theophrastian Character*, 53–135. See also Lake, *Moderate Puritans*, for more on Hall's politics. As regards the Theophrastian influence, as McCabe points out, its source was not quite Theophrastus, but Theophrastus as misinterpreted by his Renaissance translator Isaac Casaubon (*Joseph Hall*, 110–31). Also, as Boyce indicates, Hall himself owed a great deal to the medieval Christian traditions of hortatory and homiletic literature.

75. Hall, *Characters of Virtues and Vices*, 175.

76. Ibid., 144. On the need to show vice (and virtue) in their nakedness, see 146. My quotation leaves out Hall's remarks on the usefulness of his "Characters of Virtue."

77. McCabe, *Joseph Hall*, 112.

78. See Boyce, *Theophrastian Character*, on the flexibility of the form. Some writers of charactery, moreover, described specific social settings. John Earl (a member of the Great Tew) included in his collection of characters, *Microcosmography*, descriptions of a tavern and the walk at St. Paul's Cathedral. Such "charactery" of a social milieu resembles the instance to follow from Hobbes. Earl, *Microcosmography*.

79. *De Cive*, 1.2.

80. *Lev.*, 18.5.

81. Ibid., "A Review and Conclusion," 16.

82. Ibid. In *Lev.*, chap. 30, "*Of the* OFFICE *of the Sovereign Representative*," Hobbes makes it clear that he believes that "appointing teachers and examining what doctrines are conformable or contrary to the defense, peace, and good of the people" (sec. 3) is one of the sovereign's responsibilities. Again, in section 6, we learn that it is the sovereign's duty, but also to "his benefit . . . and security against the danger that may arrive to himself in his natural person from rebellion." Moreover, in presenting the doctrine that the sovereign is responsible for inculcating, he speaks in the sections that follow of what the people are to be "taught." Moreover (sec. 10), this teaching is take to place among the people on the Sabbath, by persons appointed to instruct them (namely, university-trained divines; see sec. 14 on the uses of the universities).

83. Skinner's conclusion is particularly hard to square with the antirhetorical/antidemocratic comments in *Behemoth*. Indeed, unless one gives up the notion that Hobbes lets down his guard in a general way against the use of rhetoric in matters of civic and ethical philosophy, the *Behemoth* seems in conflict with the new leniency Skinner finds. On the one hand, those who use rhetoric (notably the Presbyterians, but also the schools) are sharply attacked for gulling the multitudes. On the other hand, the text itself is a dialogue and a history. Why would a philosopher now reconciled with his own use of rhetoric feel so sure-footed in attacking the rhetoric of his opponents? If, however, we attribute to Hobbes an understanding of these matters that does not simply ask about philosophy and rhetoric in the abstract, but concerns itself as well with concrete questions such as who is speaking, to whom, and for what purposes, the *Behemoth* seems to stand more securely in its use of eloquence. Rhetoric before the masses, particularly that which tends to sedition, is always decried. Rhetoric before an elevated audience is fitting and proper (*Behemoth* was first presented to the king, although he denied Hobbes permission to publish).

84. The question of its status once it had become the text of and for the commonwealth is another matter. On this, see Strong, "How to Write Scripture."

Chapter 7

1. These sentiments were particularly acute among those gentlemen who had once hoped to live out their idealistic ambitions by becoming a part of the patronage network of the Earl of Essex (Robert Devereux). During Elizabeth's last years Essex's faction at Court had been in a mammoth conflict with that of Robert Cecil and had lost. In the desperate state that followed, Essex's exploits eventually resulted in his execution for treason in 1601. For an example of an expression of this despondency, see the essays of an Essex protégé, William Cornwallis (1579–1614). Cornwallis, *Essays*.

2. Richard Tuck offers an analysis of Tacitism and couples it in some instances with skepticism among humanists within war-torn countries in Europe. See Tuck, *Philosophy and Government*, esp. 104–19. On Tacitism specifically, see Smuts, "Court-Centered Politics"; Burke, "Tacitism, Scepticism, and Reason of State"; and Burke, "Tacitism," esp. 160–62. These authors also offer interpretations relating Tacitism to Machiavelli's writings. For a description of the effects of disillusionment and disappointment in politics at this time, see Levin, "Jonson's Metempsychosis," which is useful (although Levin does a better job of explaining the phenomena and attitudinal shifts than he does in making the case in applying this diagnosis to Jonson). Sharpe, in "The Foundation of the Chairs of History," explores the dissatisfactions with James (and certain Elizabethan nostalgia) expressed in the creation of the history chairs at Oxford and Cambridge by Camden and Fulke Greville. Salmon identifies Jonson as the "echo" of the "English Devotees of Seneca and Tacitus," in "Seneca and Tacitus in Jacobean England." See also Oestreich and Koenigsberger, *Neostoicism and the Early Modern State*.

3. The most recent efforts to make this identification are in Noel Reynolds and Arlene Saxenhouse, "Hobbes and the *Horae Subsecivae*," in Hobbes, *Three Discourses*, 3–19.

4. Burke, "Tacitism, Scepticism, and Reason of State"; Hobbes, "A Discourse of Rome," in *Three Discourses*, 95: "Wars are necessary only where they are just, and just only in case of defense. First, of our lives, secondly, of our right, and lastly, of our honor. As for enlargement of Empire, or hope of gain, they have been held just causes of war by such only, as prefer the Law of State before the Law of God."

5. Two clear examples are: "Caesar knew the Republic to be feminine, and that it would yield sooner to violence, than flattery; and therefore with all his power assaulted and overcame it," Hobbes, "A Discourse upon the Beginning of Tacitus," in *Three Discourses*, 36. Machiavelli, *The Prince*, chap. 25, in which Machiavelli speaks of Fortune as a woman: "It may be it was no less advantageous to the designs of Augustus, that some of his own faction were slain, than was the slaughter of those that took part with Anthony, and Lepidus. For they might have expected, for the requital of their service, to have been paid with participation of his authority, which he might not suffer, or else have grown averse, and plucked him down, though they had with his fall crushed themselves to death. But Augustus was now rid of those stubborn companions." Hobbes, "A Discourse upon the Beginning of Tacitus," in *Three Discourses*, 46. Cf. *The Prince*, chap. 3, where Machiavelli notes that the new prince cannot keep the friends who helped install him in power.

6. Hobbes emphasizes that the Roman colonies had reason to be rid of their republican masters: "A Popular State, if the great men grow once too mighty for the laws, is to the Provinces not as one, but many tyrants; so that not knowing to which faction to adhere, they procure the enmity always of some, and sometimes of all, and become subject to rapine." Hobbes, "A Discourse upon the Beginning of Tacitus," in *Three Discourses*, 47. Hobbes's observations here resonate with later invidious comparisons of democratic with monarchical rule in his Thucydidean work.

7. Ibid., 41–47. For example: "Augustus had hitherto dealt with the State, as one that tames wild horses; first, he did beat and weary them; next, took care not to frighten them with shadows; then, sowed them hope of ease, and made provision of corn for them; and now he begins gently to back [i.e., mount] the State. For it is not wisdom for one that is to convert a free

State into a Monarchy, to take away all the show of their liberty at one blow." Ibid., 45. See ibid., 44 and 52, where Hobbes uses the language of absolute sovereignty in describing Augustus's goals and accomplishments. See also ibid., 34, on the republic's (temporarily) appointed dictators, and ibid., 49–50, for Hobbes's admiration for Augustus's assertion, through his nephew (Claudius Marcellus), of "Supremacy in matters Ecclesiastical," which Hobbes characterizes as a sign of his "absolute sovereignty."

8. Ibid., 60–61.

9. Ibid., 57.

10. Ibid. Agrippa lost the right to succession and his reputation through these machinations. Hobbes notes that "whereas he is said to be undetected of any crime, that made not much for the matter at hand; for though he might prove no ill man, he might be nevertheless an ill governor." He suggests that Agrippa's real virtues and vices were less important than the incompetence he demonstrated in finding himself suspected of vice. This inability to "govern himself" is what Hobbes associates with his bad education and fall from grace.

11. Ibid., 58.

12. Aubrey, *"Brief Lives,"* 1:330, notes that his first schoolmaster at Magdalen Hall, James Hussee, was knighted by James I and made Chancellor of Sarum, and succeeded by John Wilkinson. Hussee he describes as "a great encourager of towardly youth" and was the individual who recommended Hobbes to the service of the Cavendish family as tutor.

13. Ibid., 65.

14. On this point, see Tuck, *Philosophy and Government*, 100–101, 280–81, and Thucydides, *The Peloponnesian War*.

15. In the letter, Hobbes tells this William Cavendish (the third Earl of Devonshire) that the book is not dedicated to him, but to the memory of his father (also William Cavendish), the second Earl of Devonshire. Nevertheless, he addresses the third Earl, and concerns himself with *his* instruction.

16. Hobbes, "To the Right Honorable Sir William Cavendish," in the Hobbes translation of Thucydides, *The Peloponnesian War*, xx. See also, Hobbes, "To the Reader," on Thucydides: "So that look how much a man of understanding might have added to his experience, if he had then lived a beholder of their proceedings, and familiar with the men and business of the time: so much almost may he profit now, by attentive reading of the same here written. He may from the narrations draw out lessons to himself, and of himself be able to trace the drifts and councels of the actors to their seats." Ibid., xxii.

17. Hobbes, "Of the Life and History of Thucydides" (Grene), 571. Antiphon was Thucydides's tutor.

18. For a discussion of seventeenth-century Stoic themes of political disengagement, see Maus, *Ben Jonson and the Roman Frame of Mind*. Flathman has also linked Hobbes to a proscription for political disengagement. See *Toward a Liberalism*, 68. Flathman has also recently issued his own interpretation of Hobbes, *Thomas Hobbes: Skepticism, Individuality, and Chastened Politics*. See especially 146. Contra Flathman, I do not think we need lose what is distinctive about Hobbes's thought by concentrating on his abiding concern for political education. On the contrary, understanding Hobbes's pedagogy is a precondition for understanding most of what he wrote on politics. His distinctiveness (including the understanding of the contingencies of knowledge that Flathman emphasizes) stands out against this background.

19. Smuts, "Court-Centered Politics," 42.

20. On this point, compare Jonson's *Sejanus, His Fall*, especially the conclusion in which Sejanus is betrayed by the Senate, and reported torn apart by an angry mob which had once exalted him. See Jonson, *Ben Jonson*, 5:100, 170, 323–98, 430–31, esp. 755–70 and 803–35.

21. Hobbes, "Of the Life and History of Thucydides" (Grene), 571–72.

22. See *EL*, 2.5.8 and 2.2.5. See also Johnston, *Rhetoric of Leviathan*, 59–65.

23. *De Cive*, 10.6–7. See also *Lev.*, 19.8.

24. *De Cive*, 12.12–13; *EL*, 2.9.14–15. In *Leviathan* Hobbes also warns against "popular men" as a source of the trouble (29.20), but the examples of Catiline and Medea are put to use in the contexts of different warnings. *Lev.*, 11.18–20, 30.7. For the narration of Medea's plot against Pelias that best matches Hobbes's, see Diodorus Siculus, *Library of History*, bk. 4, secs. 50–53.

25. *Lev.*, 19.5.

26. Ibid., 25.15–16. See also 11.13 and 16.

27. Hobbes, "Of the Life and History of Thucydides" (Grene), 579.

28. Mintz, *The Hunting of Leviathan*, 6 n. 1; Aubrey, "Brief Lives," 1:365, see also 332 for the mutual admiration said to exist between Hobbes and Jonson. See also Shillinglaw's letter to the *Times Literary Supplement* on the possibility that Hobbes may have shared with Jonson a tribute to Bacon used in Jonson's *Discoveries*.

29. A statement of his philosophy can be found in the prologue to Jonson, *Every Man in His Humor*.

> He rather prays you will be pleased to see
> One such, today, as other plays should be:
> Where neither Chorus wafts you o'er the seas;
> Nor creaking throne comes down, the boys to please;
> Nor nimble squib [firecracker] is seen, to make afeared
> The gentlewomen; nor rolled bullet heard
> To say, it thunders; nor tempestuous drum
> Rumbles to tell you when the storm doth come;
> But deeds and language such as men do use,
> And persons such as Comedy should choose
> When she would show an image of the times,
> And sport with human follies, not with crimes—
> Except we make 'em such by loving still
> Our popular errors, when we know they're ill.
> I mean such errors as you'll all confess
> By laughing at them—they deserve no less;
> Which when you heartily do, there's hope left, then,
> You that have so graced monsters may like men.
>
> (ll. 13–30)

30. Hobbes, *A Briefe of Aristotle's Rhetorique*, 581.

31. Ibid., 585. In refraining from speculating on motive Hobbes also seems to anticipate some of his later work. See, for example, *Lev.*, 27.2.

32. Hobbes, *Behemoth*, vii.

33. For a brief history of the Restoration reflecting recent revisions in historical scholarship, see Seaward, *Restoration*. Seaward's work contains a useful bibliography. See also Harris, Seaward, and Goldie, *Politics of Religion*, 1–28, and Seaward, *Cavalier Parliament*.

34. Seaward, *Restoration*, 36–39. It is in this context that we should also read Hobbes's anonymously published *Considerations upon the Reputation, Loyalty, Manners, and Religion of Thomas Hobbes of Malmesbury*. Hobbes was not the only one to publish such an apology. As Seaward, *Cavalier Parliament*, notes, it was not an uncommon form of expression among Royalists who felt the settlement had left them with insufficient reward for their efforts on behalf of the cause.

35. Burnet, *History of His Own Time*, 1:298.

36. Ibid., 323.

37. Ibid., 323–24.

38. Ibid., 411.

39. Seaward, *Restoration*, 49.

40. Burnet, *History of His Own Time*, 1:411.
41. Ibid., 182–83; Alan Marshall, "Bennet, Henry, first earl of Arlington," *ODNB*.
42. Hobbes, *Behemoth*, 40, 57, 58.
43. Ibid., 2.
44. Ibid., 2–4.
45. The campaign against Rome, it should be noted, continues unabated in *Behemoth*. He states, for example, that the popes created the universities for purposes of maintaining obedience to the papacy, and that this power was to the detriment of kings: "The profit that the Church of Rome expected from them [universities and their students], and in effect received, was the maintenance of the Pope's doctrine, and of his authority over kings and their subjects, by schooldivines; who . . . make good many points of faith incomprehensible [with the assistance of] . . . the philosophy of Aristotle." Hobbes, *Behemoth*, 17. See also 40–47.
46. Discussions of these differences, sometimes conflicting, can be found in Tuck, *Philosophy and Government*, and Tuck, *Thomas Hobbes*; cf. Sommerville, *Thomas Hobbes*, on this point. Johnston, in *The Rhetoric of Leviathan*, develops an analysis of Hobbes's rationalized theology in *Leviathan* as an effort to use doctrine to remove all credibility from those claiming authority over the Church of England. Johnston, *Rhetoric of Leviathan*, and Jacob, *Henry Stubbe*, emphasize the political salience of Hobbes's ridding the universe of spiritual entities in favor of a strict materialism—fear and authority in the nation had to have a single, earthly source, the sovereign. See also Springborg, "*Leviathan* and the Problem of Ecclesiastical Authority," and Pocock, "Time, History, and Eschatology." Pocock argues, in effect, that one must separate the scientific and theological elements of Hobbes's work. This view is challenged by Springborg and by Johnston (see *Rhetoric of Leviathan*, 117–20). See also Probst, "Infinity and Creation."
47. Sommerville, *Thomas Hobbes*, 105–34, argues that no significant break occurs in Hobbes's religious doctrine, and that the distinctions between *De Cive* and *Leviathan* have more to do with Hobbes's need to protect himself from angry Anglicans in the former work, than with some shift or evolution in his thinking in the latter. Tuck, *Hobbes*, 85–86, 314–35.
48. The idea of royal supremacy over the church, however, was tempting to the Stuarts, not least because they were likely seeking a greater toleration for Catholic factions. See Seaward, *Restoration*, 52–54, on the temporary success of Charles II's Declaration of Indulgence in 1672 and the ironic position this placed many Presbyterians in.
49. See *Lev.*, 44.17, 47.4 (in which the power to excommunicate is discussed), and 47.17–20 (esp. 17, "And therefore, by the aforesaid rule of *cui bono* we may justly pronounce for the author of all this spiritual darkness the Pope, the Roman clergy, and all those besides that endeavor to settle in the minds of men this erroneous doctrine: that the Church now on earth is that kingdom of God mentioned in the Old and New Testament"). The undoing of the Presbyterians is represented as the last step in the undoing of the knots that wove men into a web of deception. (See section 20.) It was on the basis of these passages that Clarendon painted Hobbes as an Independent. Clarendon, *A Brief View*, 308–9. Jacob, *Henry Stubbe*, 24–40, discusses some of the differences between Hobbes and the Independency of Henry Stubbe.
50. Collins, *Allegiance of Thomas Hobbes*, 97–98, 152–53.
51. See Miller, "Two Deaths of Lady Macduff."
52. Ibid.
53. See Sommerville, *Thomas Hobbes*, 108–13.
54. Hobbes felt a certain ambivalence concerning the translation of scripture. Ultimately, he accepts it while trying to mediate what he sees as its most dangerous elements by disallowing interpretations contrary to those proclaimed by the king. Hobbes also claimed that there are lessons in scripture that are straightforward, easily understood, and that "no seducer is able to dispossess the mind (of any ordinary reader)." See Hobbes, *Behemoth*, 53–54. They all concern the duty of obedience to one's superiors. See also 21–22, 47–56, and especially 51–56, on the risks concerning the dissemination of scripture and the need to control these risks by taking control of the universities.

55. Ibid., 54–55. See also Johnston, *Rhetoric of Leviathan*, 134–84, for a detailed interpretation of the relation between sovereigns, scriptural interpretation, and Hobbes's conflict with the Presbyterians.

56. *Lev.*, 32.2. See also Johnston's discussion in *The Rhetoric of Leviathan*, 138–39. Hobbes's originality lay not in claiming that scripture's meaning is not inconsistent with human reason; it lies in the particulars of what he claimed right reason to have in fact dictated, namely, his own doctrine concerning a subject's obedience. See also Springborg, "*Leviathan* and the Problem of Ecclesiastical Authority," and Mulligan, "'Reason.'"

57. See Sommerville, *Thomas Hobbes*, 105–13.

58. *Lev.*, 37.13. For Schmitt, *The Leviathan in the State Theory*, as I noted in Chapter 4, this liberty of private thought was too much to grant.

59. For example, in *Lev.*, 7.7, Hobbes ensures that any distrust one might have in prophecy is directed (or displaced) from God onto persons who claim knowledge of the supernatural. See also *Lev.*, 8.25–26. In 32.5–6, Hobbes wrote: "How God speaketh to a man immediately may be understood by those well enough to whom he hath so spoken; but how the same should be understood by another is hard, if not impossible, to know. For if a man pretend to me that God hath spoken to him supernaturally and immediately, and I make doubt of it, I cannot easily perceive what argument he can produce to oblige me to believe it. . . . To say he hath spoken to him in a dream is no more than to say he dreamed that God spake to him."

60. See Johnston, *Rhetoric of Leviathan*.

61. The Presbyterians, of course, took a very different view. As Richard Tuck has argued, the Presbyterians (as distinguished from the Independents) were attempting to use princes throughout Europe in order to bolster their own authority. Tuck, *Philosophy and Government*, 202–5. Hobbes and Seldon were united in attempting to diminish the power of the Presbyterians. Ibid., 218, 319.

62. Sommerville, *Thomas Hobbes*, 122; Tuck, *Philosophy and Government*.

63. Sommerville, *Thomas Hobbes*, 128. See also Tuck, *Philosophy and Government*, 338.

64. Hobbes, *Behemoth*, 58.

65. Ibid.

66. See Hobbes's discussion on the disobedience of the armies during the Civil War and Interregnum in ibid., 109, 140–41.

67. Ibid., 59. Hobbes here refers to the Ottoman Emperor's guard composed of Christian slaves (the Janissaries). Famously loyal to the emperors for many years, they had turned against the unpopular Osman in 1622.

68. On the attitudes toward the theater and actors, see Agnew, *Worlds Apart*, and Barish, *Anti-Theatrical Prejudice*, 222–54.

69. Hobbes, *Behemoth*, 24–26. See also his *Considerations upon the Reputation*, in *EW*, 4:409–40, esp. 430.

70. Hobbes, *Behemoth*, 24.

71. Ibid.

72. Agnew, *Worlds Apart*. See also Barish, *Anti-Theatrical Prejudice*; Greenblatt, *Renaissance Self-Fashioning*, 222–54, for a discussion of the use of this fear in Shakespeare; Greene, "Flexibility of the Self," 241–64; and Burke, *Popular Culture*, 207–43. Burke illustrates that counterfeiting was not necessarily disapproved of by some reformers when they could use it for their own ends. Focusing on Hobbes's theatrically modeled notion of representation, Agnew argues that Hobbes found theatrical metaphors an apt means of expressing the kind of (market contractual) relations he had hoped to promote. See Agnew, *Worlds Apart*, esp. 98–104.

73. See Agnew, *Worlds Apart*, 57–73, who lays particular emphasis on those who imitated persons truly deserving of charity. Antitheatricality of this kind is a continual theme in Jonson's works. It is present in epigrams such as *On Court-Worm*, in Jonson, *Epigrams*, XV, in *Ben Jonson*, vol. 2: "All men are worms: but this is no man. In silk/'Twas brought to court first wrapped, and white as milk;/Where, afterwards, it grew a butterfly:/Which was a caterpillar. So 'twill die."

Some prominent examples of characters imitating persons truly deserving of charity include Mosca in *Volpone*, Bobadill in *Every Man in His Humour*, and Subtle and Face in *The Alchemist*. The theme also appears in the masques, such as *Mercury Vindicated from the Alchemists at Court* (performed before James I in 1615), in which Jonson counsels the Crown to rid his court of the philosophers who make false promises in order to gain the favor of the king and courtiers.

74. Hobbes, *Behemoth*, 24.

75. Hobbes's use of Diodorus Siculus's narrative concerning the powers of philosophy and divinity (ibid., 90–94) might also be classed with the polemics against the Presbyterians, but Hobbes seems to be up to something larger in this interesting part of the dialogue. This larger goal is most likely to impress readers with the power that might be exercised in civil matters "by the conjuncture of philosophy and divinity" (92), a conclusion which could conceivably speak against learned Presbyterians, or for Hobbes's own doctrine, which also conjoins philosophy and divinity in the service of the sovereign. Whatever else might be said of this passage, it is clear that Hobbes intended to put Charles in mind of the potential dangers faced by sovereigns who rule under the sway of a powerful priesthood. He cites the case of the Ethiopian kings; when the Ethiopian priesthood "has a mind to it," it sends a message to the king to kill himself—a command which the king obeys (94).

76. Ibid., 158–59.

77. Ibid., 159.

78. Ibid. Hobbes also connects the Presbyterians with the preference for Greek and Roman authors who teach men to lawfully oppose tyrants, and links them specifically to the democratic prejudices of the Protestant exiles during the reign of Queen Mary. Ibid., 20, 22–23, 26. See also 30, 89, 109, 136, 155. An issue Hobbes fails to address is how to connect these exiles who taught the Greek and Roman histories at the universities to the actual revolutionaries. The revolutionaries would, of course, have been of a different generation.

79. *Lev.*, 30.14.

80. Hobbes, *Behemoth*, 159–60.

81. Ibid., 95.

82. On the status of the public sphere under monarchy, see Walzer's introduction to *Regicide and Revolution*.

83. Webster, *Great Instauration*, 102–3.

84. Twigg, *University of Cambridge*, 211; Trevor-Roper, "Three Foreigners."

85. According to Hartlib, the "foundation of a reformed commonwealth, without which no other work of reformation will ever be effectual" is a reformed school and university system in which there would be separate schools for training the "vulgar" in the mechanic life, the gentry and nobles to "bear the charges of the commonwealth," scholars, "who are to teach other humane arts and sciences," and "the sons of the prophets, who are a seminary of the ministry." From *Considerations Tending to the Happy Accomplishment of England's Reformation*; quoted in Cressy, *Education in Tudor and Stuart England*, 23. In general, it is difficult to distinguish between instruments of governance and instruments for public instruction in Hartlib's work. See, for example, Hartlib's *Description of the Famous Kingdome of Marcaria*.

86. Hartlib, *A Description of the Famous Kingdome of Marcaria*, 79–90.

87. The Scholar has just learned that in Marcaria all Divines are also trained as physicians in the "Colledge of Experience, where they deliver out yeerly such medicines as they find out by experience; and all such as shall be able to demonstrate any experiment for the health or wealth of men." Ibid., 83.

88. Ibid., 84. Hartlib's scheme did, however, allow for yearly meetings of the Great Council in which dispute is allowed to take place. Anyone who can make his case at the council has his claim "generally received for truth; if he be overcome, then it is declared to be false." Ibid. There are parallels between Hartlib's Great Council and the role imagined by the proponents of the Royal Society for that organization. See Shapin and Schaffer, *Leviathan and the Air-Pump*.

89. Webster, *Academiarum Examen*, 6–8, 18–32, on humanities. With regard to mathematics, one can draw parallels between Hobbes and the reformers, but a partiality for mathematics (even for specific disciplines, such as geometry) is far too general a category on which to assume agreements. See Feingold, *Mathematician's Apprenticeship*, for a different view of the mathematical skills of the London community.

90. Twigg, *University of Cambridge*, 212–33, explores the conflict while emphasizing the limits of the popularly accepted (conservative) notion of the role of the university in society.

91. Webster, *Great Instauration;* Hill, *World Turned Upside Down*, 75, 287–305.

92. Explicit links between politics and education reform can also be found in John Dury's *The Reformed School* and Milton's *Of Education* (and in Milton's views on political education). For a view of the period which emphasizes the Protestant "international" of education reformers, see Trevor-Roper, "Three Foreigners." See also Webster, *Great Instauration*, 214–17. Also see Shapin and Schaffer's discussion of Dury's political opposition to Hobbes in *Leviathan and the Air-Pump*, 298–300. Skinner, "Context," 81–82, discusses conceptual similarities between the two.

93. See Webster, *Great Instauration*. For a competing view, see Jacob, *Henry Stubbe*.

94. Twigg, *University of Cambridge*, 182–85. See also, Hill, "Radical Critics," 107–32.

95. Twigg, *University of Cambridge*, 170–71.

96. See ibid., 206–33.

97. On the status of both Wallis and Ward at the universities and their vulnerability (because they had both compromised their principles to secure posts at Oxford during the Commonwealth), see Schaffer, "Wallification." See also Malcolm, "Hobbes and the Royal Society." Malcolm notes that Ward had been on better terms with Hobbes before the Civil War.

98. On Wilkins, see Shapiro, *John Wilkins*.

99. [Ward], *Vindiciae Academiarum*, 1.

100. For a discussion, see Jacob, *Henry Stubbe*, 8–24. See, however, Malcolm, "Hobbes and the Royal Society." Aside from criticizing Jacob, Malcolm has suggested a common, pragmatic concurrence between Ward and Hobbes on the need for authority. He sees Ward's attack on Hobbes in "Against Resistance of Lawful Powers" as "obligatory," an attempt to distance himself and other scientific elite of the Royal Society from Hobbes as Hobbes grew increasingly "disreputable." Malcolm, "Hobbes and the Royal Society," 57–58. On 61–66, Malcolm claims that painting Hobbes as a dogmatic atheist also fit with Latitudinarian propaganda strategies. This interpretation suggests an interesting set of possibilities that we may add to the list of Ward's possible motivations. Malcolm's account, however, does not do a great deal to explain Hobbes's reaction to Ward's antagonism. I would suggest that Ward's motivations for painting Hobbes as a dogmatist could have been something aside from an attempt to distance himself and the Royal Society from Hobbes in public opinion. By 1661 Ward may have wanted to answer Hobbes's accusations: he and the Society may have felt some need to defend themselves from Hobbes in the more conventional sense. See esp. Schaffer, "Wallification," on the threat Hobbes may have posed to the Society as it sought Charles II's favor in 1663–64. See Shapin and Schaffer, *Leviathan and the Air-Pump*. See also the letters exchanged between Hobbes and Stubbe now available in Malcolm, *Correspondence*, and Malcolm's discussion of Ward in "Hobbes and the Royal Society," 2:230 n. 8.

101. The constellation of (sometimes contradictory) factors associated with gentlemanly credibility was also a major determinant in helping create a scientific establishment in seventeenth-century England. See Shapin, *Social History of Truth*, esp. 65–125. See also Shapin and Schaffer, *Leviathan and the Air-Pump*, esp. 129–39.

102. [Ward], *Vindiciae Academiarum*, 5.

103. Ibid.

104. See Jacob, *Henry Stubbe*, 8–40, for the links between Hobbes and more radical critics of Presbyterians.

105. Ibid., 51.

106. Ibid., 51–52.

107. *Lev.*, chap. 31; quoted in [Ward], *Vindiciae Academiarum*, 52.

108. [Ward], *Vindiciae Academiarum*, 52.

109. Ibid.

110. Ibid., 53.

111. Ibid., 53–54.

112. Shapin and Schaffer, *Leviathan and the Air-Pump*, 129–39, have emphasized that charges of dogmatism were also a part of the Royal Society's attack on Hobbes. As Shapin and Schaffer point out, the question of Hobbes's character in the context of his conflict with the Royal Society (Wallis and Ward were both important figures in the Society) was a *political* issue.

113. Wallis, *Hobbius Heauton-timorumenos*, 4–5.

114. Ibid., 3. "Exploded" in this context means held in contempt or rejected. "To explode" in this era is often a reference to the act of hissing an actor offstage.

115. Terence, "Heautontimorumenos," 132–96. Only fragments of the original Menander play survive.

116. One might include Hobbes's argument here among those in which he argues *in utramque partem* (see Kahn, *Rhetoric, Prudence, and Skepticism*). In this context this form of argument (using the basis of one's opponent's argument in order to argue the opposite) is an ostentatious rebuff. In a debate where the foremost stakes are the moral character of the accused, the reversal becomes a potent means of suggesting the moral backwardness of one's accusers, namely, their very accusation becomes the basis for your vindication.

117. The *Vindiciae Academiarum* is mentioned in lesson 6 of *Six Lessons*, in *EW*, 7:335–36.

118. *Six Lessons*, lesson 6, in *EW*, 7:335. In ΣΤΙΓΜΑΙ; *or, Marks of the Absurd Geometry, Rural Language, Scottish Church Politics, and Barbarisms of John Wallis, Professor of Geometry and Doctor of Divinity*, Hobbes states: "Concerning the Universities of Oxford and Cambridge, I ever held them for the greatest and noblest means of advancing learning of all kinds, where they should be therein employed, as being furnished with large endowments and other helps of study, and frequented with abundance of young gentlemen of good families and good breeding from their childhood. On the other side, in case the same means and the same wits could be employed in the advancing of the doctrines that tend to the weakening of the public, and strengthening of the power of any private ambitious party, they would also be very effectual for that; and consequently that if any doctrine tending to the diminishing of the civil power were taught there, not that the Universities were to blame, but only those men that in the universities, either in lectures, sermons, printed books, or theses, did teach such doctrine to their hearers or readers." *EW*, 7:399–400.

119. Ibid., 335–36. Note that Wallis makes the adjustment in *Hobbius Heauton-timorumenos*, 3.

120. *EW*, 7:344. Boyle's collaborator, Thomas Barlow (who also authored a refutation of Hobbes's *Historical Narration Concerning Heresie*), eventually accused Hobbes of "papist" methods for having attempted to force his works on the universities. See Shapin and Schaffer, *Leviathan and the Air-Pump*, 302–3 and note 38. See also Thomas Barlow to Thomas Hobbes, December 23, 1656/January 12, 1657, Letter 109, in Malcolm, *Correspondence*, 1:420–22, in which Barlow discusses the uses and abuses of universities, and Malcolm, *Correspondence*, 2:785–87. Despite disagreeing with him, Barlow is quite civil in this letter to Hobbes. Like Stubbe, his dislike of the Presbyterians may have been responsible for a temporary alliance between the two. See Jacob, *Henry Stubbe*.

121. Jacob, *Henry Stubbe*, discusses the relation between Hobbes and Stubbe. See esp. 8–40, 71, for discussions of similarities and differences. Jacob may be following Stubbe on the matter of Hobbes's opinion on the universities. This may, however, pass over Hobbes's own construal. As a part of what may have been Stubbe's efforts to rehabilitate Hobbes at Oxford, Jacob states that Hobbes had *revised* his view concerning the universities from the one in *Leviathan*, which was entirely negative. Ibid., 22. Stubbe made this claim based on Hobbes's remarks in one of the polemics against John Wallis. Since, however, he says that he "ever held them [the universities]

for the greatest and noblest means of advancing learning of all kinds," he suggests that he is not revising his view, but merely clarifying what he had said before. It is true that Hobbes has more positive things to say concerning the universities here than in *Leviathan*, but he maintains throughout his work that the universities *could be* used either for or against the production of an obedient and peaceable commonwealth. As Jacob notes, Stubbe was attempting to make a connection for Hobbes with Thomas Barlow (then his superior at the Bodleian Library); in his letter to Hobbes Barlow goes out of his way to acknowledge this continuity in Hobbes's thought. See Malcolm, *Correspondence*, 1:420.

122. See Malcolm, *Correspondence*, 1:xxxv, 2:904–13. For the numerous letters from François du Verdus to Thomas Hobbes, see esp. Malcolm, *Correspondence*, 1:248–69, 344, and 359, and 2:588 and 592. In the dedication to *Les Elemens*, his translation of *De Cive* (although he omits Hobbes's third section on religion), du Verdus enthusiastically encourages Louis XIV to follow the Mosaic model in which the civil authority takes charge of both religious and secular matters.

Chapter 8

1. Hobbes, untitled sketch-plans, Hobbes MS, Devonshire Collections, Chatsworth, C. vii, 11. Hobbes, "Fortifications," Hobbes MS, Devonshire Collections, Chatsworth, C. vii, 10, is a much more elaborate, handwritten, set of specifications for a fortification, including three-dimensional measures for walls, parapet, a bank, ditch, and discussion of a possible counterscarp. Here again we see evidence of Hobbes's participation in the work of practical mathematics.

2. It seems very unlikely that Hobbes's fortress in the C. vii, 11 manuscript was designed to defend anything other than his reputation for squaring the circle. Aside from its grouping with circle-in-square garden designs, a good sign of its memorializing intent is its deviation from what was then standard fortification technique. Fortification technology at this time typically called for designs built around concentric polygonal shapes: the curtain walls of the fortress would be paralleled by the lines drawn by connecting the points (the tips) formed by the front sides of the battlements. Had Hobbes followed this rule, he would have enclosed a square within a square, not a circle within a square. Two examples of square fortress design can be found in Papillon, *A Practicall Abstract*, plates 6, 10, and Staynred, *A Compendium of Fortification*, 1–2.

3. Although made in the context of the practices of experimental inquiry, this point is made most convincingly in Shapin, *Social History of Truth*.

4. See the discussion of Wallis, *Hobbius Heauton-timorumenos*, in Chapter 7. See also Eachard, another proponent of mathematical education, in *Some Opinions of Mr. Hobbs Considered*. In *Some Opinions of Mr. Hobbs Considered*, 40–42, Eachard's stand-in for Hobbes, Philautus, is rebuked for his attack on the Anglican Church and traditional logic:

> [*Timothy*] . . . Now say I, *Philautus*, give me again my *Actus primus*, and *Actus secundus*, my *terminus à quo*, and *terminus ad quem*, my *quidditas, quodditas, entitas*, and all the rest of my little, barbarous *Metaphysical* implements; rather than such childish, ridiculous, non-sensical querks and subtilties, adres'd up into eloquent stile, with soft and *Roman* expressions. You had best now complain to his *Majesty* that the boys laught at you. . . .

> [*Philautus*] . . . thou art a most rude and ungentile *scribler*, a most unmannerly, and scurrilous *libeller*, a most ignorant, pragmatical, and malicioius *despiser* of *age, gravity, observation*, and every thing else that is becoming and venerable: a very *Boy, Toy*, flie-flap, shittlecock, nut-crack, that ought not to speak to one that has *read a good Book*, or seen a *wise man*: the very sediment, fag-end, stump, and snuff of mankind; that snears and blinks at stars of reason: and that shirk'd only into humane race, to vex *old men*, and stum sober company: and therefore I do defie thee, and abhor thee, and spit on thy face. . . .

5. *EL*, "Epistle Dedicatory," xvii.

6. Strauss, *Political Philosophy of Hobbes*, 15–29.

7. See *Lev.*, 3.5, 6.35, 8.25, 11.25, and 12.2; *EL*, 1.9.18; and *Dec. Phys.*, chap. 1, in *EW*, 7:71–72. My thanks to Verna Gehring for bringing this to my attention.

8. *Lev.*, 13.2.

9. See Burckhardt, *Civilization of the Renaissance*, esp. pt. 2. Burckhardt can be endorsed, but with caveats. Some of these caveats, concerning "individuality," can be found in Gundersheimer, "Patronage in the Renaissance." The Burckhardtian perspective can miss the corporate nature of a patron's role and his reliance on available resources. There is, necessarily, a strongly calculative aspect to the reason of patrons: they ask who or what skills are available. Some rethinking of "the individual," moreover, may indicate a greater compatibility between these two perspectives than might be expected. In Biagioli, *Galileo, Courtier*, these and other elements of the calculus of patronage relations are shown as part of the self-fashioning of clients and patrons. In my view, this resonates with a more Nietzschean reading of Burckhardt's text. See Weissman, "Taking Patronage Seriously," for an excellent and suggestive criticism of neo-Burckhardtian perspectives on patronage and the general willingness to see patronage as a holdover from medieval feudal relations. Weissman argues that patronage must be seen as an urban phenomenon—a practice he traces to ancient Rome, a way of dividing the world into friends and strangers, and not necessarily a set of relations that, *pace* feudalism, necessarily asserts solid, unbreakable, hierarchical gaps between patrons and clients. Finally, Burkhardt has been augmented and corrected by writers such as Cassirer, *The Individual and the Cosmos*, and Trinkaus, "Humanism and Science," for having not appreciated the philosophical character of humanist accomplishments.

10. Burckhardt, *Civilization of the Renaissance*, 149–50.

11. Alberti, *Ten Books on Architecture*. Alberti made a point of distancing himself from the less eloquent style of the original. Observing decorum, he chose instead to deliver the message in eloquent prose, fitting for a work presented to his patrons. See ibid., 111. Also see Goldthwaite, *The Building of Renaissance Florence*, esp. 97–98.

12. For example, in *De Corpore*, 1.7: "But what the utility of philosophy is, especially of natural philosophy and geometry, will be best understood by reckoning up the chief commodities of which mankind is capable, and by comparing the manner of life of such as enjoy them, with that of others which want the same. Now, the greatest commodities of mankind are the arts; namely, of measuring matter and motion; of moving ponderous bodies; of architecture; of navigation; of making instruments for all uses; of calculating the celestial motions, the aspects of the stars, and the parts of time; of geography, &c. By which sciences, how great benefits men receive is more easily understood than expressed."

13. Trinkaus, *In Our Image and Likeness*, 2:482.

14. This is not to suggest the two were not combined. They were, perhaps frequently. See, for example, Francesco Stelluti's laudatory poem published with Galileo's *The Assayer*, 156–62. See also Rose, *Italian Renaissance of Mathematics*. My point is that the constellation of criteria by which mathematics could be praised made it possible for Hobbes to claim success without having to use his art to offer descriptions of the world.

15. Hobbes, *Verse Autobiography*, lv.

16. Jacquot, "Sir Charles Cavendish and His Learned Friends"; Tuck, *Hobbes*, 11–13; Skinner, *Reason and Rhetoric*, 250–52.

17. Jacquot, "Sir Charles Cavendish and His Learned Friends"; Trease, *Portrait of a Cavalier*, 31–36.

18. Frederick Hand, "Introduction," in Wotton, *Elements of Architecture*, esp. lxv–lxxx. Wittkower, *Palladio and English Palladianism*, 62, 99, 139. Wittkower also describes the international success of Vitruvian ideals sparked by Palladio's *I Quattro Libri dell'Architettura* (1570). Vitruvius had, however, been known to mathematical Englishmen. Dee, for example, was well aware of him. See Dee, *Mathematicall Praeface*. On Wotton, see Smith, *The Life and Letters of Sir Henry Wotton*.

19. Girouard, *Robert Smythson*, 2–38. On Elizabethan parsimony and Jacobean extravagance, see Stone, *Crisis in the Aristocracy*. Elizabeth's courtiers paid for their own extravagance, and for the privilege of making theirs hers, when she elected to visit their estates. Jacobean and Carolinian patronage, by contrast, not only increased the state's expenditures, but connected the sovereign and the architect directly. This is not to suggest that mathematical patronage was not a part of Elizabeth's regime. John Dee was her tutor and was employed in other capacities as well—if never to his own satisfaction. For a somewhat different view on the particularly English origins of "the architect," see Gerbino and Johnston, *Compass and Rule*. For discussions of Tudor and Stuart mathematical patronage, see Feingold, *Mathematician's Apprenticeship*, 190–213.

20. Rogow, *Thomas Hobbes*, 68n. Like surveying, "hydraulic engineering"—draining marshes and constructing aqueducts, waterways, exquisite ponds for the homes of the nobility, and city fountains—was considered a form of practical mathematics. See Dee, *Mathematicall Praeface*, sig. d.j–ij, and de Caus, *New and Rare Inventions of Water-Works*. (The latter is based on Salomon de Caus, *Les Raison de forces movvantes auec diverses machines*.) See also Westfall, "Science and Technology," 67–68, who notes that "anyone known to have mathematical skills might find himself drafted into such work," including Pascal, whose efforts were engaged in the draining of a marsh. On Bess of Hardwick as an architectural patron, see Girouard, *Robert Smythson*.

21. Thomson, *Renaissance Architecture*, 41–42.

22. Rogow, *Thomas Hobbes*, 57–77; Wittkower, *Palladio and English Palladianism*, 74–75.

23. *OP*, 5:325–40. Hobbes focuses his praise on the hydrological engineering work at Chatsworth. It created an artificial stream to fill a fish pond and supply the house with water. Likewise, Bess of Hardwick's accomplishment in creating "Caesarian" castles, which Hobbes says were suitable for a king to have built, is trumpeted, along with the nobility and magnanimity of his more immediate patrons, her children. William Crook published a parallel Latin and English translation in 1678.

24. See Girouard, *Robert Smythson*, who notes that Bolsover was a part of a late Elizabethan chivalric revival. Bolsover is a fantasy, or "sham," castle built not with actual military uses in mind, but to evoke gothic and chivalric life. William Newcastle remained attached to this culture; he attended the ceremonial tilts, and his entertainments at Bolsover, *Love's Welcome at Bolsover*, emphasized chivalric virtues. See Raylor and Brice, "Manuscript Poem." See also the Hobbesian sentiments expressed in Newcastle's letter of advice to Charles II, reprinted in Slaughter, *Ideology and Politics*. Here Newcastle blends the chivalric themes of martial kingship and reverence for ceremony and order with Hobbesian political advice. See Slaughter, *Ideology and Politics*, xi–xxxiv.

25. See Slaughter, *Ideology and Politics*, on in the influence of Jones and the Palladian style on Cavendish's architect, Smythson, although Smythson pursued an eclectic style. See also Trease, *Portrait of a Cavalier*, 38–39, 44, 50, 62–63, 206–8.

26. Trease, *Portrait of a Cavalier*, 160–61.

27. Ibid., 61–87.

28. Hulse, "Apollo's Whirligig." Until recently, the manuscript "On the Motions of a Horse" was attributed to Hobbes. Malcolm argues Robert Payne, another mathematically learned individual patronized by Newcastle and known by Hobbes, authored the work. See Malcolm, *Correspondence*, 2:813–14, and Skinner, *Reason and Rhetoric*, 251. Newcastle himself was responsible for two treatises on training horses: *La Méthod Nouvelle et Invention Extraordinaire de dresser les Chevaux*, and its (altered) English version, *A New and Extraordinary Method to Dress Horses*. See "To the Readers," in Trease, *Portrait of a Cavalier*, 175, 196.

29. "A Discourse of Rome," in Hobbes, *Three Discourses*, 81–83.

30. Ibid., 90.

31. Girouard, *Robert Smythson*. This is not to suggest that Elizabeth did not dress herself in the symbolism of magnificence. Elizabethan artists, however, often chose to represent the magnificence of their monarch through more traditional means, especially through the meticulous display of her finery. Smuts, "Art and the Material Culture"; Mauss, *The Gift*.

32. When Spain was anxious for peace in 1629, it prudently chose Peter Paul Rubens as its envoy to Charles I. Sharpe, *Personal Rule*, 67.

33. James, like the Renaissance pedagogues who preceded him, did not want a son lost in mathematical contemplation, but he clearly thought mathematical learning useful: "As for the study of other liberall arts and sciences, I would have you reasonably versed in them, but not preassing to bee a passe-master in any of them: for that cannot but distract you from the points of your calling, as I shewed you . . . by the enemie winning the towne, yee shall be interrupted in your demonstration, as *Archimedes* was . . . I graunt it is meete yee haue some entrance, specially in the Mathematicks; for the knowledge of the arte militarie, in situation of Campes, ordering of battles, making Fortifications, placing of batteries, or such like. And let not this your knowledge be dead without fruites . . . but let it appeare in your daily conuersation, and in all the actions of your life." *Basilicon Doron*, in Stuart, *Political Writings*, 46–47.

34. Smuts, *Court Culture*; Sharpe, *Criticism and Compliment*, esp. on the political salience of symbolism of Platonic love; Orgel and Strong, *Inigo Jones*; Orgel, *Illusion of Power*; Orgel, "Royal Theatre." See also Feingold, *Mathematician's Apprenticeship*, 190–213.

35. Both techniques are used, for example, in Anthony Van Dyck's *Charles I at the Hunt* (1635, The Louvre). See Smuts, *Court Culture*, 171–77. See also Peacock, "Politics of Portraiture." Solomon de Caus, inventor of water-driven automata for elaborate royal gardens, dedicated a work on perspective line drawing, *La Perspective*, to James I.

36. Newman, "Inigo Jones and the Politics of Architecture"; Wittkower, *Palladio and English Palladianism*; Ackerman, "Rudolph Wittkower's Influence." Jones was not, however, the only Vitruvian of his day. Ben Jonson was also a careful student of Vitruvius, and in matters concerning the scope of the architect's authority over learned subjects, Jonson takes a position in greater conformity with Vitruvius. See Johnson, *Ben Jonson: Poetry and Architecture*, 16.

37. Johnson, *Ben Jonson: Poetry and Architecture*, 19–26. See the discussion of Quintilian in chapter 2. Perhaps the best-known illustration of this form of thought in the Renaissance is Leonardo's *Vitruvian Man*.

38. This vision of order could be made to affirm the cult of Platonic love that Charles and Henrietta promoted. Orgel and Strong, *Inigo Jones*, 49–75. Cf. Sharpe, *Criticism and Compliment*, 265–301.

39. Smuts, *Court Culture*, 166–68; Newman, "Inigo Jones and the Politics of Architecture." Cf. Jones, *Most Notable Antiquity*, esp. 6–11, 44–45, 67–72.

40. Jones, *Most Notable Antiquity*, 43, 71.

41. Cited in Strong, *Henry, Prince of Wales*, 107. Strong also provides a brief account of Salomon de Caus's career with Henry (106–10). *Les Raisons* was in fact published after Henry's death. Part 1 is dedicated to Louis XIII, part 2 to Elizabeth of Bohemia (Henry and Charles I's) sister. Strong cites a Paris edition of 1624. See also Isaak de Caus, *New and Rare Inventions of Water-Works*, which is a translation of a French work based on Salomon de Caus, *Les Raison de forces movvantes auec diverses machines*.

42. See Smuts, *Court Culture*, 149–52, and de Caus, *New and Rare Inventions of Water-Works*.

43. Smuts, *Court Culture*, 155.

44. Cited in ibid., 153. Smuts raises the possibility that Charles may not have actually understood all that he professed to know. For our purposes the mere fact that he would have himself known as mathematically knowledgeable holds the greater significance. See also Sharpe, *Personal Rule*, 182.

45. One of the foremost guides to gentlemanly mathematics was Sir Henry Peacham's *The Complete Gentleman*. The topic of gentlemanly mathematics is discussed in Kelso, *Doctrine of the English Gentleman*, 137–39. See also Shapin, "'A Scholar and a Gentleman,'" and *Social History of Truth*.

46. Trease, *Portrait of a Cavalier*; Westwood, *Royal Journey Ode, or The Royal Journey*, in Raylor and Bryce, "Manuscript Poem"; Rowe, "'My Best Patron'"; Brown, "Courtesies of Place"; Raylor and Bryce, "Manuscript Poem," 173–78.

47. Ben Jonson, *The King's Entertainment at Welbeck*, in Jonson, *Ben Jonson*, 7:787–803; Ben Jonson, *Love's Welcome at Bolsover*, in ibid., 804–14. Martinich has speculated that Hobbes may have played the character of Fitz-ale in *The King's Entertainment at Welbeck*. Martinich, "Thomas Hobbes."

48. Bruce, *Calendar of State Papers*, 434; Brown, "Courtesies of Place." See also Rowe, "'My Best Patron.'"

49. Suspected of being involved in the Army Plot, Cavendish was removed from this post at Parliament's request in 1641. By 1646, when Hobbes was made tutor to the prince at the exile court, the king was made prisoner of the Scottish army and then Parliament. Moreover, Newcastle retained his role as adviser to Charles II in the years that followed. See Malcolm, *Correspondence*, 2:814, and Slaughter, *Ideology and Politics*.

50. Although her specific interests were more broadly scientific, Margaret Cavendish's prodigious output also bolstered the family's reputation for scientific learning later in the century. Cavendish's *Blazing World*, which plays on a theme of a world created in fancy and a world discovered through reason, is particularly interesting. See Cavendish, *The Blazing World and Other Writings*, esp. 122–24, which includes an opening poem where William Cavendish demonstrates his awareness of the distinction between worlds made and worlds found. For a list of Cavendish's works, see ibid., xxxvii. Cavendish offers her own materialist metaphysic in *Philosophical and Physical Opinions*.

51. See Johnson, *Ben Jonson: Poetry and Architecture*; Sharpe, *Criticism and Compliment*; Orgel and Strong, *Inigo Jones*; and Gordon, "Poet and Architect."

52. Jonson, *Epigrams*, XCVII, CXV, and CXXIX, in *Ben Jonson*, 8:62–63, 74–75, and 81. See also ibid., 8:402–8 and 218–19, and 7:807–14. There are references to Jones in the *Conversations with Drummond*, in ibid., 1:145, and in *Underwood*, XLVII, in *Ben Jonson*, 8:218–20. The cook in *Neptune's Triumph*, and *The Staple of the News*, act 4, scene 1, and the character "In-and-In Medlay" in *A Tale of a Tub*, all of which can also be found in *Ben Jonson*, mock Jones. Gordon, "Poet and Architect," offers an extensive review of the quarrel.

53. Ben Jonson, *An Expostulation with Inigo Jones*, lines 52 and 74, in *Ben Jonson*, 8:404–5.

54. Jonson writes in the *Epostulation:* ". . . O Showes! Showes! Mighty Showes!/ The Eloquence of Masques! What need of prose/Or Verse, or Sense t'express Immortal you?/ You are ye Spectacles of State!" In *Ben Jonson*, 8:403–4.

55. Gordon, "Poet and Architect"; Orgel, "Introduction," in *CM*. Sharpe, *Criticism and Compliment*, 179–264, has noted the didacticism of the court masque did not disappear after the collaboration between Jonson and Jones ended.

56. Taylor, *Mathematical Practitioners*, 196.

57. Johnson, *Ben Jonson: Poetry and Architecture*; Greene, "Ben Jonson and the Centered Self." See also Jonson, *Ben Jonson*, 1:93 and 11:259, 582–85.

58. Jonson, *Expostulation*, l. 64, in *Ben Jonson*, 8:404.

59. Johnson, *Ben Jonson: Poetry and Architecture*, 16, see also Newman "Inigo Jones and the Politics of Architecture."

60. Riggs, *Ben Jonson: A Life*, 325–37; Jonson, *Ben Jonson*, 7:787–814. In the second entertainment, *Love's Welcome*, Jonson took aim at Jones again in the character of Coronell Vitruvius. See the discussion of this character later in this chapter.

61. "Similarly, in the members of a temple there ought to be the greatest harmony in the symmetrical relations of the different parts to the general magnitude of the whole. Then again, in the human body the central point is naturally the navel. For if a man can be placed flat on his back, with his hands and feet extended, and a pair of compasses centered at his navel, the fingers and toes of his two hands and feet will touch the circumference of a circle described therefrom. And just as the human body yields a circular outline, so too a square figure may be found from it. For if we measure the distance from the soles of the feet to the top of the head, and then apply that measure to the outstretched arms, the breadth will be found to be the same as the height, as in the case of plane surfaces which are completely square." Vitruvius, *De Architectura* 3.1.3.

62. Johnson, *Ben Jonson: Poetry and Architecture*. See, for example, Jonson, *Pleasure Reconciled with Virtue* (1618), where Daedalus, the archetypal artisan, brings order to the chaotic scene of performers dressed as wine bottles and casks, signifying indulgent and undisciplined pleasures, on the masque stage through the promise of "a guide that gives them laws/ To all their motions. . . ." Here it is affirmed that these precepts are "in sacred harmony." *CM*, 272.

63. Jonson, *Discoveries*, ll. 2030–35, in *Ben Jonson*, 8:625. The passage is drawn from Vives, but here too there is a link to Vitruvius and to mathematical learning.

64. From *News from the New World Discovered in the Moon* (1621), in Orgel and Strong, *Inigo Jones*, 311.

65. In "The Author's Preface," in *Gondibert*, written to Hobbes, Davenant uses the language of architecture to describe his poem. Davenant was one of the "Son's of Ben [Jonson]." He speaks, for example, of the poem as "his building," of the acts as his "underwalks" and as its "Frame," of its various attributes as the poem's "large rooms, furniture, and ornaments," and speaks of himself as the "builder." Davenant, "The Author's Preface," in *Gondibert*, 15, 16, 18, 20, 44. Like Solomon, Davenant writes that he was aided in the construction by a variety of learned men, most notably Hobbes himself. This he compares to building with a variety of materials: "Fellers of Wood, Hewers of Stone, as of learned Architects: Nor have I refrained to be obliged to men of any science, as mechanical, as liberall." Ibid., 22.

66. Jonson, *Discoveries*, ll. 2030–35, in *Ben Jonson*, 8:625.

67. Gauthier, *Logic of Leviathan*.

68. This was also an element of Jonson's attack on Jones. See Jonson, *Epigrams*, CXV, "On the Townes Honest Man," in *Ben Jonson*, 8:74–75.

69. Bobadill's aspiration, moreover, was not without corollaries in the print culture. See Hood, *A Copie of the Speache;* Hylles, *The Arte of Vulgar Arithmetick;* and Bedwell, *Via regia ad geometriam*.

70. Ben Jonson, *Every Man in His Humour (Folio of 1616)*, act 4, scene 7, ll. 73–94, in *Ben Jonson*, vol. 3. I have not quoted from the version published in 1598, but from the later Folio revision. *Bobadilla*, in the original, speaks a mathematically infused boast very much like the one quoted.

71. Turner, "Mathematical Instruments."

72. Although it did not come to fruition, Sir Humphey Gilbert had in fact proposed that the state itself dedicate its efforts to the production of mathematical gentlemen toward the end of Elizabeth's reign: he put forward a plan for an academy for gentlemen ("Queen Elizabeth's Academy"), where practical mathematics would be part of training for warfare. Gilbert, "Queen Elizebethes Achademy." See also the discussion of mathematics in gentlemanly education in Kelso, *Doctrine of the English Gentleman;* Mason, *Gentlefolk in the Making;* and Peacham, *Complete Gentleman*. An extensive bibliography can be found in Shapin, "'A Scholar and a Gentleman.'" I borrow the term "self-fashioning" from Greenblatt, *Renaissance Self-Fashioning*. See also Greenblatt, "Psychoanalysis and Renaissance Culture." The practices and rejection of histrionics have been explored in ways that will interest Hobbes scholars in Agnew, *Worlds Apart*. Other important works that speak to the issue of theatricality are Barish, *Anti-Theatrical Prejudice*, and Greene, "Flexibility of the Self." Critiques of new historicist literature abound. For a useful critique, as well as cites to other important critiques, see Levine, *Men in Women's Clothing*.

73. On tripping speech in Jonson, see Barish, *Ben Jonson and the Language of Prose Comedy*.

74. Jonson's Coronell, as with his other dramatic parody of Jones, In-and-In Medlay, in *A Tale of the Tub*, is more focused on ridiculous claims to omnicompetence, the characteristic in Jones that Jonson particularly resented. On this, see Gordon, "Poet and Architect." Coronell Vitruvius, accompanied by a collection of dancing mechanics, describes himself in *Love's Welcome at Bolsover* as a surveyor (Jones was appointed the King's Surveyor): "Doe you know what a Surveyour is now? I tell you, a Supervisor! A hard word, that; but it may be softned, and brought in, to signify something. An Overseer! One that oversee-eth you. A busie man! And yet I must seeme busier than I am." Jonson, *Ben Jonson*, 7:809.

75. Mandey, "A Garden of Geometrical Roses" and "Some Principles and Problems in Geometry, &c.," in *Mellificium Mensionis*, 40–109, 110–185. Mandey also coauthored with Moxon *Mechanick Powers*, a systematic explanation of simple machines and the principles of various engines. In their address to the readers, however, these authors praise Hobbes's nemesis, John Wallis, for his work on mechanics. In the translated works by Hobbes, Wallis is strongly criticized. Mandey's basic geometrical definitions in *Mellificium*, however, echo Hobbes's preferred definitions, not Wallis's. See my discussion in the appendix on these definitions.

76. Parker, *Military Revolution*.

77. Johnston, "Mathematical Practitioners." For a very extensive, if now occasionally questioned account, see Taylor, *Mathematical Practitioners*. See Hylles, *The Arte of Vulgar Arithmeticke*; Bedwell, *Via regia ad geometriam*; and Digges, *An arithmeticall warlike treatise*.

78. Johnston, "Mathematical Practitioners"; Turner, "Mathematical Instruments," 51–88.

79. Willmoth, "Mathematical Sciences and Military Technology"; Taylor, *Mathematical Practitioners*; Hall, *Ballistics in the Seventeenth Century*.

80. An important example is Hood, *A Copie of the Speache*. Hood was made the official mathematics teacher to the city of London in response to the call for more expert use of mathematical techniques among England's fighting forces. See Johnston, "Mathematical Practitioners."

81. See, for example, Bedwell, *Via regia ad geometriam*, a translation of Ramus. On Ramus and practical geometry, see Hooykaas, *Humanisme, science et réforme*, and Margolin, "L'enseignement des mathématiques en France."

82. Taylor, *Mathematical Practitioners*; Hall, *Ballistics in the Seventeenth Century*; Willmoth, "Mathematical Sciences and Military Technology."

83. Nethercot, *Sir William D'avenant*, 21–37, 166, 200–265, esp. 257.

84. Miller, "Uniqueness of *Leviathan*," 75–104.

85. *Lev.*, 46.23; *Lev.*, 44.11.

86. Sharpe, *Criticism and Compliment*, 180. This may also be the influence of Geertz. See Geertz, *Negara*.

87. The offended Venetian ambassador, Osio Busino, describes Jonson and Jones's masque *Pleasure Reconciled to Virtue* as closing with the masquers falling on a table of food, "like so many harpies . . . the first assault threw the table to the ground." In Orgel and Strong, *Inigo Jones*, 279–84.

88. Sharpe, *Personal Rule*, 209–74; Sharpe, *Criticism and Compliment*.

89. "Whereas all representations, especially those of this nature in court, public spectacles, either have been or ought to be the mirrors of man's life, whose ends, for the excellence of their exhibitors . . . ought always to carry a mixture of profit with them no less than delight; we, the inventors, being commanded from the king to think on some thing worthy of his majesty's putting in act . . . for the honor of his court." *Love's Triumph Through Callipolis* (1631), in *CM*, 454.

90. Shakespeare, *The Tempest*. The Orgel edition includes his analysis of Shakespeare's masque, and of masques in general.

91. Orgel, *Illusion of Power*, 39.

92. The presence of music and dance meant that mathematics was a part of this form of royal entertainment from the start, but mathematical contributions to the masque reached their high point in the seventeenth century under James I and Charles I. Following the Civil War, the genre did continue. Two masques were performed for Cromwell. Sharpe, *Criticism and Compliment*, 181 n. 6. Masques were also performed during the Restoration; see Walkling, "Politics and the Restoration Masque," 52–69.

93. There were, however, private theaters like the Cockpit-in-Court (an attachment to Whitehall). In these theaters a play's audience and the masque audience might have been equally exclusive. The seating arrangements may have also reflected differences in status among the playgoers.

94. Palme, *Triumph of Peace;* Newman, "Inigo Jones and the Politics of Architecture." See, however, Sharpe, *Criticism and Compliment,* 259, and Orgel and Strong, *Inigo Jones,* for costume design.

95. For a meditation on just how different the typical audience for a masque was from the typical audience for a publicly presented play, particularly with regard to readings of masques as *public* spectacles, see Smuts, "Art and the Material Culture." This is not to suggest, however, that plays were not also performed before more exclusive audiences. Whitehall itself was used; the *Tempest* may have played there. Orgel, "Introduction" to *The Tempest,* 2.

96. Orgel, *Illusion of Power,* 6–9.

97. Orgel, "Royal Theatre"; Orgel, *Illusion of Power;* Orgel and Strong, *Inigo Jones.*

98. These techniques began to be used in England in 1605. Orgel, *Illusion of Power,* 10. Library records suggest, however, that English interest in perspective can be dated to the 1590s. See Strong, *Henry, Prince of Wales,* 109.

99. Orgel, *Illusion of Power,* 26–36; Orgel and Strong, *Inigo Jones,* 15–27, and esp. 736–62 for the illustrations and diagrams of the mechanics and design of the machinery of *Salmacida Spolia.*

100. Marin, *Portrait of the King,* esp. 168–79. The "absolute power" of the absolute monarch, according to Marin, is itself represented in the geometrically perfect representation of the king's city, Paris, in the map by Gomboust, his engineer. The king's view is total, and totalizing: "*Veritas index sui:* the representation represents itself by offering the marks of its truth. There is no need to seek others, and these marks of truth and of the power of truth are indissolubly those of the truth of power—that is, of all-powerful truth and absolute power. Thus representation according to the *true order* has for effect a *power without limits, that of the absolute monarch.* Thus, inversely, the glory and liberality of the king, as well as his wisdom and omniscience according to political truth, have for effect a faithful and exact representation that is absolute because absolutely *subjugated,* in each of its points and each of its lines, to its principle, which is the prince" (175).

Marin's analysis of absolutism and representation echoes with Hobbesian themes (*Portrait of the King,* 7, and his discussion of fables and the state of nature in *Food for Thought*). The relationship to Hobbes, however, is not fully explored, and is certainly made that much more complicated by the fact that Hobbes attacks the figure that is at heart of all of Marin's analysis, the Eucharist. For Marin, the totalizing power of the absolute sovereign is measured against the speech act of Christ, "This is my body." He draws his analyses from the defense of the Catholic reading of the Eucharist from the Port Royal logicians' defense against the Calvinists. Hobbes was an absolutist par excellence, and yet he was a merciless critic of the Eucharist. As we shall see, Hobbes represents a subtle but monumental shift in the appropriation of divinity in the legitimation of sovereignty.

101. This kind of design is informatively contrasted with the more republican theater design of Jones's Italian predecessors, Andrea Palladio and Vincenzo Scamozzi, for the Teatro Olimpico. Orgel, *Illusion of Power,* 11–15.

102. Sharpe, *Criticism and Compliment,* 180.

103. For a discussion of differences between masques commissioned by Charles I and those commissioned by Henrietta Maria, see Sharpe, *Criticism and Compliment,* esp. 257.

104. Jones's seating plans are preserved from a play privately performed for Charles I, *Florimène.* Orgel, *Illusion of Power,* 26–36.

105. Orgel, *Illusion of Power,* 39. Professional actors were also a part of the court masque. They took the speaking roles. Decorum dictated that nobles could dance but not speak on stage. They could not risk the social pollution of being mistaken for stage-players. Henrietta Maria, however, was accustomed to French entertainments; in these nobles took speaking parts. She did take speaking parts in the masques. Charles I was particularly defensive about this practice. See Sharpe, *Criticism and Compliment,* and in particular, the analysis of the circumstances surrounding the *Triumph of Peace.*

106. Orgel, *Illusion of Power,* 9.

107. Ronald Knowles, "Introduction," in Ogilby, *The Entertainment of His Most Excellent Majestie*, 18, on the use of archways in Charles II's royal procession.

108. Marin, *Portrait of the King*, on the doubleness of representation. By walking on stage, the sovereign represents himself in the act of representation.

109. See Sharpe, *Criticism and Compliment*, 186–89. There is a danger in generalizing here. There is a tension between the masque's didactic and celebratory functions. These tensions are manifest, for example, in the contemporary readings and contemporaneous receptions of James Shirley and Inigo Jones's masque, *The Triumph of Peace*. This masque was created for Charles, ostensibly as an apology by the Inns of Court, following the publication of *Histrio-Mastix, or the Scourge of Players*, by William Prynne, a member of Lincoln's Inn. The performance certainly contradicts the critical spirit of Prynne's attack on the stage, but it also incorporated subtle criticism of the insularity of the monarch's entertainments. See the readings of Orgel, *Illusion of Power*, 43–44, 77–85; Sharpe, *Criticism and Compliment*, 214–23; and Venuti, *Our Halcyon Dayes*, 165–211.

110. Orgel, "Introduction" to *The Tempest*; Orgel, *Illusion of Power*.

111. Orgel and Strong, *Inigo Jones*, 660–785.

112. How far could one go in offering counsel? Could one risk offending the Crown? This question has been intelligently addressed in Sharpe, *Criticism and Compliment*, esp. 256–64; in Marcus, *Politics of Mirth*; and especially in Butler, "Ben Jonson and the Limits of Courtly Panegyric," 91–115.

113. The entrance of such a character representing the disruptive forces of the antimasque can be found in Thomas Carew and Inigo Jones's *Coelum Britannicum* (1634), in Orgel and Strong, *Inigo Jones*, 567–97. He introduces himself: "My name is Momus-ap-Sommos-ap-Erebus-ap-Chaos-ap-Demagorgon-ap-Eternity. My offices and titles are the Supreme Theomastix, Hypercritic of Manners, Protonotary of Abuses, Arch-informer, Dilator General, Universal Calumniator, Eternal Plaintiff, and Perpetual Foreman of the Grand Inquest. My privileges are an ubiquitary, circumambulatory, speculatory, interrogatory, redargutory, immunity over all the privy lodgings, behind hangings, doors, curtains, through keyholes, chinks, windows, about all venereal lobbies, . . . in and at all courts of civil and criminal judicature, all councils, consultations and parliamentary assemblies" (ll. 133–46).

114. Ben Jonson, *The Golden Age Restored*, ll. 39–47, in *CM*, 224–32.

115. Ibid., esp. 215. Before Jove's triumph is announced, however, Pallas has to coax "Astraea, goddess of Justice" (and a figure often linked with Elizabeth) and "Golden Age" to come down from heaven and dwell with mortals. James here then receives the blessing of the deceased Elizabeth. See Butler and Lindley, "Restoring Astraea," 807–27.

116. For reflections on the movement of the masque away from mere dance and its eventual integration with the theatrical and literary elements of drama, see Orgel, *Jonsonian Masque*, 147–85.

117. To say that masques mirrored these challenges to the monarch's rule, therefore, would be wrong. This is so for two, related reasons: first, the masque maker might claim to show the real truth behind the disturbance, instead of its appearance; second, this claim to show the disturbance as it really was could be quite a distortion itself. See, for example, the analysis by Lindley, "Embarrassing Ben," 343–59. See also Venuti, *Our Halcyon Dayes*, 165–211.

118. Orgel, *Illusion of Power*, 43; Marcus, *Politics of Mirth*; Sharpe, *Criticism and Compliment*; Butler and Lindley, "Restoring Astraea"; Lindley, "Embarrassing Ben"; Venuti, *Our Halcyon Dayes*. Thus it was particularly instructive when the forces of disruption were allowed to remain a part of the masque, as Sharpe has noted.

119. *CM*, 75–106.

120. The four humors are melancholy, phlegm, blood, and choler. Physical and mental well-being, according to Galen, required that the four be balanced. The affections are joy, hope, dread, and sorrow. Here too, balance was the key to health.

121. *CM*, 97–104.

122. Ibid., 105–14.
123. See Jonson's note, in Orgel, "Introduction," in *CM*, 515–16. Cf. *Lev.*, 16.3.
124. *CM*, 115–19. On Jonson's source, Ripa's *Iconologia*, see Gordon, "*Hymenaei*" and "The Imagery of Ben Jonson's *Masques of Blackness* and *Beautie*."
125. These themes are particularly strong in James's address to (his first) Parliament, where marriage, union, and the sanctification of the unification of the kingdoms—the "inward Peace annext to my Person"—are stressed. See Stuart, *Political Writings*, 135. Referring to the two kingdoms, James said: "What God hath conioyned then, let no man separate. I am the Husband, and all the whole Isle is my lawfull Wife; I am the Head, and it is my Body; I am the Shepherd, and it is my flocke: I hope therefore no man will be so vnreasonable as to thinke that I that am a Christian King vnder the Gospel, should be a Polygamist and a husband to two wiues; that I being the Head, should have a diuided and monstrous Body." Ibid., 136.
126. On the marriage themes in *Hymenaei*, see Gordon, "*Hymenaei*"; Lindley, "Embarrassing Ben"; and Loughlin, "'Love's Friend and Stranger to Virginitie,'" 833–49.
127. On James's status as a political philosopher, see Sommerville's introduction to Stuart, *Political Writings*, xv–xxviii. I have discussed Charles I's attempts to associate himself with mathematical learning, but on his larger efforts to portray himself in the royal propaganda as a philosopher-king, see Sharpe, *Personal Rule*, 179–274. To be sure, Charles I was not trying to be the same philosopher-king as his father. James wished to be known for his arguments, Charles for the images and practices of a morally well ordered life and court. Sharpe dwells on these differences, arguing that Charles I's Neoplatonist rectitude defined itself against the lascivious and slovenly practices of the Jacobean court. Both, however, made use of Neoplatonic thought: Charles I was less determined to argue from it than to live according to it, and to have others follow his example. Hence, the increased importance of symbolism and ceremony at his court.
128. *CM*, 80, ll. 120–23.
129. Ibid., 84, ll. 245–49.
130. Gordon, "Poet and Architect"; Gordon, "*Hymenaei*."
131. *CM*, 86, ll. 286–97.
132. For an interpretation that also connects Hobbes to poetic traditions, although argued through a very different framework, see Prokhovnik, *Rhetoric and Philosophy in Hobbes's Leviathan*.
133. *Lev.*, 16.5, 13–15; *Lev.*, 17.13; *Lev.*, 18.1.
134. Strong, "How to Write Scripture," 128–59.
135. *Lev.*, "Introduction," 4.
136. *Lev.*, 21.21; *Lev.*, 29.15, 23; *Lev.*, 42.125.
137. Sharpe, *Criticism and Compliment*, 181 n. 6. Rumors spread by Hobbes's enemy John Dowel that Cromwell had read *Leviathan* and wished to reward him for it are unsubstantiated. See Rogow, *Thomas Hobbes*, 155 n. 7.
138. See Rogow, *Thomas Hobbes*, 153–55, and Clarendon, *Brief View*, 8–9. In his *Verse Autobiography* Hobbes writes of the events following the death of Charles I. He refers to Charles II:

> King Charles at Paris who did then reside,
> Had right to England's Scepter undenied.
> A rebel rout the kingdom kept in awe,
> And ruled the giddy rabble without law,
> Who boldly Parliament themselves did call,
> Thought but a poor handful of men in all.
> Blood-thirsty leeches, hating all that's good,
> Gutted with innocent and noble blood.
> . . . .
> Hence many scholars to the King did go,
> Expelled, Sad, indigent, burthensome too.
> As yet my studies undisturbed were,

> And my grand climacteric past one year.
> When that book [*Leviathan*] was perused by knowing men,
> The gates of Janus temple opened them;
> And they accused me to the King, that I
> Seemed to approve Cromwell's impiety,
> And countenance the worst of wickedness:
> This was believed, and I appeared no less
> Than a grand enemy, so that I was for't
> Banished both the King's presence and his court.
>
> . . . .
>
> Then I came home, not sure of safety there,
> Though I could not be safer anywhere.
>
> . . . .
>
> At London, lest I should appear a spy,
> Unto the state myself I did apply;
>
> (ll. 217–52)

139. *Lev.*, 17.13–14.

140. *Lev.*, 13.11. Although Hobbes insists that a war of "every man against every man" exists in America, and between nations (13.12), he concedes in the English edition of *Leviathan* that the grand anthropological connotations do not correspond to matters of historical fact. That is, he does not hold that there was a prehistoric state when all were truly against all. In the Latin edition, however, Hobbes flirts with the idea that it might be true and offers the example of Cain and Abel: "He would not have dared it if there had at that time been a common power which could have punished him." See Curley's note 7 in *Leviathan*. In my view, the state of nature is best read in an allegorical (or masque-like) light. It was a way for Hobbes to articulate to his contemporaries all that was threatening in their conduct before and during the Civil War, and a way to make clear that his doctrine could, with sovereign sanction and power, produce a world without these troubles.

141. Thus, according to Hobbes, when the sovereign can no longer protect the subjects, the soul has left the body politic: "For the right men have by nature to protect themselves, when none else can protect them, can by no covenant be relinquished. The sovereignty is the soul of the commonwealth, which, once departed from the body, the members do no more receive their motion from it. The end of obedience is protection, which, wheresoever a man seeth it, either in his own or in another's sword, nature applieth his obedience to it, and his endeavor to maintain it." *Lev.*, 21.21. It is noteworthy that in Hobbes's treatment of man it is not souls, but the interactions of sense, our desires, and our aversions, which account for voluntary bodily motions. *Lev.*, chap. 6. That Hobbes finds himself returning to the visions of an animate soul suggests how strong a grip the old framework still had on his thoughts about the newly autonomous "body politic."

142. *Leviathan* was published in 1651. By May 1650 he was up to chapter 37. *The Author's Preface to His Much Honor'd Friend, M. Hobbes*, was published by Davenant, without his poem, *Gondibert*, but with "The Answer of Mr. Hobbes to Sir Will. D'Avanant's Preface Before Gondibert," signed January 10, 1650. (Editions that included the first book of the poem were published in 1651.) Davenant notes that Hobbes has given the poem "a daylie examination as it was writing." Davenant, *Gondibert*, 3. For Davenant's masques with Jonson, with illustrations, see Orgel and Strong, *Inigo Jones*. For the text of all of his masques and plays, see *The Dramatic Works of Sir William Davenant*.

143. Goldie, "The Reception of Hobbes."

144. See Robert Filmer's *Observations Concerning the Originall of Government, upon Mr Hobs "Leviathan," Mr Milton against Salmasias, H. Grotius "De Jure Belli,"* in Filmer, *Patriarchia and Other Works*. On Royalist opposition to Hobbes's use of consent, the insistence on divine sanction, and

the revolutionary claim to strip the Crown of its power based on consent, see Skinner, "Hobbes and the Purely Artificial Person of the State." On the connection made between the individual right of self-preservation and the collective right of Parliament as the people's representative, see Sommerville, *Thomas Hobbes*, 33–37, 51–52, and 59–63.

145. Goldie, "The Reception of Hobbes."

146. King James VI and I Stuart, *Basilicon Doron*, in Stuart, *Political Writings*, for example, 1–2 ("The Argument"), 12–13, 20, 24, 32, 37. 59–61; King James VI and I Stuart, *The Trew Law of Free Monarchies; or, The Reciprock and Mutual Duetie Betwext A Free King, And His naturall Subiects* (1616), in Stuart, *Political Writings*.

147. *Lev.*, 12.13. It was not just men; women, birds, crocodiles, and leeks were also deified. They "filled almost all places with spirits called *demons:* the plains, with *Pan* and *Panisies*, or Satyres; the woods, with Fawns and Nymphs," filled hell with Furies, Charon, and Cerebus, and built temples to "mere accidents and qualities, such as are time, night, day, peace, concord, love, contention, virtue, honour, health, rust, fever, and the like." *Lev.*, 12.16.

148. Ibid., 17.

149. Ibid., 20.

150. In fact, for a mathematician of his day, Hobbes is remarkably quiet concerning the study of harmony. He makes a brief reference to Galileo's observations on harmony in *EL*, 1.8.2.

151. Sharpe, *Personal Rule*, 182.

152. The frontispiece can even be interpreted in this light, the crosier and the sword in the hands of the Leviathan each forming the arm of a compass held by the mortal god who plots the square and even streets of the walled city pictured beneath him.

Chapter 9

1. On the logic of gift-exchange, see Mauss, *The Gift*. See Biagioli, *Galileo, Courtier*, for an important discussion of gift-exchange in early modern scientific, as well as absolutist, contexts.

2. Clarendon, *Brief View*. The Commonwealth's news sheet, *Mercurius politicus*, records: "They write also from Paris, that M. Hobbs (he that wrote the Book of *Common-wealth*) sent one of his Books as a Present to the King of Scots, which he accepted, . . . but being afterward informed by some of his Priests, that that Book did not only contain many Principles of Atheism and grosse Impiety (for so they call every thing that squares not with their corrupt Clergy-Interest[)] . . . and reflected dangerously upon the Majesty of Sovereign Princes, therefore when M. Hobbs came to make a tender of his service to him in person, he was rejected . . . the King would not admit him, . . . by which means M. Hobbs declines in credit with his friends there of the Royal stamp." *Mercurius politicus* 84 (January 8–15, 1652): 1344.

Hobbes's verse biography mentions "knowing men" who accused him to the king of approving of "Cromwell impiety," and "countenance[ing] the worst of wickedness." He speaks of the "gates of Janus Temple" opening the pages of *Leviathan*. A temple to Janus, the two-faced god, had two doors, which were opened in ancient Rome during times of war. Hobbes here delivers a double message concerning his view of his accusers, and their hostile intents. He claims not to blame the king for following those "intrusted with his government." Hobbes, *Verse Autobiography*, ll. 234–46. Richard Tuck, whose edition of *Leviathan* reproduces the presentation manuscript's frontispiece, suggests that Clarendon's own criticism was most influential, and puts the date of Hobbes's presentation of the manuscript to Charles II in November or December of 1651; see Tuck, "Note on the Text."

3. "A Discourse upon the Beginning of Tacitus," in Hobbes, *Three Discourses*, 51–52; *Lev.*, 11.7; *Lev.*, 14.12; *Lev.*, 14.15; *Lev.*, 42.63; MacPherson, *Political Theory of Possessive Individualism*.

4. Mauss, *The Gift*; Biagioli, *Galileo, Courtier*.

5. *Lev.*, 11.7.

6. Ibid.

7. *Lev.*, "A Review and Conclusion," 16.

8. Clarendon, *Brief View*, 8.

9. Ibid., 8–9; Hobbes, *Verse Autobiography*, ll. 217–52. Hobbes speaks of the king being persuaded by persons surrounding him at the time. Clarendon states that Hobbes was forced to flee the court before his own arrival, but suggests that he had in fact criticized *Leviathan* to Charles.

10. See note 2.

11. He was tutoring Edmund Waller's son. See Thomas Hobbes to Edmund Waller, July 29/August 8, 1645, Letter 39, in Malcolm, *Correspondence of Thomas Hobbes*, 1:124–25. On Hobbes's relationship with Davenant, see Chapter 7 and my "Uniqueness of *Leviathan*."

12. *EL*, 1.10.4. Judgment and "fancy" (itself a faculty necessary but not sufficient for sound poets) are the marks of a person with "wit": the capacity to find among things uncommonly detected similarities and distinctions (the opposite of which Hobbes defines as the characteristic of "dull" persons). See also *Lev.*, 8.1–10, although here Hobbes allows that one may be a wit on the basis of judgment alone. Understood as faculties, Hobbes always allowed for their cooperation in able persons. Skinner, *Reason and Rhetoric*, 365–75, takes a different view of fancy and judgment's relations over the course of Hobbes's works.

13. *Lev.*, 25.9. The immediate contrast to this way of sweetening commands is exhortation and dehortation in the giving of counsel, which is to Hobbes a sign of a councilor who is thinking of his own interests, rather than the good of the sovereign. Cf. *Lev.*, 25.6. Skinner, in my view, misreads paragraph 9 in that he associates the commander's sweetened language with giving orders that "can be taken not as acts of commanding but rather of counselling and offering advice." See Skinner, *Reason and Rhetoric*, 359. It is true that the bitter pill of a command difficult to accept may be sweetened, but Hobbes is adamant in chapter 25 that counsel and command remain logically distinct. Were commands viewed as mere counsel, they would give the false impression of being optional, a thing Hobbes was keen to avoid (*Lev.*, 25.4). Viewed, however, as a gesture toward the unity of selves between sovereign and subject, this passage suggests that the sweetening effect of the commander's eloquence is to imply that what is in your interest (as sovereign) is in my interests as subject.

14. Wolin, *Hobbes and the Epic Tradition of Political Theory*, 3–11. Wolin also emphasizes the role of education in bringing Hobbes's plans to fruition. Ibid., 45–49. Wolin reaffirms his views of Hobbes in Wolin, *Tocqueville Between Two Worlds*, esp. 22–33, 45–49.

15. Strauss, *Political Philosophy of Hobbes;* Strauss, "Notes on Carl Schmitt."

16. James, *Life of Reason;* Jacobson, *Pride and Solace*, 51–92.

17. Schmitt, *Political Theology*, esp. 33–52; Schmitt, *Concept of the Political*, esp. 65–67; Schmitt, *The Leviathan in the State Theory*.

18. Wolin, *Hobbes and the Epic Tradition of Political Theory*, 13–15, 30–35, 38. Wolin writes: "One cannot help wondering whether Hobbes was a faithful Hobbist or, more precisely, whether Hobbes the [epic] theorist and Hobbes the methodist followed the same precepts." Ibid., 32. Wolin, *Tocqueville Between Two Worlds*, 46–47. I hope I have shown that what Wolin describes as Hobbes's epic qualities and his claim to superior, mathematical methods were driven by the same precepts.

19. White, *Sustaining Affirmation;* Connolly, *Ethos of Pluralization*. Both refer to Heidegger's influence.

20. Connolly, *Ethos of Pluralization*, 2.

21. Ibid., esp. 4.

22. The important exception is Brandt, *Thomas Hobbes' Mechanical Conception of Nature*. Hoping to find a practitioner of the New Science as it had been idealized, his admirably close reading of Hobbes leads him to acknowledge how and why his expectations were disappointed.

23. Foucault, "What Is an Author?," in *Language, Counter-Memory, Practice*, 113–38.

24. This is a political ethos "in which alternative perspectives support space for each other to exist through the agonistic respect they practice toward one another. In a world where a plurality

of ontopolitical perspectives is credible, perhaps it is ethically laudable for the proponents of alternative perspectives to reconsider the ethics of engagement between contending constituencies. Maybe the drive to knockdown argument in ontopolitical interpretation is a corollary to the drive to fundamentalism in political life." Connolly, *Ethos of Pluralization*, 16.

25. Ibid., 105–6.

26. It was the later natural law thinkers, those who wished to reclaim moral and political knowledge rooted in strong foundational claims, who had to disavow Hobbes. A notable example is Cumberland, *De Legibus Naturae*.

27. This, it seems to me, is what Michael Ryan claims to be doing in his now famous deconstruction of Hobbes in *Marxism and Deconstruction*, 1–8. Hobbes is not "masking" the arbitrary power of the "conservative liberal" political philosophy. This is not because he is not arbitrary (although it may also be because he is not liberal), but because he has no desire to mask his use of arbitrary power.

28. In contemporary debates one may either be political or metaphysical, but seemingly not both. See Rawls, "Justice as Fairness," and "Lecture One," although cf. "Lecture One," 29 n. 31, wherein Rawls allows that some metaphysical views "not relevant" to his political concept may be involved. With his first philosophy, Hobbes was like his Aristotelian predecessors and contemporaries in this regard. The assertion of a metaphysics was part and parcel of being political. Hobbes is particularly clear that one must simply accept the claims of his first philosophy if one is to proceed further within his system. These assertions are not, therefore, put forward as hypothetical claims waiting for potential falsification. Mintz, *The Hunting of Leviathan*, 67. See esp. *De Corpore*, 4.1.

29. Toulmin, *Cosmopolis*.

30. Cited in ibid., 66.

31. Ibid., 69–70.

32. *De Cive*, 13.1. Here the language of first mover (and ordinary and extraordinary divine powers) enters into Hobbes's distinction between the right and exercise of the sovereign's power. He specifically compares the sovereign's use of delegated authority to the control of God as first mover over the universe through an ordinary course (implemented through secondary causes), and the sovereign's right to intervene and involve himself in any particular matter to the exercise of God's extraordinary powers.

33. Hobbes, "A Discourse upon the Beginnings of Tacitus," in Hobbes, *Three Discourses*, 59–60.

34. Morrill and Walter, "Order and Disorder in the English Revolution," 137.

35. Reprinted in Hobbes, *De Cive: The English Version*, plate 4. On Royston, see Potter, *Secret Rites and Secret Writing*, esp. 165–67 (where the image is also reproduced), and Goldsmith, "Picturing Hobbes's Politics?," 232–37.

36. Charles I, *Eikon Basilike*; on Gauden's role, see Potter, *Secret Rites and Secret Writing*, 170–84. Potter nicely illustrates how the polemical antitheatrical rhetoric (see my Chapter 5) informed both the critics (who emphasized that an imposter had written the book for Charles I) and Royalist defenders of this text.

37. For example: "I would rather chuse to ware a Crown of Thornes with My Saviour, then to exchange that of Gold (which is due to Me) for one of lead, whose embased flexiblenesse shall be forced to bend, and comply to the various, and oft contrary dictates of any Factions; when instead of Reason, and Publick concernments, they obtrude nothing but what makes for the interest of parties, and flowes from the partialities of private wills and passions." Charles I, *Eikon Basilike*, 38. "My Enemies (being more solemnly cruell) will, it may be, seeke to adde (as those did, who Crucified Christ) the mockery of Justice, to the cruelty of Malice: That I may be destroyed, as with greater pomp and artifice, so with less pity, it will be but a necessary policy to make My death appeare as an act of Justice." Ibid., 256.

38. Ibid., 17, 18.

39. Ibid., 19–20.

40. Ogilby, *The Entertainment of His Most Excellent Majestie;* Knowles, "Introduction," in Ogilby, *The Entertainment of His Most Excellent Majestie,* 18.

41. *Lev.,* 29.14.

42. Ibid., 8.21.

43. Ibid., 29.1. The poet and royalist Thomas Shipman praised Hobbes in a letter to him near the end of Hobbes's life by comparing the greatness of his patron's home, Hardwick Hall, to himself and to *Leviathan:* "I have seen 2 mighty Wonders—Mr. Hobs & Hardwic . . . The Marbles must yield to that durableness of Name wil giue it . . . Tho' Empires haue their fatal periods Yet I look upon this Palace & that other (His Leviathan) as the mightyst & lastingst Structures yt any Age has rays'd." Thomas Shipman to Thomas Hobbes, September 1678, Letter 203, in Malcolm, *Correspondence,* 2:768. The "Marbles" may be a reference to the exceptionally ornate plasterwork in Hardwick Hall's Great High Chamber.

44. Eachard, *Some Opinions of Mr. Hobbs Considered.*

45. Cowley, *Pindarique* ODES, 26.

46. *The True Effigies of the Monster of Malmesbury,* 4, 7–8. On the reception of Hobbes, see Goldie, "The Reception of Hobbes." Historians today find themselves divided over how to understand the reaction to claims concerning the scope and justification for monarchical sovereignty. Some recent and important treatments include Wootton, "Introduction"; Sommerville, *Politics and Ideology in England* and *Thomas Hobbes;* Tuck, *Philosophy and Government;* and Burgess, "On Hobbesian Resistance Theory" and *Absolute Monarchy and the Stuart Constitution.*

47. Rorty, *Philosophy and the Mirror of Nature,* 5; Bernstein uses the phrase "Cartesian Anxiety" in *Beyond Objectivism and Relativism.*

48. Connolly, *Ethos of Pluralization,* 136–37.

49. Ricoeur, "Political Paradox." Although Schmitt's defense of the autonomy of "the political" in *The Concept of the Political* goes unmentioned in Ricoeur's piece, we can think of it as a Schmittian perspective thrown into moral reverse. Like Schmitt, Ricoeur argues for the autonomy of the political. Implicitly against the Schmittian perspective, he appeals to his readers to resist exercising the very kind of violent and arbitrary political decisions that Schmitt trumpets as his cause in his fight against depoliticization or neutralization. From the Schmittian point of view, Ricoeur's insistence that there is political *evil* is a failure to preserve the autonomy of politics that Ricoeur professes.

50. Ricoeur, "Political Paradox," 252.

51. Rousseau, *On the Social Contract,* 69.

52. Connolly, *Ethos of Pluralization,* 138.

53. Ibid.

54. Durkheim brings things full circle. He delivers his positivist *bon mot* in the course of a refutation of a received view concerning the origins of religion. Although he goes unmentioned, Hobbes could have been the source; see *Lev.,* chap. 12. Durkheim rejects the view that attributes the origins of religion to the search for explanations. The supernatural, Durkheim notes, is a concept that must be preceded by the relatively recent view of the universe as ordinarily governed by natural laws, a universal determinism. Durkheim then condemns those in the social sciences who are only just becoming accustomed to believing in their subject's law-like behavior: "It follows that veritable miracles are believed to be possible there [in the deficient social sciences]. It is admitted, for example, that a legislator can create an institution out of nothing by a mere injunction of its will, or transform one social system into another, just as believers in so many religions have held that the divine will created the world out of nothing, or can arbitrarily transmute one thing into another." Those who know of "social facts" know better than these "primitives." Durkheim, *Elementary Forms of Religious Life,* 41–42.

55. Perhaps because political evil must show itself to be a problem in even the most admirable formulation of the social contract, Ricoeur all but names Hobbes as the exemplar he will not consider (rather than Rousseau). Ricoeur, "Political Paradox," 251–52. He does consider Machiavelli (see 257–58), but, it seems, as a stand-in for Schmitt's friend/enemy distinction, and

as evidence of the "implacable logic of political action." Machiavelli is proof that we cannot resolve the political paradox, but he might have been more fully considered—as might have Hobbes—as evidence of another danger: a potential indifference to this paradox among those who are not unaware of it.

Appendix

1. For many years, what was typically said about the conflict was that it was nasty and vindictive (it was), and that Hobbes was on the losing side. That has now changed. Historians of mathematics and of science have linked the conflict with Hobbes's struggles with the Royal Society. It has been connected to the *Quaestio* debate (discussed in Chapter 5), and to other key mathematical debates of the seventeenth century. See Robertson, *Hobbes*; Schaffer, "Wallification"; Mancosu, *Philosophy of Mathematics* and "Aristotelian Logic and Euclidean Mathematics"; Grant, "Hobbes and Mathematics"; Jesseph, "Of Analytics and Indivisibles" and "Hobbes and Mathematical Method"; and Pycior, "Mathematics and Philosophy."

2. Jesseph, *Squaring the Circle*, esp. 293–339.
3. Scott, *Mathematical Work of John Wallis*, 133–65.
4. Jesseph, "Hobbes and Mathematical Method."
5. Descartes, *La Geometrie*, 2–5.
6. This view of its purpose was put forward by its Renaissance promoter, François Viète (1540–1603). On this, see Grant, "Hobbes and Mathematics," 108–28, esp. 114–17, and Scott, *History of Mathematics*, 105–19, esp. 109–15.
7. Jesseph also makes this point in "Hobbes and Mathematical Method" and "Of Analytics and Indivisibles."
8. *Elements of Philosophy*, pt. 3, chap. 20, sec. 6, in *EW*, 1:309–17.
9. Criticisms of Descartes for being nothing more than an analyst rather than one who could produce a priori demonstrations are, as David Lachterman has argued, merely the tip of the iceberg. Lachterman's brilliant work highlights the important fact that Descartes vehemently opposed such criticism. One of Descartes's coups was to argue that his analytic method was in fact the beginning of a process that could provide a priori demonstrations through the reconstruction of figures. In light of Lachterman's analysis of both Euclidean geometry and the important deviations from Euclid's didactic goals, Hobbes's remark demoting analytic geometry to a kind of prudence is particularly ironic. Lachterman argues that Euclidean geometry did in fact accord with standards of prudence, prudence designed to aid the student in coming to know the geometrical figures already known to him (Lachterman connects Euclidean with Platonic teaching styles). With the introduction of radicals such as Descartes, however, he argues that prudence fell out of geometry, and gave way to a constructive agenda. Lachterman's work illustrates, furthermore, that topics of creation, and the human imitation of God, are productive topics for the consideration of Descartes's work as well. Lachterman, *Ethics of Geometry*, see esp. 148–61 concerning analysis, synthesis, and a priori proofs. Shapin, *Scientific Revolution*, 158 n. 7. On this subject, see also Mancosu, *Philosophy of Mathematics*, 83–84.
10. *Six Lessons*, lesson 5, in *EW*, 7:329. Oughtred describes the analytic method in Oughtred, *Mr. William Oughtred's Key* (*Clavis Mathematicae*), chap. 1, sec. 14.
11. It should be noted that Hobbes could not have consistently opposed the use of symbols or marks *tout court*. Names, after all, were marks in his philosophy, and it is only with the help of these that we become capable of science. (See, for example, *EL*, 1.5.1–4.) Hobbes's objection, rather, was that the system of symbols used by the algebraic practitioners further removed the names we used from the matter that begat the phantasm in our mind. See Pycior, "Mathematics and Philosophy."
12. *Elements of Philosophy*, pt. 3, chap. 20, sec. 6, in *EW*, 1:309–17. See, for example, 316, where he writes: "But what! are the ancient geometricians to be blamed, who made use of the quadratrix for the finding out of a strait line equal to the arch of a circle? And Pappus himself,

was he faulty, when he found out the trisection of an angle by the help of an hyperbole? Or am I in the wrong, who think I have found out the construction of both these problems by the rule and compass only? Neither they, nor I. For the ancients made use of this analysis which proceeds by the powers; and with them it was a fault to do that by a more remote power, which might be done by a nearer; as being an argument that they did not sufficiently understand the nature of the thing."

He begins with a defense of his botched attempts at squaring the circle. He is suggesting that he is no more blameworthy than his ancient counterparts (or Pappus), who also used traditional geometrical methods in their attempts to square the circle or trisect an angle. By "powers" he means the use of roots. In other words, methods of algebraic reasoning were available to the ancients, but they chose not to use these "remote powers" when they might be "done by nearer," that is to say, "rule and compass only." On squaring the circle, see Grant, "Hobbes and Mathematics"; Pycior, "Mathematics and Philosophy"; and Robertson, *Hobbes*, esp. 104–5.

13. *Six Lessons*, lesson 5, in *EW*, 7:329.

14. Jesseph, "Hobbes and Mathematical Method"; Jesseph, "Of Analytics and Indivisibles"; Pycior, "Mathematics and Philosophy"; Grant, "Hobbes and Mathematics"; Brandt, *Thomas Hobbes' Mechanical Conception of Nature*, 213–16.

15. Barrow, furthermore, criticized Hobbes. See Mahoney, "Barrow's Mathematics."

16. This puts Hobbes in a paradoxical position when our point of departure is Aristotle's rule against metabasis. Because each science has its own set of first principles, one is cautioned against trying to export inferences — or inferential styles — from one science to the next. Most notably, one should not try to export the methods of mathematics to politics (*Nicomachean Ethics*, bk. 6). Hobbes's idealized geometry becomes the basis for a gross violation of the rule against metabasis. He devises a science that is meant to supersede the major Aristotelian divisions, including Aristotle's division between productive arts (*techne*), contemplative philosophy (*episteme*), and political thought (*praxis*). On the other hand, Hobbes and Barrow protest loudly when the analytic geometricians import the tools of arithmetic into geometry. For an interesting discussion of this subject in Euclid, Descartes, and modern thinkers in general, see Lachterman, *Ethics of Geometry*. On metabasis, see Funkenstein, *Theology and the Scientific Imagination*.

17. *De Corpore*, 6.13–17; *Six Lessons*, lesson 2, in *EW*, 7:211–13.

18. *Six Lessons*, lesson 1, in *EW*, 7:202.

19. Ibid.

20. Hobbes was particularly concerned when Euclid seemed to risk, in his definitions, violations of his metaphysics. Take Hobbes's considerations of Euclid's definition of a point in the *Six Lessons*, lesson 1, in *EW*, 7:200–202, for example. Hobbes translates it, "a mark is that of which there is no part." but it could also be translated as suggesting that a point or mark is "indivisible." This worried Hobbes because that which is indivisible "is no quantity; and if a point be not quantity, seeing it is neither substance nor quality, it is nothing." This is not, according to Hobbes, what Euclid meant, but it is what some of his less candid interpreters (namely, Hobbes's opponent John Wallis) maintained. Were a point nothing, were it to lack all quantity, it would fit into the same category as the soul or angels according to many theologians — incorporeal entities. Hobbes's doctrine dictated that all was matter; he rejected extramaterial entities as philosophical absurdity and the treachery of the Kingdom of Darkness — seditious religious doctrines that conjured up threatening spirits in order to lull citizens into acts of disobedience. Extended criticism and analysis of Euclid can be found in *Six Lessons*, lesson 1, in *EW*, 7:191–211, esp. 196–97, and 199–211; Hobbes, *De Principiis et Ratiocinatione Geometrarum*, in *OP*, vol. 4; and the second dialogue of *Examinatio et Emendatio Mathematicæ Hodiernæ*, in *OP*, 4:53–88.

21. *Six Lessons*, lesson 1, in *EW*, 7:214–15.

22. Ibid., 215.

23. *De Corpore*, 6.6; *Six Lessons*, lesson 1, in *EW*, 7:191. For some useful remarks on how Hobbes's incorporation of motion into geometry represents a blurring of the distinctions between statics and dynamics maintained in traditional physics and contradicts points of view

that have come subsequent to him, see Brandt, *Thomas Hobbes' Mechanical Conception of Nature*, 217–49.

24. Jesseph, "Of Analytics and Indivisibles"; Jesseph, "Hobbes and Mathematical Method."

25. Rogow, *Thomas Hobbes*, 200. The quotation is from Hobbes, *Considerations upon the Reputation*, in *EW*, 4:440.

26. Wallis, *Hobbiani puncti dispunctio*. Hobbes takes note of the remark in "An Extract of a Letter from Henry Stubb," in *EW*, 7:426.

27. See Hobbes, *Marks of the Absurd Geometry*, in *EW*, 7:386.

28. Hobbes's full title is *Six Lessons to the Professors of Mathematics, one of Geometry, the other of Astronomy in the Chairs set up by the Noble and Learned Sire Henry Savile, in the University of Oxford*.

29. The *Six Lessons* were more than just a response to the *Vindiciae;* Hobbes was also responding to the opportunistic attacks by Wallis on his own attempts to square the circle—attempts into which Hobbes had been goaded by Ward and Wilkins in the *Vindiciae*. See Chapter 7 herein. Jesseph, *Squaring the Circle*, 67–72.

30. Jesseph, *Squaring the Circle*, 341.

31. Ibid., 339. Jesseph's claim that neither side seemed to have suffered as a result of these accusations seems off the point. What they argued and why are questions we can distinguish from whether they achieved their full polemical intent.

32. "Language most shows a man: speak that I may see thee. It springs out of the most retired, and inmost parts of us, and is the image of the parent of it, the mind. No glass renders a man's form or likeness, so true as his speech." Jonson, *Discoveries*, ll. 2030–35, in *Ben Jonson*, 8:625.

33. *Six Lessons*, lesson 1, in *EW*, 7:191. Hobbes would go on to define geometry as "the science of determining the quantity of anything, not measured, by comparing it with some other quantity or quantities measured." Ibid. He also refers to the nuts and bolts of geometry as the business of determining the magnitudes of bodies, that is to say, the lengths of lines and the dimensions of planes and three-dimensional bodies. See ibid., 193: "The science of geometry, so far forth as it contemplateth bodies only, is no more but by measuring the length of one or more lines, by the position of others known in one and the same figure, to determine by ratiocination, how much is the superfices; and by measuring length, breadth, and thickness, to determine the quantity of the whole body." See also *Lev.*, 46.1.

34. For example, *Six Lessons*, lesson 2, in *EW*, 7:219: "To them therefore that deny a point to have quantity, that is, a line to have latitude, the forenamed principles are not possible, and consequently no proposition in geometry is demonstrated or demonstrable. You therefore that deny a point to have quantity, and a line to have breadth, have nothing at all of the science of geometry. The practice you may have, but so hath any man that hath learned the bare propositions by heart; but they are not fit to be professors either of geometry or of any other science that dependeth on it." Also see ibid., lesson 3, in *EW*, 7:220, 225, 238, and 242, which reads: "[You] pretend no less to natural philosophy than to geometry. . . . But you swim upon other men's bladders in the superfices of geometry, without being able to endure diving . . . I am the first that hath made the grounds of geometry firm and coherent." This plays, again, on the matter/spirit conflict.

35. Wallis, *Elenchus geometriae Hobbianae*.

36. *Six Lessons*, lesson 2, in *EW*, 7:213. See Shapin and Schaffer, *Leviathan and the Air-Pump*, and Shapin, *Social History of Truth*, on Hobbes's objection to the use of witnesses as a part of philosophical argument.

37. Perhaps this is why he felt compelled to add "and when your witnesses appear, they will not take your part." *Six Lessons*, lesson 2, in *EW*, 7:213.

38. Ibid., lesson 1, in *EW*, 7:204–5. For other examples, see 184, 200–202, and 203.

39. See ibid., 201, on the definition of a point (an argument that parallels Hobbes's argument against the nonsubstantive definitions), and ibid., lesson 4, in *EW*, 7:290–92, on the norms of criticism between geometricians. In most cases, Hobbes is concerned to show that Savile simply approved definitions that both he and Euclid's commentator Proclus approved, and to

point to the difference between these substantive definitions of points, lines, and figures and the nonsubstantive definitions adopted by Wallis and the algebraic camp.

40. Ibid., lesson 3, in *EW*, 7:237, 243.

41. Ibid., lesson 6, in *EW*, 7:349.

42. Hobbes, *Marks of the Absurd Geometry*, in *EW*, 7:379–80. See also *Six Lessons*, lesson 6, in *EW*, 7:349, and lesson 4, in *EW*, 7:281–82, where Hobbes comments on one element of his work where he and Wallis do not disagree: "[These] you say are sound. True. But never the more to be thought so for your approbation, but the less; because you are not fit, neither to reprehend, nor praise, and because all that you have hitherto condemned as false, hath been proved true. Then you show me how you could demonstrate the sixth and seventh articles a shorter way. But though there be your symbols, yet no man is obliged to take them for demonstration. And though they be granted to be dumb demonstrations, yet when they are taught to speak as they ought to do, they will be longer demonstrations than these of mine."

43. Warrender, *Political Philosophy of Hobbes*, 2:13–16. Hobbes returned to England at the end of 1651. Malcolm, "Summary Biography," 13–44.

44. See *EW*, 7:427, where Hobbes goads Wallis with this problem. Jesseph, *Squaring the Circle*, 334–35; Aubrey, "Brief Lives," 2:569; Wood, *Athenae Oxonienses*, 414–15; Stubbe, *The Savilian Professours Case Stated*.

45. *EW*, 7:401–28. While defending Hobbes, Wallis is consistently painted as an ill-lettered scholar incapable of matching Hobbes (or the author) on matters of language. It is also noteworthy that Stubbe is willing to associate Wallis's algebra with inarticulacy: "It is a pity the Doctor [Wallis] could not argue in symbols too, that so we might not understand him; but suppose all his papers to carry evidence with them, because they are *mathematically* scratched." Ibid., 409. Interestingly, Stubbe's criticism appears to have been encouraged by the Independent vice-chancellor at Oxford, John Owen. See Henry Stubbe to Thomas Hobbes, October 7/17, 1656; October 25/November 4, 1656; November 9/19, 1656; and November 29/December 9, 1656, Letters 91, 96, 97, 98, and 101, in Malcolm, *Correspondence*, 1:311–12, 333–41, and 378–79. Also see Jesseph, *Squaring the Circle*, 303–4.

46. Hutton, *Restoration*, 131.

47. Clearly a very large number of antagonistic remarks were published during his lifetime. Mintz, *The Hunting of Leviathan*, 157–59. For an interesting treatment of the norms of controversies, and what failure to respond to critics meant in Renaissance Italy, see Biagioli, *Galileo, Courtier*.

48. *EW*, vol. 4.

49. Seaward, *Cavalier Parliament*.

50. Jesseph, *Squaring the Circle*, 335–39. Jesseph notes that after the Restoration Wallis had his two positions affirmed by the Parliament and "was even admitted as one of the king's chaplains in ordinary and appointed in 1661 to the group of divines charged with revising the Book of Common Prayer." Ibid., 335. It is worth noting that there remained a ready audience for anti-Presbyterian writings. In fact, resolute Anglican bishops resisted the proposed changes to the Book of Common Prayer, rejecting concessions made to Presbyterians. As a result of this, when the Acts of Uniformity were imposed in 1662, hundreds of Presbyterians ministers were removed from their offices. Seaward, *Restoration*, 49. See also Chapter 7 herein.

51. *EL*, 1.13.3.

52. *Lev.*, 5.7. See also *Lev.*, 4.12 and 5.16, 18, 46, and 11.

53. Ibid., 8.27. Citing a few examples of scholastic language, all premised on the existence of incorporeal substances, Hobbes adds: "When men write whole volumes of such stuff, are they not mad, or intend to make others so? And particularly, in the question of transubstantiation; where after certain words spoken, they that say, the whiteness, roundness, magnitude, quality, corruptibility, all which are incorporeal, &c. go out of the wafer, into the body of our blessed Saviour, do they not make those nesses, tudes, and ties, to be so many spirits possessing his body? For by spirits, they mean always things, that being incorporeal, are nevertheless moveable

from one place to another. So that this kind of absurdity, may rightly be numbered amongst the many sorts of madness; and all the time that guided by clear thoughts of their worldly lust, they forbear disputing, or writing thus, but lucid intervals. And thus much of the virtues and defects intellectual." Ibid.

54. Hobbes, *Marks of the Absurd Geometry*, in *EW*, 7:386–87.

55. "To judge of poets is only the faculty of poets; and not of all poets, but the best." Jonson, *Discoveries*, ll. 2578–79, in *Ben Jonson*, 8:642.

56. Ibid., ll. 587–605, in *Ben Jonson*, 8:581–82.

57. Ibid., ll. 2346–820, in *Ben Jonson*, 8:635–49.

58. Ben Jonson, *Epigrams*, XLIX, in *Ben Jonson*, 8:42.

59. "The times was, when men would learne, and study good things; not envie those that had them . . . now letters only make men vile. Hee is upbraydingly called a *Poet*, as if it were a most contemptible Nick-name. But the *Professors* (indeed) have made the learning cheape. Rayling, and tinckling *Rimers*. . . . Hee shall not have a Reader now, unlesse he jeer and lye." Jonson, *Discoveries*, ll. 278–86, in *Ben Jonson*, 8:571.

60. Full title: *De Principiis et Ratiocinatione Geometrarum: ubi ostenditur incertitudinem falsitatemque non minorem inesse scriptis eorum quam scriptis physicorum et ethicorum. Contra Fastum professorum Geometriae.*

61. "Contra geometras, amice lector, non contra geometriam haec scribo. Artum ipsam, artuim navigandi, aedificandi, pingendi, computatndi, et denique (scientiae omnium nobilissimae) physicae matrem, aeque ac qui maxime laudibus extollendam censeo." *OP*, 4:389–90.

62. The attack on his former collaborator Inigo Jones is a case in point (see Chapter 8), but in the *Epigrams* Jonson flaunts his discerning and censorious eye. See esp. "To Alchemists" (VI), "On Something, that Walks Somewhere" (XI), "On Court-Worm" (XV), and "To Courtling" (LXXII).

63. The connection between this kind of suspicion and the practices of self-fashioning is best drawn in Whigham, *Ambition and Privilege*.

64. Burton, *Philosophaster*.

65. Ibid., 39.

66. Although I will not attempt to do so here, there are interesting and productive parallels between Hobbes and the various figures involved either in attempted reforms of language, or who attempted to fashion universal languages. These included Ben Jonson, Seth Ward, Comenius, and Mersenne. Particularly interesting points of comparison would include attitudes linking the corruption of speech and the corruption of learned professions (Comenius's *The Labyrinth of the World*), and debates over the possibility of rediscovering an Adamic language, or whether to impose norms on usage. On these subjects, see Padley, *The Latin Tradition* and *Trends in Vernacular Grammar;* Slaughter, *Universal Languages;* and Dear, *Mersenne*.

67. The argument could well extend to other philosophers. Although Descartes certainly was an accomplished algebraist, he fell short of his own promise to deliver a wholly mathematical natural philosophy. The *Principles of Philosophy* (*Principia*), in spite of asserting that the only acceptable principles of explanation in physics are those of geometry and pure mathematics, is not mathematics per se. His failure to deliver on this promise has prompted speculation on his capacity to apply his mathematics to physics. For a review of the issue and defense of his abilities on this count, see Garber, "A Different Descartes," 113–30. See Dear, *Discipline and Experience*, for another approach to the development of physico-mathematics.

BIBLIOGRAPHY

Ackerman, James S. "Rudolf Wittkower's Influence on the History of Architecture." *Source: Notes in the History of Art* 8, no. 9 (1989): 86–90.
Agamben, Giorgio. *Homo Sacer: Sovereign Power and Bare Life.* Translated by Daniel Heller-Roazen. Stanford: Stanford University Press, 1998.
———. *State of Exception.* Translated by Kevin Attell. Chicago: University of Chicago Press, 2005.
Agnew, Jean-Christophe. *Worlds Apart: The Market and the Theater in Anglo-American Thought, 1550–1750.* Cambridge: Cambridge University Press, 1986.
Alberti, Leone Battista. *Ten Books on Architecture.* Translated into Italian by Cosimo Bartoli and from Italian into English by James Leoni. 1755. Reprint. Edited by Joseph Rykwert. London: Alec Tiranti, 1955.
Aquinas. *See* Thomas Aquinas
Arendt, Hannah. *The Human Condition.* Chicago: University of Chicago Press, 1958.
Aristotle. *De Anima.* Translated by R. D. Hicks. Cambridge: Cambridge University Press, 1907.
———. *Metaphysics.* Translated by Richard Hope. Ann Arbor: University of Michigan Press, 1960.
———. *Nicomachean Ethics.* Translated by Martin Ostwald. Indianapolis: Bobbs-Merrill, 1962.
———. *The Politics.* Translated by Carnes Lord. Chicago: University of Chicago Press, 1984.
———. *Posterior Analytics.* Translated by Hugh Tredennick. Cambridge: Harvard University Press, 1960.
———. *Prior Analytics.* Translated by H. P. Cooke and Hugh Tredennick. Cambridge: Harvard University Press, 1938.
Aron, Raymond. *Main Currents in Sociological Thought.* Vol. 2. Translated by Richard Howard and Helen Weaver. Garden City, N.Y.: Doubleday, 1970.
Ascham, Roger. *The Scholemaster.* 1570. Reprint. Edited by John Mayor. London, 1863.
Ashcraft, Richard. "Hobbes's Natural Man: A Study in Ideology Formation." *Journal of Politics* 33 (1971): 1076–1171.
———. "Ideology and Class in Hobbes' Political Theory." *Political Theory* 6 (1978): 27–62.
Ashton, Robert. *Counter-Revolution: The Second Civil War and Its Origins, 1646–48.* New Haven: Yale University Press, 1994.
Aubrey, John. *Aubrey on Education.* Edited by J. E. Stephens. London: Routledge and Kegan Paul, 1972.
———. *"Brief Lives" Chiefly of Contemporaries, Set Down by Aubrey, Between the Years 1669 and 1696.* Edited by Andrew Clark. 2 vols. Oxford, 1898.
Augustine, Saint. *City of God.* Translated by Henry Bettenson. Harmondsworth, U.K.: Penguin, 1984.
Bacon, Francis. *The Works of Francis Bacon.* 15 vols. Edited by R. L. Ellis, J. Spedding, and D. D. Heath. London, 1887–92.
Ball, Terrence. "Hobbes's Linguistic Turn." *Polity* 17 (1985): 739–60.
Barber, Benjamin. *Strong Democracy: Participatory Politics for a New Age.* Berkeley and Los Angeles: University of California Press, 1984.
Barish, Jonas. *The Anti-Theatrical Prejudice.* Princeton: Princeton University Press, 1979.
———. *Ben Jonson and the Language of Prose Comedy.* Cambridge: Cambridge University Press, 1960.
Barker, William. "Introduction." In Richard Mulcaster, *Positions Concerning the Training Up of Children,* edited by William Barker. Toronto: University of Toronto Press, 1994.

Barnouw, Jeffrey. "Hobbes's Causal Account of Sensation." *Journal of the History of Philosophy* 17 (1980): 115–30.

———. "Hobbes's Psychology of Thought: Endeavours, Purpose, and Curiosity." *History of European Ideas* 10, no. 5 (1989): 519–45.

Baron, Hans. *Crisis of the Early Italian Renaissance*. Princeton: Princeton University Press, 1966.

Barton, Anne. *Ben Jonson: Dramatist*. Cambridge: Cambridge University Press, 1984.

Bauman, Zygmunt. "Seeking in Modern Athens an Answer to the Ancient Jerusalem Question." In *Man and His Enemies: Essays on Carl Schmitt*, edited by Svetozar Minkov and Piotr Nowak, 211–33. Białystok: Wydawnictwo Uniwersitetu w. Białymstoku, 2008.

Baumgold, Deborah. *Hobbes's Political Theory*. Cambridge: Cambridge University Press, 1988.

Bedwell, William. *Via regia ad geometriam. The vvay to geometry. Being necessary and usefull, for astronomers. Geographers. Landmeaters. Sea-men. Engineres. Architecks. Carpenters. Paynters. Carvers, &c. Written in Latine by Peter Ramvs, and now translated and much enlarged by the learned Mr. William Beadvvell*. London, 1636.

Beiner, Ronald. *Political Judgment*. Chicago: University of Chicago Press, 1983.

Bell, Daniel. *The End of Ideology*. Cambridge: Harvard University Press, 1960.

Bernstein, Richard. *Beyond Objectivism and Relativism: Science, Hermeneutics, and Praxis*. Philadelphia: University of Pennsylvania Press, 1988.

———. *The New Constellation: Ethical-Political Horizons of Modernity/Postmodernity*. Cambridge: MIT Press, 1992.

Beyssade, Jean-Marie. "On the Idea of God: Incomprehensibility or Incompatibilities." In *Essays on the Philosophy and Science of René Descartes*, translated by Charles Paul, edited by Stephen Voss, 85–94. Oxford: Oxford University Press, 1993.

Bhaskar, Roy. *Reclaiming Reality: A Critical Introduction to Contemporary Philosophy*. London: Verso, 1989.

Biagioli, Mario. *Galileo, Courtier: The Practice of Science in the Culture of Absolutism*. Chicago: University of Chicago Press, 1993.

———. "The Social Status of Italian Mathematicians, 1450–1600." *History of Science* 27 (1989): 41–95.

Biancani, Giuseppe. *De Mathematicarum Natura*. Translated by Gyula Klima. In Paolo Mancosu, *Philosophy of Mathematics and Mathematical Practice in the Seventeenth Century*, 178–212. Oxford: Oxford University Press, 1996.

Bienvenu, Richard, and Mordechai Feingold, eds. *In the Presence of the Past: Essays in Honor of Frank Manuel*. Dordrecht: Kluwer Academic Publishers, 1991.

Bird, Alexander. "Squaring the Circle: Hobbes on Philosophy and Geometry." *Journal of the History of Ideas* 57 (1996): 217–31.

Blair, Ann, and Anthony Grafton. "Reassessing Humanism and Science." *Journal of the History of Ideas* 53, no. 4 (1992): 535–40.

Blumenberg, Hans. *The Legitimacy of the Modern Age*. Translated by Robert Wallace. Cambridge: MIT Press, 1983.

Bobbio, Norberto. *Thomas Hobbes and the Natural Law Tradition*. Translated by Daniela Gobetti. Chicago: University of Chicago Press, 1993.

Boonin-Vail, David. *Thomas Hobbes and the Science of Moral Virtue*. Cambridge: Cambridge University Press, 1994.

Borot, Luc. "History in Hobbes's Political Thought." In *The Cambridge Companion to Hobbes*, edited by Tom Sorell, 305–28. Cambridge: Cambridge University Press, 1996.

Bourdieu, Pierre. *Distinction: A Social Critique of the Judgement of Taste*. Translated by Richard Nice. Cambridge: Harvard University Press, 1984.

———. *The Logic of Practice*. Translated by Richard Nice. Stanford: Stanford University Press, 1990.

———. *Outline of a Theory of Practice*. Translated by Richard Nice. Cambridge: Cambridge University Press, 1977.

———. "The Sentiment of Honor in Kabyle Society." In *Honour and Shame*, edited by J. Peristiany. Chicago: University of Chicago Press, 1966.
Bowle, John. *Hobbes and His Critics: A Study in Seventeenth-Century Constitutionalism*. Oxford: Oxford University Press, 1952.
Boyce, Benjamin. *The Theophrastian Character in England to 1642*. Cambridge: Harvard University Press, 1947.
Brandt, Frithiof. *Thomas Hobbes' Mechanical Conception of Nature*. Copenhagen: Levin and Munksgaard, 1928.
Breidert, Wolfgang. "Les mathématiques et la méthode mathématique chez Hobbes." *Revue Internationale de Philosophie* 129 (1979): 415–31.
Brown, Cedric. "Courtesies of Place and Arts of Diplomacy in Ben Jonson's Last Two Entertainments for Royalty." *Seventeenth Century* 9 (1994): 147–71.
Bruce, John, ed. *Calendar of State Papers, Domestic Series, of the Reign of Charles I (1637–1638)*. London, 1869.
Buck, Peter. "Seventeenth-Century Political Arithmetic: Civil Strife and Vital Statistics." *Isis* 241 (1977): 67–84.
Buckley, William. *Arithmetica memorativa, sive Brevis, et compendaria arithmetica tractatio*. . . . London, 1567.
Burckhardt, Jacob. *The Civilization of the Renaissance in Italy*. Vol. 1. Translated by S. G. C. Middlemore. New York: Harper and Row, 1958.
Burgess, Glenn. *Absolute Monarchy and the Stuart Constitution*. New Haven: Yale University Press, 1996.
———. "Contexts for the Writing and Publication of Hobbes's *Leviathan*." *History of Political Thought* 11 (1990): 675–702.
———. "The Divine Right of Kings Reconsidered." *English Historical Review* 107, no. 425 (1992): 837–61.
———. "On Hobbesian Resistance Theory." *Political Studies* 42 (1994): 62–83.
———. "Reviews and Short Notices: *Three Discourses*." *History* 82 (1997): 496–97.
Burke, Kenneth. *A Rhetoric of Motives*. Berkeley and Los Angeles: University of California Press, 1969.
Burke, Peter. *Popular Culture in Early Modern Europe*. New York: Harper and Row, 1978.
———. "Tacitism." In *Tacitus*, edited by T. A. Dorey. London: Routledge and Kegan Paul, 1969.
———. "Tacitism, Skepticism, and Reason of State." In *The Cambridge History of Political Thought, 1450–1700*, edited by J. H. Burns and Mark Goldie, 479–98. Cambridge: Cambridge University Press, 1991.
Burnet, [Bishop] Gilbert. *History of His Own Time*. 1833. Reprint. Edited by Martin Joseph Routh. 6 vols. Hildesheim: Georg Olms Verlagsbuchhandlung, 1969.
Burton, Robert. *Anatomy of Melancholy*. 1621. Reprint. Edited by Floyd Dell and Paul Jordan-Smith. New York: George H. Doran, 1927.
———. *Philosophaster*. Edited and translated by Connie McQuillen. Binghamton, N.Y.: Medieval and Renaissance Texts and Studies, 1993.
Butler, Martin. "Ben Jonson and the Limits of Courtly Panegyric." In *Culture and Politics in Early Stuart England*, edited by Kevin Sharpe and Peter Lake, 91–115. Stanford: Stanford University Press, 1993.
Butler, Martin, and David Lindley. "Restoring *Astraea:* Jonson's Masque for the Fall of Somerset." *ELH* 61 (1994): 807–27.
Butterfield, Herbert. *The Whig Interpretation of History*. London: G. Bell and Sons, 1931.
Cantalupo, Charles. *A Literary Leviathan: Thomas Hobbes's Masterpiece of Language*. Lewisburg: Bucknell University Press, 1991.
Cardano, Girolamo. *Les Livres de Hierome Cardanus, Medecin, Millanois . . . Traduis de Latin en Françoys, par Richard le Blanc*. Paris, 1566.
Cascardi, Anthony. *The Subject of Modernity*. Cambridge: Cambridge University Press, 1992.

Case, John. *Speculum moralium quaestionum in universalam ethicen Aristotelis.* . . . Oxford, 1585.

Cassirer, Ernst. *The Individual and the Cosmos in Renaissance Philosophy.* Translated by Mario Domandi. New York: Harper and Row, 1963.

Castiglione, Baldessare. *The Book of the Courtier.* 1528. Translated by Charles S. Singleton. Garden City, N.Y.: Doubleday, 1959.

Caus, Isaak de. *New and Rare Inventions of Water-Works: Shewing the Easiest waies to Raise Water higher then the Spring.* Translated by John Leake. London, 1659.

Caus, Salomon de. *La Perspective, Avec la Raison des ombres et miroirs.* London, 1612.

Cavendish, Margaret, Duchess of Newcastle. *The Description of a New World Called the Blazing World.* Edited by Kate Lilley. In *The Blazing World and Other Writings.* London: Penguin Books, 1992.

———. *The Philosophical and Physical Opinions, Written by Her Excellency the Lady Marchionesse of Newcastle.* London, 1655.

Cavendish, William, Earl of Newcastle. "Considerations touching the facility or Difficulty of the Motions of a Horse on Streight Lines, & Circular." In *A Catalogue of Letters and Other Historical Documents Exhibited in the Library at Welbeck,* edited by Arthur Strong. London: John Murray, 1903.

———. *The Covntry Captaine: A Comoedye Lately Presented By his Majesties Servants at Blackfryers.* The Hague, 1649.

———. *A declaration of the Right Honourable the Earle of Nevvcastle His Excellency, &c in answer of six groundlesse aspersions cast upon him by the Lord Fairefax, in his late warrant bearing date Feb. 1642.* York, 1643.

———. *La Méthod Nouvelle et Invention Extraordinaire de dresser les Chevaux.* Antwerp, 1658.

———. *A New and Extraordinary Method to Dress Horses.* London, 1677.

Celenza, Christopher S. *The Lost Italian Renaissance: Humanists, Historians, and Latin's Legacy.* Baltimore: Johns Hopkins University Press, 2005.

Charles I, King of England, and John Gauden. *Eikon Basilike [The Pourtraicture of His Sacred Majestie in his Solitudes and Sufferings].* London, 1648.

Charleton, Kenneth. *Education in Renaissance England.* London: Routledge and Kegan Paul, 1965.

Child, Arthur. "Making and Knowing in Hobbes, Vico, and Dewey." *University of California Publications in Philosophy* 16 (1953): 271–310.

Clarendon, Earl of [Edward Hyde]. *A Brief View and Survey of the Dangerous Errors of Church and State in Mr. Hobbes's Book, entitled Leviathan.* Oxford, 1676.

———. *Two Dialogues: Of the Want of Respect Due to Age, and Concerning Education.* Los Angeles: William Andrews Clark Memorial Library, 1984.

Clarke, Donald. *John Milton at St. Paul's School: A Study of Ancient Rhetoric in English Renaissance Education.* Hamden, Conn.: Archon Books, 1948.

Clarke, Stuart. "The Rational Witchfinder: Conscience, Demonological Naturalism, and Popular Superstitions." In *Science, Culture, and Popular Belief in Renaissance Europe,* edited by Stephen Pumfrey, Paolo Rossi, and Maurice Slawinski, 222–49. Manchester: Manchester University Press, 1991.

Clucas, Stephen. "The Atomism of the Cavendish Circle: A Reappraisal." *Seventeenth Century* 9 (1994): 247–73.

———. "In Search of 'The True Logick': Methodological Eclecticism Among the 'Baconian Reformers.'" In *Samuel Hartlib and the Universal Reformation: Studies in Intellectual Education,* edited by Mark Greengrass, Michael Leslie, and Timothy Raylor, 51–91. Cambridge: Cambridge University Press, 1994.

Cochrane, Eric. "Science and Humanism in the Italian Renaissance." *American Historical Review* 81 (1976): 1039–57.

Collins, Jeffrey. *The Allegiance of Thomas Hobbes.* Oxford: Oxford University Press, 2005.

Comenius, John Amos. *The Great Didact.* Translation of *Didacta Magna* (1657) by M. W. Keatinge. New York: Russell and Russell, 1967.

———. *The Labyrinth of the World*. Translated by Matthew Spinka. Ann Arbor: University of Michigan, 1972.
Condren, Conal. "On the Rhetorical Foundations of *Leviathan*." *History of Political Thought* 11 (1990): 703–20.
Conley, Tom. *The Self-Made Map: Cartographic Writing in Early Modern France*. Minneapolis: University of Minnesota Press, 1996.
Connolly, William E. *The Ethos of Pluralization*. Minneapolis: University of Minnesota Press, 1995.
———. *Political Theory and Modernity*. Oxford: Basil Blackwell, 1988.
Copenhaver, Brian P., and Charles B. Schmitt. *Renaissance Philosophy*. New York: Oxford University Press, 1992.
Copleston, Frederick. *A History of Philosophy*. Vol. 3, pt. 1. Westminster, Md.: Newman Press, 1953.
Cormack, Lesley B. "'Good Fences Make Good Neighbors': Geography as Self-Definition in Early Modern England." *Isis* 82 (1991): 639–61.
Cornwallis, William. *Essays*. Baltimore: Johns Hopkins University Press, 1946.
Costello, William. *The Scholastic Curriculum at Early Seventeenth-Century Cambridge*. Cambridge: Harvard University Press, 1958.
Cowley, Abraham. *Pindarique ODES, Written in Imitation of the Stile & Manner of the Odes of Pindar*. London, 1669.
Cranston, Maurice, and Richard Peters, eds. *Hobbes and Rousseau*. Garden City, N.Y.: Doubleday, 1972.
Cressy, David. *Education in Tudor and Stuart England*. New York: St. Martin's Press, 1976.
———. *Literacy and the Social Order*. Cambridge: Cambridge University Press, 1980.
Crewe, Jonathan. "The Hegemonic Theater of George Puttenham." In *Renaissance Historicism*, edited by Arthur Kinney and Dan Collins, 93–107. Amherst: University of Massachusetts Press, 1987.
Croll, Morris. *Attic and Baroque Style*. Princeton: Princeton University Press, 1969.
Crombie, Alistair C. "Mathematics and Platonism in the Sixteenth-Century Italian Universities and in Jesuit Educational Policy." In *Prismata: Naturwissenschaftsgeschichtliche Studien*, edited by Y. Maeyama and W. G. Slatzer, 63–94. Wiesbaden: Franz Steiner Verlag, 1977.
Cumberland, Richard. *De Legibus Naturae*. 1672. Translated by John Maxwell under the title *A Treatise of the Laws of Nature*. 1727. Reprinted with an introduction by Jon Parkin. Indianapolis: Liberty Fund, 2005.
Curtis, Mark. "The Alienated Intellectuals of Early Stuart England." *Past and Present* 23 (1962): 25–43.
———. *Oxford and Cambridge in Transition, 1558–1642: An Essay on Changing Relations Between the English Universities and English Society*. Oxford: Clarendon Press, 1959.
Cusa, Nicolaus [C. Cusanus]. *Idiota de mente*. Translated by Clyde Lee Miller. New York: Abaris Books, 1979.
———. *Idiota de mente*. In *Opera Omnia, Iussu et auctoritate Literarum Heidelbergensis ad codicum fidem edita*, edited by L. Bauer, vol. 5. Leipzig: Felix Meiner, 1983.
———. *The Idiot in Four Books. The first and second of Wisdome. The third of the Mind. The fourth of statick Experiments, Or experiments of the Balance*. London, 1650.
Cust, Richard. *The Forced Loans and English Politics, 1626–1628*. Oxford: Oxford University Press, 1987.
Davenant, Sir William. *The Dramatic Works of Sir William Davenant*. Edited by W. Patterson. London, 1873.
———. *Gondibert*. Edited by David Gladish. Oxford: Clarendon Press, 1971.
Davis, Natalie Zemon. "Beyond the Market: Books as Gifts in Sixteenth-Century France." *Transactions of the Royal Historical Society* 33 (1983): 69–88.
Deane, William, ed. and trans. ΣΟΦΙΑ ΣΑΛΩΜΩΝ: *The Book of Wisdom*. Oxford, 1881.

Dear, Peter. *Discipline and Experience: The Mathematical Way in the Scientific Revolution.* Chicago: University of Chicago Press, 1995.

———. "Jesuit Mathematical Science and the Reconstruction of Experience in the Early Seventeenth Century." *Studies in the History and Philosophy of Science* 18 (1987): 133–75.

———. *Mersenne and the Learning of the Schools.* Ithaca: Cornell University Press, 1988.

———. "Miracles, Experiments, and the Ordinary Course of Nature." *Isis* 81 (1990): 663–83.

Debus, Allen. "Introduction." In John Dee, *The Mathematicall Praeface to the Elements of Geometrie of Euclid of Megara.* 1570. Reprint. New York: Science History Publications, 1975.

———. "Mathematics and Nature in Chemical Texts of the Renaissance." *Ambix* 15 (1968): 1–28, 211.

Dee, John. *The Mathematicall Praeface to the Elements of Geometrie of Euclid of Megara.* 1570. Reprint. New York: Science History Publications, 1975.

DeMolen, Richard. *Richard Mulcaster (c. 1531–1611): Educational Reform in the Renaissance.* Nieuwkoop: De Graaf, 1991.

Derrida, Jacques. *The Beast and the Sovereign.* Translated by G. Bennington. Edited by Michel Lisse et al. Chicago: University of Chicago Press, 2009.

———. *Rogues: Two Essays on Reason.* Translated by Pascale-Anne Brault and Michael Naas. Stanford: Stanford University Press, 2005.

Descartes, Rene. *La Geometrie.* A reprint of the 1637 edition with a translation by David Eugene Smith and Marcia L. Latham. La Salle, Ill.: Open Court, 1952.

———. *Oeuvres.* Revised edition. Edited by C. Adam and P. Tannery. 11 vols. Paris: Vrin, 1974.

———. *The Philosophical Works of Descartes.* Edited by Elizabeth S. Haldane and G. R. T. Ross. Vol. 1. Cambridge: Cambridge University Press, 1961.

Dewey, John. "The Motivation of Hobbes's Political Philosophy." 1918. Reprinted in John Dewey, *Middle Works,* 11:18–40. Carbondale: Southern Illinois University Press, 1988.

———. *The Quest for Certainty: A Study of the Relation of Knowledge and Action.* New York: Minton, Balch, 1929.

Dickens, A. G. *The Marian Reaction in the Diocese of York, Part II.* York: St. Anthony Hall Publications, 1957.

Dietz, Mary. "Hobbes's Subject as Citizen." In *Thomas Hobbes and Political Theory,* edited by Mary Dietz. Lawrence: University Press of Kansas, 1990.

Digges, Thomas, and Leonard Digges. *An arithmetical warlike treatise named* STRATIOTICOS *compendiously teaching the science of numbers as well in fractions as integers, and so much of the rules and æquations algebraicall, and art of nombers cossicall, as are requisite for the profession of a souldier. . . .* London, 1590.

Dilthey, Wilhelm. "The Rise of Hermeneutics." Translated by Fredric Jameson. In *The Hermeneutic Tradition from Ast to Ricoeur,* edited by Gayle L. Ormiston and Alan D. Schrift. Albany: State University of New York Press, 1990.

Diodorus Siculus. *Library of History.* Vol. 2. Translated by C. H. Oldfather. Loeb Classical Library no. 303. Cambridge: Harvard University Press, 1935.

Dodd, Mary. 1952. "The Rhetorics in Molesworth's Edition of Hobbes." *Modern Philology* 50 (1952): 36–42.

Dollimore, Jonathan. *Radical Tragedy: Religion, Ideology, and Power in the Drama of Shakespeare and His Contemporaries.* Chicago: University of Chicago Press, 1984.

Douglas, Andrew Halliday. *The Philosophy and Psychology of Pietro Pomponazzi.* Edited by Charles Douglas and R. P. Hardie. Reprint. Hildesheim: Georg Olms Verlagsbuchhandlung, 1962.

Douglas, Mary. *Purity and Danger: An Analysis of the Concepts of Pollution and Taboo.* London: Routledge and Kegan Paul, 1966.

Dryden, John. *Selected Works.* Edited by William Frost. New York: Holt, Rinehart, and Winston, 1953.

Duhem, Pierre. "Nicolas de Cues et Leonard de Vinci." In *Etudes sur Leonard de Vinci.* Paris: Librarie Scientifique, 1909.

Dumm, Thomas. "Response to Michael Rogin." *Political Theory* 17 (1989): 291–95.
Dumouchel, Paul. "Hobbes: La course à la souveraineté." *Stanford French Review* 10 (1986): 153–76.
———. "Hobbes and Secularization: Christianity and the Political Problem of Religion." *Contagion* 2 (1995): 39–56.
———. "*Persona*: Reason and Representation in Hobbes's Political Philosophy." *Cahiers d'épistémologie*, 9606. University of Quebec, Montreal, 1996.
———. "Voir et craindre un lion: Hobbes et la rationalité des passions." *Cahiers d'épistémologie*, 9413. University of Quebec, Montreal, 1994.
Durkheim, Emile. *The Elementary Forms of Religious Life*. Translated by Joseph Ward Swain. New York: Macmillan, 1965.
———. "The Nature and Method of Pedagogy." In *Education and Sociology*, translated by Sherwood D. Fox, 91–112. Glencoe, Ill.: The Free Press, 1956.
Dury, John. *The Reformed School*. London, 1649.
Eachard, John. *The Grounds and Occasions of the Contempt of the Clergy and Religion Enquired into in a Letter written to R. L.* 10th edition. London, 1696.
———. *Mr. Hobbs's State of Nature Considered: In a Dialogue Between Philautus and Timothy*. 4th edition. London, 1696.
———. *Some Opinions of Mr. Hobbs Considered in a Second Dialogue between Philautus and Timothy, By the same author*. London, 1673.
Earl, John. *Microcosmography, or a Piece of the World Discovered in Essays and Characters*. Edited by Harold Osborne. St. Claire Shores, Mich.: Scholarly Press, 1978.
Elias, Norbert. *The Court Society*. Oxford: Basil Blackwell, 1983.
Elton, G. R. *Reform and Renewal: Thomas Cromwell and the Common Weal*. Cambridge: Cambridge University Press, 1973.
Elyot, Thomas. *The Book named The Governor*. 1513. Reprint. Edited by S. E. Lehmberg. London: Everyman's Library, 1962.
Erasmus. *The Education of a Christian Prince*. Translated by N. M. Cheshire and M. J. Heath. Edited by Lisa Jardine. Cambridge: Cambridge University Press, 1997.
Euclid. *The Thirteen Books of Euclid's Elements*. 1926. Edited by Thomas Heath. 4 vols. Reprint. New York: Dover, 1956.
Ewin, R. E. *Virtues and Rights: The Moral Philosophy of Thomas Hobbes*. Boulder, Colo.: Westview Press, 1991.
Farrington, Benjamin. "Hobbes's Autobiography." *Rationalist's Annual*, 1958, 22–31.
Feingold, Mordechai, ed. *Before Newton: The Life and Times of Isaac Barrow*. Cambridge: Cambridge University Press, 1990.
———. *The Mathematician's Apprenticeship: Science, Universities, and Society in England, 1560–1640*. Cambridge: Cambridge University Press, 1984.
Ferguson, Arthur. *The Articulate Citizen and the English Renaissance*. Durham: Duke University Press, 1965.
Ficino, Marsilio. *Theologia Platonica, sive de immortalitate animorum (Théologie platonicienne de l'immortalité des ames)*. 3 vols. Edited by R. Marcel. Paris: Société d'Édition Les Belles Lettres, 1964–70.
Field, Judith V., and Frank James, eds. *Renaissance and Revolution: Humanists, Scholars, Craftsmen, and Natural Philosophers in Early Modern Europe*. Cambridge: Cambridge University Press, 1993.
Figgis, John Neville. *The Divine Right of Kings*. New York: Harper and Row, 1965.
Filmer, Robert. *Patriarchia and Other Writings*. Edited by Johann Sommerville. Cambridge: Cambridge University Press, 1991.
Fish, Stanley. *Self-Consuming Artifacts: The Experience of Seventeenth-Century Literature*. Berkeley and Los Angeles: University of California Press, 1972.
Flathman, Richard. *Thomas Hobbes: Skepticism, Individuality, and Chastened Politics*. Newbury Park, Calif.: Sage, 1993.

———. *Toward a Liberalism*. Ithaca: Cornell University Press, 1989.
Fletcher, Anthony. "Honor, Reputation, and Local Officeholding in Elizabethan and Stuart England." In *Order and Disorder in Early Modern England*, edited by Anthony Fletcher and John Stevenson. Cambridge: Cambridge University Press, 1985.
Fortier, John C. "Hobbes and 'A Discourse of Laws': The Perils of Wordprint Analysis." *Review of Politics* 59 (1997): 861–87.
———. "Last Word." *Review of Politics* 59 (1997): 905–14.
Foucault, Michel. *Language, Counter-Memory, Practice*. Ithaca: Cornell University Press, 1980.
———. *The Order of Things: An Archaeology of the Human Sciences*. New York: Random House, 1970.
Fox, Alistair, and John Guy. *Reassessing the Henrican Renaissance*. Oxford: Basil Blackwell, 1986.
Francis, Mark. "The Nineteenth-Century Theory of Sovereignty and Thomas Hobbes." *History of Political Thought* 1 (1980): 517–40.
Frost, Samantha. *Lessons from a Materialist Thinker: Hobbesian Reflections on Ethics and Politics*. Stanford: Stanford University Press, 2008.
Funkenstein, Amos. *Theology and the Scientific Imagination from the Middle Ages to the Seventeenth Century*. Princeton: Princeton University Press, 1986.
Gabbey, Alan. "Between *Ars* and *Philosophia Naturalis*: Reflections on the Historiography of Early Modern Mechanics." In *Renaissance and Revolution: Humanists, Scholars, Craftsmen, and Natural Philosophers in Early Modern Europe*, edited by Judith Veronica Field and Frank James, 133–47. Cambridge: Cambridge University Press, 1993.
Gadamer, Hans-Georg. *Heidegger's Ways*. Translated by John Stanley. Albany: State University of New York Press, 1994.
———. *Reason in the Age of Science*. Translated by Frederick Lawrence. Cambridge: MIT Press, 1981.
———. *Truth and Method*. Revised edition. Translated by Joel Weinsheimer and Donald Marshall. New York: Crossroads, 1990.
Galileo [Galilei]. *The Assayer*. 1623. Translated by Drake Stillman and C. D. O'Malley. In *The Controversy on the Comets of 1618*, 151–336. Philadelphia: University of Pennsylvania Press, 1960.
Garber, Daniel. "A Different Descartes: Descartes and the Programme for a Mathematical Physics in His Correspondence." In *Descartes' Natural Philosophy*, edited by Stephen Gaukroger, John Schuster, and John Sutton, 113–30. London: Routledge, 2000.
Garin, Eugenio. "The Philosopher and the Magus." In *Renaissance Characters*, edited by E. Garin, translated by L. G. Cochrane, 123–53. Chicago: University of Chicago Press, 1991.
———. *Science and Civil Life in the Italian Renaissance*. Translated by Peter Munz. Garden City, N.Y.: Doubleday, 1969.
Gaukroger, Stephen. *Descartes: An Intellectual Biography*. Oxford: Clarendon Press, 1995.
———. *Descartes: Philosophy, Mathematics, and Physics*. Totowa, N.J.: Barnes and Noble Books, 1980.
———. "Descartes' Project for a Mathematical Physics." In Gaukroger, *Descartes: Philosophy, Mathematics, and Physics*, 97–140. Totowa, N.J.: Barnes and Noble Books, 1980.
Gauthier, David. *The Logic of Leviathan: The Moral and Political Theory of Thomas Hobbes*. London: Oxford University Press, 1969.
Geertz, Clifford. *Negara: The Theatre State in Nineteenth-Century Bali*. Princeton: Princeton University Press, 1980.
Gerbino, Anthony, and Stephen Johnston. *Compass and Rule: Architecture as Mathematical Practice in England, 1500–1750*. New Haven: Yale University Press, 2009.
Gert, Bernard. "Hobbes and Psychological Egoism." In *Hobbes's Leviathan: Interpretation and Criticism*, edited by Bernard Baumrin, 107–26. Belmont, Calif.: Wadsworth, 1969.
———. "Hobbes's Psychology." In *The Cambridge Companion to Hobbes*, edited by Tom Sorell, 157–74. Cambridge: Cambridge University Press, 1996.
———. "Introduction." In Thomas Hobbes, *Man and Citizen*. Garden City, N.Y.: Anchor Books, 1972.

Gilbert, Sir Humphrey. "Queen Elizebethes Achademy." Edited by F. J. Furnivall. *Early English Text Society* 8, extra series (1869).
Gilbert, Neal. *Renaissance Concepts of Method*. New York: Columbia University Press, 1960.
Gilson, Etienne. *The Christian Philosophy of St. Thomas Aquinas*. Translated by L. K. Shook. New York: Random House, 1956.
Girard, René. *Violence and the Sacred*. Translated by Patrick Gregory. Baltimore: Johns Hopkins University Press, 1977.
Giroeard, Mark. *Robert Smythson and the Elizabethan Country House*. New Haven: Yale University Press, 1983.
Goldberg, Jonathan. *James I and the Politics of Literature*. Stanford: Stanford University Press, 1989.
Goldie, Mark. "The Reception of Hobbes." In *The Cambridge History of Political Thought, 1450–1700*, edited by J. H. Burns and Mark Goldie. Cambridge: Cambridge University Press, 1991.
Goldsmith, M. M. "Hobbes on Law." In *The Cambridge Companion to Hobbes*, edited by Tom Sorell, 274–304. Cambridge: Cambridge University Press, 1996.
———. *Hobbes's Science of Politics*. New York: Columbia University Press, 1966.
———. "Picturing Hobbes's Politics? The Illustrations to *Philosophical Rudiments*." *Journal of the Warburg and Courtauld Institutes* 44 (1981): 232–37.
Goldthwaite, Richard. *The Building of Renaissance Florence: An Economic and Social History*. Baltimore: Johns Hopkins University Press, 1980.
———. *Wealth and the Demand for Art in Italy, 1300–1600*. Baltimore: Johns Hopkins University Press, 1993.
Gordon, D. J. "*Hymenaei:* Ben Jonson's Masque of Union." In D. J. Gordon, *The Renaissance Imagination*, edited by Stephen Orgel, 157–84. Berkeley and Los Angeles: University of California Press, 1975.
———. "The Imagery of Ben Jonson's *Masques of Blackness* and *Beautie*." In D. J. Gordon, *The Renaissance Imagination*, edited by Stephen Orgel, 134–56. Berkeley and Los Angeles: University of California Press, 1975.
———. "Poet and Architect: The Intellectual Setting of the Quarrel Between Ben Jonson and Inigo Jones." *Journal of the Warburg and Courtauld Institutes* 12 (1949): 152–78.
Gordon, G. S. "Introduction." In Henry Peacham, *Peacham's Compleat Gentleman, 1634*. Oxford: Clarendon Press, 1906.
Gossen, Stephan. *The School of Abuses*. 1579. Reprint. Edited by Edward Arber. London, 1868.
Grafton, Anthony, and Lisa Jardine. *From Humanism to the Humanities: Education and the Liberal Arts in Fifteenth- and Sixteenth-Century Europe*. Cambridge: Harvard University Press, 1986.
Graham, Kenneth. *The Performance of Conviction: Plainness and Rhetoric in the Early English Renaissance*. Ithaca: Cornell University Press, 1994.
Grant, Hardy. "Hobbes and Mathematics." In *The Cambridge Companion to Hobbes*, edited by Tom Sorell, 108–28. Cambridge: Cambridge University Press, 1996.
Greenblatt, Stephen. "Psychoanalysis and Renaissance Culture." In Stephen Greenblatt, *Learning to Curse: Essays in Early Modern Culture*. London: Routledge, 1990.
———. *Renaissance Self-Fashioning: From More to Shakespeare*. Chicago: University of Chicago Press, 1980.
Greene, Thomas. "Ben Jonson and the Centered Self." *Studies in British Literature* 10 (1970): 352–98.
———. "The Flexibility of the Self in Renaissance Literature." In *The Disciplines of Criticism*, edited by Peter Demetz, Thomas Greene, and Lowry Nelson Jr., 241–64. New Haven: Yale University Press, 1968.
Greengrass, Mark, Michael Leslie, and Timothy Raylor, eds. *Samuel Hartlib and the Universal Reformation: Studies in Intellectual Education*. Cambridge: Cambridge University Press, 1994.
Greenleaf, W. H. 1972. "Hobbes: The Problem of Interpretation." In *Hobbes and Rousseau*, edited by Maurice Cranston and Richard Peters. Garden City, N.Y.: Doubleday, 1972.

Grendler, Paul. "Schooling in Western Europe." *Renaissance Quarterly* 43 (1990): 775–87.

Gundersheimer, Werner. 1981. "Patronage in the Renaissance: An Exploratory Approach." In *Patronage in the Renaissance*, edited by Guy Fitch Lytle and Stephen Orgel. Princeton: Princeton University Press, 1981.

Habermas, Jürgen. *Theory and Practice*. Translated by John Viertel. Boston: Beacon Press, 1971.

Hacking, Ian. *The Emergence of Probability*. Cambridge: Cambridge University Press, 1975.

Hall, Joseph. *Characters of Vertues and Vices*. 1608. Reprint. Edited by Rudolf Kirk. New Brunswick: Rutgers University Press, 1975.

Hall, Marie Boas. "Galileo's Influence on Seventeenth-Century English Scientists." In *Galileo, Man of Science*, edited by Ernam McMullin, 405–14. New York: Basic Books, 1967.

Hall, Rupert. *Ballistics in the Seventeenth Century*. Cambridge: Cambridge University Press, 1952.

Hall, Trevor H. *Old Conjuring Books: A Bibliographical and Historical Study with a Supplementary Check-List*. London: Duckworth, 1972.

Hammer, Paul E. J. "The Use of Scholarship: The Secretariat of Robert Devereux, Second Earl of Essex, c. 1585–1601." *English Historical Review* 109 (1994): 26–51.

Hampton, Jean. *Hobbes and the Social Contract Tradition*. Cambridge: Cambridge University Press, 1986.

Hanson, Donald. "The Meaning of 'Demonstration' in Hobbes's Science." *History of Political Thought* 11 (1990): 587–626.

Hardin, Russell. "Hobbesian Political Order." *Political Theory* 19 (1991): 156–80.

Harris, Tim, Paul Seaward, and Mark Goldie, eds. *The Politics of Religion in Restoration England*. Oxford: Basil Blackwell, 1991.

Harwood, John. "Introduction." In *The Rhetorics of Thomas Hobbes and Bernard Lamy*, edited by John Harwood. Carbondale: Southern Illinois University Press, 1986.

Hartlib, Samuel. *A Description of the Famous Kingdome of Marcaria; shewing its Excellent Government: wherein The inhabitants live in great Prosperity, Health, and Happiness; the King obeyed, the Nobles honoured; and all good men respected, Vice punished, and vertue rewarded. An Example to other Nations. In a Dialogue between a Schollar and a Traveller*. 1641. In *Samuel Hartlib and the Advancement of Learning*, edited by Charles Webster, 79–90. Cambridge: Cambridge University Press, 1970.

Hatfield, Gary. "Reason, Nature, and God in Descartes." In *Essays on the Philosophy and Science of René Descartes*, edited by Stephen Voss, 259–87. Oxford: Oxford University Press, 1993.

Heidegger, Martin. *The Basic Problems of Phenomenology*. Translated by Albert Hofstadter. Bloomington: University of Indiana Press, 1982.

———. *Being and Time*. Translated by John Macquarrie and Edward Robinson. San Francisco: Harper and Row, 1962.

Helgerson, Richard. *Forms of Nationhood: The Elizabethan Writing of England*. Chicago: University of Chicago Press, 1992.

———. *Self-Crowned Laureates*. Berkeley and Los Angeles: University of California Press, 1983.

Hempel, Carl. 1966. *Philosophy of Natural Science*. Englewood Cliffs, N.J.: Prentice Hall, 1966.

Herbert, Gary. *Thomas Hobbes: The Unity of Scientific and Moral Wisdom*. Vancouver: University of British Colombia Press, 1989.

Hesse, Mary. "Reason and Evaluation in the History of Science." In *Changing Perspectives in the History of Science: Essays in Honour of Joseph Needham*, edited by Mikulas Teich and Robert Young, 127–66. London: Heinemann, 1973.

Hexter, J. H. "The Education of the Aristocracy in the Renaissance." In *Reappraisals in History*, 45–71. New York: Harper and Row, 1961.

———. "Thomas Hobbes and the Law." *Cornell Law Review* 65 (1980): 471–90.

Hill, Christopher. *Intellectual Origins of the English Revolution*. Oxford: Clarendon Press, 1965.

———. "The Radical Critics of Oxford and Cambridge in the 1650s." In *Universities in Politics*, edited by J. W. Baldwin and Richard A. Goldwaite, 107–32. Baltimore: Johns Hopkins University Press, 1972.

———. *The World Turned Upside Down*. Harmondsworth, U.K.: Penguin, 1972.
Hill, Thomas. *A briefe and pleasaunt treatise, entituled, Naturall and Artificiall Conclusions: Written first by sundrie scholers of the Universitie of Padua in Italie, at the instant request of one Barthelmewe a Tuscane: And now Englished by Thomas Hill Londoner, as well for the commoditie of sundrie Artificers, as for the matters of pleasure, to recreate wittes at vacant tymes*. London, 1581. Reprinted under the title *A Book of Elizabethan Magic*, edited by Thomas Ross. Regensburg, Ger.: Verlag Hans Carl, 1974.
———. *Naturall and artificiall conclusions. Compiled first in Latine, by the worthiest and best authors, both of the famous University of Padua in Italy, and divers other places. . . . And now againe published with a new addition of rarities, for the practice of sundry artificers; as also to recreate wits withall at vacant times*. London, 1650.
Hylles, Thomas. *The Arte of Vulgar Arithmeticke, both in Integers and Fractions, deuided into two Bookes*. London, 1600. [Sometimes attributed to Thomas Hill.]
Hilton, John L., Noel B. Reynolds, and Arlene W. Saxenhouse. "Hobbes and 'A Discourse of Laws': Response to Fortier." *Review of Politics* 59 (1997): 889–903.
Hine, William. "Marin Mersenne: Renaissance Naturalism and Renaissance Magic." In *In Defense of Rhetoric*, edited by Brian Vickers, 165–76. Oxford: Oxford University Press, 1989.
Hintikka, Jaakko, and Unto Remes. *The Method of Analysis: Its Geometrical Origins and Its General Significance*. Dordrecht: D. Reidel, 1974.
Hirst, Derek. *Authority and Conflict: England, 1603–1658*. Cambridge: Harvard University Press, 1986.
Hobbes, Thomas. *Ad nobilissimum dominum Guilielmum Comitem Devoniae, &c. De mirabilibus pecci, Carmen Thomae Hobbes*. London, 1627.
———. "The Answer of Mr. Hobbes to Sir Will. D'Avenant's Preface Before Gondibert." In Sir William Davenant, *Gondibert*, edited by David Gladish, 45–55. Oxford: Oxford University Press, 1971.
———. *Behemoth, or the Long Parliament*. Edited by Ferdinand Tönnies. Chicago: University of Chicago Press, 1990.
———. *A Briefe of Aristotle's Rhetorique*. In *The Rhetorics of Thomas Hobbes and Bernard Lamy*, edited by John Harwood. Carbondale: Southern Illinois University Press, 1986.
———. *Computatio Sive Logica / Logic*. Edited, and with an introductory essay, by Isabel C. Hungerland and George R. Vick. Translated by Aloysius Martinich. New York: Abaris Books, 1981.
———. *De Cive: The English Version* [*Philosophical Rudiments Concerning Government and Society*]. Edited by Howard Warrender. Oxford: Oxford University Press, 1983.
———. *De Cive: The Latin Version*. Edited by Howard Warrender. Oxford: Oxford University Press, 1983.
———. *De Homine*. Translated by Charles Wood, T. S. K. Scott-Craig, and Bernard Gert. In *Man and Citizen: "De Homine" and "De Cive" by Thomas Hobbes*, edited by Bernard Gert. New York: Anchor Books, 1972.
———. *De Mirabilibus Pecci: Being the Wonders of the Peak in Darbyshire*. London, 1678.
———. *A Dialogue Between a Philosopher and a Student of the Common Laws of England*. Edited by Joseph Cropsey. Chicago: University of Chicago Press, 1971.
———. *The Elements of Law, Natural and Politic*. Edited by Ferdinand Tönnies. Cambridge: Cambridge University Press, 1928.
———. *The Elements of Philosophy, The First Section, Concerning Body, written in Latin, by Thomas Hobbes of Malmesbury and translated into English*. In *The English Works of Thomas Hobbes of Malmesbury*, edited by William Molesworth, vol. 1. London, 1839.
———. *The English Works of Thomas Hobbes of Malmesbury*. Edited by William Molesworth. 11 vols. London, 1839–45.
———. "Fortification." Hobbes MS, Devonshire Collections, Chatsworth, C. vii. 10.

———. *Leviathan*. With selected variants from the Latin edition of 1668. Edited by Edwin Curley. Indianapolis: Hackett, 1994. [Curley's paragraph numbers conform to those of the Molesworth edition.]

———. "Little Treatise." In Thomas Hobbes, *The Elements of Law, Natural and Politic*, edited by Ferdinand Tönnies, 193–210. Cambridge: Cambridge University Press, 1928.

———. "Of the Life and History of Thucydides." In *The English Works of Thomas Hobbes of Malmesbury*, edited by William Molesworth, 8:xiii–xxxii. London, 1843.

———. "Of the Life and History of Thucydides." In *Thucydides, The Peloponnesian War: The Complete Hobbes Translation*, edited by David Grene, 569–86. Chicago: University of Chicago Press, 1989.

———. *On the Citizen*. Edited by Richard Tuck and Michael Silverthorn. Translated by Michael Silverthorn. Cambridge: Cambridge University Press, 1998.

———. *Opera Philosophica quae Latine scripsit omnia*. Edited by William Molesworth. 5 vols. London: John Bohn, 1839–45.

———. *Thomas White's "De Mundo" Examined*. Translated by Harold Whitmore Jones. Bradford: Bradford University Press, 1976.

———. *Three Discourses: A Critical Modern Edition of Newly Identified Works of the Young Hobbes*. Edited by Noel Reynolds and Arlene Saxenhouse. Chicago: University of Chicago Press, 1995.

———. "To the Readers." In *The History of the Grecian War, Written by Thucydides*, translated by Thomas Hobbes. Vol. 8 of Thomas Hobbes, *The English Works*, edited by Sir William Molesworth. London, 1839.

———. *Tractatus Opticus*. Edited by F. Alessio. *Rivista critica di storia della filosofia* 18 (1963): 147–228.

———. Untitled sketch-plans. Hobbes MS, Devonshire Collections, Chatsworth, C. vii. 11.

———. *Verse Autobiography*. Translator unknown. In *Leviathan*, edited by E. Curley. Indianapolis: Hackett, 1994.

Holmes, Stephen. "Introduction." In Hobbes, *Behemoth; or, The Long Parliament*, edited by Ferdinand Tönnies. Chicago: University of Chicago Press, 1990.

Hood, F. C. *The Divine Politics of Thomas Hobbes*. Oxford: Clarendon Press, 1964.

Hood, Thomas. *A Copie of the Speache: Made by the Mathematical Lecturer*. London, 1588.

Hooker, Richard. *Of the Laws of Ecclesiastical Polity*. Vols. 1–3. Cambridge: Harvard University Press, 1977–81.

Hooykaas, Reijer. *Humanisme, science et réforme: Pierre de la Ramée (1515–1572)*. Leiden: E. J. Brill, 1958.

Hotson, Howard. "Philosophical Pedagogy in Reformed Central Europe Between Ramus and Comenius: A Survey of the Continental Background of the 'Three Foreigners.'" In *Samuel Hartlib and the Universal Reformation: Studies in Intellectual Education*, edited by Mark Greengrass, Michael Leslie, and Timothy Raylor, 29–50. Cambridge: Cambridge University Press, 1994.

Hulse, Lynn. "Apollo's Whirligig: William Cavendish, Duke of Newcastle and His Music Collection." *Seventeenth Century* 9 (1994): 213–46.

Hurstfield, Joel. *Freedom, Corruption, and Government in Elizabethan England*. Cambridge: Harvard University Press, 1973.

Hutton, Ronald. *The Restoration: A Political and Religious History of England and Wales, 1658–1667*. Oxford: Oxford University Press, 1985.

Jacob, James. *Henry Stubbe: Radical Protestantism and the Early Enlightenment*. Cambridge: Cambridge University Press, 1983.

Jacob, James, and Timothy Raylor. "Opera and Obedience: Thomas Hobbes and *A Proposition for Advancement of Moralitie*, by Sir William Davenant." *Seventeenth Century* 6 (1991): 205–50.

Jacobson, Norman. *Pride and Solace: The Functions and Limits of Political Theory*. London: Methuen Books, 1978.

Jacquot, Jean. "Sir Charles Cavendish and His Learned Friends." Pts. 1 and 2. *Annals of Science* 8 (1952): 13–27, 175–91.

James, D. G. *The Life of Reason: Hobbes, Locke, Bolingbroke*. London: Longmans, Green, 1949.
Jardine, Lisa. *Francis Bacon: Discovery and the Art of Discourse*. Cambridge: Cambridge University Press, 1974.
Jardine, Nicholas. *The Birth of History and Philosophy of Science: Kepler's "A Defense of Tycho Against Ursus" with Essays on Its Provenance and Significance*. Cambridge: Cambridge University Press, 1984.
———. "The Epistemology of the Sciences." In *The Cambridge History of Renaissance Philosophy*, edited by C. B. Schmitt, Quentin Skinner, and E. Kessler, 685–711. Cambridge: Cambridge University Press, 1988.
———. "Galileo's Road to Truth and the Demonstrative Regress." *Studies in History and Philosophy of Science* 7 (1976): 277–318.
Jaspers, Karl. *Anselm and Nicholas of Cusa*. Edited by Hannah Arendt. Translated by Ralph Manheim. New York: Harcourt, Brace, Jovanovich, 1966.
Javitch, Daniel. "Il Cortegiano and the Constraints of Despotism." In *Castiglione: The Ideal and the Real in Renaissance Culture*, edited by Robert Hanning and David Rosand, 17–28. New Haven: Yale University Press, 1983.
———. *Poetry and Courtliness in Renaissance England*. Princeton: Princeton University Press, 1978.
Jenson, H. James. *The Muses' Concord: Literature, Music, and the Visual Arts in the Baroque Age*. Bloomington: Indiana University Press, 1976.
Jesseph, Douglas. "Hobbes and Mathematical Method." *Perspectives on Science* 1 (1993): 306–41.
———. "Hobbes and the Method of the Natural Sciences." In *The Cambridge Companion to Hobbes*, edited by Tom Sorell, 86–107. Cambridge: Cambridge University Press, 1996.
———. "Of Analytics and Indivisibles: Hobbes on the Method of Modern Mathematics." *Revue d'histoire des sciences* 46 (1993): 153–93.
———. *Squaring the Circle: The War Between Hobbes and Wallis*. Chicago: University of Chicago Press, 1999.
Johnson, A. W. *Ben Jonson: Poetry and Architecture*. Oxford: Clarendon Press, 1994.
Johnston, David. "Hobbes's Mortalism." *History of Political Thought* 10 (1989): 647–63.
———. *The Rhetoric of Leviathan*. Princeton: Princeton University Press, 1986.
Johnston, Stephen. "Mathematical Practitioners and Instruments in Elizabethan England." *Annals of Science* 48 (1991): 319–44.
Jones, Inigo. *Coelum Britannicum*. 1634. Reprinted in *Inigo Jones and the Theater of the Stuart Court*, edited by Steven Orgel and Roy Strong, 2:566–97. Berkeley and Los Angeles: University of California Press, 1973.
———. *The Most Notable Antiquity of Great Britain Vulgarly Called Stonehenge . . . Restored*. Edited by John Webb. London, 1655.
Jonson, Ben. *Ben Jonson*. 11 vols. Vols. 1–5 edited by C. H. Herford and Percy Simpson. Vols. 6–11 edited by C. H. Herford, Percy Simpson, and Evelyn Simpson. Oxford: Clarendon Press, 1925–52.
———. *Ben Jonson: The Complete Masques*. Edited by Stephen Orgel. New Haven: Yale University Press, 1969.
———. *Ben Jonson: The Complete Poems*. Edited by George Parfitt. Harmondsworth, U.K.: Penguin, 1988.
———. *Every Man in His Humor*. Edited by Gabriele Jackson. New Haven: Yale University Press, 1969.
———. *Sejanus, His Fall*. Edited by W. F. Bolton. London: Benn, 1966.
———. *Volpone*. Edited by Alvin Kernan. New Haven: Yale University Press, 1962.
Kahan, Alan S. *Aristocratic Liberalism: The Social and Political Thought of Jacob Burckhardt, John Stuart Mill, and Alexis de Tocqueville*. Oxford: Oxford University Press, 1992.
Kahn, Victoria. "Margaret Cavendish and the Romance of Contract." *Renaissance Quarterly* 50 (1997): 526–66.

———. *Rhetoric, Prudence, and Skepticism in the Renaissance*. Ithaca: Cornell University Press, 1985.
Kantorowicz, Ernst. *The King's Two Bodies*. Princeton: Princeton University Press, 1957.
Kavka, Gregory. *Hobbesian Moral and Political Theory*. Princeton: Princeton University Press, 1986.
Keller, A. G. "Mathematicians, Mechanics, and Experimental Machines in Northern Italy in the Sixteenth Century." In *The Emergence of Science in Western Europe*, edited by Maurice Crosland, 15–34. London: Macmillan, 1975.
Kennedy, George. *Classical Rhetoric and Its Christian and Secular Tradition from Ancient to Modern Times*. Chapel Hill: University of North Carolina Press, 1980.
———. *Quintilian*. New York: Twayne Publishers, 1969.
Kelso, Ruth. *The Doctrine of the English Gentleman in the Sixteenth Century*. University of Illinois Studies in Language and Literature 14. Urbana: University of Illinois Press, 1929.
Klaaren, Eugene. *Religious Origins of Modern Science*. Grand Rapids, Mich.: Eerdmans, 1977.
Koselleck, Reinhart. *Critique and Crisis: Enlightenment and the Pathologies of Modern Society*. Oxford: Berg, 1988.
Koyre, Alexandre. *From the Closed World to the Infinite Universe*. Baltimore: Johns Hopkins University Press, 1957.
Kraus, Jody. *The Limits of Hobbesian Contractarianism*. Cambridge: Cambridge University Press, 1993.
Kraye, Jill. "The Philosophy of the Italian Renaissance." In *The Renaissance and Seventeenth-Century Rationalism*, edited by G. H. R. Parkinson, 16–69. London: Routledge, 1993.
Kraynak, Robert P. *History and Modernity in the Thought of Thomas Hobbes*. Ithaca: Cornell University Press, 1990.
———. "Speculations on the Earliest Writings of Hobbes." *Review of Politics* 58 (1996): 813–14.
Kristeller, Paul Oskar. *Eight Philosophers of the Italian Renaissance*. Stanford: Stanford University Press, 1964.
———. *Renaissance Thought: The Classic, Scholastic, and Humanist Strains*. New York: Harper and Row, 1961.
Krook, Dorothea. "Thomas Hobbes's Doctrine of Meaning and Truth." *Philosophy: The Journal of the Royal Institute of Philosophy* 31 (1956): 3–22.
Kuhn, Thomas. *The Essential Tension: Selected Studies in Scientific Tradition and Change*. Chicago: University of Chicago Press, 1979.
———. *The Structure of Scientific Revolutions*. 2nd edition. Chicago: University of Chicago Press, 1970.
Lachterman, David. *The Ethics of Geometry: A Genealogy of Modernity*. London: Routledge, 1989.
———. "*Objectum Purae Matheseos*: Mathematical Construction and the Passage from Essence to Existence." In *Essays on Descartes' "Meditations,"* edited by A. O. Rorty. Berkeley and Los Angeles: University of California Press, 1986.
Laird, John. *Hobbes*. London: E. Benn, 1934.
Laird, W. R. "Archimedes Among the Humanists." *Isis* 82 (1991): 629–38.
Lake, Peter. *Moderate Puritans and the Elizabethan Church*. Cambridge: Cambridge University Press, 1982.
Laudan, Larry. "The Clock Metaphor and Hypothesis: The Impact of Descartes on English Methodological Thought, 1650–1670." In Larry Laudan, *Science and Hypothesis: Historical Essays on Scientific Methodology*. Dordrecht: D. Reidel, 1981.
Leijenhorst, Cees. *The Mechanisation of Aristotelianism: The Late Aristotelian Setting of Thomas Hobbes' Natural Philosophy*. Leiden: E. J. Brill, 2002.
Lenoble, Robert. *Mersenne ou la naissance du mécanisme*. Paris: Vrin, 1971.
Levin, Harry. "Jonson's Metempsychosis." *Philological Quarterly* 22 (1943): 231–39.
Levine, Laura. *Men in Women's Clothing: Anti-theatricality and Effeminization, 1579–1642*. Cambridge: Cambridge University Press, 1994.
Lévi-Strauss, Claude. *The Elementary Structures of Kinship*. Boston: Beacon Press, 1969.
Lindberg, David C., and Robert Westman, eds. *Reappraisals of the Scientific Revolution*. Cambridge: Cambridge University Press, 1990.

Lindley, David. "Embarrassing Ben: The Masques for Frances Howard." *English Literary Renaissance* 16 (1986): 343–59.
Lloyd, G. E. R. *Magic, Reason, and Experience: Studies in the Development of the Greek Sciences.* Cambridge: Cambridge University Press, 1979.
Lloyd, S. A. *Ideals as Interests in Hobbes's "Leviathan": The Power of Mind Over Matter.* Cambridge: Cambridge University Press, 2003.
Locke, John. "Thoughts Concerning Education." In *The Educational Writings of John Locke.* Cambridge: Cambridge University Press, 1968.
Long, Pamela. "Humanism and Science." In *Renaissance Humanism: Foundations, Forms, and Legacy*, vol. 3, *Humanism and the Disciplines*, edited by Albert Rabil Jr., 486–512. Philadelphia: University of Pennsylvania Press, 1988.
———. "Power, Patronage, and the Authorship of *Ars:* From Mechanical Know-How to Mechanical Knowledge in the Last Scribal Age." *Isis* 88 (1997): 1–41.
Loughlin, Marie. "'Love's Friend and Stranger to Virginitie': The Politics of the Virginal Body in Ben Jonson's *Hymenaei* and Thomas Campion's *The Lord Hay's Masque.*" *ELH* 63 (1996): 833–49.
Lucian. *Works in Eight Volumes.* Vols. 1–5 translated by A. M. Harmon. Vol. 6 translated by K. Kilburn. Vols. 7–8 translated by M. D. MacLeod. Cambridge: Harvard University Press, 1953–67.
Lytle, Guy Fitch, and Stephen Orgel, eds. *Patronage in the Renaissance.* Princeton: Princeton University Press, 1981.
Machiavelli, Niccolo. *The Prince.* Translated by Harvey Mansfield. Chicago: University of Chicago Press, 1998.
MacPherson, C. B. "Hobbes's Bourgeois Man." In *Hobbes Studies*, edited by K. C. Brown. Oxford: Basil Blackwell, 1965.
———. "Introduction." In Hobbes, *Leviathan.* Harmondsworth, U.K.: Penguin, 1968.
———. *The Political Theory of Possessive Individualism.* Oxford: Oxford University Press, 1962.
Mahoney, Michael. "Barrow's Mathematics: Between Ancients and Moderns." In *Before Newton: The Life and Times of Isaac Barrow*, edited by Mordechai Feingold, 179–249. Cambridge: Cambridge University Press, 1990.
Malcolm, Noel. *The Correspondence of Thomas Hobbes.* Vol. 1, *1622–1659.* Vol. 2, *1660–1679.* Oxford: Oxford University Press, 1994, 1997.
———. "Hobbes and the Royal Society." In *Perspectives on Hobbes*, edited by J. A. G. Rogers and Alan Ryan, 43–80. Oxford: Oxford University Press, 1988.
———. "Hobbes, Sandys, and the Virginia Company." *Historical Journal* 24 (1981): 297–321.
———. "A Summary Biography of Hobbes." In *The Cambridge Companion to Hobbes*, edited by Tom Sorell. Cambridge: Cambridge University Press, 1986.
Malet, Antoni. "Isaac Barrow on the Mathematization of Nature: Theological Voluntarism and the Rise of Geometric Optics." *Journal of the History of Ideas* 58 (1997): 265–87.
Mancosu, Paolo. "Aristotelian Logic and Euclidean Mathematics: Seventeenth-Century Developments of the *Quaestio de certitudine mathematicarum.*" *Studies in History and Philosophy of Science* 23 (1992): 241–65.
———. *Philosophy of Mathematics and Mathematical Practice in the Seventeenth Century.* Oxford: Oxford University Press, 1996.
Mandey, Venterus. *Mellificium Mensionis; or, The Marrow of Measuring.* London, 1682.
Mandey, Venterus, and James Moxon. *Mechanick Powers; or, The Mistery of Nature and Art Unvail'd.* London, 1696.
Marcus, Leah. *The Politics of Mirth: Jonson, Herrick, Milton, Marvell, and the Defense of Old Holiday Pastimes.* Chicago: University of Chicago Press, 1986.
Margolin, Jean-Claude. "L'enseignement des mathématiques en France (1540–1570): Charles de Bovelles, Fine, Peletier, Ramus." In *French Renaissance Studies, 1540–1570: Humanism*

and the Encyclopedia, edited by Peter Sharratt, 109–55. Edinburgh: Edinburgh University Press, 1969.
Marin, Louis. *Food for Thought*. Translated by Mette Hjort. Baltimore: Johns Hopkins University Press, 1989.
———. *Portrait of the King*. Translated by Martha Houle. Minneapolis: University of Minnesota Press, 1988.
Martin, Julian. *Francis Bacon, the State, and the Reform of Natural Philosophy*. Cambridge: Cambridge University Press, 1992.
Martinich, A. P. "Book Reviews: Three Discourses." *Journal of the History of Philosophy* 35 (1997): 465–67.
———. "Thomas Hobbes in Ben Jonson's *The King's Entertainment at Welbeck*." *Notes and Queries* 45 (1998): 370–71.
———. *The Two Gods of Leviathan: Thomas Hobbes on Religion and Politics*. Cambridge: Cambridge University Press, 1992.
Mason, John E. *Gentlefolk in the Making: Studies in the History of English Courtesy Literature and Related Topics from 1531 to 1774*. Philadelphia: University of Pennsylvania Press, 1935.
Mathie, William. "Reason and Rhetoric in Hobbes's *Leviathan*." *Interpretation* 14 (1986): 281–98.
Maus, Katherine. *Ben Jonson and the Roman Frame of Mind*. Princeton: Princeton University Press, 1984.
Mauss, Marcel. *The Gift*. New York: W. W. Norton, 1967.
Mayer, T. F. "Thomas Starkey's Aristocratic Reform Programme." *History of Political Thought* 7 (1986): 439–60.
McCabe, Richard. *Joseph Hall: A Study in Satire and Meditation*. Oxford: Clarendon Press, 1982.
McClure, Kirstie. *Judging Rights: Lockian Politics and the Limits of Consent*. Ithaca: Cornell University Press, 1996.
McConica, James. *English Humanists and Reformation Politics Under Henry VIII and Edward VI*. Oxford: Oxford University Press, 1965.
McCormick, John. "Fear, Technology, and the State: Carl Schmitt, Leo Strauss, and the Revival of Hobbes in Weimar and National Socialist Germany." *Political Theory* 22 (1994): 619–52.
McKeon, Richard. "The Uses of Rhetoric in a Technological Age: Architectonic Productive Arts." In McKeon, *Rhetoric: Essays in Invention and Discovery*, edited by Mark Backman, 1–24. Woodbridge, Conn.: Ox Bow Press, 1987.
McMullin, Ernan. "Conceptions of Science in the Scientific Revolution." In *Reappraisals of the Scientific Revolution*, edited by David C. Lindberg and Robert Westman, 27–92. Cambridge: Cambridge University Press, 1990.
McNeilly, F. S. *The Anatomy of Leviathan*. New York: St. Martin's Press, 1969.
Meier, Heinrich. *Carl Schmitt and Leo Strauss: The Hidden Dialogue*. Translated by J. Harvey Lomax. Chicago: University of Chicago Press, 1995.
Miller, Perry. *The New England Mind: The Seventeenth Century*. New York: Macmillan, 1939.
Miller, Ted H. "Oakeshott's Hobbes and the Fear of Political Rationalism." *Political Theory* 29 (2001): 806–33.
———. "The Two Deaths of Lady Macduff: Antimetaphysics, Violence, and William Davenant's Restoration Revision of Macbeth." *Political Theory* 36, no. 6 (2008): 856–82.
———. "The Uniqueness of *Leviathan*: Authorizing Poets, Philosophers, and Sovereigns." In *Leviathan After 350 Years*, edited by Tom Sorell and Luc Foismeau. Oxford: Oxford University Press, 2004.
Miller, Ted, and Tracy Strong. "Meanings and Contexts: Mr. Skinner's Hobbes and the English Mode of Political Theory." *Inquiry* 40 (1997): 323–56.
Milton, Anthony. "'The Unchanged Peacemaker'? John Dury and the Politics of Irenicism in England, 1628–1643." In *Samuel Hartlib and the Universal Reformation: Studies in Intellectual

Education, edited by Mark Greengrass, Michael Leslie, and Timothy Raylor, 95–117. Cambridge: Cambridge University Press, 1994.

Milton, John. *Of Education*. In *The Complete Poetry and Select Prose of John Milton*, edited by Cleanth Brooks. New York: Random House, 1950.

Mintz, Samuel. *The Hunting of Leviathan: Seventeenth-Century Reactions to the Materialism and Moral Philosophy of Thomas Hobbes*. Cambridge: Cambridge University Press, 1962.

Monfasani, John. "Humanism and Rhetoric." In *Renaissance Humanism: Foundations, Forms, and Legacy*, vol. 3, *Humanism and the Disciplines*, edited by Albert Rabil Jr., 171–235. Philadelphia: University of Pennsylvania Press, 1988.

Montrose, Louis. "Of Gentlemen and Shepherds: The Politics of Elizabethan Pastoral Form." *ELH* 50 (1983): 415–59.

Morgan, John. *Godly Learning: Puritan Attitudes Towards Reason, Learning, and Education, 1560–1640*. Cambridge: Cambridge University Press, 1986.

Morison, Richard. "Two Tracts Against the Pilgrimage of Grace." In *Humanist Scholarship and Public Order*, edited by David Berkowitz. Washington, D.C.: Folger Books, 1984.

Morrill, J. S., and J. D. Walter. "Order and Disorder in the English Revolution." In *Order and Disorder in Early Modern England*, edited by Anthony Fletcher and John Stevenson, 137–65. Cambridge: Cambridge University Press, 1985.

Mulcaster, Richard. *The First Part of the Elementary*. 1582. Facsimile of the first edition. Menston, U.K.: Scolar Press, 1970.

———. *Positions [W]herein Those Primitive Circumstances Be Examined, which are Necessarie for the Training up of children, either for skill in their booke, or health in their bodies*. London, 1581. Huntington, 62699, C 18253.

Mulligan, Lotte. "'Reason,' 'Right Reason,' and 'Revelation' in Mid-Seventeenth-Century England." In *Occult and Scientific Mentalities in the Renaissance*, edited by Brian Vickers, 375–401. Cambridge: Cambridge University Press, 1984.

Nauert, Charles. "Humanist Infiltration into the Academic World: Some Studies of Northern Universities." *Renaissance Quarterly* 43 (1990): 799–812.

Neal, Patrick. "Hobbes and Rational Choice Theory." *Western Political Quarterly* 40 (1987): 645–52.

Nedham, Marchamont. *A Discourse Concerning Schools: Offered to Publick Consideration*. London, 1663.

Nelson, John, Allan Megill, and Donald McCloskey, eds. *The Rhetoric of the Human Sciences*. Madison: University of Wisconsin Press, 1987.

Nethercot, Arthur H. *Sir William D'avenant: Poet Laureate and Playwright-Manager*. Chicago: University of Chicago Press, 1938.

Newcastle, Margaret. *The Life of the 1st Duke of Newcastle*. 1667. Reprint. London: E. P. Dent, 1916.

Newman, J. "Inigo Jones and the Politics of Architecture." In *Culture and Politics in Early Stuart England*, edited by Kevin Sharpe and Peter Lake, 229–55. Stanford: Stanford University Press, 1993.

Nietzsche, Friedrich. *Untimely Meditations*. Translated by R. J. Hollingdale. Cambridge: Cambridge University Press, 1983.

Oakeshott, Michael. "Introduction to *Leviathan*." In *Rationalism in Politics and Other Essays*, 2nd edition, edited by Timothy Fuller. Indianapolis: Liberty Press, 1991.

———. *Rationalism in Politics and Other Essays*. 2nd edition. Edited by Timothy Fuller. Indianapolis: Liberty Press, 1991.

———. "Thomas Hobbes." *Scrutiny* 4 (1935–36): 263–77.

Oakley, Francis. "The Absolute and Ordained Power of God and King in the Sixteenth and Seventeenth Centuries: Philosophy, Science, Politics, and Law." *Journal of the History of Ideas* 59 (1998): 669–90.

———. "The Absolute and Ordained Power of God in Sixteenth- and Seventeenth-Century Theology." *Journal of the History of Ideas* 59 (1998): 437–39.

———. "Jacobean Political Theology: The Absolute and Ordinary Powers of the King." *Journal of the History of Ideas* 29 (1968): 323–46.
———. *Omnipotence, Covenant, and Order*. Ithaca: Cornell University Press, 1984.
Oestreich, Gerhard, and H. G. Koenigsberger, eds. *Neostoicism and the Early Modern State*. Translated by David McClintock. Cambridge: Cambridge University Press, 1982.
Ogilby, John. *The Entertainment of His Most Excellent Majestie Charles II in His Passage Through the City of London to His Coronation*. 1662. Facsimile of the first edition, with an introduction by Ronald Knowles. Binghamton, N.Y.: Medieval and Renaissance Texts and Studies, 1988.
Okin, Susan Moller. "'The Sovereign and His Counsellours': Hobbes's Reevaluation of Parliament." *Political Theory* 10 (1982): 49–75.
Ong, Walter J. "Hobbes and Talon's Ramist Rhetoric in English." *Transactions of the Cambridge Bibliographic Society* 1 (1951): 260–69.
———. *Ramus, Method, and the Decay of Dialogue: From the Art of Discourse to the Art of Reason*. Cambridge: Harvard University Press, 1983.
Orgel, Stephen. *The Illusion of Power*. Berkeley and Los Angeles: University of California Press, 1975.
———. "Introduction." In *Ben Jonson: The Complete Masques*. New Haven: Yale University Press, 1969.
———. "Introduction." In William Shakespeare, *The Tempest*, 1–87. Oxford: Oxford University Press, 1987.
———. *The Jonsonian Masque*. 2nd edition. New York: Columbia University Press, 1981.
———. "The Royal Theatre and the Role of King." In *Patronage in the Renaissance*, edited by Guy Fitch Lytle and Stephen Orgel. Princeton: Princeton University Press, 1981.
Orgel, Stephen, and Roy Strong, eds. *Inigo Jones and the Theater of the Stuart Court*. 2 vols. Berkeley and Los Angeles: University of California Press, 1973.
Ormiston, Gayle, and Alan Schrift, eds. *The Hermeneutic Tradition from Ast to Ricoeur*. Albany: State University of New York Press, 1990.
Osler, Margaret. *Divine Will and Mechanical Philosophy: Gassendi and Descartes on Contingency and Necessity in the Created World*. Cambridge: Cambridge University Press, 1994.
Oughtred, William. *Mr. William Oughtred's Key of the Mathematicks with Notes*. Translated anonymously. London, 1694. [Originally published as *Clavis Mathematica*.]
Oxford Dictionary of National Biography. Oxford: Oxford University Press, 2004.
Pacchi, Arrigo. "Hobbes and the Problem of God." In *Perspectives on Hobbes*, edited by J. A. G. Rogers and Alan Ryan, 171–87. Oxford: Oxford University Press, 1988.
Padley, G. A. *Grammatical Theory in Western Europe, 1500–1700: The Latin Tradition*. Cambridge: Cambridge University Press, 1976.
———. *Grammatical Theory in Western Europe, 1500–1700: Trends in Vernacular Grammar*. Vol. 1. Cambridge: Cambridge University Press, 1985.
Palme, Per. *Triumph of Peace: A Study of the Whitehall Banqueting House*. London: Thames and Hudson, 1957.
Papillon, David. *A Practicall Abstract of the Arts of Fortification and Assailing*. London, 1645.
Parker, Geoffrey. *The Military Revolution: Military Innovation and the Rise of the West, 1500–1800*. 2nd edition. Cambridge: Cambridge University Press, 1996.
Parry, Graham. *The Seventeenth Century: The Intellectual and Cultural Context of English Literature, 1603–1700*. London: Longman, 1989.
[Payne, Robert.] "Considerations touching the facility or Difficulty of the Motions of a Horse on Streight Lines, & Circular." In *A Catalogue of Letters and Other Historical Documents Exhibited in the Library at Welbeck*, edited by Arthur Strong. London: John Murray, 1903.
Peacham, Henry. *The Complete Gentleman*. 1622. In *The Complete Gentleman, The Truth of Our Times*, and *The Art of Living in London*, edited by Virgil Heltzel. Ithaca: Cornell University Press, 1962.
Peacock, John. "The Politics of Portraiture." In *Culture and Politics in Early Stuart England*, edited by Kevin Sharpe and Peter Lake, 199–228. Stanford: Stanford University Press, 1993.

Pearl, Valerie. "London's Counter-Revolution." In *Interregnum: The Quest for Settlement*, edited by G. E. Aylmer, 29–56. New York: Macmillan, 1972.

Peck, Linda Levy. *Court Patronage and Corruption in Early Stuart England*. Boston: Unwin Hyman, 1990.

Pérez-Ramos, Antonio. 1993. "Francis Bacon and Man's Two-Faced Kingdom." In *Renaissance and Seventeenth-Century Rationalism*, edited by G. H. R. Parkinson. London: Routledge, 1993.

———. *Francis Bacon's Idea of Science and the Maker's Knowledge Tradition*. Oxford: Clarendon Press, 1989.

Peters, Richard. *Hobbes*. Harmondsworth, U.K.: Penguin, 1956.

Peters, Richard, and Henri Tajfel. "Hobbes and Hull: Metaphysicians of Behavior." In *Hobbes and Rousseau*, edited by Maurice Cranston and Richard Peters, 165–83. Garden City, N.Y.: Doubleday, 1972.

Petty, William. *The Economic Writings of Sir William Petty*. Edited by Charles Henry Hull. Cambridge, 1899.

———. *The Petty Papers: Some Unpublished Writings of Sir William Petty; Edited from the Bowood Papers by the Marquis of Lansdowne*. 2 vols. New York: Houghton Mifflin, 1927.

Pine, Martin L. *Pietro Pomponazzi: Radical Philosopher of the Renaissance*. Padua: Antenore, 1986.

Plato. *Meno*. Translated by G. M. A. Grube. 2nd edition. Indianapolis: Hackett, 1981.

———. *Republic*. Translated by G. M. A. Grube. Edited by C. D. C. Reeve. Indianapolis: Hackett, 1992.

———. *Timaeus*. Translated by Francis Cornford. London: K. Paul, Trench, Trubner, 1937.

Plutarch. "Table Talk." Translated by Edwin L. Minar. In *Moralia*, vol. 8. Loeb Classical Library no. 424. Cambridge: Harvard University Press, 1961.

Pocock, J. G. A. "Political Ideas as Historical Events: Political Philosophers as Historical Actors." In *Political Theory and Political Education*, edited by Melvin Richter, 139–58. Princeton: Princeton University Press, 1980.

———. "Time, History, and Eschatology in the Thought of Thomas Hobbes." In *Politics, Language, and Time*, 148–201. New York: Athenaeum, 1973.

Polin, Raymond. *Politique et philosophie chez Thomas Hobbes*. Paris: Presses Universitaires de France, 1953.

Popkin, Richard. "Hartlib, Dury, and the Jews." In *Samuel Hartlib and the Universal Reformation: Studies in Intellectual Education*, edited by Mark Greengrass, Michael Leslie, and Timothy Raylor, 118–36. Cambridge: Cambridge University Press, 1994.

———. *The History of Skepticism from Erasmus to Spinoza*. Berkeley and Los Angeles: University of California Press, 1979.

———. "Hobbes and Skepticism I" and "Hobbes and Skepticism II." Reprinted in *The Third Force in Seventeenth-Century Thought*, 9–49. London: E. J. Brill, 1992.

———. "Prophecy and Skepticism in the Sixteenth and Seventeenth Century." *BJHP* 4 (1996): 1–20.

Potter, Lois. *Secret Rites and Secret Writing: Royalist Literature, 1641–1660*. Cambridge: Cambridge University Press, 1989.

Prins, Jan. "Hobbes on Light and Vision." In *The Cambridge Companion to Hobbes*, edited by Tom Sorell, 129–59. Cambridge: Cambridge University Press, 1996.

———. "Ward's Polemic with Hobbes on the Sources of His Optical Theories." *Revue d'histoire des sciences* 46 (1993): 195–224.

Probst, Siegmund. "Infinity and Creation: The Origins of the Controversy Between Thomas Hobbes and the Savilian Professors Seth Ward and John Wallis." *British Journal of the History of Science* 26 (1993): 271–79.

Proclus. *A Commentary on the First Book of Euclid's Elements*. Translated by Glenn Morrow. Princeton: Princeton University Press, 1992.

Proctor, Robert. "The *Studia Humanitatis*: Contemporary Scholarship and Renaissance Ideals." *Renaissance Quarterly* 43 (1990): 813–18.

Prokhovnik, Raia. *Rhetoric and Philosophy in Hobbes's "Leviathan."* New York: Garland Press, 1991.

Puttenham, George. *The Arte of English Poesie.* 1588. Edited by Gladyse Willcock and Alice Walker. Cambridge: Cambridge University Press, 1936.
Pycior, Helena. "Mathematics and Philosophy: Wallis, Hobbes, Barrow, and Berkeley." *Journal of the History of Ideas* 55 (1987): 265–86.
Querela geometrica; or, Geometry's complaint of the injuries lately received from Mr. Thomas White in his late tract entitled, Tutela geometrica. London, 1660.
Quintilian. *Institutio oratoria.* 4 vols. Translated by H. E. Butler. London: William Heinemann, 1920–22.
Randall, John Herman. *The School of Padua and the Emergence of Modern Science.* Padua: Antenore, 1961.
Rawls, John. "Justice as Fairness: Political Not Metaphysical." *Philosophy and Public Affairs* 14 (1985): 223–51.
———. "Lecture One." In *Political Liberalism.* New York: Columbia University Press, 1996.
Raylor, Timothy, and Jackson Bryce. "A Manuscript Poem on the Royal Progress of 1634: An Edition and Translation of John Westwood's 'Carmen Basileuporion.'" *Seventeenth Century* 9 (1994): 173–95.
Reik, Miriam. *The Golden Lands of Thomas Hobbes.* Detroit: University of Michigan Press, 1977.
Remer, Gary. "Hobbes, the Rhetorical Tradition, and Toleration." *Review of Politics* 54 (1992): 5–33.
Richter, Melvin, ed. *Political Theory and Political Education.* Princeton: Princeton University Press, 1980.
Ricoeur, Paul. "The Political Paradox." In *History and Truth,* translated by Charles A. Kelbley, 247–70. Evanston: Northwestern University Press, 1965.
Riggs, David. *Ben Jonson: A Life.* Cambridge: Harvard University Press, 1989.
Robertson, George Croom. *Hobbes.* London, 1886.
Rogers, J. A. G., and Alan Ryan, eds. *Perspectives on Hobbes.* Oxford: Oxford University Press, 1988.
Rogin, Paul Michael. *The Intellectuals and McCarthy: The Radical Specter.* Cambridge: MIT Press, 1967.
———. "Review of Thomas Dumm, *Democracy and Punishment: Disciplinary Origins of the United States.*" *Political Theory* 17 (1989): 141–48.
Rogow, Arnold. *Thomas Hobbes: Radical in Service of Reaction.* New York: W. W. Norton, 1986.
Rorty, Richard. *Consequences of Pragmatism.* Minneapolis: University of Minnesota Press, 1982.
———. *Contingency, Irony, and Solidarity.* Cambridge: Cambridge University Press, 1989.
———. *Philosophy and the Mirror of Nature.* Princeton: Princeton University Press, 1979.
———. "Postmodernist Bourgeois Liberalism." *Journal of Philosophy* 80 (1983): 583–89.
———. "Thugs and Theorists: A Reply to Richard Bernstein." *Political Theory* 15 (1987): 564–80.
Rose, Paul Lawrence. *The Italian Renaissance of Mathematics: Studies on Humanists and Mathematicians from Petrarch to Galileo.* Geneva: Librarie Droz, 1975.
Rossi, Paolo. *Francis Bacon: From Magic to Science.* Translated by Sacha Rabinovitch. Chicago: University of Chicago Press, 1968.
Rousseau, Jean-Jacques. *On the Social Contract.* Translated by Judith Masters. Edited by Roger Masters. New York: St. Martin's Press, 1978.
Rowe, Nick. "'My Best Patron': William Cavendish and Jonson's Caroline Drama." *Seventeenth Century* 9 (1994): 197–212.
Rummel, Erika. *The Humanist-Scholastic Debate in the Renaissance and Reformation.* Cambridge: Harvard University Press, 1995.
Russell, Conrad. *The Crisis of Parliaments: English History, 1509–1660.* Oxford: Oxford University Press, 1971.
———. "Divine Rights in the Early Seventeenth Century." In *Public Duty and Private Conscience in Seventeenth-Century England: Essays Presented to G. E. Aylmer,* edited by John Morrill, Paul Slack, and Daniel Wolfe, 101–20. Oxford: Oxford University Press, 1993.
———. *Parliaments and English Politics, 1621–1629.* Oxford: Oxford University Press, 1979.
Russell, Elizabeth. "The Influx of Commoners into the University of Oxford Before 1581: An Optical Illusion." *English Historical Review* 92 (1997): 721–45.

Ryan, Alan. "Hobbes's Political Philosophy." In *The Cambridge Companion to Hobbes*, edited by Tom Sorell, 208–45. Cambridge: Cambridge University Press, 1996.

Ryan, Michael. *Marxism and Deconstruction: A Critical Articulation*. Baltimore: Johns Hopkins University Press, 1982.

Sacksteder, William. "Hobbes: Geometrical Objects." *Philosophy of Science* 48 (1980): 573–90.

———. "Hobbes: Teaching Philosophy to Speak English." *Journal of the History of Philosophy* 16 (1978): 33–45.

———. "Hobbes' Philosophical and Rhetorical Artifice." *Philosophy and Rhetoric* 17 (1984): 30–46.

———. *Hobbes Studies (1879–1979): A Bibliography*. Bowling Green: Philosophy Documentation Center, Bowling Green State University, 1982.

———. "Three Diverse Sciences in Hobbes: First Philosophy, Geometry, and Physics." *Review of Metaphysics* 45 (1992): 739–72.

Sahlins, Marshall. *Stone Age Economics*. Chicago: Aldine, Atherton, 1972.

Salkever, Stephen. "'Lopp'd and Bound': How Liberal Theory Obscures the Goods of Liberal Practices." In *Liberalism and the Good*, edited by R. Bruce Douglas, Gerald Mara, and Henry Richardson, 167–202. New York: Routledge, 1990.

Salmon, J. H. M. "Seneca and Tacitus in Jacobean England." In *The Mental World of the Jacobean Court*, edited by L. L. Peck. Cambridge: Cambridge University Press, 1991.

Sarasohn, Lisa. *Gassendi's Ethics: Freedom in a Mechanistic Universe*. Ithaca: Cornell University Press, 1996.

———. "Was *Leviathan* a Patronage Artifact?" *History of Political Thought* 21 (2000): 606–31.

Scarisbrick, J. J. *Henry VIII*. Berkeley and Los Angeles: University of California Press, 1968.

Schaffer, Simon. "Making Certain." *Social Studies of Science* 14 (1984): 137–52.

———. "Wallification: Thomas Hobbes on School Divinity and Experimental Pneumatics." *Studies in History and Philosophy of Science* 19 (1988): 275–98.

Schmitt, Carl. *The Concept of the Political*. Translated by George Schwab. Chicago: University of Chicago Press, 1996.

———. *The Leviathan in the State Theory of Thomas Hobbes: Meaning and Failure of a Political Symbol*. Translated by George Schwab and Erna Hilfstein. Chicago: University of Chicago Press, 2008.

———. *Political Theology: Four Chapters on the Concept of Sovereignty*. 1922. Translated by George Schwab. Chicago: University of Chicago Press, 2005.

———. "The State as Mechanism in Hobbes and Descartes." 1937. In Carl Schmitt, *The Leviathan in the State Theory of Thomas Hobbes*, translated by George Schwab and Erna Hilfstein, 89–103. Chicago: University of Chicago Press, 2008.

Schmitt, Charles B. *Aristotle and the Renaissance*. The Martin Classical Lectures 27. Cambridge: Harvard University Press, 1983.

———. *John Case and Aristotelianism in Renaissance England*. Montreal: McGill-Queen's University Press, 1983.

———. "Science in the Italian Universities in the Sixteenth and Early Seventeenth Centuries." In *The Emergence of Science in Western Europe*, edited by Maurice Crosland. New York: Science History Publications, 1976.

Schochet, Gordon. *Patriarchalism in Political Thought: The Authoritarian Family and Political Speculation and Attitudes, Especially in the Seventeenth Century*. New Brunswick, N.J.: Transaction Books, 1988.

Scott, J. F. *A History of Mathematics: From Antiquity to the Beginning of the Nineteenth Century*. London: Taylor and Francis, 1960.

———. *The Mathematical Work of John Wallis, D.D., F.R.S. (1616–1703)*. 1938. Reprint. New York: Chelsea Publishing, 1981.

Scott, Jonathan. *England's Troubles: Seventeenth-Century English Political Instability in European Contexts*. Cambridge: Cambridge University Press, 2000.

Seaward, Paul. *The Cavalier Parliament and the Reconstruction of the Old Regime, 1661–1667.* Cambridge: Cambridge University Press, 1988.
———. *The Restoration.* London: Macmillan, 1991.
Seigel, Jerrold. *Rhetoric and Philosophy in Renaissance Humanism: The Union of Eloquence and Wisdom, Petrarch to Valla.* Princeton: Princeton University Press, 1968.
Shakespeare, William. *The Tempest.* Edited by Stephen Orgel. Oxford: Oxford University Press, 1987.
Shapin, Steven. "Robert Boyle and Mathematics: Reality, Representation, and Experimental Practice." *Science in Context* 2 (1988): 32–58.
———. "'A Scholar and a Gentleman': The Problematic Identity of the Scientific Practitioner in Early Modern England." *History of Science* 29 (1991): 279–327.
———. *The Scientific Revolution.* Chicago: University of Chicago Press, 1996.
———. *A Social History of Truth: Civility and Science in Seventeenth-Century England.* Chicago: University of Chicago Press, 1994.
Shapin, Steven, and Simon Schaffer. *Leviathan and the Air-Pump: Hobbes, Boyle, and the Experimental Life.* Princeton: Princeton University Press, 1985.
Shapiro, Alan. "The *Optical Lectures* and the Foundation of the Theory of Optical Imagery." In *Before Newton: The Life and Times of Isaac Barrow,* edited by Mordechai Feingold, 105–78. Cambridge: Cambridge University Press, 1990.
Shapiro, Barbara. *John Wilkins, 1614–1672: An Intellectual Biography.* Berkeley and Los Angeles: University of California Press, 1969.
———. *Probability and Certainty in Seventeenth-Century England: A Study of the Relationship Between Natural Science, Religion, Law, and Literature.* Princeton: Princeton University Press, 1983.
Shapiro, Gary. "Reading and Writing in the Text of Hobbes's *Leviathan.*" *Journal of the History of Philosophy* 18 (1980): 147–57.
Shapiro, Ian. *Political Criticism.* Berkeley and Los Angeles: University of California Press, 1990.
Sharpe, Kevin. "Archbishop Laud and the University of Oxford." In *History and the Imagination,* edited by Lloyd Jones, V. Pearl, and B. Wordon, 176–78. London: Duckworth, 1981.
———. *Criticism and Compliment: The Politics of Literature in the England of Charles I.* Cambridge: Cambridge University Press, 1987.
———. "The Foundation of the Chairs of History at Oxford and Cambridge: An Episode in Jacobean Politics." In *History of Universities,* edited by L. W. B. Brockliss, 2:127–52. Oxford: Oxford University Press, 1982.
———. *The Personal Rule of Charles I.* New Haven: Yale University Press, 1992.
Sharpe, Kevin, and Peter Lake, eds. *Culture and Politics in Early Stuart England.* Stanford: Stanford University Press, 1993.
Sharratt, Peter. "Peter Ramus and the Reform of the University: The Divorce of Philosophy and Eloquence?" In *French Renaissance Studies, 1540–70: Humanism and the Encyclopedia,* edited by Peter Sharratt, 4–20. Edinburgh: Edinburgh University Press, 1976.
Shillinglaw, Arthur. "Letter." *Times Literary Supplement,* April 18, 1936, 336.
Shugar, Deborah. *Habits of Thought in the English Renaissance: Religion, Politics, and the Dominant Culture.* Berkeley and Los Angeles: University of California Press, 1990.
Shulman, George. "Metaphor and Modernization in the Political Thought of Thomas Hobbes." *Political Theory* 17 (1989): 392–416.
Sidney, Philip. *The Defense of Poesy.* Edited by Katherine Duncan-Jones. Oxford: Oxford University Press, 1989.
Silver, Victoria. "The Fiction of Self-Evidence in Hobbes's *Leviathan.*" *ELH* 55 (1988): 351–79.
———. "Hobbes on Rhetoric." In *The Cambridge Companion to Hobbes,* edited by Tom Sorell, 329–45. Cambridge: Cambridge University Press, 1996.
———. "A Matter of Interpretation—Critical Response." *Critical Inquiry* 20 (1993): 160–71.
Silverthorne, Michael. "Thomas Hobbes Tutor." *International Journal of the Classical Tradition* 4 (1998): 411–18.

Simon, Joan. *Education and Society in Tudor England*. Cambridge: Cambridge University Press, 1966.
Skinner, Quentin. "Conquest and Consent: Thomas Hobbes and the Engagement Controversy." In *The Interregnum: The Quest for Settlement*, edited by G. E. Aylmer, 79–98. London: Macmillan, 1974.
———. "The Context of Hobbes's Theory of Obligation." In *Hobbes and Rousseau*, edited by Maurice Cranston and Richard Peters, 109–42. Garden City, N.Y.: Doubleday, 1972.
———. *The Foundations of Modern Political Thought*. 2 vols. Cambridge: Cambridge University Press, 1978.
———. "Hobbes and the Purely Artificial Person of the State." *Journal of Political Philosophy* 7 (1999): 1–29.
———. "The Ideological Context of Hobbes's Political Thought." *Historical Journal* 9 (1966): 286–317.
———. *Meaning and Context: Quentin Skinner and His Critics*. Edited by James Tully. Cambridge: Polity Press, 1988.
———. *Reason and Rhetoric in the Philosophy of Hobbes*. Cambridge: Cambridge University Press, 1996.
———. "Thomas Hobbes: Rhetoric and the Construction of Morality." *Proceedings of the British Academy* 76 (1991): 1–61.
———. "Thomas Hobbes and His Disciples in France and England." *Comparative Studies in Society and History* 8 (1966): 153–67.
———. "Thomas Hobbes and the Nature of the Early Royal Society." *Historical Journal* 12 (1969): 217–39.
Slaughter, M. M. *Universal Languages and Scientific Taxonomy in the Seventeenth Century*. Cambridge: Cambridge University Press, 1982.
Slaughter, Thomas. *Ideology and Politics on the Eve of the Restoration: Newcastle's Advice to Charles II*. Philadelphia: American Philosophical Society, 1984.
Slomp, Gabriella. "Hobbes, Thucydides, and the Three Greatest Things." *History of Political Thought* 40 (1990): 565–86.
Smith, D. K. *The Cartographic Imagination in Early Modern England: Re-writing the World in Marlowe, Spencer, Raleigh, and Marvell*. Burlington, Vt.: Ashgate, 2008.
Smith, Logan Pearsall. *The Life and Letters of Sir Henry Wotton*. Oxford: Oxford University Press, 1907.
Smuts, R. Malcolm, ed. "Art and the Material Culture in Early Stuart England." In *The Stuart Court and Europe: Essays in Politics and Political Culture*. Cambridge: Cambridge University Press, 1996.
———. "Court-Centered Politics and the Uses of Roman Historians, c. 1590–1630." In *Culture and Politics in Early Stuart England*, edited by Kevin Sharpe and Peter Lake, 21–43. Stanford: Stanford University Press, 1993.
———. *Court Culture and the Origins of a Royalist Tradition in Early Stuart England*. Philadelphia: University of Pennsylvania Press, 1987.
Solt, Leo. *Church and State in Early Modern England, 1509–1640*. Oxford: Oxford University Press, 1990.
Sommerville, Johann P. "English and European Political Ideals in the Early Seventeenth Century: Revisionism and the Case for Absolutism." *Journal of British Studies* 35, no. 2 (1996): 168–94.
———. "Lofty Science and Local Politics." In *The Cambridge Companion to Hobbes*, edited by Tom Sorell, 246–73. Cambridge: Cambridge University Press, 1996.
———. *Politics and Ideology in England, 1603–1640*. London: Longman, 1986.
———. "The Science in Hobbes's Politics." In *Perspectives on Hobbes*, edited by J. A. G. Rogers and Alan Ryan, 67–80. Oxford: Oxford University Press, 1988.
———. *Thomas Hobbes: Political Ideas in Historical Contexts*. New York: St. Martin's Press, 1992.

Sorell, Tom, ed. *The Cambridge Companion to Hobbes.* Cambridge: Cambridge University Press, 1996.
———. *Hobbes.* London: Routledge and Kegan Paul, 1986.
———. "Hobbes's Persuasive Civil Science." *Philosophical Quarterly* 40 (1990): 342–51.
———. "Hobbes's Scheme of the Sciences." In *The Cambridge Companion to Hobbes*, edited by Tom Sorell. Cambridge: Cambridge University Press, 1996.
———. "Hobbes's UnAristotelian Political Rhetoric." *Philosophy and Rhetoric* 23 (1990): 96–108.
Southern, R. W. *The Making of the Middle Ages.* New Haven: Yale University Press, 1953.
Southgate, Beverley C. "Blackloism and Tradition: From Theological Certainty to Historiographical Doubt." *Journal of the History of Ideas* 61 (2000): 97–114.
———. "'Cauterising the Tumor of Pyrrhonism': Blackloism Versus Skepticism." *Journal of the History of Ideas* 53 (1992): 631–45.
———. *"Covetous of Truth": The Life and Work of Thomas White, 1593–1676.* Dordrecht: Kluwer Academic Publishers, 1993.
Spragens, Thomas. *The Politics of Motion: The World of Thomas Hobbes.* Lexington: University Press of Kentucky, 1973.
Springborg, Patricia. "Hobbes on Religion." In *The Cambridge Companion to Hobbes*, edited by Tom Sorell, 346–80. Cambridge: Cambridge University Press, 1996.
———. "*Leviathan* and the Problem of Ecclesiastical Authority." *Political Theory* 3 (1975): 289–303.
Spufford, Margaret. *Small Books and Pleasant Histories.* Cambridge: Cambridge University Press, 1981.
Starkey, Thomas. *A Dialogue Between Pole and Lupset.* Edited by Kathleen Burton. London: Chatto and Windus, 1948.
Staynred, Philip. *A Compendium of Fortification: both Geometrically and Instrumentally by a Scale.* London, 1683.
Stillman, Robert. "Hobbes's *Leviathan:* Monsters, Metaphors, and Magic." *ELH* 62 (1995): 791–819.
Stone, Lawrence. *The Crisis in the Aristocracy, 1558–1641.* Oxford: Oxford University Press, 1965.
———. "The Educational Revolution in England, 1560–1640." *Past and Present* 28 (1964): 41–80.
Strong, Roy. *Henry, Prince of Wales and England's Lost Renaissance.* New York: Thames and Hudson, 1986.
Strong, Tracy B. "Carl Schmitt and Thomas Hobbes: Myth and Politics." Foreword in Carl Schmitt, *The Leviathan in the State Theory of Thomas Hobbes*, translated by George Schwab and Erna Hilfstein. Chicago: University of Chicago Press, 2008.
———. "How to Write Scripture: Words, Authority, and Politics in Thomas Hobbes." *Critical Inquiry* 20 (1993): 128–59.
———. "When Is a Text Not a Pretext? A Rejoinder to Victoria Silver." *Critical Inquiry* 20 (1993): 172–78.
Strauss, Leo. *Natural Right and History.* Chicago: University of Chicago Press, 1953.
———. "Notes on Carl Schmitt, *The Concept of the Political.*" Translated by J. Harvey Lomax. In Carl Schmitt, *The Concept of the Political*, translated by George Schwab, 82–107. Chicago: University of Chicago Press, 1996.
———. "On the Basis of Hobbes's Political Philosophy." In Leo Strauss, *What Is Political Philosophy and Other Essays*, 170–96. Chicago: University of Chicago Press, 1988.
———. "On the Intention of Rousseau." In *Hobbes and Rousseau*, edited by Maurice Cranston and Richard Peters, 254–90. Garden City, N.Y.: Doubleday, 1972.
———. *Persecution and the Art of Writing.* Chicago: University of Chicago Press, 1988.
———. *The Political Philosophy of Hobbes: Its Basis and Genesis.* Translated by Elsa Sinclair. Chicago: University of Chicago Press, 1963. [Originally published in 1936.]
[Stuart], King James VI and I. *Political Writings.* Edited by Johann Sommerville. Cambridge: Cambridge University Press, 1994.
Stubbe, Henry. *The Savilian Professors Case Stated. . . .* London, 1658.

Tarcov, Nathan. *Locke's Education for Liberty*. Chicago: University of Chicago Press, 1984.
Taylor, Charles. "Atomism." In *Philosophical Papers*, vol. 2, *Philosophy and the Human Sciences*, chap. 7. Cambridge: Cambridge University Press, 1985.
———. "Neutrality in Political Science." In Charles Taylor, *Philosophical Papers*, vol. 2, *Philosophy and the Human Sciences*, chap. 2. Cambridge: Cambridge University Press, 1985.
———. *Sources of the Self: The Making of the Modern Identity*. Cambridge: Harvard University Press, 1989.
———. "What's Wrong with Negative Liberty?" In Charles Taylor, *Philosophical Papers*, vol. 2, *Philosophy and the Human Sciences*, chap. 8. Cambridge: Cambridge University Press, 1985.
Taylor, E. G. R. *The Mathematical Practitioners of Tudor and Stuart England*. Cambridge: Cambridge University Press, 1954.
Teich, Mikulas, and Robert Young, eds. *Changing Perspectives in the History of Science: Essays in Honour of Joseph Needham*. London: Heinemann, 1973.
Tenison, Thomas. *The Creed of Mr. Hobbes Examined: In a feigned Conference Between Him and a Student of Divinity*. London, 1670.
Terence. "Heautontimorumenos: The Self-Tormentor." Translated by Henry Thomas Riley. In *The Comedies of Terence*, 132–96. London, 1877.
Thomas, Keith. *Religion and the Decline of Magic*. Harmondsworth, U.K.: Penguin, 1973.
———. *Rule and Misrule in the Schools of Early Modern England*. The Stenton Lecture, 1975. Reading: University of Reading, 1976.
———. "The Social Origins of Hobbes' Political Thought." In *Hobbes Studies*, edited by K. C. Brown, 185–236. Oxford: Basil Blackwell, 1965.
Thomas Aquinas. *Summa theologica*. Translated by Fathers of the English Dominican Province. New York: Benziger Brothers, 1947–48.
Thomson, David. *Renaissance Architecture: Critics, Patrons, Luxury*. Manchester: Manchester University Press, 1993.
Thorpe, Clarence DeWitt. *The Aesthetic Theory of Thomas Hobbes*. Michigan: University of Michigan Press, 1940.
Thucydides. *The Peloponnesian War: The Complete Hobbes Translation*. Edited by David Grene. Chicago: University of Chicago Press, 1989.
de Tocqueville, Alexis. *Democracy in America*. Translated by George Lawrence. Edited by J. P. Mayer. Garden City, N.Y.: Anchor Books, 1969.
———. *The Old Regime and the French Revolution*. Translated by Stuart Gilbert. New York: Anchor Books, 1955.
Todd, Margo. *Christian Humanism and the Puritan Social Order*. Cambridge: Cambridge University Press, 1987.
Tönnies, Ferdinand. *On Social Ideas and Ideologies*. Edited by E. G. Jacoby. New York: Harper and Row, 1974.
Toulmin, Stephen. *Cosmopolis: The Hidden Agenda of Modernity*. Chicago: University of Chicago Press, 1990.
Trease, Geoffrey. *Portrait of a Cavalier: William Cavendish, First Duke of Newcastle*. London: Macmillan, 1979.
Trevor-Roper, Hugh R. "Three Foreigners: The Philosophers of the Puritan Revolution." In *Religion, the Reformation, and Social Change and Other Essays*, 2nd edition, 237–93. London: Macmillan, 1972.
Tricaud, François. "'Homo homini Deus,' 'Homo homini Lupus': Recherche des sources des deux formules de Hobbes." In *Hobbes-Forschungen*, edited by Reinhart Koselleck and Roman Schnur, 61–70. Berlin: Duncker und Humblot, 1969.
———. "Quelques éléments sur la question de l'accès aux textes dans les études hobbiennes." *Revue Internationale de Philosophie* 129 (1979): 393–414.

Trinkaus, Charles. "Humanism and Science: Humanist Critiques of Natural Philosophy." In *The Scope of Renaissance Humanism*, 140–68. Ann Arbor: University of Michigan Press, 1983.
———. *In Our Image and Likeness: Humanity and Divinity in Italian Humanist Thought*. 2 vols. Chicago: University of Chicago Press, 1970.
———. "Marsilio Ficino and the Ideal of Human Autonomy." In *Renaissance Transformations of Late Medieval Thought*. Brookfield, Vt.: Ashgate, 1999.
———. *The Scope of Renaissance Humanism*. Ann Arbor: University of Michigan Press, 1983.
The True Effigies of the Monster of Malmesbury; or, Thomas Hobbes in his Proper Colours. London, 1680.
Tuck, Richard. "Grotius, Carneades and Hobbes." *Grotiana* 4 (1983): 43–62.
———. *Hobbes*. Oxford: Oxford University Press, 1989.
———. "Hobbes and Descartes." In *Perspectives on Hobbes*, edited by J. A. G. Rogers and Alan Ryan, 11–42. Oxford: Oxford University Press, 1988.
———. "Hobbes and Locke on Toleration." In *Thomas Hobbes and Political Theory*, edited by Mary Dietz, 153–71. Lawrence: University Press of Kansas, 1990.
———. "Hobbes's Moral Philosophy." In *The Cambridge Companion to Hobbes*, edited by Tom Sorell, 175–207. Cambridge: Cambridge University Press, 1996.
———. "Introduction." In Thomas Hobbes, *On the Citizen*, edited and translated by Richard Tuck and Michael Silverthorne. Cambridge: Cambridge University Press, 1998.
———. "Note on the Text." In Thomas Hobbes, *Leviathan*, edited by Richard Tuck, xxvii–xxxvii. Cambridge: Cambridge University Press, 1991.
———. *Philosophy and Government, 1572–1651*. Cambridge: Cambridge University Press, 1993.
Turner, A. J. "Mathematical Instruments and the Education of Gentlemen." *Annals of Science* 30 (1973): 51–88.
Turner, Henry. "Literature and Mapping in Early Modern England, 1520–1688." In *The History of Cartography*, vol. 3, *Cartography in the European Renaissance*, edited by David Woodward, 412–26. Chicago: University of Chicago Press, 2007.
Twigg, John. *The University of Cambridge and the English Revolution, 1625–1688*. Cambridge: Boydell Press, 1990.
Venuti, Lawrence. *Our Halcyon Dayes: English Prerevolutionary Texts and Postmodern Culture*. Madison: University of Wisconsin Press, 1989.
du Verdus, François. *Les Elemens Politique de Monsieur Hobbes*. Paris, 1660.
Vickers, Brian, ed. *In Defense of Rhetoric*. Oxford: Oxford University Press, 1989.
Vico, Giambattista. *The New Science of Giambattista Vico*. 3rd edition. 1744. Translated by Thomas Bergin and Max Fisch. Ithaca: Cornell University Press, 1984.
Vitruvius, Marcus. *De architectura*. Translated by Morris Hicky Morgan. New York: Dover, 1982.
Vives, Juan Luis. *De tradendis disciplinis*. 1531. Translated by Foster Watson. Cambridge: Cambridge University Press, 1913.
Voss, Stephen, ed. *Essays on the Philosophy and Science of René Descartes*. Oxford: Oxford University Press, 1993.
Walkling, Andrew. "Politics and the Restoration Masque: The Case of *Dido and Aeneas*." In *Culture and Society in the Stuart Restoration*, edited by Gerald MacClean, 52–69. Cambridge: Cambridge University Press, 1995.
Wallace, William A. *Causality and Scientific Explanation*. 2 vols. Ann Arbor: University of Michigan, 1972–74.
———. *Galileo and His Sources: The Heritage of the Collegio Romano in Galileo's Science*. Princeton: Princeton University Press, 1984.
Wallis, John. "The Autobiography of John Wallis, F.R.S." Edited by Christopher Scriba. *Notes and Records of the Royal Society of London* 25 (1970): 17–46.
———. *Due correction for Mr. Hobbes. Or Schoole discipline, for not saying his lessons right. In answer to his six lessons, directed to the professors of mathematicks. By the professor of geometry*. Oxford, 1656.
———. *Elenchus geometriae Hobbianae. Sive, Geometricorum, quae in ipsius Elementis philosophiae, à Thoma Hobbes Malmesburiensi proferuntur, refutatio*. Oxford, 1655.

———. *Grammar of the English Language with an introductory grammatico-physical Treatise on Speech.* Translated by J. A. Kemp. London: Longman, 1972. [Originally published in Latin in 1653 under the title *Grammatica Linguae Anglicanae.* Kemp's translation and the Latin of the original are printed herein as parallel texts.]

———. *Hobbiani puncti dispunctio; or, The Undoing of Mr Hobs's Points; in answer to M. Hobs's Stigmai, id est, Stigmata Hobbii.* Oxford, 1657.

———. *Hobbius Heauton-timorumenos; or, A consideration of Mr. Hobbes his dialogves. In an epistolary discourse, addressed to the Honourable Robert Boyle, Esq.* Oxford, 1662.

Walsham, Alexandra. "The Parochial Roots of Laudianism Revisited: Catholics, Anti-Calvinists and 'Parish Anglicans' in Early Stuart England." *Journal of Ecclesiastical History* 49 (1998): 620–51.

Walzer, Michael. "Good Aristocrats/Bad Aristocrats: Thomas Hobbes and Early Modern Political Culture." In *In the Presence of the Past: Essays in Honor of Frank Manuel,* edited by Richard Bienvenu and Mordechai Feingold, 41–53. Dordrecht: Kluwer Academic Publishers, 1991.

———. "Philosophy and Democracy." *Political Theory* 9 (1981): 379–99.

———. "Political Decision-Making and Political Education." In *Political Theory and Political Education,* edited by Melvin Richter, 159–76. Princeton: Princeton University Press, 1980.

———. *Regicide and Revolution: Speeches at the Trial of Louis XIV.* Translated by Miriam Rothstein. New York: Columbia University Press, 1974.

Ward, Seth. "Against Resistance of Lawful Powers: A Sermon preached at White-Hall, Novemb. Vth. 1661." London, 1661.

[Ward, Seth?]. *Vindiciae Academiarum, containing Some briefe Animadversions upon Mr. Webster's Book stiled "The Examination of Academies," Together with an Appendix concerning what M. Hobbs, and M. Dell have published on this Argument.* Preface attributed to John Wilkins. Oxford, 1654. STC 832.

Warnke, George. *Gadamer: Hermeneutics, Tradition, and Reason.* Stanford: Stanford University Press, 1987.

Warrender, Howard. *The Political Philosophy of Hobbes: His Theory of Obligation.* 2 vols. Oxford: Clarendon Press, 1957.

Watkins, J. W. N. *Hobbes's System of Ideas: A Study in the Political Significance of Philosophical Theories.* London: Hutchinson University Library, 1973.

Watts, Pauline Moffitt. *Nicolas Cusanus: A Fifteenth-Century Vision of Man.* Leiden: E. J. Brill, 1982.

Wayne, Don. "Mediation and Contestation: English Classicism from Sidney to Jonson." *Criticism* 25 (1983): 211–37.

———. *Penshurst: The Semiotics of Place and the Poetics of History.* Madison: University of Wisconsin Press, 1984.

Webster, Charles. "Benjamin Worsley, Engineering for Universal Reform from the Invisible College to the Navigation Act." In *Samuel Hartlib and the Universal Reformation: Studies in Intellectual Education,* edited by Mark Greengrass, Michael Leslie, and Timothy Raylor, 213–35. Cambridge: Cambridge University Press, 1994.

———. *The Great Instauration: Science, Medicine, and Reform, 1626–1660.* New York: Holmes and Meier, 1975.

Webster, Charles. *Samuel Hartlib and the Advancement of Learning.* Cambridge: Cambridge University Press, 1970.

Webster, John. *Academiarum Examen.* 1653. In *Science and Education in the Seventeenth Century: The Webster-Ward Debate,* edited by Allan Debus. New York: Elsevier, 1970.

Weintraub, Karl. *The Value of the Individual: Self and Circumstance in Autobiography.* Chicago: University of Chicago Press, 1978.

Weissman, Ronald. "Taking Patronage Seriously." In *Patronage, Art, and Society in Renaissance Italy,* edited by F. W. Kent, P. Simon, and J. C. Eade. Oxford: Oxford University Press, 1987.

Westfall, Richard. "Science and Technology During the Scientific Revolution: An Empirical Approach." In *Renaissance and Revolution: Humanists, Scholars, Craftsmen, and Natural Philosophers in Early Modern Europe*, edited by J. V. Field and Frank James, 63–72. Cambridge: Cambridge University Press, 1993.

Westman, Robert. "The Astronomer's Role in the Sixteenth Century: A Preliminary Study." *History of Science* 18 (1980): 105–47.

———. "Kepler's Theory of Hypothesis and the 'Realist Dilemma.'" *Studies in History and Philosophy of Science* 3 (1972): 233–64.

———. "Proof, Poetics, and Patronage: Copernicus's Preface to *De Revolutionibus*." In *Reappraisals of the Scientific Revolution*. Cambridge: Cambridge University Press, 1990.

Westwood, John. *Carmen Basileuporion (Royal Journey Ode, or The Royal Journey)*. Translated from 1634 edition by Jackson Bryce, in "A Manuscript Poem on the Royal Progress of 1634: An Edition and Translation of John Westwood's 'Carmen Basileuporion.'" *Seventeenth Century* 9 (1994): 173–95.

Whigham, Frank. *Ambition and Privilege: The Social Tropes of Elizabethan Courtesy Theory*. Berkeley and Los Angeles: University of California Press, 1984.

White, Stephen K. *Political Theory and Postmodernism*. Cambridge: Cambridge University Press, 1991.

———. *Sustaining Affirmation: The Strengths of Weak Ontology in Political Theory*. Princeton: Princeton University Press, 2000.

White, Thomas. *Chrysaspis, seu, Scriptorum suorum in scientiis obscurioribus apologiae vice propalata tutela geometrica*. London, 1659.

———. *Chrysaspis to Querela*. London, 1660.

Willmoth, Frances. "Mathematical Sciences and Military Technology: The Ordnance Office in the Reign of Charles II." In *Renaissance and Revolution: Humanists, Scholars, Craftsmen, and Natural Philosophers in Early Modern Europe*, edited by Judith V. Field and Frank James, 117–31. Cambridge: Cambridge University Press, 1993.

Winch, Peter. "Man and Society in Hobbes and Rousseau." In *Hobbes and Rousseau*, edited by Maurice Cranston and Richard Peters, 232–53. Garden City, N.Y.: Doubleday, 1972.

Wittkower, Rudolf. *Palladio and English Palladianism*. London: Thames and Hudson, 1974.

Wolin, Sheldon. *Hobbes and the Epic Tradition of Political Theory*. Los Angeles: Clark Memorial Library, 1970.

———. *Politics and Vision: Continuity and Innovation in Western Political Thought*. Boston: Little, Brown, 1960.

———. *Tocqueville Between Two Worlds: The Making of a Political and Theoretical Life*. Princeton: Princeton University Press, 2001.

Wood, Anthony à. *Athenae Oxonienses*. Reprint of the 1691 edition, edited by Philip Bliss. New York: B. Franklin, 1967.

Wood, Neal. "Thomas Hobbes and the Crisis of the English Aristocracy." *History of Political Thought* 1 (1980): 437–52.

Woods-Marsden, Joanna. "Images of Castles in the Renaissance: Symbols of 'Signoria'/Symbols of Tyranny." *Art Journal* (1989): 130–37.

Wootton, David. "Introduction." In *Divine Right and Democracy*, edited by David Wootton, 21–90. Harmondsworth, U.K.: Penguin, 1986.

Wotton, Sir Henry. *Elements of Architecture*. A facsimile of the 1624 edition with an introduction by Frederick Hand. Charlottesville: University of Virginia Press, 1968.

Xenophon. *Memorabilia*. Translated by E. C. Marchant. Loeb Classical Library no. 168. Cambridge: Harvard University Press, 1923.

Yates, Frances. *Giordano Bruno and the Hermetic Tradition*. Chicago: University of Chicago Press, 1964.

Zagorin, Perez. "Clarendon and Hobbes." *Journal of Modern History* 57 (1985): 593–616.

———. *The Court and the Country: The Beginning of the English Revolution*. New York: Athenaeum, 1971.

Zappen, James. "Aristotelian and Ramist Rhetoric in Thomas Hobbes's *Leviathan:* Pathos Versus Ethos and Logos." *Rhetorica* 1 (1983): 65–91.

Zarka, Yves Charles. "First Philosophy and the Foundations of Knowledge." In *The Cambridge Companion to Hobbes*, edited by Tom Sorell, 62–85. Cambridge: Cambridge University Press, 1996.

INDEX

absolutism: Hobbes's discussion of, 1–2, 14, 69–70, 77–80, 147–48, 240n.15, 259n.77; Marin's analysis of, 290n.100; modern legacy of, 216–19; patronage networks and, 169; uncertainty and, 211–16. *See also* sovereignty
Act of Oblivion and Indemnity (1661), 145
Act of Uniformity (1661), 145
Agamben, Giorgio, 70, 257n.57
Agricola, Rudolph, 30, 244n.48
Agrippa, 276n.10
Alberti, Leone Battista, 170–72, 284n.11
algebra (analytic geometry), 221–37, 252n.86, 253n.88
analytic method. *See* demonstration
Anglican Church, 145–49, 198, 230, 278n.47, 283n.4
antifoundationalism, Hobbes and, 208–9
antitheatricality, Hobbes's use of, 149–50, 279nn.72–73
architecton: Hobbes's concept of, 81–114, 259n.1; Jesuit defense of mathematics and, 101–8
architecture, 17, 23, 29, 165, 170–80, 234, 285n.19, 288n.65; Hobbes's, 161, 164, 165
Archytas, 171
Aristotle, 15, 16, 58, 60, 76, 83, 92, 95–97, 100, 119, 120, 131, 132, 151, 244n.38, 252n.81, 260n.3, 263nn.53, 57, 266n. 90, 267nn.99, 101, 269n.118, 278n.45, 299n.16; *Nichomachean Ethics*, 120–21; *Posterior Analytics*, 95–96, 100, 265n.80, 266n.95
Ascham, Roger, 32, 166; *Scholemaster*, 22–24
Assyria, natural philosophy in, 84
astronomy, 23, 51, 88, 93, 171, 245n.68, 266nn.91, 95
atheism, Hobbes's philosophy and, 230, 253n.94, 281n.100
Aubrey, John, 9–10, 13, 116, 127, 134, 230, 242n.12, 258n.75, 270n.8, 276n.12
audience thesis, 115–20
Augustine, 250n.67, 267n.106, 275n.7
Augustus, Caesar, 138–40
Averlino, Antonia, 124

Bacon, Francis, 5, 63, 81, 141, 172, 260n.2
Banqueting House (Whitehall), 176, 186

Barlow, Thomas, 225, 282n.120
Bennett, Henry (Earl of Arlington), 146
Bess of Hardwick, 173, 285n.23
Biagioli, Mario, 94, 262n.37
Blancanus, Josephus, 94, 97–108, 112–13, 225, 265nn.75, 79–80, 266n.87
Book of Common Prayer, 145
Boyle, Robert, 123, 157–58, 268n.112
Brahe, Tycho, 94
Bruno, Giordano, 66
Buckingham. *See* Villiers, George (1st Duke of Buckingham)
Buckley, William, *Arithmetica memorativa*, 25–26, 245n.67
Burckhardt, Jacob, 169–71, 284n.9
Burnet, Gilbert (Bishop), 145
Burton, Robert, 233–37; *Anatomy of Melancholy*, 235; *Philosophaster*, 235

Calvin, John, 66
Cardano, Girolamo, 254n.18
cartography, 9–11, 171–72, 242nn.4, 8, 290n.100; Hobbes's, 9, 242nn.4, 6
Castiglione, Baldessare, *Book of the Courtier*, 124
Catholicism, 146–49, 158, 278nn.45, 49
Cavendish, Charles, 177–78
Cavendish, Margaret, *Blazing World and Other Writings*, 287n.50
Cavendish, William (and Cavendish family) (Earl of Newcastle), 126–29, 165, 273n.62; architecture and, 171–74, 286n.24; Charles II and, 287n.49; as Hobbes's patron, 13–16, 24, 120, 141, 177–83, 270n.8, 273n.65, 276nn.12, 15–16; mathematical learning and, 177–78
Cavendish, William (Earl of Devonshire), 126, 173–74, 279n.65
Cecil, Robert, 275n.1
certainty: and Aristotelianism, 97–98; quest for, 66, 210–11
charactery, 131–32, 274n.78
Charles I (King of England): *Eikon Basilike*, 28, 212, 296n.37; English Civil War and, 126, 128, 141, 146, 153, 229–30; execution of, 211–12, 229–30; Hobbes and, 14, 165, 292n.138; masques constructed for,

178–83, 188–93; mathematical interests of, 123–24, 174–86, 198, 286n.44; Neoplatonism and, 292n.127; Parliament and, 126, 128, 141

Charles II (King of England): Act of Oblivion and Indemnity, 145; Hobbes's audience, as, 134, 149, 193–99, 201–4, 270n.2, 294n.2; Hobbes and, 79, 87, 118, 134, 165, 201–2, 258n.75; as mortal god, 79, 193–99; patronage, 126–27, 165, 177, 183, 281n.100, 285n.24, 287n.49; restoration, 124–25, 144–46, 212, 230, 278n.48

Chatsworth, 173, 285n.23
Cheke, John, 24–26, 245n.67
Cicero, 58, 138
civil science, Hobbes's concept of, 55–58, 67, 76, 87, 124–26, 253n.3
Civil War (British), 28, 137, 144–58, 211–12
Clarendon Code, 145
Clarendon, Earl of. *See* Hyde, Edward (Earl of Clarendon)
Clavius, Christopher, 89, 94, 97, 99–100, 103–5, 113, 262n.51, 266n.95
Collegio Romano, 95
Collins, Jeffery, 147–48
Comenius, 123, 302n.66
composition, causal reasoning and, 51–54
Connolly, William, 206–9, 216–19
Copernicus, Nicolaus, 5, 66
Cowley, Abraham, 214–15
creation, mathematics and science of, 51–54
Cromwell, Oliver, 123, 154–55, 193–94, 230, 270n.2
Cusanus, Nicolas, Hobbes compared with, 251n.76

Davenant, William, 123–24, 147, 186, 189, 195, 203, 270n.16, 293n.142; *Gondibert*, 183, 288n.65; *Proposition for Advancement of Moralitie, A*, 123, 271n.34
Da Vinci, Leonardo, 179
Dear, Peter, 98–99, 267n.106
De Caus, Salomon, *Les Raisons des forces Mouvantes*, 177
decorum, 125, 133, 139–40, 172–74, 179–80, 184–87, 194, 202–4, 271n.40, 290n.105
Dee, John, 264n.65, 265n.71, 285n.19
Dell, William, 90–92, 155–56
democracy, 4–8, 14, 130, 134–35, 137–44, 146–53, 185, 193–98, 212–13, 216–19, 240nn.10–11, 272n.42, 280n.78
demonstration, a priori/ aposteriori (synthetic/ analytic method), 51–52, 85, 101–8, 251n.72, 253n.88, 259n.1, 266n.89, 298n.9; *tou dioti/tou hoti*, 95–96, 99–102, 263n.57; *demonstatio propter quid* (demonstration of the reasoned fact), 263n.57; *demonstratio quia* (demonstration of fact), 263n.57

Descartes, René: "Cartesian anxiety," 215–16; education of, 94; *La Geometrie*, 222–28; Heidegger's discussion of, 257n.66; Hobbes and, 215–16, 223–24, 250n.61, 268n.111, 269n.12, 298n.9; mathematics and, 302n.67; on physics, 82, 302n.67; *Principles of Philosophy*, 268n.111, 306n.67; Schmitt's discussion of, 70–75, 257n.50; Toulmin's discussion of, 66, 210; voluntarism of, 109, 268n.111, 269n.123; Wallis and, 222–28

De Tocqueville, Alexis, *Democracy in America*, 1–8, 240n.10
Devereux, Robert (Earl of Essex), 275n.1
Dewey, John, 210
Dionysius of Halicarnassius, 143–44
divine right, 4, 64, 148, 187, 192, 195, 196, 198, 203, 240n.15
Durkheim, Emile, 297n.54
du Verdus, François, 158, 283n.122

Eachard, John, 119, 214, 283n.4
Egypt, natural philosophy in, 83–84
Elizabeth I, Queen of England, 187–88, 259n.80, 264n.65, 271n.35, 275n.1, 285n.19, 286n.31
eloquence. *See* rhetoric
engineering, 171, 173, 177, 285nn.20, 23
epic theory, 11, 116–17, 205–6, 295n.18
equality, 1–2, 139, 168, 240n.10
Erasmus, 32, 56, 243n.32, 244n.43
Essence: mathematics and the grasp of Aristotelian forms, 95–101; and Hobbes, 106, 269n.119
Essex, Earl of, 191
Ethiopia, natural philosophy in, 83–84, 280n.75
Euclid, 95–97, 100; Hobbes's discovery of, 9–10, 12, 225–26, 228–37, 241n.1, 270n.8, 298n.9, 299n.20; Mulcaster on, 26

fact, knowledge of, Hobbes's discussion of, 44–45, 247n.11, 249n.57; Bacon on purpose of, 5; prudence and, 249n.55
Feingold, Mordechai, 91, 93
Ficino, Marsilio, *Theologica platonica*, 62–63, 254n.12
first philosophy *(philosophia prima)*, 119–20, 259n.1, 260n.7, 269n.119
Five Mile Act, 145–46

forced loan of 1626–27, 126
Foucault, Michel, 207
fundamentalism, 208, 215

Galileo, 66, 94, 267n.97; Hobbes's references to, 19, 31, 113
Garin, Eugenio, 65–66, 241n.26
Gauden, John, 212
geometer, who is, 228–37
geometry: and algebra, 222–28, 298n.12; Hobbes's architectonic ambitions, and 81–92, 101–8, 112–14, 259n.1; Aristotelian scientific standards and, 95–101; as a means of autonomous creation, 49–50, 52, 205; philosophical language and, 41; commodious life through practical uses of 48–49, 161–66, 182; Hobbes's so-called discovery of, 7, 9–17, 116, 119–20, 173; Hobbes and humanist educators affinity for, 27–33, 165–66, 171–72; as orderly thought, 29–33; physics and, 81–108, 252n.84, 299n.23; Quintilian and, 19–20, 244n.37; Vives and, 22–23; Wallis and, 221–37
Germanicus, 140
Gilbert, Humphrey, 288n.72
Girard, René, 65

Hall, Joseph (Bishop), 131, 274n.74
Hardwick Hall, 173
Harmony, 18–20, 23, 176, 179, 192, 197–98, 278n.61, 288n.62, 294n.150
Hartlib, Samuel, 123, 280nn.85, 88; *Marcaria*, 154, 280n.87
Heidegger, Martin, 5, 71, 74, 257n.66
Helgerson, Richard, 242n.8, 243n.30
Henrietta Maria (Queen of England), 183, 188, 194
Henry VIII (King of England), 21, 183, 244n.43, 245n.67; court masques for, 186
Herodotus, 143–44
Hill, Thomas, *Naturall and Artificiall Conclusions*, 63–65, 254n.18
Hobbes, Thomas, WORKS
  Anti-White, 82–83, 85–87, 109–10
  Behemoth, 16, 126, 135, 274n.83; antitheatricality rhetoric in, 149–50; as history, 137, 144–49; Presbyterians in, 182–83; rhetoric in, 149; on the causes of the English Civil War, 150–53
  Considerations upon the Reputation, Loyalty, Manners, and Religion of Thomas Hobbes of Malmesbury, 230, 277n.34

De Cive, 67, 115, 118–20, 194, 211–12, 260n.2, 278n.47, 283n.122, 296n.32; audience and argument, 129–34; civil science in, 55–58, 67, 253n.3; on democratic assemblies, 142–44; geometry in, 86, 91; publication and distribution of, 270n.6; reason in, 123; rhetoric in, 125–26, 131–32, 134, 270n.6, 273n.70
De Corpore, 35, 42, 50; demotion of physics in, 82–83, 85–87, 106; formation of definitions in, 247n.29; imitation of God discussed in, 35, 50–51, 199; mathematical education in, 91–92, 102, 106, 265n.81, 284n.12; philosophical knowledge defined, 42–44, 47, 85, 102; physics discussed in, 81–82; "separate essences" in, 89; voluntarism in, 109–12
De Homine, 38–39, 49–52, 77–80, 247n.25
De Mirabilibus Pecci (The Wonders of the Peak), 13, 173
De Principiis et Ratiocinatione Geometrarum, 234
Decameron Physiologicum, 48, 82–85
Discourse of Rome, A, 174–76
Discourse Upon the Beginning of Tacitus, A, 138–40, 211–12, 275n.5
Elements of Law, 19, 30–31, 104–5, 115, 118, 119, 120–21, 142, 166–67, 172; audience and argument, 126–29, 133–34
History of the Peloponnesian War (Thucydides, trans. Hobbes), 9–10, 13–16, 58, 140–44, 271n.25
Leviathan: audience and argument, 4, 115–20, 125, 132–35, 184–85, 193–99, 201–4; as gift, 4, 201–4, 230, 292n.137; and the high culture of practical mathematics, 16–17, 161, 184–99; on human nature, 67–70; and humanism, 7–8, 31, 77, 115–20; imitation of God in, 50, 52–54, 62, 66–70, 79–80, 196–99, 218, 253n.94; on language, 37–38, 41, 232; as masque-text, 7–8, 161, 193–99, 203–4, 293n.140; as mirror for a prince, 4, 185, 193–99, 203; and the plea to the sovereign to teach his doctrine, 66–67, 90–91, 132–33, 156–58, 282n.121; on reasoning and science, 41, 45, 67–70, 86, 89, 109–11, 231–32, 247nn.11, 25, 251n.72; and rhetoric, 7–8, 115–20, 132–35, 184–85; Schmitt on, 70–75, 77–78, 241n.18, 256nn.44, 46, 48, 257n.62
"On the Life and History of Thucydides," 14, 141, 143, 147

Principia et Problemata aliquot geometrica, 182–83
Rosetum Geometricum, 182–83
Seven Philosophical Problems, 48, 82, 87
Six Lessons to the (Savilian) Professors of Mathematics, 157–58, 182–83, 227–29, 282n.118, 300n.29
homo faber, 61, 171
Hooker, Richard, *Of the Laws of Ecclesiastical Polity*, 59–61
Hooykaas, Reijer, 245n.68
Howard, Frances, 191
humanism, renaissance: contra scholasticism, 20–27; education and, 17–33, 143–44; eloquence and, 124–26; history and, 137–60; Hobbes's so-called transition from, 7–17, 61–66, 116–20, 159–60, 241n.26, 242n.10; imitation of God and, 61–66; mathematics and, 9–33, 161–99, 221–37; modernity and, 9–17, 241n.1
Hussee, James, 276n.12
Hyde, Edward (Earl of Clarendon), 119, 145, 198, 201–4, 230, 270n.2, 294n.2, 295n.9

Independents, 146–47, 278n.49

Jacob, James, 271n.34
Jacobson, Norman, 251n.71
James, D. G., 241n.23
James I (King of England/ Scotland), 79, 177–83, 186, 188, 190–92, 258n.76, 286n.33, 292nn.125, 127; *Basilicon Doron*, 175–76, 258n.76
Javitch, Daniel, 271nn.35, 40
Jesseph, Douglas, 87–92, 221–22, 227–28, 230, 300n.31, 301n.50
Jesuit defense of mathematics, 94; Hobbes contrasted, 101–8, 264n.70, 266n.95
Johnston, David, 116–19
Jones, Inigo, 172–73, 176–83, 186–89, 192–93, 195, 197–98, 246n.90, 286n.36, 291n.109
Jonson, Ben: antitheatricality and, 150; charactery and, 131, 277n.29; court masques of, 186–93, 195, 197–98, 288nn.62, 74; defense of poetic identity by, 233–37, 302n.66; *Every Man in His Humour*, 180–83; *Golden Age Restored, The*, 189–90; Hobbes and, 143, 177, 271n.25, 273n.71, 274n.73; *Hymenaei, or the Solemnities of Masque and Barriers at a Marriage*, 190–93; Jones, Inigo conflict with, 178–83; mathematical learning, and, 178–83, 192; Vitruvian aesthetics and, 286n.36

Kahan, Alan S., 2
Kahn, Victoria, 12

Lachterman, David, 298n.9
La Fontaine, Jean de, "Wolf and the Lamb, The," 72–73
La Mettrie, Julien (Offray de), 257n.68
Latimer, Richard, 13
Laud, William, Archbishop of Canterbury, 123, 153–54
laws of nature, 35, 78, 129, 272n.42
Lipsius, 138
Long Parliament, 126, 212
Louis XIV (King), 72–73
Luther, Martin, 66

Machievelli, Niccoló, 8, 56–57, 66, 138, 208–9, 218, 253n.3, 275n.2, 297n.55; *Prince, The*, 275n.5
MacPherson, C. B., 241n.1
Malcolm, Noel, 91
Mancosu, Paulo, 92, 263nn.54, 57, 267n.99
Mandey, Venterus, *Mellificum Mensionis; or, The Marrow of Measuring*, 182–83, 289n.75
Manetti, Giannozzo, *De dignitate et excellentia hominis* (Manetti), 61–62
Marin, Louis, 290n.100
Martinich, Aloysius, 266n.90
masques: Jonson and Jones collaboration on, 178–83, 289n.87; *Leviathan* as masque-text, 193–99; political significance of, 185–93, 291nn.109, 113, 117
materialism: of Hobbes, 6–8, 107–8; physics and mathematics, 89–90
mathematics. *See* algebra, architecture, astronomy, cartography, engineering, geometry, humanism, natural philosophy, *and the entries under Hobbes and Wallis*
Medea, 277n.24
Mersenne, Marin, 19, 63, 72, 94, 172, 242n.12, 243n.36, 246n.7, 250n.67, 254n.15, 264n.59, 267n.106, 302n.66
metabasis, 299n.16
Michelangelo, 66
mimesis, 65
miracles, 62–64, 255nn.38–39
modernity, 5, 9–17, 166–69
Monck, George (General), 145
Montrose, Louis, 271n.35
More, Thomas, 244n.43
Morrill, John, 211–12

Mulcaster, Richard, 12, 23–27, 30, 165–66, 245n.71, 246n.87; *First Part of the Elementary, The*, 32; *Positions*, 26
music, and mathematics, 18–20

natural philosophy, 6, 8, 46, 68, 81–114; Hobbes's disparagement of, 68–70, 82–87; and mathematics, 81–114
Neoplatonism: architecture of Inigo Jones and, 176; and Aristotelianism, 98–99
Neostoics, 138
Newcastle, Earl of. *See* Cavendish, William (and Cavendish family)
nominalism, 250n.67; and Hobbes, 42–43, 246n.7
Oakeshott, Michael, 46–48, 240n.1
Ockham, William of, 246n.7
Ogilby, John, 125
Ordnance Office (England), 183
Orgel, Stephen, 188, 194

Parliament: English Civil War and, 153–58; Hobbes's views of, 126, 128–29, 141–44, 151–53, 194, 198; Stuart Restoration and, 144–49
passion, reason and, 166–69
Payne, Robert, 286n.28
Peacham, Henry, 11
Pedro da Fonseca, 264n.70
Pell, John, 123
Pereira, Benedict, 263n.56, 95–96, 107
Perringchief, William, 177
Peters, Richard, 11, 241n.1
Piccolomini, Alessandro, 23n.54, 95, 98, 107
Pius II (Pope), 95
Plato, 18, 25, 58, 59; on essences, 99–100; Ficino's translation of, 62–63; geometry and influence of, 267n.106; Hobbes and, 31, 58, 67, 74, 86, 107, 121–23; on human nature, 60; on philosophy, 25; reason and philosophy and, 167–68; *Republic, The*, 74; Vitruvian architecture and, 176
poetry: divine imitation in works of, 64–65, 255nn.23, 25; eloquence in, 124–26; identity in, 233–37; Vitruvian aesthetics and, 180–83
"Political Paradox, The" (Ricoeur), 216–17
Pomponazzi, Pietro, 63, 65–66, 218, 254nn.16, 18
Presbyterians, 144–53, 182–83, 229–30, 278n.49, 279n.61, 280nn.75, 78
probabilism, 250n.67
Protectorate, 123, 155, 194

prudence, 14, 37–41, 44, 45, 217, 224, 247n.9, 249n.55
Prynne, William *Histirio-Mastix, or the Scourge of Players*, 291n.109
Puttenham, George, *Art of English Poesy, The*, 64–65, 79, 255n.23, 259n.80, 271nn.35, 40
Pythagoras, 18–19, 171, 242n.3; Vitruvian architecture and, 176
Pythagorean theorem, 9–10, 242n.3

Quaestio de certitudine mathematicarum, 92, 267n.99, 298n.1
Quakers, 146
Quintilian, *Institutio oratoria*, on the orator's education and mathematics, 17–20, 27, 243nn.32, 34, 244n.37

Randall, John Herman, 263n.57
Rawls, John, 296n.28
Raylor, Timothy, 271n.34
Reformation (English), 147–49
republicanism, 57–58, 124, 125, 130, 138–40, 211, 212, 272n.42, 275n.6, 290n.101
resolution, causal reasoning and, 51–54
Reynolds, Noel, 174–76
rhetoric (eloquence), 7–8, 12, 15, 17, 19–20, 93, 105, 115–35, 137, 149–50, 156, 159–60, 169, 172, 204, 205, 214, 242n.10, 243n.32, 270n.6, 271n.40, 274n.83, 282n.116, 295n.13
Ricoeur, Paul, 216–17, 297nn.49, 54
Rorty, Richard, 209–16
Rousseau, Jean-Jacques, 217–18
Royal Society, 119, 155, 230, 250n.67, 280n.88, 281n.100, 282n.112, 298n.1
Royston, Richard, 211–12
Rubens, Peter Paul, 174–75, 286n.32
Ryan, Michael, 296n.27

Savile, Henry, 228–29, 300n.39
Saxenhouse, Arlene, 174
Schmitt, Carl, 5, 70–75, 205, 241n.18, 256nn.46, 48, 257nn.50, 62, 297n.49; *Political Theology*, 71–72, 256n.44, 257n.72
Schmitt, Charles B., 93
Shakespeare, *Tempest, The*, 186, 188–89
Shapin, Steven, 23, 268n.112; and Schaffer, 247n.11, 281n.100, 282n.12
Shipman, Thomas, 297n.43
Shirley, James, 291n.109
Siculus, Diodorus, 83–84, 280n.75
Sidney, Philip, *Defense of Poesy, The*, 65, 255n.23

Skinner, Quentin, 11–12, 17, 116–27, 131, 159–60, 242nn.10, 12, 270nn.8, 16, 271n.40, 273nn.70, 72, 274n.83, 296n.13
Smuts, Malcolm, 141
Socrates, 58, 245n.68
Sorbière, Samuel, 130
Sorell, Tom, 260n.2
sovereignty, 1–2, 4–8, 69–70, 148–49, 184–85, 211–19, 293n.141; in *Leviathan*, 120, 132–35, 183–99, 272n.42, 274n.82; represented in court masques, 186–93; Schmitt's discussion of, 70–75, 256n.44
Spinoza, Baruch, 71
Spragens, Thomas, 241n.1
Stoics, 138, 276n.18
Stonehenge, 176
Strafford, Earl of, 126
Strauss, Leo, 5, 8, 11–12, 205, 241n.1, 243n.14; on Hobbes's phases, 11–12, 241n.1, 243n.14; *Persecution and the Art of Writing*, 240n.11; Schmitt and, 256n.44, 256n.46
Strong, Tracy, 193
Stubbe, Henry, 158, 230, 282nn.120–21
studia humanitatis, 124–26
synthetic method. *See* demonstration

Tacitus, 138–40, 275nn.2, 5–7
Theophrastus, 131, 274n.74
Thucydides, *History of the Peloponnesian War* (trans. Hobbes), 9–10, 13–16, 58, 140–44, 271n.25
Thirty Years War, 66
Tomkins, Nathaniel, 272n.49
Tönnies, Ferdinand, 11, 44, 256n.46
Toulmin, Stephen, *Cosmopolis*, 66, 210–11
Trinkaus, Charles, 254nn.7, 10
Tuck, Richard, 110, 115, 275n.2

universities: Hobbes's doctrine by sovereign command, to be made to teach, 7, 78, 79, 81, 90–91, 94, 119, 123, 129, 132–33, 149, 152, 153–58, 169, 202, 203, 230–31, 246n.6, 274n. 82, 278n.118, 282n.121; mathematics within, 91, 92–94, 229, 262n.47, 282n.120; as in the Papacy's grip, 269n.119, 278n.8, 282n.121; and reform schemes, 153–56; resistance there from, 7, 90–91, 145; as sources of sedition, according to Hobbes, 149, 152, 280n.78, 282n.118

Valla, Lorenzo, 243n.32, 245n.73
Van Dyke, Anthony, 175
Villiers, George (1st Duke of Buckingham), 126–29, 141
vir civilus, 118–20
Vitruvian ideals, 176–77, 179–80, 286n.36, 287n.61
Vives, Juan Luis: *Commentaries on the Civitas Dei*, 21; *De tradendis disciplinis*, 21–23, 27, 29–30, 32–33, 166, 244nn.42–44
voluntarism, 108–12, 250nn. 58–62, 268nn. 109–11

Waller, Edmund, 126–27, 272n.49
Wallis, John, 85–92, 148–49, 155–57, 182, 209, 221–37, 289n.75, 298n.1, 300n.39, 301n.45; *Hobbius Heuton-timorumenus; or A Consideration of Mr. Hobbes his Dialogues*, 157–58
Walter, J. D., 211–12
Ward, Seth, 85, 90–92, 153, 155–58, 227, 230, 261n.31, 281nn.97, 287n.100, 302n.66; *Vindiciae Academiarum*, 90–92, 155–58, 227
Warner, Walter, 172
Webster, Charles, 153–54
Webster, John, 90–92, 154–56
Whigham, Frank, 271n.35
White, Stephen, 206–7
White, Thomas, 85–87, 92, 260n.7
Wilkins, John, 90–92, 156–58
Wilkinson, John, 276n.12
Wolin, Sheldon, 205, 206, 240n.1, 295nn.14, 18
Wolsey, Thomas (Cardinal), 244n.43
word-pictures, Hobbes's use of, 16, 247n.8
Wotton, Henry, 172–73

Xenophon, 245n.68

www.ingramcontent.com/pod-product-compliance
Lightning Source LLC
Chambersburg PA
CBHW021353290426
44108CB00010B/217